CONFESSIONS OF A FREE SPEECH LAWYER

Confessions of a Free Speech Lawyer

Charlottesville and the Politics of Hate

Rodney A. Smolla

Cornell University Press
Ithaca and London

To my family

First published 2020 by Cornell University Press

Printed in the United States of America

Library of Congress Cataloging-in-Publication Data
Names: Smolla, Rodney A.
Title: Confessions of a free speech lawyer : Charlottesville and the politics of hate / Rodney A. Smolla.
Description: Ithaca [New York] : Cornell University Press, 2020. | Includes bibliographical references and index.
Identifiers: LCCN 2019049063 (print) | LCCN 2019049064 (ebook) | ISBN 9781501749650 (hardcover) | ISBN 9781501749667 (epub) | ISBN 9781501749674 (pdf)
Subjects: LCSH: Unite the Right Rally (2017 : Charlottesville (Va.)) | Demonstrations—Virginia—Charlottesville—History—21st century. | Freedom of speech—United States. | Hate speech—Law and legislation—United States. | Right-wing extremists—Virginia—Charlottesville. | Racism—Virginia—Charlottesville. | White supremacy movements—United States. | White nationalism—United States. | Hate groups—United States.
Classification: LCC HN90.S62 S75 2020 (print) | LCC HN90.S62 (ebook) | DDC 303.48/409755481—dc23
LC record available at https://lccn.loc.gov/2019049063
LC ebook record available at https://lccn.loc.gov/2019049064

CONTENTS

ACKNOWLEDGMENTS

I thank Anna Smolla, Connie Sweeney, Sara Evans, Evan Ryser, Stephen Wesley, Jessica O'Hearn, Emily Andrew, and Joshua Brownlie for their assistance and support.

1

A Call from the Task Force

I received a call from the governor's office in Richmond, Virginia, on the Monday following Labor Day weekend in September 2017. The call came from Shannon Dion, who was working in the office of Governor Terry McAuliffe. Dion had been my student at the University of Richmond School of Law, where I had served as the school's dean. She was phoning on behalf of the governor and Virginia's secretary of public safety, Brian Moran. Governor McAuliffe had created a governor's task force to study the racial violence in the city of Charlottesville during the summer of 2017. That violence had claimed the life of Heather Heyer on August 12, when a white supremacist, James Alex Fields Jr., slammed his speeding car pell-mell into a crowd of counterprotesters confronting a "Unite the Right" rally.

The work of the task force, Dion explained, would require it to delve deeply in the constitutional protections of freedom of speech and freedom of assembly and the rules of engagement governing what society could or could not do when confronted with racial supremacist groups rallying in a city, surrounded by opposing groups determined to confront and shout down the messages of racism and hate. The governor and the secretary were hoping I would be willing to serve as an expert consultant to the task force on those First Amendment rules of engagement. The request came on very short notice. The task force would commence its meetings in just two weeks. But I instantly agreed to serve, assuring Dion that I would do whatever needed to adjust my schedule to travel from Delaware, where I lived and worked as dean of the Delaware Law School, to travel to Richmond, Virginia's capital, for the task force hearings.[1]

Dion knew me as a law professor and law school dean and as a constitutional law litigator and scholar. When we hung up on the call, I wondered if she remembered that I had been the lead attorney in a famous free speech case involving vicious racist hate speech, *Virginia v. Black*.[2] The case involved a cross-burning rally of the Ku Klux Klan in rural western Virginia in 1998, and a second cross-burning incident in Virginia Beach, Virginia, also in 1998, in the yard of an African American, James Jubilee. The case went all the way to the Supreme Court of the United States, where I represented and argued on behalf of the racist cross-burners, asserting that the First Amendment protected their right to brandish symbols of racism, though it did not protect actual incitement to violence, or true threats intended to intimidate victims.

I had watched with horror the television images of racist violence in Charlottesville the month before. With so much of the nation, I had been shocked and traumatized by the gruesome video of James Fields slamming his car into the crowd of innocent counterprotesters, murdering Heather Heyer. Not so much with the rest of the nation, however, I felt special pangs of guilt, doubt, and remorse over the violence that engulfed Charlottesville, and the death of Heyer. For I had personally argued the Supreme Court case fighting for the rights of racist groups like the Ku Klux Klan and American neo-Nazis to spread their bile on the streets and parks of Virginia. What had my advocacy wrought? I felt vaguely complicit in the hate speech, in the violence, in the carnage and the death.

In accepting the invitation to join the efforts of the task force, I vowed to myself that I would check all preconceptions and prejudices and approach the effort with an open mind about the meaning of freedom of speech and assembly and the tensions between our American commitment to freedom of expression and our concurrent commitments to equality and human dignity. It was in that spirit that I approached the work of the Charlottesville Task Force. It was in that spirit that I came to see that the events of Charlottesville in the superheated, hateful summer of 2017 had meaning and resonance far beyond that time and place. This story is the chronicle of my exploration of that meaning and resonance.

A few months before I received Dion's call, I had received another call, inviting me to represent Jason Kessler, one of the leaders of the alt-right supremacists who had organized the Unite the Right rally that led to Heather Heyer's death. In August 2017, just days before the scheduled Unite the Right rally, the City of Charlottesville sought to move the rally from the streets and parks in downtown Charlottesville, near the University of Virginia campus, to McIntire Park, a spacious forest preserve and recreational park on the outskirts of the city. Kessler and Richard Spencer, the national alt-right leader and driving force behind the Unite the Right rally, did not want the rally moved. The two monuments to the Confederate generals Robert E. Lee and Stonewall Jackson were in the city's downtown parks. One of the announced purposes of the Unite the Right rally was to fight attempts by Charlottesville to remove or relocate the monuments. Kessler and Spencer, both graduates of the University of Virginia, also wanted to march through the UVA campus in a kind of "in your face" defiance of the UVA community, which they perceived as captured by radical progressive political correctness.

Why would I be called to represent the likes of Kessler and Spencer? For starters, I had been a stalwart free speech lawyer who had represented racists before—the Ku Klux Klan, for god's sake—in *Virginia v. Black*, all the way to the Supreme Court. I also had long-standing ties to two nonprofits in Virginia that often brought litigation on free speech issues: the American Civil Liberties Union of Virginia, and the Rutherford Institute. I had just finished writing an amicus curiae (friend of the court) brief on behalf of the Virginia ACLU and the Rutherford Institute in the Supreme Court of Virginia, in a case involving the free speech rights of judges to speak on issues of public concern. The Virginia ACLU and the Rutherford Institute volunteered to represent Kessler in his lawsuit against Charlottesville.

When I was approached by the legal director of the Virginia ACLU, Leslie Chambers Mehta, I was in the midst of a family vacation and preparing for the wedding of my eldest daughter. This was an emergency request for legal assistance, and I had not been following the breaking day-by-day and hour-by-hour events. Based on my outsider's view from the news coverage of the pending Unite the Right rally, and my own knowledge of the topography of Charlottesville, it was very difficult to make any clean and clear judgment as to whether the efforts of the city to move the rally were or were not legally permissible. I had often taken my children, including my daughter who was about to have her wedding, to McIntire Park. I knew the park well and could see why, given the pressure-cooker atmosphere building in Charlottesville, there was some common-sense logic to moving the entire event to McIntire Park. I also had some gauzy, inarticulate, vague intuition that something did not seem right—though at the time I was still quite far from any thoughtful understanding of what was bothering me. I took a pass, telling the Virginia ACLU that I would not participate as counsel for Kessler and his group.

The decision not to take the case had consequences for me. It kept me at an objective distance from the events, which would ultimately keep me free to accept the later offer from the office of Governor McAuliffe to participate, as a disinterested scholarly expert, offering testimony and advice to the task force that was convened to review the Charlottesville events.

And it kept me free to write this book.

All of us are constantly influenced by what's on the air and in the air. My exploration for the "meaning of Charlottesville" was constantly influenced by all that was in and on the air as I worked. As I was writing this book in 2018, Spike Lee, a visionary movie director, released a film masterpiece, *BlacKkKlansman*. The movie tells the true story of an African American police detective who managed to infiltrate the Ku Klux Klan in Colorado Springs, Colorado, in the 1970s. The white supremacist David Duke is featured prominently as the celebrity supremacist who is duped by the black detective. Duke also features prominently in this book as the precursor to the next generation of supremacists who orchestrated the bloody confrontations in Charlottesville in the summer of 2017. Spike Lee chose to end his movie with footage from Charlottesville in 2017, including the carnage that led to the death of Heather Heyer.

BlacKkKlansman exhibits Spike Lee's masterly ability to tell a moral tale without getting in your face. It is not polemical, or manipulative, or dishonest, artistically or intellectually. Lee's decision to cut to images of Charlottesville at the end of his film speaks for itself. It reminded me that the dark comedy he has conjured from events in the 1970s, in which a clever black cop dupes the white supremacists of that day, remains the stuff of dark tragedy at large in America today.

The year 2018 also marked the fiftieth anniversary of the death of Martin Luther King Jr., who was struck down by an assassin's bullet in Memphis on April 4, 1968. I was invited to partner with Rev. John G. Moore of Wilmington, Delaware, to stage a creative event commemorating Dr. King's death. Moore had perfected performances in which he reenacted King's many famous speeches. His "act" was brilliant. As I watched him demonstrate his performance, I felt as if Martin Luther King had been brought back from the past and stood before me. The plan for our program was somewhat edgy. I would "interview" Dr. King, played by Moore, who would respond in character, borrowing as much as possible from King's own words. It was part historical drama, part theater improv. I was researching for our performance as I was writing this book and in the process became fixed on one moment in King's life.

King stirred the conscience of the nation from the steps of the Lincoln Memorial on the Washington Mall in 1963, declaring in a tremolo voice that seemed transported from the Promised Land, "I have a dream that one day this nation will rise up and live out the true meaning of its creed: 'We hold these truths to be self-evident, that all men are created equal.'" Only eighteen days after King's "I Have a Dream" speech, four African American teenage girls, Addie Mae Collins, Denise McNair, Carole Robertson, and Cynthia Wesley, were killed in a bombing of the Sixteenth Street Baptist Church in Birmingham, Alabama, their dreams silenced and their families shattered in the screams and shrapnel of a race-hate bomb. King descended from the Lincoln Memorial highs to the Birmingham mourning depths.

In his eulogy for the slain girls, King challenged the grieving congregation to consider not *who* killed the four girls, but *what* killed them. The nation would ask both questions when King himself was cut down. I, however, could not stop asking simply *who* killed Heather Heyer in Charlottesville on August 17, 2017, but *what* killed her. And as I explored both the who and the what, I was constantly haunted by the nightmare that perhaps among the who in the cast of those complicit was *me*. And with that nightmare, its companion night-terror, that the *what* included my many blind spots on issues of American history, culture, and law on matters touching the intersection of freedom of speech and "identity" in all its complex forms—race, gender, sexuality, religion, national origin, citizenship, and politics.

As these thoughts were swirling, I happened to attend a program in my role as dean of the Delaware Law School, sponsored by the law school's Black Law Students Association, on the writings and speeches of James Baldwin, as reflected in a posthumously published book, and then a film, *I Am Not Your Negro*.[3] In a 1985 speech at Cambridge University, Baldwin may have shocked his audience in criticizing Attorney General Robert Kennedy's suggestion that in forty years, America might have a black president. Baldwin noted that to white people, Kennedy's observation probably seemed like a very emancipated statement. For me—a white civil rights and civil liberties lawyer reflecting on what Kennedy said—Kennedy's notion would indeed seem emancipated, and even prophetic, given the election of President Barack Obama. Yet Baldwin warned that many black people saw it differently. White people, he observed, were not in Harlem to sample the reaction to Kennedy's statement. "They did not hear (and possibly will never hear) the laughter and the bitterness and the scorn with which this statement was greeted," Baldwin said. "Bobby Kennedy only got here yesterday and now he's already on his way to the presidency," Baldwin continued. "We've been here for four hundred years and now he tells us that maybe in forty years, if you're good, we may let you become president."[4] Baldwin's remarks haunted me as I considered how I, thinking myself enlightened on issues of freedom of speech and emancipated on issues of race, could not entirely perceive the crosscurrents of perception and emotion spurred by images of Ku Klux Klan members burning a cross, or a monument to Confederate general Robert E. Lee placed in prominent display in the center of a southern city.

The long hot 2017 summer in Charlottesville was also the first summer of the presidency of Donald Trump, and certainly not the winter of his opponents' discontent. Many of those who reacted with fear and loathing at the election of President Trump interpreted his election as a rearguard yearning for America's racist and xenophobic past, a yearning for an America in which "greater" is code for "whiter," conjuring images of ethno-state revivals of America in 1924 or Germany in 1933. The chants of the newly coined alt-right movement, shouting slogans such as "you will not replace us" or "blood and soil," were perceived in some quarters as surrogates for Trump's own subliminal (and at times explicit) messages of racism and xenophobia.[5]

My ruminations naturally included reflections on the multiple roles I have played as a professional, including lawyer, scholar, teacher, and university administrator. The Unite the Right rally was not just a rally in the city of Charlottesville. It was a rally at the University of Virginia. I'd spent the bulk of my professional career on American college and university campuses, and I was aware that the crossfire hurricane of conflict that descended on Charlottesville in 2017 spun off multiple tornados on the campus of that great university.

The University of Virginia did not admit women until the 1970s, when ordered to cease its all-male admissions policy by a federal court. UVA would become the epicenter of the American maelstrom over campus gender politics when an article published in *Rolling Stone* magazine described a brutal ritual gang rape of a UVA freshman at a campus fraternity event. I was a lawyer in the ensuing litigation, representing the fraternity. The story accusing the fraternity turned out to be entirely false—a fabrication. The painful raw-nerve firestorm ignited by the immediate reaction to the story, however, was entirely real.

For all this, however, Charlottesville and the University of Virginia were also, by 2017, among the American bastions of left-wing progressive liberal activist opposition to racism, sexism, xenophobia, and homophobia. Charlottesville and the University of Virginia were claiming a seat next to other famous American campuses, like the University of California at Berkeley, or Yale, as ardently active beacons of the rights of the oppressed and dispossessed. The mayor of Charlottesville declared the city the capital of the progressive resistance. It stood for the rights of people of color, religious minorities, gay, lesbian, bisexual, and transgender persons—the champion of all colors and causes that the supremacists of the alt-right despised. Here were fear and loathing in Charlottesville, fueled from the right and the left, isobar highs and lows of love and hate, generating a perfect storm.

If Charlottesville may be defined as a crossroads for politics, it has also proven a ripe environment for creativity. It has been home to musicians, actors, and writers, from Dave Matthews to Sissy Spacek, Edgar Allan Poe to William Faulkner to John Grisham. It has been home to great eccentrics, including Anna Anderson, the putative sole survivor of the massacre of the Romanov royal family during the Russian Revolution, who claimed to be the Grand Duchess Anastasia. (We now know that her claim to be Anastasia was concocted.)

William Faulkner lived in Charlottesville for five years, from 1957 until his death in 1962. In 1957 and 1958 he was the University of Virginia's first Balch Writer in Residence. When he strolled the university's famous "Academical Village" in the late 1950s, sporting his signature collegiate tweed suit, the famous literary gentleman from Mississippi had already won the Nobel Prize for literature, a Pulitzer Prize, and two National Book Awards. While some at stately UVA had feared bringing him to the campus—Faulkner was as notorious for the hardness of his drinking as he was acclaimed for the fluidity of his prose—he did his duties to his students and his colleagues, if not also to his bourbon, living in Charlottesville to be close to his only child Jill, whose husband was attending the UVA Law School.[6] In his masterpiece novel *Absalom, Absalom!* one of Faulkner's characters, Rosa, explains that she became "more than even love; I became all polymath love's androgynous advocate."[7] Charlottesville in 2017 seemed to capture advocacy for all polymath love, and all polymath hate. The city became the symbol of America's ongoing struggle to reconcile its ever-optimistic dreams for the future with the haunting nightmares of its history. Or to again borrow from Faulkner, as his character the lawyer Gavin Stevens says in *A Requiem for a Nun*, "The past is never dead. It's not even past."[8]

2

THE CHARLESTON MASSACRE

On June 17, 2015, Dylann Storm Roof, a white supremacist, brutally murdered nine African Americans at the Emanuel African Methodist Episcopal Church in Charleston, South Carolina. Roof's evil massacre of innocents would have ripple effects far beyond Charleston. His actions renewed debates over guns and the Second Amendment and the right to bear arms. His actions also changed the dynamics of American debate over symbols of the Confederacy, including the Confederate battle flag and monuments to Confederate leaders such as Jefferson Davis, Stonewall Jackson, and Robert E. Lee. The ripple effects reached across the South, and the nation, and took on special intensity in Charlottesville.

Prior to committing the murders, Roof toured South Carolina historical sites with links to the Civil War and slavery, posting photographs and selfies of his visits. Four of the photographs on Roof's site showed him with the Confederate battle flag.[1] His online narrative, styled as his "manifesto," was the story of his racist radicalization. Roof's rambling screed was infested with attacks on African Americans, Hispanics, and Jews.

"I have no choice," Roof asserted. "I am not in the position to, alone, go into the ghetto and fight. I chose Charleston because it is most historic city in my state, and at one time had the highest ratio of blacks to Whites in the country."[2] Roof portrayed himself as one of the few with the courage to do what it takes. "We have no skinheads, no real KKK, no one doing anything but talking on the internet," he stated. "Well someone has to have the bravery to take it to the real world, and I guess that has to be me."[3]

Recall that Martin Luther King's eulogy for the four African American girls killed in the Sixteenth Street Baptist Church bombing in Birmingham had challenged mourners to ask not who killed the girls, but what killed them, echoing themes King had raised in his famous *Letter from Birmingham Jail*. The Charleston massacre, like so many other recent acts of mass violence, focused the country yet again on the *what* question. The *what* question often centers on gun control, the Second Amendment, and the right to bear arms. The gun debate would be part of the aftermath of Dylann Roof's Charleston shooting, as it has been with mass shootings before and since.

But the *what* question is not so cleanly separated from the *who* question. When the shooter or bomber has ties to the international war on terrorism, to ISIS or Al-Qaeda or other strains of violent Islamic jihad, the *what* question also turns to radical elements in the Middle East and their radical domestic lone-wolf followers. In Dylann Roof's case, however, the radical terroristic impulses were not foreign, but domestic. Soon after the shooting, images from Roof's social media postings depicting him wrapped in the racist symbols of the Confederacy went viral on the internet. Soon thereafter, the internet was abuzz with reports about the various social media sites that Roof claimed had influenced him in his journal of radicalization and violence.

Roof was radicalized by material he read on websites. One of the organizations that had influenced him was the "Council of Concerned Citizens."[4] "The first website I came to was the Council of Conservative Citizens," Roof stated.[5] Among the Council's stated guiding principles is opposition to "all efforts to mix the races of mankind."[6] The material on the Council of Concerned Citizens site, coupled with Roof's views of the controversy surrounding George Zimmerman's shooting of Trayvon Martin, an unarmed black Florida teenager, "truly awakened" him.[7]

Roof thought Zimmerman was right to shoot Martin. But more than that, Roof perceived murders of whites by blacks as a call to whites to murder blacks. The Council of Concerned Citizens materials contained "pages upon pages of these brutal black on White murders,"[8] Roof explained. "I was in disbelief. At this moment I realized that something was very wrong. How could the news be blowing up the Trayvon Martin case while hundreds of these black on White murders got ignored?"[9]

As news that the material posted by the Council of Concerned Citizens had influenced Roof surfaced in the media, the Council reacted. In a message posted for the organization, and in a more personalized message posted by the organization's president, Earl Holt III, Roof's murders were condemned, but Roof's message was affirmed.

Jared Taylor, a spokesperson for the Council, proclaimed that the Council "unequivocally condemns" Roof's actions.[10] Yet Taylor also stood behind the content of the material on the Council's website, and the conclusions to be drawn from that content. Taylor asserted that the Council "stands unshakably behind the facts on its website, and points out the dangers of denying the extent of black-on-white crime." Taylor asserted that every year "there are about 500,000 violent, interracial crimes," of which "about 85 percent are committed by blacks against whites."[11]

The reverse, Taylor maintained, was not true. "Every year, there are some 20,000 rapes of white women by blacks, but rapes by white men of black women are so unusual, they scarcely appear in crime statistics," he asserted. Taylor argued that if "these figures were reversed—if there were wide-spread white-on-black rape and violence—it would be constant national news. Instead, the true nature of interracial violence is ignored." Taylor claimed that this pattern led to the "frustration" of persons like Dylann Roof and predictably led to acts such as Roof's violence.[12]

Jared Taylor's writings had influenced the thought of Richard Spencer. Taylor graduated from Yale in 1973, where he majored in philosophy, and then received a master's degree in international studies from the Paris Institute of Political Studies. He was born in Japan, the child of Christian missionaries, and lived in Japan until he was sixteen. His work as a white nationalist included leadership roles in many various supremacist groups, with interlocking relationships. Taylor was the founder of an online racial supremacist magazine, American Renaissance. He had been a director of the National Policy Institute, which Richard Spencer would come to lead. Taylor, like Spencer, brought a quality of urbanity, sophistication, elite education, and intellectualism to white supremacy. If Spencer was no dumb Nazi, Taylor was no dumb Ku Kluxer. As the Southern Poverty Law Center put it, Taylor is "a courtly presenter of ideas that most would describe as crudely white supremacist—a kind of modern-day version of the refined but racist colonialist of old."[13]

The Council of Concerned Citizens had contributed money to the campaigns of several candidates for the Republican nomination for president, as well as Republican candidates running for Congress and state political posts. Four of the Republican presidential hopefuls, Scott Walker, Rand Paul, Ted Cruz, and Rick Santorum, led many Republicans in immediately cutting ties to the Council of Concerned Citizens, stating that they would either return contributions or donate to charity money contributed by Earl Holt or the Council.[14]

I was in South Carolina when the funerals for the victims of the Charleston massacre were held. President Obama delivered a stirring eulogy, which ended with his spontaneously leading the assembled mourners in the singing of "Amazing Grace." While the funeral was being held, I was driving through Columbia, the capital of South Carolina, with members of my family. When I had been president of Furman University in South Carolina, I'd quietly worked behind the scenes to see if a deal could be brokered that would finally get the Confederate battle flag removed from the South Carolina state capitol grounds. But those efforts never got anywhere. I drove with my family past the capitol building, and we stopped our car in front of the flagpole where the Confederate battle flag was still flying. I took a picture of it on my iPhone and got into the car. "Maybe this shooting will finally get the damn flag removed," I told my wife, Anna. At that moment I had little confidence that it would. That night I wrote an opinion piece for *Washington Monthly* magazine urging that the flag be taken down. But at that point I still had very little hope that any such thing could happen.

But I was wrong. The South Carolina governor Nikki Haley, who would later serve at the US ambassador to the United Nations in the early administration of President Donald Trump, was present in Charleston with President Obama at the funeral service for the Emanuel African American Methodist Church victims. Following the funeral, Governor Haley rose to the historic moment. With her urging, the South Carolina legislature voted to remove the Confederate battle flag. I savored this victory. With so many others, I saw it as a rare moment of bipartisan unity spurred by the recognition of our shared humanity, a light shining in the face of tragic darkness.

My savoring was ill-considered and short-lived. The decision by South Carolina to remove the flag led to a tsunami across the South. Many civil rights leaders and other progressives began questioning the legitimacy of all symbols of the Confederacy. There were calls in many quarters to remove monuments to famous Confederate leaders, such as Jefferson Davis, Robert E. Lee, and Stonewall Jackson.

The swelling calls to remove the Confederate symbols in turn triggered a massive countermovement, as if an echo-boom to the South's period of massive resistance in the wake of the 1954 desegregation decision in *Brown v. Board of Education*.[15] What I had seen as the simple commonsense, compassionate exercise in human decency reflected in the removal of the Confederate battle flag from the South Carolina capitol suddenly erupted in a national referendum over whether the country should expurgate all symbols honoring the cause and leaders of the Confederacy. Faulkner was right. The past is never dead.

BECOMING RICHARD SPENCER

Richard Bertrand Spencer was born in Boston in 1978.[1] He grew up in Dallas, a son of privilege. His father was a respected Dallas ophthalmologist. His mother was an heiress to cotton farms in Louisiana. He attended St. Mark's of Texas, an elite private all-male prep school.[2]

Spencer started college at Colgate University in upstate New York but transferred after his freshman year to the University of Virginia, majoring in music history and English. After graduating from UVA, he went to the University of Chicago, where he got a master's degree, and then entered a doctoral program at Duke. He left Duke in 2007 before getting his doctorate, spurred by the Duke lacrosse team case. As Spencer put it, he decided to drop out of Duke "to pursue a life of thought-crime."[3]

Before his time at Duke, Spencer traveled to Germany in 2002, living on Lake Chiemsee, in Bavaria southeast of Munich. He worked for the Bavarian State Opera and immersed himself in the study of German history and literature. He was particularly moved by the writings of Friedrich Nietzsche, the nineteenth-century philosopher whose work would be co-opted by the Nazis. It was during his time in Germany that his ideas about race began to form.

Spencer's work as an active conservative intellectual and political player began in the conservative mainstream. His first gig, which grew directly from the Duke lacrosse scandal, was with the *American Conservative*, which he joined after leaving Duke. The *American Conservative* had been founded in 2002 by Scott McConnell, Patrick Buchanan, and Taki Theodoracopulos, to add a more aggressively conservative publication voice to the marketplace than the *National Review* or the *Weekly Standard*. Spencer then became executive editor of Taki's Magazine, an online publication founded by Taki Theodoracopulos, the conservative Greek journalist popularly known as Taki. In an article in the *Spectator* called "Cult of Victimhood," Taki opined, "I was brought up to believe that one never pays a woman for her conversation, but only for her silence."[4]

Taki, some might think, could have influenced Donald Trump's playbook. In the same article Taki explained his views of race. "Race is more than skin deep, no ifs or buts about it," Taki wrote. "On average, Orientals are slower to mature, less randy, less fertile, and have larger brains and higher IQ scores. Blacks are at the other pole, and whites fall somewhere in the middle, although closer to the Orientals than the blacks."[5] If Taki was Spencer's mentor, it was plain enough in what direction Spencer would be moving.

Spencer's evolution can be seen in a 2009 piece he wrote in Taki's Magazine titled "White Like Us." In the article Spencer attacks affirmative action, diversity, and political correctness. But Spencer in "White Like Us" is not yet over the edge, any more than racy erotic scenes from *Sex in the City* should be confused with hard-core porn. Spencer was not yet radically supremacist, not yet visioning America as a white ethno-state.

"As I've learned from some friends who work at large law firms at New York," Spencer wrote in the article,

> the entry fee for the game is an abiding respect for diversity and the institution of gay marriage and an intuitive knowledge of when and when not Asians and Jews are considered protected classes and when and when not to mention in a hiring session that a gay applicant might "add to diversity." (I've even noted that megafirms like Kirkland and Ellis have taken to holding outreach hiring fares for potential "GLBT" associates—which, no

doubt, have inspired many straight white guys to do Tootsie routines, camp it up a bit and hope to land a super job as a diversity hire.)[6]

Lamenting the confused state of "white consciousness," Spencer argued that "whites have instituted the PC [politically correct] regime on themselves (and rigorously enforce and maintain it)." Spencer observed, "No alien power or coalition of disgruntled minorities have forced whites to act is such stupid ways and believe such stupid things; it's all been the fault WASPs, Jews, and other shades of *blanche*." Spencer claimed that while many blacks might enjoy the benefits of affirmative action, "very, very few of them genuinely believe in Diversity Dogma quite like whites do." Rather, Spencer claimed, "most blacks I've known are refreshingly heretical when it comes to PC (that is to say, honest-er.)"[7]

In his 2009 piece, Spencer mused that an "activist white consciousness is probably not possible, regardless of whether it's desirable." Nevertheless, Spencer concluded, "there remains a pressing need for the people of the West to develop dignified and rational ways of relating to peoples of other races and cultures—and without resorting to the nauseating 'anti-racism' and one-world-ism we've all been hooked on since the '60s. For this, real honesty about ourselves is a good place to start."[8]

The Spencer in this essay was not yet the most dangerous racial supremacist in America, but he was well on his way. What made so many regard him as the ultimate danger, however, was not simply the extremity of the views he would finally come to embrace, but the suave slickness of the persona in which they were packaged.

He was dangerous because he was smart. Spencer was no dumb Nazi. The smarts were not just in his credentials—St. Mark's, Colgate, UVA, Chicago, Duke—but what he knew of history and politics and culture, and how he used what he knew. Spencer evolved as the illiberal product of a liberal education, pressing his study of music, language, history, philosophy, politics, and culture into the service of ethnic cleansing.

Spencer was not just smart. He could flat-out write. Spencer could turn a phrase and flip a pun with the best. And he dressed well. His clothes were expensive, stylish, and cosmopolitan. He could speak with disarming wit and charm when he wanted to, even make himself sound perfectly reasonable. Spencer would begin to create his own mythology as one of America's most disarming far-right activists, relishing the attention as his myth grew. To his opponents, it was the very fact that Spencer did not look or sound like radical right extremists were supposed to look or sound that made him all the more formidable.

Richard Spencer kept migrating, moving righter and whiter. His breakthrough came in 2011. Louis Andrews, the head of the National Policy Institute, a white nationalist policy think tank, became ill and had to step down. The National Policy Institute was founded in 2005 by William Regnery II. Regnery was a member of a wealthy conservative publishing family, and a white nationalist. The National Policy Institute's mission was "to elevate the consciousness of whites, ensure our biological and cultural continuity, and protect our civil rights."[9] Andrews also ran a related publishing company, Washington Summit Publishers. Spencer was recruited to succeed Andrews as head of the National Policy Institute and head of the publishing company. Spencer took the job and promptly moved the two entities to Whitefish, Montana, where his mother owned a commercial building and a vacation home.

Spencer then grew increasingly radical in his white supremacist thinking. At a 2013 conference of white nationalists called the American Renaissance, Spencer gave a speech urging "the creation of a White Ethno-State on the North American continent." He became an advocate for "ethnic cleansing." History, Spencer asserted, had unfortunately given ethnic cleansing a bad name. "Today, in the public imagination, 'ethnic-cleansing' has been associated with civil war and mass murder (understandably so)." Spencer, however, believed that ethnic cleansing could be peaceful, accomplished without mass murder, but simply through the fiat of law mandating "ethnic redistribution." Spencer envisioned this as a living and breathing future reality, as something that could really happen, asserting, "It is perfectly feasible for a white state to be established on the North American continent."[10]

By this time Spencer had coined the phrase—and laid claim to the founding of—the "alt-right." Spencer started Alternative Right, an online magazine, in 2011. He began to think of himself as having the potential to play a major role in history, which would require him to live dangerously and cultivate controversy.[11]

Spencer's views of race were heavily influenced by the German conception of *Volksgeist*, a word that means "the spirit of a people." Johann Gottfried von Herder, a nineteenth-century German philosopher, theologian, and literary critic, captured the *Volksgeist* ideal in his lament: "But now! Again I cry, my German brethren! But now! The remains of all genuine folk-thought is rolling into the abyss of oblivion with a last and accelerated impetus. For the last century we have been ashamed of everything that concerns the fatherland."[12] Spencer would come to channel this theme in his thoughts on white consciousness and the need for whites to shed their shame over their race. Spencer would also be influenced by a German legal thinker, Carl Schmitt. Schmitt was a lawyer and legal philosopher who became one of the leading jurists of the Third Reich. He was editor-in-chief of the Nazi newspaper for lawyers, the *Deutsche Juristen-Zeitung*, the "German Jurists' Journal," and was a law professor at the University of Berlin. Schmitt led the Nazi book-burning rallies, arguing for the destruction of all "un-German" ideas.[13] Schmitt had a brutal conception of politics and power, believing effective governments had to possess elements of totalitarianism and dictatorship.

Graeme Wood, Spencer's former classmate from St. Mark's School in Dallas, interviewed Spencer for an article in the *Atlantic*. "There's this notion of parliament as an 'endless debate,'" Spencer told Wood. But Spencer, following the writings of Schmitt, rejected the views of classic liberalism, which defended the give-and-take of points and counterpoints in a democracy. Spencer instead argued that the real job of the state is to ensure that one side wins and that the losing side submits. "Politics is inherently brutal," Spencer told Wood. "It's nonconsensual by its very nature. The state is crystallized violence."[14]

Spencer may have attended Thomas Jefferson's university, but in the service of a state dedicated to crystallized violence, it would become for Spencer essential that Jefferson's most famous statement, that "all men are created equal," be rejected. In an article Spencer wrote for the National Policy Institute's online Radix Journal, Spencer explained his rejection of Jefferson:

> A century and a half ago, Alexander Stephens, vice-president of the Confederate States of America, was faced with the prospect of the victory or annihilation of his nation and fledgling state in what is now referred to as the American civil war.
>
> In his greatest address, "the cornerstone of the confederacy," he did not speak (mendaciously) about "states rights" or any kind of constitutional

legality. he instead cut to the heart of the social order he was opposing. he stressed that the confederacy was based on the conclusion that Thomas Jefferson was wrong; the "cornerstone" of the new state was the "physical, philosophical, and moral truth" of human inequality.

Ours, too, should be a declaration of difference and distance—"we hold these truths to be self-evident; that all men are created unequal." in the wake of the old world, this will be our proposition.[15]

It is but a short step from crystallized violence to Kristallnacht. It is not much of longer step to the sort of violence that led to Heather Heyer's death in Charlottesville. In his transition from the mainstream right to the alt-right, Spencer often tried to position himself as just another provocative conservative intellectual who loved to tweak the politically correct left. But when pressed, Spencer would admit that his vision of an ethno-state would inevitably be bloody.[16] America is a country with more than 102 million African Americans, Latinos, and Asians. When the *Washington Post* challenged Spencer as to how America could become a white ethno-state without violence, he admitted, "Look, maybe it will be horribly bloody and terrible. That's a possibility with anything."[17]

Spencer's casual acceptance of the possibility that the logical end to his crusade was violence did not seem to bother him deeply. Spencer appeared to treat a cataclysmic race war as just good sport, like dissing lefties. Or as writer Eli Brown observed of Spencer: "What's good for the goose is good for the goose-stepper."[18]

4

REVEREND EDWARDS

In the wake of the Charleston murders, Rev. Dr. Alvin Edwards, pastor of Mount Zion First African Baptist Church in Charlottesville, reflected on whether something like the Charleston massacre could occur in Charlottesville, and what religious groups in Charlottesville could do to prevent such a violent explosion of race hate.

Edwards grew up in Joliet, Illinois, in what he calls his "B.C. days," for "before Christ."[1] After Christ, he attended the prestigious Wheaton College in Illinois, receiving a BA in biblical studies. He went to the Virginia Union School of Theology for a master's in divinity, then obtained a PhD in education from George Mason University in Fairfax, Virginia. After serving in churches in Plymouth and Richmond, Virginia, Edwards in 1981 became pastor of Mount Zion in Charlottesville. Edwards was mayor of Charlottesville from 1990 to 1992. He was also a former Charlottesville city councilor, a former member of the Charlottesville School Board, a member of the board of Piedmont Virginia Community College, and former chair of the Charlottesville Democratic Party. He also served on the Monticello Area Community Action Agency, the Alliance for Interfaith Ministries, the Charlottesville Redevelopment Housing Authority, the board of the Charlottesville/Albemarle Boys and Girls Club, the Charlottesville Planning Coordinating Council, the Dr. Martin Luther King, Jr., Celebration Committee, and the African American Summit Committee.[2]

After the Charleston murders, Edwards wondered if the pastors in Charlottesville knew and trusted each other enough to organize a quick and coordinated response if such an event took place in Charlottesville. He had to admit that the answer was no.[3] As Edwards saw it, the black clergy and white clergy in Charlottesville had been largely separated since the days of segregation, had very little interaction, and barely knew each other.

That lack of interaction between the black and white clergy in Charlottesville symbolized a broader theme in American life, the difference between *diversity* and *integration*. Viewed statistically, Charlottesville's religious community was racially "diverse." But the lack of meaningful interaction between black and white clergy exposed a lack of authentic integration.

Gregory B. Fairchild is the Isadore Horween Research Professor of Business Administration at the University of Virginia Darden School of Business. In his reflections on the summer of 2017 in Charlottesville, Fairchild emphasized the difference between diversity and integration.[4] He noted that scholars Gary Orfield and Chungmei Lee released a study on the fiftieth anniversary of the landmark school desegregation decision, *Brown v. Board of Education*, which had the provocative title "*Brown* at 50: King's Dream or *Plessy*'s Nightmare?"[5] Viewed quantitatively, American public schools were more diverse than ever. Qualitatively, however, integration did not exist, because "most white students have little contact with minority students."[6]

To counter this habit of estrangement, Edwards formed the Charlottesville Clergy Collective. As explained on its website, the Clergy Collective was "a God-centered faith community of prayer, solidarity, and impact within the Charlottesville-Albemarle Region of Central Virginia."[7] The declared mission of the Clergy Collective was "to establish, develop, and promote racial unity within the faith leadership of the Charlottesville-Albemarle Region through fellowship, collaborative partnership, and relationship-building." The declared methods for advancing the mission were to conduct regular meetings to foster communication, to engage in events highlighting issues of racial and social justice, to partner with other community leaders "to promote mutual cooperation between law enforcement, city government, and the faith leadership of this region," and to "support marginalized and historically under-served populations in our community."[8] The Charlottesville Clergy Collective grew to over ninety religious and lay persons from many differently faith traditions.

5

THE CHARLOTTESVILLE MONUMENTS

Philanthropist Paul Goodloe McIntire donated the Robert E. Lee statue to the city of Charlottesville in 1924. McIntire was born in Charlottesville in 1860. He attended the University of Virginia from 1878 to 1879 and then left, as he put it, "since I had to make a living." McIntire went to Chicago to make his living, starting as a coffee trader with a seat he purchased on the Chicago Stock Exchange. In 1901 he moved to New York and took a seat on the New York Stock Exchange. By 1918 he had become rich and was ready to retire and head home to Charlottesville.

The Lee sculpture that McIntire commissioned depicted Lee riding his legendary horse, Traveller, in a heroic, dignified pose. The equestrian statue was placed in what would be named Lee Park, a formal urban square. The statue was conceived by sculptor Henry Shrady, who died before the project was completed.[1] Another artist, Leo Lentelli, completed the bronze sculpture.[2]

The Thomas "Stonewall" Jackson statue commissioned by McIntire was similar in design. Jackson was also depicted atop his horse, named

Little Sorrel. The work of the artist Charles Keck, the statue was set on a granite base carved with the allegorical figures of Faith and Valor.

Both the Lee and Jackson statues were unveiled with great pomp, and both unveilings were replete with circumstance.[3]

The Lee statue was presented to the City of Charlottesville on May 21, 1924. The dedication ceremony was conducted under the leadership of the Charlottesville chapters of groups dedicated to venerating the nobility of the Confederacy, including the Confederate Veterans, the Sons of Confederate Veterans, and the United Daughters of the Confederacy. The ceremony included a parade of one hundred cadets from the Virginia Military Institute, who marched through the center of Charlottesville, which was decorated with Confederate colors. Dr. Henry Louis Smith, president of Washington and Lee University, formally presented the statue to the city. The crowd burst into cheers as Mary Walker Lee, a three-year-old great-granddaughter of Robert E. Lee, pulled the Confederate flag draped over the sculpture away to unveil it. The president of the University of Virginia, Edwin A. Alderman, then delivered a speech to accept the statute on behalf of city. The events at Lee Park would be toasted that evening with parties and balls throughout the city.

The Lee and Jackson statues embodied the "lost cause" interpretation of the Civil War, a phrase first attributed to Edward A. Pollard, a graduate of UVA and apologist for slavery.[4] In the dedication address for the Lee statue, Lee was celebrated as a hero who embodied "the moral greatness of the Old South" and as a proponent of reconciliation between the two sections. The Civil War itself was remembered as a conflict between "interpretations of our Constitution" and between "ideals of democracy."[5] This view of the monuments of the Confederacy and the cause for which it stood at once romanticized and sanitized the Civil War. Robert E. Lee, claimed one of the speakers, "abhorred slavery."[6] Seen through this prism, Lee was just a good soldier. Slavery was not Lee's crusade. Fighting for the sovereignty of his home state of Virginia and its southern sisters was what the Civil War was about. It was a war over honorable principle, a war over differing interpretations of the meaning of the Constitution. And the South, though it lost on the battlefield, still had the better of the constitutional debate, or so the story went.

Elizabeth R. Varon is the Langbourne M. Williams Professor of American History and associate director of the John L. Nau III Center for Civil

War History at the University of Virginia. Varon describes the "lost cause" narrative as the original "false equivalency," and she places the blame for the false equivalency narrative squarely on the shoulders of Robert E. Lee.[7]

After the Civil War, Lee was summoned to testify before Congress, in front of the Joint Committee on Reconstruction. Lee's testimony became a beacon for southerners. As Varon explains, Lee clung to the "prewar Southern fantasy of 'paternalism': the idea that masters had been the kindly custodians of their black wards, extending them care in exchange for their submission."[8] Lee in turn advanced a postwar corollary to that fantasy, insisting that only southern whites could steward the newly freed former slaves. Varon points out that this was not a stewardship toward authentic equality, but "to a new form of benign subordination as a class of perpetual serfs."[9]

For southerners who embraced the "lost cause" view of the Civil War, it was easy to simultaneously embrace a regime of institutionalized public and private discrimination against blacks.[10] The mayor of New Orleans Mitch Landrieu took up this theme in a 2017 speech arguing that the statues had originally been erected in an effort to "rebrand" the Confederate cause.[11] "These monuments purposefully celebrate a fictional, sanitized Confederacy; ignoring the death, ignoring the enslavement, and the terror that it actually stood for," Landrieu proclaimed.[12]

On the surface, what became the South's official reality was the myth that the Civil War was not about slavery and not about race. Beneath the surface, however, it was all about slavery, and all about race.

6

BLUT UND BODEN

The chant "Blood and Soil," popular among alt-right American supremacists, conjured an idealized German past. "Blood and Soil," or *Blut und Boden* in German, paid homage to idealized pure German "blood" and the organic connection of pure German blood to the physical German landscape.

Blut und Boden was appropriated by the Nazis and used to conjure an almost mystical union between the authentic German-Nordic race and the territorial state of Germany. The phrase contemplated those who were not of pure German blood as invading nomadic races. Jews were the worst of the invaders. In a book published in 1930 titled *Neuadel aus Blut und Boden* (A new nobility based on blood and soil), writer Richard Walther Darré argued that Germany should pursue a systematic eugenics program to purify the German race and strengthen the nation.

Nazi Germany did indeed embark on a radical eugenics program to purify the human race. Remarkably, the German eugenics experiment had its roots in Virginia. The story of that Virginia experiment in eugenics, an experiment that would be followed by Hitler and the Third Reich, is best told through the saga of a Virginia woman, Carrie Elizabeth Buck, who lived a large part of her life in Charlottesville.

Some six blocks from Charlottesville's Downtown Mall, and the parks where the statues of Robert E. Lee and Stonewall Jackson are placed, there is a Virginia historical marker commemorating the saga of Carrie Buck. The marker, on Preston Avenue just south of Grady Avenue, is roughly halfway between the University of Virginia campus and McIntire Park.

Buck's story is profound, connected to the prejudices of the Old and New South, the theories of Charles Darwin and the "eugenics movement," Adolf Hitler's "final solution," and the fame and the infamy of Supreme Court justice Oliver Wendell Holmes.[1] Buck was a victim, used, abused, exploited. Yet like the most resolute characters in the novels of William Faulkner, Buck *endured*.

Carrie Elizabeth Buck was born in Charlottesville in 1906, the daughter of Frank and Emma Buck, who were married in 1896. When Carrie was about three or four years old, she was placed with foster parents, Mr. and Mrs. J. T. Dobbs, with whom she lived for fourteen years. By all accounts Carrie was a normal child. She attended school through the fifth grade and was recommended for promotion to sixth grade. Her fifth-grade teacher entered the comment "very good—deportment and lessons."[2]

When she was seventeen, Carrie became pregnant, and suddenly the Dobbses were desperate to have her committed to an institution. The Dobbses were not simply chagrined by the perceived shame of an unwed pregnancy within the family. In the summer of 1923, when Mrs. Dobbs was away from home because of an illness, Carrie was raped by Mrs. Dobbs's nephew. The Dobbses wanted Carrie put away to avoid the family rape scandal.[3]

In the same year that the Robert E. Lee statue was unveiled in Charlottesville, the Virginia General Assembly passed two laws dealing with race and eugenics. Both were enacted on March 20, 1924. Senate Bill 219 was the Racial Integrity Act. Senate Bill 281 was the Sterilization Act, an act "to provide for the sexual sterilization of inmates of State institutions in certain cases."

The Racial Integrity Act recognized the existence of only two races, "white" and "colored." It adopted the "one-drop rule," defining as "colored" any person with even "one drop" of African ancestry. Virginia had previously resisted adoption of the one-drop rule. In a letter to the editor of the Charlottesville newspaper in 1853, a writer opposed to the rule warned that if it were adopted, "I doubt not, if many who are reputed to be white, and are in fact so, do not in a very short time find themselves instead of being elevated, reduced by the judgment of a court of competent jurisdiction, to the level of a free negro."[4] The Racial Integrity Act required that the race of every person be recorded at birth. It made criminal any marriage between a white person and a "colored."

The companion legislation, the Sterilization Act, read,

> Whereas, both the health of the individual patient and the welfare of society may be promoted in certain cases by the sterilization of mental defectives under careful safeguard and by competent and conscientious authority, and
>
> Whereas, such sterilization may be effected in males by the operation of vasectomy and in females by the operation of salpingectomy, both of which said operations may be performed without serious pain or substantial danger to the life of the patient, and
>
> Whereas, the Commonwealth has in custodial care and is supporting in various State institutions many defective persons who if now discharged or paroled would likely become by the propagation of their kind a menace to society but who if incapable of procreating might properly and safely be discharged or paroled and become self-supporting with benefit both to themselves and to society, and
>
> Whereas, human experience has demonstrated that heredity plays an important part in the transmission of sanity, idiocy, imbecility, epilepsy and crime, now, therefore
>
> 1. Be it enacted by the general assembly of Virginia, That whenever the superintendent of the Western State Hospital, or of the Eastern State Hospital, or of the Southwestern State Hospital, or of the Central State Hospital, or the State Colony for Epileptics and Feeble-Minded, shall be of opinion that it is for the best interests of the patients and of society that any inmate of the institution under his care should be sexually sterilized, such superintendent is hereby authorized to perform, or cause to be performed by some capable physicians or surgeon, the operation of sterilization on any such patient confined in such institution afflicted with hereditary forms of insanity that are recurrent, idiocy, imbecility, feeble-mindedness or epilepsy;

provided that such superintendent shall have first complied with the requirements of this act.

2. Such superintendent shall first present to the special board of directors of his hospital or colony a petition stating the facts of the case and the grounds of his opinion, verified by his affidavit to the best of his knowledge and belief, and praying that an order may be entered by said board requiring him to perform or have performed by some competent physician to be designated by him in his said petition or by said board in its order, upon the inmate of his institution named in such petition, the operation of vasectomy if upon a male and of salpingectomy if upon a female.[5]

Both the Racial Integrity Act and the Sterilization Act were products of the work of a person named Harry Laughlin, who wrote an influential work titled *Model Eugenical Sterilization Law: A Report of the Psychopathic Laboratory of the Municipal Court of Chicago*, published in 1922.[6] Laughlin's report, originating under the auspices of the Municipal Court of Chicago, would change the world.

The University of Virginia became one of the world capitals of eugenics thought.[7] One UVA student wrote in a paper in 1934, "In Germany, Hitler has decreed that about 400,000 persons be sterilized. This is a great step in eliminating the racial deficients."[8]

The State Colony for Epileptics and Feeble-Minded, one of the Virginia institutions mentioned in the 1924 Virginia Sterilization Act, was known simply as the "Colony." It was in Madison Heights, near Lynchburg, the town that would later gain fame for being the headquarters of conservative televangelist Jerry Falwell and his Liberty University.

The Colony, created in 1906, was the brainchild of Colonel Aubrey Strode, Dr. Albert Priddy, and Dr. Joseph DeJarnette. All three were devotees of the American eugenics movement. Priddy was the Colony's founding superintendent. The first board of directors of the Colony included a lawyer named Irving P. Whitehead. Whitehead would later prove to be instrumental in the life of Carrie Buck.

The original idea behind the Colony was that it would serve as an alternative institution for disabled Virginians who needed to be institutionalized, many of whom would have previously been imprisoned. In 1914, Priddy persuaded the Virginia legislature to enlarge the Colony's mission to include institutionalization of the "feeble-minded."

Yet there were, it appeared, too many of the feebleminded in Virginia for the Colony to keep up. And what was worse, the feebleminded had a proclivity to repopulate. Dr. Priddy's ally, Dr. Joseph DeJarnette, was director of the Western State Hospital in Staunton, west of Charlottesville.

DeJarnette did not want Virginia, or America, to lose the sterilization race with Germany. Years after the creation of the Colony, DeJarnette lamented in a 1938 article, "Germany in six years has sterilized about 80,000 of her unfit while the United States—with approximately twice the population—has only sterilized about 27,869 in the past 20 years. . . . The fact that there are 12,000,000 defectives in the U.S. should arouse our best endeavors to push this procedure to the maximum. . . . The Germans are beating us at our own game."[9] The twelve million "defectives" DeJarnette lamented were plainly blacks and other American ethnic minorities.[10] DeJarnette wrote a poem to give literary voice to his racial solution, which he often recited in public speeches as he proselytized for the sterilization of misfits and defectives, who sought to "breed back to the monkey's nest." An excerpt from the poem read:

> Oh, why do we allow these people
> To breed back to the monkey's nest,
> To increase our country's burdens
> When we should only breed the best?
> Oh, you wise men take up the burden,
> And make this your loudest creed,
> Sterilize the misfits promptly—
> All are not fit to breed!
> Then our race will be strengthened and bettered,
> And our men and our women be blest,
> Not apish, repulsive and foolish,
> For the best will breed the best.[11]

Albert Priddy entirely agreed with DeJarnette, and though he expressed his views with less literary license, he began to urge the state of Virginia to consider the strain placed on the state's fiscal resources by having to institutionalize an ever-growing population of defective citizens. The state, Priddy suggested, should instead consider the option of sterilizing those defectives, thereby diminishing the strain they placed on society. Priddy urged the Virginia General Assembly "to give thought to the practicability of a law permitting the sterilization of inmates of our eleemosynary and penal institutions."[12]

In a report to the state legislature titled *Mental Defectives in Virginia*, Priddy proposed that the state address the growing "blight on mankind," urging mass sterilization to curb behavioral defects. Priddy believed behavior were passed on through heredity. The defects that passed through our genes included, in Priddy's view, crime, prostitution, alcoholism, and the proliferation of "non-producing and shiftless persons, living on public and private charity."[13] The Virginia General Assembly found Priddy's arguments persuasive and passed the Sterilization Act.

Sterilizations were already under way when Carrie Buck was committed to the Colony. Indeed, sterilizations had been conducted at the Colony even before passage of the 1924 Sterilization Act. But all had not gone smoothly.

In 1916 board member Irving Whitehead had recommended approval of sterilizations of two women, Jessie and Willie Mallory, from Richmond. Willie Mallory was married to George Mallory, and they had twelve children. George was working away from home in September 2016 at a sawmill in Hanover, outside Richmond. Willie was at their home in Richmond, where eight of their children resided. Two male friends were visiting her. The Richmond police arrived at the home and arrested Willie for running a disorderly house, claiming that she was running a brothel. The children were taken to a juvenile court and transferred to the custody of a Children's Home Society, on the testimony of the arresting police that the children were living in a house of prostitution. Willie and two of her older daughters, Nannie and Jessie, were committed to the Colony. While at the Colony, Willie and Jessie were sterilized and then released. Nannie, who was fourteen, remained under Albert Priddy's control at the Colony.

Nannie's father George hired a lawyer to sue Priddy, seeking Nannie's release. He also sued to have his children returned from the custody of the Children's Home. In yet a third lawsuit, George Mallory sued Albert Priddy for $5,000 in damages, alleging that Willie Mallory had been illegally committed and sterilized against her will. Priddy responded aggressively, defending himself and warning George Mallory that he would have him arrested and brought to the Colony as well—perhaps also to be sterilized. Priddy won the lawsuit, relying on the defense that once the Mallory women were committed to the Colony, it was within Priddy's "therapeutic discretion" to have them sterilized. But the case raised concerns for Priddy and the leaders of the Colony. The trial judge in the case appeared skeptical and warned Priddy not to sterilize others until Virginia passed a law clearly authorizing such actions.[14]

Yet even with the passage of the Virginia Sterilization Act, Priddy and other leaders at the Colony wanted to litigate a test case that would finally resolve the legality of their regime of involuntary sterilization. To stage a test case, the leaders of the Colony needed to select an inmate for involuntary sterilization, and then needed to have that inmate contest the proposed sterilization in court. If the Colony prevailed against the inmate, the legality of involuntary sterilizations would be firmly established.

Carrie Buck was the inmate selected for this test. From the beginning, the fix was in. Relying on the testimony of Priddy, Carrie was classified as "feebleminded," of the "Moron Class," and a "moral delinquent."[15] Carrie had, after all, borne an illegitimate child. An administrative board conducted a hearing and quickly endorsed Carrie's sterilization, easily finding her to be "a feebleminded inmate of this institution and by the laws of heredity . . . the probable potential parent of socially inadequate offspring, likewise afflicted," and "that she may be sexually sterilized without detriment to her general health, and that the welfare of the said Carrie Buck and of society will be promoted by such sterilization."[16]

In punctilious observance of the procedures required under the new Virginia Sterilization Act, a judicial appeal of the board's decision was arranged. While the litigation was moving through the courts, Albert Priddy died. His successor, Dr. John Hendren Bell, assumed the role as the defendant representing the Colony and its sterilization program. The lawyer appointed to represent Carrie was none other than Irving P. Whitehead—a founding member of the Colony's board of directors and an ally of Priddy and his ally Aubrey Strode. Whitehead had helped draft the Sterilization Act—the very law he was now putatively challenging. Indeed, one of the residence buildings at the Colony was named the Whitehead Building, in his honor. If only Carrie had a clue.

Carrie's lawyer Whitehead simply took a dive. Whether Carrie was *actually* feebleminded or a moral defective really did not matter to Whitehead or to the Colony. What mattered was the *principle* of the thing.

Assuming Carrie was feebleminded and morally defective, was there anything in American law, including the Constitution of the United States, that stood in the way of her being involuntarily sterilized? The point of the exercise was to establish the legal and moral legitimacy of mass sterilization of defectives. It was the science and philosophy of eugenics, and the legality of sterilization, that was on trial. Whether the particular person selected to test these issues was actually deserving did not much really matter. To Priddy, Strode, DeJarnette, and Whitehead, Carrie was well within their stereotype of a defective misfit acting as a drag on society. Carrie was poor, uneducated, and undoubtedly promiscuous. As DeJarnette's poem proclaimed, "Sterilize the misfits promptly—All are not fit to breed!"

Because it was the principle that mattered, the trial focused on principle. The evidence presented in favor of Carrie's sterilization included the deposition testimony of the eugenicist Harry Laughlin, the author whose work had largely driven the eugenics movement. Laughlin had never met Carrie. He'd never even been to Virginia. Laughlin's "scientific conclusions," entered into the judicial record, were drawn entirely from information supplied secondhand by Priddy. Channeling Priddy, Laughlin endorsed the "facts" that Carrie had lived a "life of immorality, prostitution, and untruthfulness; had never been self-sustaining; and has had one illegitimate child . . . supposed to be mental defective."[17] Carrie was within a group of people who "belong to the shiftless, ignorant, and worthless class of anti-social whites of the South."[18]

Eleven witnesses testified against Carrie, attesting to her feeblemindedness and immorality. Seven had never even met her. There was no evidence that Carrie's biological mother, Emma, was in any sense mentally disabled. Carrie herself had been deemed a normal child and had progressed through school as far as she went. And Carrie's own child, Vivian, would later turn out to be a bright child and strong student, until tragically she died of a childhood disease at seven. As to Carrie's immorality, she was pregnant because she'd been raped—then committed to protect the rapist.

But the principle of the thing was the principle of the thing. Details aside, Carrie surely fit the profile of Virginia's caricature of the defective misfit, and for that matter, of the caricature of misfits in the eyes of many Americans.

His only two qualifications for command were that he had been a United States senator from Oregon and a friend of Abraham Lincoln. Baker was shot and killed early in the battle. At first Holmes thought this was a break for his side. But the situation for the Union troops deteriorated. The Union forces had no leadership. The Confederate troops fought under the cover of the woods, and from the strategic high ground. The Union troops were in complete disarray, and Holmes's regiment was routed. At twilight, the regiment tried to retreat by scrambling down the bluff. The Confederate troops did not let up. Bullets were flying at the backs of the Union soldiers as they reached the bottom of a ravine where four small boats were waiting. There was not room on the boats to carry all the troops across the river. One of the boats was so badly overloaded it capsized. Holmes watched a tangle of men tumble into the icy water, with rebel shot raining down on them. The river became clogged with their bodies and blood.

The first bullet to hit Holmes was spent and just knocked the wind out of him. Holmes recovered and went back racing to the front line. He was shot again. At first, he felt as if a horse had kicked him and knocked him over. The regiment's first sergeant caught Holmes and pulled him to the rear. He opened Holmes's shirt and told Holmes there were two holes in his chest, and a bullet that was visible. He pulled the bullet out and handed it to Holmes. Holmes felt a sickening feeling wash over his face, like he was being doused in water. Next to Holmes a noncommissioned officer was lying on the ground, shot through the head and covered with blood.

Holmes was worried that he had been shot through the lungs. He spit, and blood came out. Yes, Holmes figured, through the lungs. Holmes knew from his experience in the field that hemorrhaging through the lungs was an agonizing death. He reached into his waistcoat for a bottle of laudanum. He could take the drug to end his own life, sparing himself an agonizing death. But Holmes chose not to give up. His comrades in the

In 1925, the Supreme Court of Appeals of Virginia ruled that Carrie could be sterilized. The Virginia Court concluded,

> At the time Carrie Buck was committed to the State Colony for Epileptics and Feeble-Minded, she was seventeen years old and the mother of an illegitimate child of defective mentality. She had the mind of a child nine years old, and her mother had theretofore been committed to the same Colony as a feeble-minded person. Carrie Buck, by the laws of heredity, is the probable potential parent is socially inadequate offspring, likewise affected as she is. Unless sterilized by surgical operation, she must be kept in the custodial care of the Colony for thirty years, until she is sterilized by nature, during which time she will be a charge upon the State. If sterilized under the law, she could be given her liberty and secure a good home, under supervision, without injury to society. Her welfare and that of society would be promoted by such sterilization.[19]

Vindication from the Supreme Court of Appeals of Virginia was one thing; vindication from the Supreme Court of the United States was another. Whitehead had lost the case for Carrie in the highest Court of Virginia—a victory for what Whitehead really believed—but he must have sensed momentum. He appealed Carrie's loss to the Supreme Court of the United States.

In the Supreme Court, Whitehead represented Carrie, and Whitehead's longtime ally, Aubrey Strode, represented the Colony. Can you spell collusion? The trumped-up facts were presented to the Supreme Court with no effort to defend Carrie. The issue was purely a matter of legal principle. Did the Constitution of the United States permit society to involuntarily sterilize defectives?

Justice Oliver Wendell Holmes wrote the opinion of the court. It was an 8–1 decision, with only one justice, Pierce Butler, dissenting. Justice Butler did not, however, write a dissenting opinion.

Holmes's entire opinion in *Buck v. Bell* (1927) was just five paragraphs

field managed to get him down from the bluff and to a surgeon. His fears were true. He had two holes in his lungs, and he was bleeding from the mouth. Once again he was tempted to take the laudanum. But once again he did not.

The decision of Holmes not to end his own life meant nothing to the resolution of the Civil War, but it would have a profound impact on the history of American law. Holmes would write the fateful decision in *Buck v. Bell*. He would also be the architect for what would eventually emerge as the dominant American conception of freedom of speech. Both ideas would exert powerful gravitational pull on the events in Charlottesville's summer of 2017.

I have a love-hate relationship with the jurisprudence of Holmes. Perhaps, as the writer James Dickey observed, "love-hate is stronger than either love or hate."[21] The brutal opinion of Holmes in *Buck v. Bell* falls on the hate side of the ledger.

"It would be strange," Holmes continued, "if it [the public welfare] could not call upon those who already sap the strength of the State for these lesser sacrifices, often not felt to be such by those concerned, in order to prevent our being swamped with incompetence."[22] If the elites of Harvard could be drafted to die in a bloody war, then certainly the misfits of Charlottesville could be called upon to give up reproducing, lest society be swamped with degenerates. "It is better for all the world, if instead of waiting to execute degenerate offspring for crime, or to let them starve for their imbecility, society can prevent those who are manifestly unfit from continuing their kind,"[23] Holmes continued. Why wait to put these reproducing criminals to death for their future crimes, or watch them "starve for their imbecility," Holmes reasoned, when it is so much easier to simply prevent them from "continuing their kind"?

The Supreme Court had already declared that citizens are not absolutely sovereign over their own bodies. In *Jacobson v. Massachusetts*,[24] decided in 1905, the court had upheld a Massachusetts law that was used by the city of Cambridge to impose compulsory vaccination on Cambridge residents against smallpox. Citing the *Jacobson* decision in *Buck v. Bell*, Holmes wrote that the "principle that sustains compulsory vaccination is broad enough to cover cutting the Fallopian tubes."[25] This was followed by six words that would go down in the history of the Supreme Court as among the cruelest ever written: "Three generations of imbeciles are enough."[26]

This would have been a prodigious day's work, but Holmes was not done. It had been argued that to sterilize the likes of Carrie Buck, an "incompetent" who had happened to find her unhappy way into the Colony, was unfair, and a denial of the equal protection of the laws, because surely there were others in the population, equally as "defective" as Carrie, who had not become wards of the state and were free to continue to have sex and populate. Holmes dismissed this argument as all but silly, stating sarcastically that it "is the usual last resort of constitutional arguments to point out shortcomings of this sort."[27] But Holmes had far more than sarcasm to bring to bear against this argument. Holmes chose to endorse the heart and soul of the eugenics movement, the notion that the more society sterilizes, the stronger society will be. Holmes saw that the faster defectives were sterilized, the quicker they could be safely released back into the general population, opening more spots in the Colony for other defectives to be captured and sterilized, thereby lessening the inequality between the defectives inside and outside the state's institutions. In the final sentence of his opinion Holmes thus wrote: "Of course so far as the operations enable those who otherwise must be kept confined to be returned to the world, and thus open the asylum to others, the equality aimed at will be more nearly reached."[28]

Following the Holmes opinion, Carrie Buck was sterilized at the Colony, on October 19, 1927. The Supreme Court's decision in *Buck v. Bell* provided legal cover for the sterilization of more than eighty-three hundred Virginians held in the state's mental institutions from 1927 until 1972. Nationwide, over sixty thousand Americans would be involuntarily sterilized under the authority of *Buck v. Bell*. Hitler's Third Reich adopted a sterilization law patterned after the Virginia statute the Supreme Court had endorsed.[29]

The leading American scholar on Carrie Buck is Paul A. Lombardo.[30] Lombardo received both his law degree and PhD from the University of Virginia. He went on to become Regents' Professor and Bobby Lee Cook Professor of Law at the Georgia State University Law School. Between 2011 and 2016 he served as a senior adviser to the Presidential Commission for the Study of Bioethical Issues. Professor Lombardo's distinguished career as a historian and legal scholar on matters relating to the intersection of law, medicine, and ethics included over twenty-five years of research on Carrie Buck's story. He was able to interview Buck before she died.[31] Buck's sister, Doris Buck, was also sterilized, but not even told of the procedure. Doris Buck married and with her husband tried to have children. She did not learn until 1980 why she could not get pregnant.[32]

Largely because of the impressive scholarship of Professor Lombardo, we now know that all of the facts upon which the Holmes opinion in *Buck v. Bell* were predicated were fabricated. There were never three generations of imbeciles. Nothing in the record demonstrated that Carrie's mother Emma had any mental infirmity. Carrie had been deemed a perfectly normal child throughout her upbringing, and following her calamity at the hands of Virginia and the United States Supreme Court she lived an admirable life. She was an avid reader, a dedicated member of her church choir, a devoted wife, married for twenty-four years, and an articulate and thoughtful citizen. Her daughter Vivian was an honor roll student before dying of a childhood disease. Carrie Buck died on January 28, 1983, at age seventy-six. Professor Lombardo was among the few at her funeral.

When the historical marker was erected in Charlottesville on May 2, 2002, Governor Mark R. Warner offered the "Commonwealth's sincere apology for Virginia's participation in eugenics."

Mr. Jefferson's University

The University of Virginia was founded in 1819 by Thomas Jefferson. Jefferson loved it so much that he insisted his gravestone mention only three of his life's accomplishments: author of the Declaration of Independence, drafter of the Virginia Statute for Religious Freedom, and father of the University of Virginia. UVA is one of America's most storied institutions of higher education. Jefferson had grown exasperated by his alma mater, the College of William and Mary, because it had become, in Jefferson's view, too religious, forcing students to recite a catechism. Jefferson, famous for his belief in a wall of separation between church and state, conceived of a new Virginia state university. He wrote of the new university to artist Charles Willson Peale, stating that it would be "on the most extensive and liberal scale that our circumstances would call for and our faculties meet," where students would come from Virginia and other states to "drink of the cup of knowledge." And over the centuries they did come, drinking of the cup of knowledge, and a variety of other cups as well.

Jefferson's spirit remains palpably alive at the university. His spirit is reflected in the architecture of "the Grounds," as the campus is often called, which the *New York Times* described at the time as "incomparably the most ambitious and monumental architectural project that had or has yet been conceived in this century." The "Lawn," a terraced green space of academic buildings and student housing, and the Rotunda, standing at the north end of the Lawn, are its definitive features.

UVA in the twenty-first century is a study in contrast and contradiction. It can boast a rightful place as one of the great research universities of the world, with faculty who are international leaders in the sciences, arts, and learned professions. For students from Virginia, the UVA in-state tuition of roughly $10,000 a year makes it one of the greatest educational bargains in the United States—an Ivy League–quality school for a small fraction of the Ivy League price. As a state university, UVA admits plenty of public-school blue-collar and rural kids each year, first-generation college students for whom UVA is an extraordinary beacon of upward mobility. Yet the university's image, part mythology and part reality, is an image of wealth and privilege. UVA might just as well be Yale or Princeton, a bastion of the sort of old-boy wealth that Norman Mailer once described as "that much-massaged look of a man whose money makes money while he sleeps."[1] Men often wear blue blazers and ties to football games, and women wear pearls.

In 2012 *U.S. News & World Report* judged UVA second in the United States among public universities in academic ranking. The same year *Playboy* magazine ranked UVA the nation's number-one party school. Both rankings seemed well deserved. To be sure, at UVA it seemed that everybody partied. Perhaps no more than they partied at Duke or Yale, to be fair, but party-on they did. Even in this, it could be argued, the influence of Jefferson might be discerned. He was author of the Declaration of Independence, drafter of the Statute of Religious Freedom, father of the University of Virginia, and, to borrow from the rock lyrics of Three Dog Night, "he always had some mighty fine wine."[2]

Yet there was also a darker side to Jefferson's legacy, a side not easily processed. Here he was the author of the magnificent declaration that "all men are created equal." Yet Jefferson owned slaves. Yet Jefferson took a slave as his mistress, and she bore his offspring. For Jefferson, for his university, for Charlottesville, for the country, matters relating to race and to sex would always be a complex work in progress.

Fast forward to the modern-bouillabaisse-stew-hot-not-your-grandparents'-melting-pot of contemporary culture-war campus politics, where issues of race and sex and power and privilege all mingle, tingle, and tangle in confounding and confusing confluence and conflict.

Richard Spencer, the mastermind behind Charlottesville's 2017 summer of violence, formed much of his obsession with modern culture-war identity politics while he was pursuing a doctorate at Duke. In the infamous 2006 Duke lacrosse team scandal, white members of the lacrosse team were accused of raping a black woman at a team house party. The accusations turned out to be false. The Duke lacrosse incident was a precipitating moment in Spencer's journey toward radicalization. In the eyes of many conservatives, the Duke lacrosse incident reflected what writer Tom Wolfe, in his novel *The Bonfire of the Vanities*, described as the "mania for the Great White Defendant." Spencer was at Duke at the time, and so was Stephen Miller. Both rode to fame in the flames surrounding Duke's own bonfire of the vanities.

Stephen Miller would become one of the most influential advisers to President Donald Trump. He was the speechwriter who authored the acceptance speech Trump delivered on his nomination for president at the Republican National Convention in 2016, and Miller helped craft Trump's inaugural address on his assuming the presidency. Under the title "senior advisor to the president for policy," Miller helped craft many of the signature initiatives of Trump's administration, including Trump's immigration travel ban, his crackdown on "sanctuary cities," the decision to fire FBI director James Comey, and efforts to adopt policies making it difficult for Chinese students to study in the United States.

Miller and Spencer met when Miller was a conservative undergraduate at Duke, as members of the Duke Conservative Union. It was the Duke lacrosse incident that galvanized Spencer's radicalism and also launched Miller's career as a movement conservative intellectual. Miller, then a senior, wrote an article in January 2007 for the Duke student newspaper titled "A Portrait of Radicalism," blasting the Duke faculty members who had, in his view, rushed to prejudge the case and assume that the members of the lacrosse team were guilty. Miller then appeared as a guest on Bill O'Reilly's Fox News *O'Reilly Factor* show. At the same time, a Thai restaurant in Alexandria, Virginia, was hosting a panel discussion on the Duke lacrosse case. One of the speakers was Richard Spencer, who delivered a blistering condemnation of the Duke faculty and administration for its actions against the lacrosse team.[3] By happenstance, in the audience at Spencer's speech were writer Scott McConnell and editor Michael Dougherty, who worked for the *American Conservative* magazine. They were impressed by Spencer's persona and by his speech. One thing led to another, and Spencer ended up leaving academia for a life of activism. The *American Conservative* commissioned Spencer to write an article about the Duke case. Spencer wrote the article, dropped out of Duke, and went to work for the magazine full time. "In this funny chain of events, the Duke lacrosse case changed the course of my career," Spencer once told journalist Reeves Wiedeman. "My life would not have taken the direction it did absent the Duke lacrosse case."[4]

In the lead-up to the Charlottesville 2017 summer of disturbance, the University of Virginia would go through its own version of the Duke lacrosse case, the second of Richard Spencer's schools to experience a communal meltdown over claims of gang rape allegedly perpetrated by elite white males.

The Phi Kappa Psi fraternity at the University of Virginia had been portrayed in a *Rolling Stone* magazine article written by journalist and contributing editor Sabrina Rubin Erdely as orchestrating a brutal ritual gang-rape of a UVA freshman woman named "Jackie."

Immediately after *Rolling Stone* broke its story, I was contacted for comment by a reporter for the *Washington Post*. Reflexively—and, on reflection, not so very reflectively—my thoughts turned to Oscar Wilde.

Oscar Fingal O'Flahertie Wills Wilde, to not be short, was a brilliant Irish poet, playwright, novelist, and raconteur. Wilde's best novel was the haunting, ghostly tale *The Picture of Dorian Gray*. Wilde's best play was impishly titled *The Importance of Being Earnest*. In one of the strange and improbable ways that history has of creating connections, Richard Spencer had performed in Wilde's *Earnest* as a college actor in his freshman year at Colgate, the college he attended before transferring to UVA.

Oscar Wilde brought a criminal libel prosecution against John Douglas, the Marquess of Queensberry, when Wilde was accused of being the gay lover of Douglas's son, Alfred. The problem for Wilde was that the allegations were true. Wilde's libel case backfired, ending in Wilde's financial ruin and a prison sentence. As a young lawyer I happened to have the occasion to spend a few nights at L'Hotel, a boutique hotel on the

Left Bank in Saint-Germain-des-Prés in Paris, where Oscar Wilde lived as an expatriate in France, and where he died. As he sipped champagne on his deathbed in the chic hotel, Wilde quipped, "I am dying beyond my means."

Rolling Stone's article, titled "A Rape on Campus: A Brutal Assault and Struggle for Justice at UVA," was a graphic exercise in "new journalism," a vivid account written in the riveting style of a Truman Capote story depicting Jackie's brutal ordeal.

Jacqueline, or "Jackie," was her real first name. Her real last name is not used in this book. Jackie was born in Boston, where she lived until her family moved to northern Virginia, in the Washington suburbs, where Jackie attended high school. Her father was a retired Vietnam veteran and military contractor. Her mother was a stay-at-home mom. Jackie was on her high school swim team and played first-chair violin for the school orchestra. She was an honor roll student and active in community service. She traveled to Costa Rica on a service mission. Yet like many college-bound students, Jackie was ready to leave home and experience the escape and freedom of college.

Jackie arrived at the University of Virginia in the fall of 2012. She faced the usual adjustments of college life, getting used to UVA's demanding academics, learning to manage her time, and finding her fit in the social scene. Like many first-year college students, her main circle of friends were roommates and other students in her residence hall. Jackie worked as a lifeguard at the University Aquatic Center. She was not a drinker or wild partier, but was no prude either, and had a normal curiosity about the party scene at UVA's many sororities and fraternities.

The *Rolling Stone* article told how Jackie was brought to a Phi Kappa Psi date function held on September 28, 2012, by a third-year undergraduate at UVA, identified as "Drew," a member of the fraternity. Jackie knew Drew from the UVA Aquatic and Fitness Center, where they both worked. The article recounted how, at the Phi Kappa Psi party, Jackie was given alcoholic punch to drink, and then brought upstairs by Drew to a dark bedroom. In the bedroom Jackie was tackled and sent backward onto a low glass table, which shattered and caused shards of glass to dig into her back. She was punched, pinned to the table, a hand clamped over her mouth, while her legs were pried apart, and she was ritually raped by seven Phi Kappa Psi members for three agonizing hours. One of the rapists began the ritual by shouting "Grab its motherfucking leg." The gang rape was a Phi Kappa Psi initiation rite. During the ritual rape one of Jackie's assailants chastised one of the other assailants, saying, "Don't you want to be a brother? We had to do it, so you do, too." Jackie was repeatedly raped, and even violated with a beer bottle, which was shoved into her. Hours later, as she staggered, bloody and violated, from the frat house, Jackie called for help from three of her student friends. But what callow friends they proved to be. Instead of providing Jackie comfort and support, they coldly sought to dissuade her from reporting her assault, warning that Jackie would be "the girl who cried rape" and that they would "never be allowed into any frat party again." All this was recounted in detail in the *Rolling Stone* article.

Under the headline "Suing Rolling Stone Might Be a 'Colossal Mistake' for the UVA Frat," the *Post* quoted me for the smug conclusion that any libel suit could backfire, exposing the fraternity's "skeletons in the closet." My first instinct, I am somewhat ashamed to say, was that surely the fraternity would be foolish to sue—just like Oscar Wilde.

As with many of my first instincts, this one turned out to be entirely wrong.

Following the story in the *Washington Post*, the Charlottesville lawyer representing the Phi Kappa Psi fraternity, Tom Albro, called me. Tom and I had known each other for years. I regarded him as the best libel lawyer in Virginia, and one of the best in the country. Tom assured me that the fraternity had no skeletons in the closet and that the rape story was entirely false. He then surprised me, asking if I'd be interested in joining him in representing Phi Kappa Psi in a suit for defamation against *Rolling Stone*.

I agreed to join Albro's team as cocounsel. One of the perspectives I brought to the team was an understanding of the political and cultural dynamics surrounding controversies over gender equality, race, sexual orientation, and sexual assault on American university campuses. While I had spent a lot of time in Charlottesville, I had never been on the University of Virginia faculty. But I had over twenty years of experience as a faculty member and administrator at three other Virginia schools: the College of William and Mary, the University of Richmond, and Washington and Lee University.

As an educator and scholar, I had been actively involved in issues relating to sexual assault on American college campuses. When I was dean of the Law School at Washington and Lee University, down the road from Charlottesville in the small Shenandoah Valley town of Lexington, I was appointed to chair a task force on sexual assault. The task force revealed that sexual assault on the campus was far more prevalent in reality than in the university's reported statistics, because so few victims of sexual assault were willing to come forward and file complaints against their assailants. The university's system for investigating and adjudicating sexual assault claims was perceived by many as biased against victims. There was also a widespread sense that those who filed complaints of sexual assault were likely to be socially ostracized. The task force recommended a comprehensive set of reforms to encourage greater reporting of assaults and create a more balanced system for investigation and adjudication of sexual assault complaints When I later became president of Furman University, in Greenville, South Carolina, I was the "court of last resort" within the university for the adjudication of sexual assault complaints. As a scholar and law professor, I had written extensively and taught classes on the handling of sexual assault allegations on American campuses, including the processes and burdens of proof mandated by the US Department of Education under Title IX. Last but by no means least, my daughter Corey was a sexual assault victims' advocate at Yale and had been at the forefront of many of Yale's struggles to deal with issues relating to sexual assault and racism on the Yale campus.

I was also an experienced libel law litigator. I had been cocounsel or lead counsel in many high-profile libel suits in state and federal courts across the nation. We were a lean team—just three lawyers, Tom, me, and Evan Mayo, who had just graduated from the University of Virginia Law School, passed the bar exam, and become a member of the Virginia state bar.

Our client, the Alpha Chapter of the Phi Kappa Psi fraternity, or "Phi Psi," was founded at the University of Virginia in 1853, as the second Phi Psi chapter in the nation. The Phi Psi brotherhood was grounded on the "great joy of helping others." The charitable mission of the fraternity remained alive and well in 2012, as Phi Psi brothers raised thousands of dollars for charitable causes and devoted more than one thousand volunteer service hours each year. Its graduates were often men of power and influence in business, politics, medicine, academia, and the military. Over the course of its history the UVA Phi Psi chapter boasted many successful alumni, including governors, congressmen, ambassadors, generals, an admiral, and a US president and Nobel Peace Prize recipient, Woodrow Wilson.

Phi Psi did not have a reputation as a wild party frat. It was no "Animal House." If anything, its reputation was on the nerdier side, with members who generally did well in academics, athletics, and university leadership. It was known as an "upper tier" fraternity, whose brothers had been offered memberships to UVA's engineering honor society, the Echols Scholars program, Tau Beta Pi, the Raven Society (named for UVA student Edgar Allan Poe's famous poem), the Order of the Cloak and Dagger, and the University Honor Committee. Its members had been Jefferson and Fulbright Scholars, participated in ROTC, been leaders in the Inter-Fraternity Council and student government, played as varsity athletes, worked as athletic coaches, and been invited to live on the university's famous Lawn, the exclusive residential units reserved for the university's best students.

Rolling Stone's indictment of Phi Psi, and more broadly all of UVA's culture, was devastating. The tenor of the article was captured in its repeated quotation from lyrics of the song "Rugby Road," which the article described as the "traditional University of Virginia fight song."

> From Rugby Road to Vinegar Hill, we're gonna get drunk tonight
> The faculty's afraid of us, they know we're in the right
> So fill up your cups, your loving cups, as full as full can be
> As long as love and liquor last, we'll drink to the U of V.

> All you girls from Mary Washington
> and RMWC, never let a Cavalier an inch above your knee.
> He'll take you to his fraternity house and fill you full of beer.
> And soon you'll be the mother of a bastard Cavalier!

"A Rape on Campus" exploded onto the American college scene, causing an immediate uproar throughout the nation. In quick reaction to the article, UVA president Teresa Sullivan ordered all Greek activities on the UVA campus suspended.

The article precipitated near-riot conditions on the UVA campus. The Phi Kappa Psi house became an overnight symbol for the scourge of rape. Massive protest rallies directed at Phi Psi emerged, in which irate members of the public, driven to outrage by *Rolling Stone*, expressed their anger. On the same night the article was published, a group of students vandalized the Phi Kappa Psi fraternity house. Slogans such as "UVA Center for Rape Studies" and "Suspend Us!" were spray-painted on the retaining wall of the house. Bottles and chunks of cinder block were hurled through the fraternity house windows. The next day, news trucks crowded the area in front of the house, as reporters peppered the deer-in-the-headlights members of the fraternity. Additional protesters arrived from Washington, DC. One protest leader used a bullhorn to demand that the protesters "burn the frat houses down." Other protesters advanced onto the porch of the Phi Psi house and refused to move until the Charlottesville Police Department arrested four of their number and forcibly removed them from the property. Many protesters used cameras and cell phones to capture images of the inside of the house and the Phi Kappa Psi brothers who lived there. A journalist used a telephoto lens to snap pictures of composite photographs through the windows and published that information online. On the night of November 23, 2014, two men attempted to break into the house through a side door.

In UVA classrooms, Phi Kappa Psi members endured extemporaneous lectures from their academic professors about the "absolutely disgusting" behavior of the Phi Kappa Psi members. In one class, a teacher interrupted a discussion about the article to request that any Phi Kappa Psi members in the class identify themselves. In a graduate school in Washington, DC, a Phi Kappa Psi alumnus listened in disbelief as his professor addressed the class shortly after the release of the article: "If you were to remove our brain, we would still be able to carry out normal daily function. If you don't believe me, just ask those fraternity brothers at UVA. You get them together, you remove their cortex, and they function perfectly—they can breathe, they can eat, they can do all kinds of things." Another Phi Psi brother was playing in a collegiate sports tournament when the news broke, and he was taunted and called a rapist throughout the ensuing game.

One Phi Kappa Psi brother who was studying abroad in Scotland chose to conceal his fraternity membership from classmates who had read and believed the story. News networks in other countries ran stories based on the belief that the accusations of gang-rape were true. *Rolling Stone*'s article destroyed Phi Kappa Psi's reputation on a worldwide scale.

As Jackie related the story to *Rolling Stone*, her brutal assault was emblematic of deeper and darker conspiracies at UVA, and perhaps on campuses across the nation. Jackie said she knew of at least two other women currently at UVA who had also been gang-raped at Phi Kappa Psi. There was evidence, she said, that the gang rape ritual dated back decades. And the culture at UVA consistently and persistently covered it all up. The university's own administrators, Jackie claimed, did all they could to aid and abet the conspiracy of silence. Jackie explained that a dean at UVA had put it clearly: "Who wants to be known as 'rape university'?"

The powerful currents that swept through the UVA campus after the *Rolling Stone* story presaged much of what would happen again as the alt-right descended on Charlottesville. Many of those most virulently repulsed by the gang-rape story and driven to stage graphic protest demonstrations on the UVA campus would also be repulsed by the racist messages of the alt-right. In both cases, the roiling anger, first directed against the perceived brutal sexual assault depicted in *Rolling Stone*, and second against the racial supremacist messages of the alt-right, was heavily fueled by communication on social media. And in both cases, many of those in the UVA community were reflexively suspicious of the leadership of the university itself—skeptical that university leaders were sufficiently aggressive in taking principled stands against sexism and sexual assault or messages of racial supremacy and violence.

My work on the *Rolling Stone* case brought home to me the passions at large on the UVA campus that would erupt once again as the debate over the fate of the Charlottesville Confederate monuments intensified, debates that set the stage for what would become a series of supremacist events in Charlottesville in the summer of 2017, culminating the deadly rally to Unite the Right.

8

KESSLER V. BELLAMY

Charlottesville became the epicenter of the national debate over Confederate monuments. The debate in Charlottesville was colored by a personal sideshow battle between Wes Bellamy, a local African American teacher, activist, and political leader, and Jason Kessler, Charlottesville's emerging alt-right supremacist man-on-the-scene.

Wes Bellamy came from Atlanta and attended college at South Carolina State University. He moved to Charlottesville in 2009. Bellamy became a teacher at Albemarle High School. (Albemarle County is the Virginia county that entirely surrounds Charlottesville, though under Virginia law the City of Charlottesville is a legally independent municipality and enclave.) While teaching and becoming engaged in community and political affairs, Bellamy continued his education, earning a master's degree in education administration in 2014 and a doctoral degree at Virginia State University in 2017. Governor Terry McAuliffe appointed Bellamy to the Virginia State Board of Education in 2016.

Bellamy was active in community service. He worked with a group called Helping Young People Evolve, a boxing and mentoring program serving boys and girls in the Charlottesville/Albemarle urban ring. Student partici-pants in the program had an overall increase in their grade point averages from 1.8 in December 2011 to 3.2 in June 2016. Bellamy served as presi-dent of a group called the "100 Black Men of Central Virginia" and was an adviser to the University of Virginia Collegiate 100 Black Men of Central Virginia chapter. Bellamy was co-chair of the Charlottesville Alliance for Black Male Achievement. He served on the Charlottesville Redevelopment and Housing Authority Board and the Charlottesville Police Citizens Advi-sory Panel. He has also served on the Charlottesville Housing Advisory Committee.

Charlottesville has a city manager form of government. The city man-ager is a professional city administrator, the chief executive officer of the city. The city manager is not elected but is rather hired and fired by the five-member city council, which has the ultimate legal authority in the city. A mayor and a vice-mayor are selected from the membership of the city council by the council members. Thus, while citizens vote for the membership of the city council, they do not directly select the mayor and vice-mayor. In cities with a city manager form of government, the mayor is not the day-to-day chief executive officer of the city but is rather more akin to a chair of the board, the presiding officer of the city council.

Wes Bellamy first ran for the Charlottesville City Council in 2013. He initially appeared tied in the Democratic Party primary voting with Bob Fenwick, with 1,088 votes each. Following a recount, however, Fenwick was declared the winner by five votes.[1] Bellamy ran again in 2015 and this time was elected, becoming the youngest person ever to serve as a member of the Charlottesville City Council. He was then chosen as vice-mayor.

Jason Kessler was Bellamy's nemesis. Kessler graduated from the Uni-versity of Virginia in 2009 with a bachelor of arts in psychology. Kes-sler fashioned himself a freelance journalist and activist. He wrote for various right-wing publications, including VDARE, the Daily Caller, and GotNews.[2] Kessler also maintained his own site, JasonKessler.us. Kessler founded a number of his own organizations, including "America First" and "Security for America."[3] Kessler's attacks on Wes Bellamy, followed by his leadership role in resisting attempts to remove Charlottesville's Confederate monuments to Robert E. Lee and Stonewall Jackson, would begin to place him in greater prominence within the alt-right universe. These efforts by Kessler were eventually what led him to meet Richard Spencer, with whom he began to orchestrate the alt-right's targeting of Charlottesville in the summer of 2017.

Wes Bellamy took on the role as the leading activist and political figure fighting to remove the Charlottesville Confederate monuments. Bellamy organized a press conference, to be held in front of the Lee statue in Lee Park, on March 22, 2016, at which he and his supporters called on the city to remove the Lee statue and the Jackson statue.[4]

Bellamy's schedule press conference was publicized in advance and drew a crowd of angry counterdemonstrators, many brandishing Confederate flags and carrying signs protesting against attempts to "erase history." The press conference grew tense as demonstrators for and against the removal of the statues traded insults and accusations.

Kessler was particularly offended by Bellamy's crusade against the Lee statue. Kessler started a crusade of his own, seeking removal of Bellamy. Kessler discovered that Bellamy was an active Twitter user, and he mined Bellamy's Twitter account for embarrassing posts. His mining struck a mother lode. Kessler published a compendium of Bellamy's tweets on his own blog and called for Bellamy's resignation or removal from office. Local Charlottesville media outlets, and then national news organizations such as CNN, picked up on the controversy and repeated Bellamy's tweets.

The University of Virginia's student newspaper, the *Cavalier Daily*, led the charge against Bellamy.[5] In an October 2011 tweet, Bellamy had answered a question prompted by another user, "Does it make males uncomfortable wen girls are so upfront about sex??" with "It only makes faggots uncomfortable." The Bellamy tweets included vulgar terms for female genitalia, and retweets on sexual assault and rape, including a retweet that stated "Eat it while she asleep if she moan it aint rape." Bellamy tweeted about too many women being teachers, and how their prevalence hurt male students, asserting, "I'm all for equal opportunity . . . but a Female Principal with a school full of female teachers is fkn a sure fire way to fk up our lil boys smh." Other Bellamy tweets appeared openly racist and hostile to whites. In 2009 Bellamy had tweeted, "I DONT LIK WHIT PEOPLE SO I HATE WHITE SNOW!!!!! FML!!!!" Bellamy in other tweets compared white women to the devil and complained of white women wearing sundresses.[6]

The *Cavalier Daily* observed that the Bellamy tweets expressing prejudice contrasted with a tweet Bellamy sent pushing for unity immediately following the mass shooting at the Orlando gay nightclub, Pulse, in June that had left forty-nine dead. "I don't care if you're gay, straight, trans, black, white, blue, or purple" Bellamy tweeted on June 13, "YOU DESERVE EQUAL RIGHTS AND YOU HAVE THE RIGHT TO BE SAFE!"[7]

In December 2016, Kessler launched a petition drive demanding that Bellamy resign or be removed "in light of recently revealed anti-white, racist and pro-rape comments." Another pro-Confederacy monument group, called the Virginia Flaggers, urged Charlottesville citizens to contact the Charlottesville City Council and demand Bellamy's removal from office.[8]

Bellamy was under siege. Albemarle High School suspended him from his teaching post, and he ultimately resigned from the high school. Yet Bellamy was resolved to retain his political position and sustain his attack on the Confederate monuments. "I am not a black supremacist, a racist, a misogynist," Bellamy stated in response to Kessler's attacks. Bellamy attributed his tweets to an immature time in his life, which no longer reflected his values. "What I am is a son, a husband, a father, a teacher and a proud member of this community who works every day to improve the city we live in."[9] Bellamy apologized, took ownership of his wrongful statements, and sought to move on. "I sincerely apologize for the inappropriate things I posted to social media many years ago," Bellamy stated in a Facebook post. "Elected officials should be held to a higher standard, and while I was not in office at the time, in this instance I came up short of the man I aspire to be."[10]

9

The Monuments Debate

On May 28, 2016, the Charlottesville City Council approved a resolution to create a "Blue Ribbon Commission on Race, Memorials, and Public Spaces" to provide the council "with options for telling the full story of Charlottesville's history of race and for changing the City's narrative through our public spaces."[1] Nine persons were appointed to the commission, which had as its principal focus the statues Robert E. Lee and Stonewall Jackson.

The commission conducted a series of public hearings. Proponents of removal attacked the statues as racist and as perpetuating the "lost cause" apology for the Civil War. Proponents of retaining the statutes defended them as appropriate homages to the history of South, arguing that there was an inherent evil to attempts to erase history. Those favoring removal argued that modern society ought not venerate an evil history; a statue of Robert E. Lee or Stonewall Jackson was no worthier of veneration than a statue of Adolf Hitler or Joseph Stalin.

On November 1, 2016, the commission issued a compromise decision. By a vote of 6–3 it decided not to recommend removal of the Lee and Jackson statues but to instead place them in a new "context," recommending that Charlottesville "retain the statues on the condition that their meaning is transformed, and their history is retold." Yet the commission also recommended that the two parks in which the statues were placed—Lee Park and Jackson Park—be renamed.[2]

University of Virginia professor of history John Edwin Mason served as the vice chair of the commission and drafted parts of its report. He was proud of the commission's work and believed that its conclusions reflected a broad consensus on the commission, though with varying degrees of enthusiasm among its members.[3]

The following week, on November 8, 2016, the election of Donald Trump as president of the United States would enter the Charlottesville narrative. Trump's election raised the intensity of debates over all matters concerning identity politics in the United States, including divisive questions surrounding the monuments to the Confederacy.

Following the election, pressure mounted on the commission to reconsider its decision. On November 18, the commission did partially modify its recommendation. It voted to move the Lee statute to McIntire Park, a large forest-preserve park outside the downtown area of Charlottesville, but to keep the Jackson statute where it was.[4] The revised report was formally submitted to the Charlottesville City Council on December 19, 2016.

As the inauguration of President Trump approached, various groups wary of the president-elect's views on race, ethnicity, poverty, and sexual orientation became increasingly virulent in their anti-Trump demonstrations. Charlottesville mayor Mike Signer aligned himself with this growing movement, declaring that he hoped Charlottesville would become the "national capital of the Resistance."[5]

The first showdown on what to do with the monuments occurred on January 17, 2017, three days before Trump took the oath of office as the nation's forty-fifth president.[6] The Charlottesville City Council had before it the question of whether to move the two monuments or allow them to stay. The council meeting was tempestuous, with passionate advocates for both sides.

Wes Bellamy and council member Kristin Szakos voted to move both the Lee and Jackson monuments. Mayor Signer and council member

Kathy Galvin opposed the move. They cited the potential expense of moving both monuments, which was likely to cost hundreds of thousands of dollars, the potential that efforts to move the monuments would embroil the city in legal challenges seeking to block the move, and the angry backlash expected from many segments of the community if the moves were made.

Council member Bob Fenwick, who had previously defeated Wes Bellamy for a seat on the council, held the swing vote. Fenwick voted to abstain, resulting in a 2–2 deadlock. "Enough symbolism. Enough with the declarations, proclamations, good intentions, and written promises. We have been down that road before—more than once," Fenwick said. "It's time to show me the money. If these words tonight have any meaning, they will find their way into the city budget. It's time to invest in our citizens."

Once Fenwick cast his abstention vote, all hell broke loose. Mayor Signer labored to maintain order. Fenwick drew the ire of the activists seeking to have the monuments moved, enduring shouts of "shame" and "coward." They perceived the council's failure to take action as an insult to African Americans, perpetuating the symbols of slavery, the Confederacy, and Jim Crow. "You're the worst type of racist. You're the one that smiles and tell us that everything is going to be OK," one of the community members shouted at Fenwick.[7]

Those opposed to moving the monuments were equally vitriolic. "It is one thing to advocate for something, but you demonize the people you're forcing to pay for your liberal agenda," city resident John Heyden told the council. "We're tired of being disrespected by carpetbagging liberals who want to voice their racial hatred on those of us who were born here," Heyden declared.[8] Before and during the meeting, defenders of the monuments focused much of their ire at Bellamy. Teresa Kay Lam, from Elkton, Virginia, accused Bellamy himself of fanning racism by labeling defenders of the monuments as "white supremacists." "My ancestors fought under General Lee. I am kin to General Lee, and I will fight with honor to keep his monument where it is and run you out of town," Lam wrote in an e-mail responding to one of Bellamy's Facebook posts.[9]

Don Gathers, who had chaired the blue ribbon commission on the monuments, was frustrated by the deadlock. "What Fenwick did was a coward's exit," Gathers said. "That was six months of work that's amounted to absolutely nothing."[10]

On February 6, 2017, the city council met again. The defenders of the monuments were present in force. Even so, Bob Fenwick now took a position, voting to move the monuments. "If you think death threats will stop me, you must not know my background. I've been through much worse," Fenwick said. "I'm aware a lawsuit's been threatened. I'd welcome one."[11] By a vote of 3–2 the council called for city staff employees to report back within sixty days on a plan to move the statues.

The formal vote to move the monuments began to galvanize the opposition. On February 21, 2017, Corey Stewart, a candidate for the Republican nomination for governor of Virginia, spoke at a political rally in Charlottesville, making the saving of the monuments a major campaign theme. Stewart was joined at the rally by Jason Kessler, who had led the earlier attack on Bellamy and would later be the pivotal Charlottesville leader of the deadly Unite the Right rally.

On March 22, 2017, Fenwick's invitation to bring the litigation on was accepted. A consortium of plaintiffs, including the Virginia division of the Sons of Confederate Veterans and a group that called itself "the Monument Fund," along with various other Charlottesville residents, led by attorney Ralph E. Main, brought a lawsuit to block the proposed removal of the statues. The group argued that the statues were insulated from removal under a Virginia state law that prohibited local governments from removing "war memorials." The Lee and Jackson statues, the suit asserted, were plainly memorials relating to the Civil War and thus could not be moved. The case was assigned to circuit judge Richard E. Moore. This was the same Judge Moore before whom the defamation lawsuit filed by Tom Albro and me for the Phi Kappa Psi fraternity against *Rolling Stone* was pending.

Richard Moore was an undergraduate at Duke at the same time that I was attending Duke Law School, though we did not then meet. He then went on to the University of Virginia Law School, served as a deputy commonwealth's attorney (the name for prosecutors in Virginia) in Charlottesville and Albemarle County, and as an assistant commonwealth's attorney in Orange County, Virginia, before becoming a judge in the Juvenile and Domestic Relations Court 2012. Two years later the Virginia General Assembly elevated him to the Charlottesville Circuit Court.

Alexis de Tocqueville, in his classic 1835 work *Democracy in America*, observed that "there is virtually no political question in the United States that does not sooner or later resolve itself into a judicial question."[12] The proposition proved true for Judge Moore, who soon seemed to find himself the arbiter of judicial questions arising from all of Charlottesville's political and cultural traumas.

Moore presided over the civil litigation arising from the murder of a University of Virginia women's lacrosse player, Yeardley Love, at the hands of a UVA men's lacrosse player. Love's murder was one of a series of murders of women connected to Charlottesville or the University of Virginia that rattled and haunted the community, as if it were possessed by some violent, malevolent curse.

On October 17, 2009, Morgan Dana Harrington, a twenty-year-old from Roanoke, Virginia, who was attending Virginia Tech University in nearby Blacksburg, traveled with three friends to Charlottesville to attend a concert by the rock group Metallica at UVA's John Paul Jones arena— the university's basketball arena and concert venue. Harrington left her friends to go to the bathroom but did not return. Her friends called her at 8:48 p.m. Harrington picked up on her cell phone and told her friends that she had gotten locked out of the arena but that she would find a way home and they should not worry. Harrington was spotted around 9:30 that evening hitchhiking on a bridge near the arena. That was the last time she was seen alive.

Harrington's purse, with her identification and cell phone, were found in a parking lot at UVA's Lannigan Athletic Field. The battery had been removed from the phone. Months later, on January 26, 2010, her body was discovered on a 742-acre farm in a rural area about ten miles from the UVA campus. She had many broken bones and had been raped. Police were able to harvest DNA evidence from Harrington's body and match the DNA to another unsolved Virginia crime, an abduction and sexual assault in Fairfax, dating back to 2005. As word got out that a possible serial rapist and killer was at large in Virginia, Crimestoppers offered a $100,000 reward for information leading to a conviction, and the band Metallica added an additional $50,000 reward. But no suspect could be identified.

It took another tragedy to finally solve Harrington's murder. Hannah Elizabeth Graham was an eighteen-year-old student at UVA. On

September 13, 2014, Graham was partying late into the night. She texted some friends at 1:20 a.m. with the message that she was leaving one party and heading for another but had gotten lost. Outside the Tempo restaurant on Charlottesville's Downtown Mall, a witness spotted Graham with an older man, who had an arm around her and was trying to coax her into an orange 1998 Chrysler Sebring. The witness testified that he did "not look friendly" and said that Graham shouted at him, "I'm not getting into that car with you." Video surveillance footage helped police identify the man as thirty-two-year-old Jesse Leeroy Matthew Jr.

Matthew had a suspicious history. In 2002 he attended Liberty University, founded by Rev. Jerry Falwell, in Lynchburg, Virginia. Matthew was accused of sexual assault at Liberty, which triggered a police investigation. He quit the school, and no charges were filed. Matthew then enrolled at Christopher Newport University in Newport News, Virginia. He was again charged with sexual assault. Police again investigated, and again Matthew quit school, and again no charges were filed.

Five weeks after Heather Graham disappeared, her remains were discovered in a rural area about ten miles from the UVA campus, only one and a half miles from the place where Dana Harrington's body had been found. Forensic evidence linked Graham's murder to Harrington's, and both matched Jesse Matthew. Matthew ultimately pleaded guilty to both the Graham and Harrington murders and was sentenced to life imprisonment without parole.

Yeardley Love and George Wesley Huguely V had been dating for two years. In the spring of 2010 Love broke up with Huguely. He reacted to the breakup violently, sending Love threatening e-mails and text messages. On one occasion Huguely attacked Love while he was drunk. On other occasion, visiting lacrosse players from the University of North Carolina broke up a violent confrontation between Huguely and Love. On May 3, 2010, Huguely appeared at the door of Love's off-campus apartment on Fourteenth Street, in Charlottesville's "Corner" district. Huguely kicked down the door to Love's bedroom, grabbed her, and shook her head repeatedly against the wall. The attack killed her.

Huguely was arrested and charged with murder and other crimes. He was tried in February 2012. After deliberating nine hours, a jury found him guilty of second-degree murder and grand larceny, rejecting Huguely's defense that he acted in "the heat of passion." He was sentenced to twenty-three years in prison.

Yeardley Love's mother, Sharon Love, filed multiple civil wrongful death suits, including suits against Huguely himself, as well as against the University of Virginia, the university's men's lacrosse coach Dom Starsia, associate lacrosse coach Marc Van Arsdale, and the university's athletic director Craig Littlepage. Her suit claimed that it "was well known to the players and coaches on the UVA men's and women's lacrosse teams that Huguely's alcohol abuse and erratic, aggressive behavior was increasingly getting out of control, especially his obsession with Love and his aggressiveness and threats to Love," and that in spite of this, no action was taken "to discipline Huguely, to suspend or remove Huguely from the lacrosse team, to refer Huguely for treatment or counseling for alcohol/ substance abuse or anger/aggressive behavior management, or to subsequently report Huguely's potential risk of violence pursuant to the UVA Policy on Preventing and Addressing Threats or Acts of Violence." The Love family ultimately dropped its suit against the university and the two coaches and athletic director but continued to pursue the case against Huguely. The case would ultimately land before Judge Moore.

It also fell upon Moore to decide whether the monuments to Robert E. Lee and Stonewall Jackson could be removed by the City of Charlottesville. The challengers relied on a number of Virginia laws restricting the power of local governments to move war memorials. Judge Moore issued his ruling on May 2, 2017. Finding that the Lee and Jackson statues did appear to qualify as war memorials, Moore issued a preliminary injunction prohibiting the City of Charlottesville from moving the statutes for six months, pending a fuller trial on the merits of the claim that any removal of the statutes would be illegal. Moore noted, after a six-hour hearing, that the Lee and Jackson statutes were offensive to some people because it was clear that they were war memorials to the Confederacy. Yet while acknowledging that the statutes caused offense to many in the community, Moore reasoned, that did not change the inescapable reality that the statutes were war memorials. Even if the cause connected with the statutes was regarded by many today as dishonorable, that did not disqualify the statutes from their protection under Virginia law. Judge Moore also gave something to the City of Charlottesville, however. He ruled that his injunction did not prevent Charlottesville from renaming Lee and Jackson Parks, actions that did not involve removal of the memorials themselves.

The fight over the removal of the monuments, including Judge Moore's ruling, led directly to plans by Richard Spencer and Jason Kessler to stage the first alt-right event in Charlottesville, a rally on Mother's Day weekend calculated to stir the alt-right base to action in defense of the monuments and advancing the movement's larger agenda. Those plans implicated a debate that had been raging across American college campuses, over whether "hate speech" was "free speech." That debate in turn implicated larger debates, centuries old, over competing conceptions about what freedom of speech means in the United States.

10

COMPETING CONCEPTIONS OF FREE SPEECH

The First Amendment to the Constitution of the United States reads, "Congress shall make no law respecting an establishment of religion, or prohibiting the free exercise thereof; or abridging the freedom of speech, or of the press; or the right of the people peaceably to assemble, and to petition the Government for a redress of grievances." It was adopted on December 15, 1791, as part of the first ten amendments to the Constitution that comprise the Bill of Rights. Debate over the meaning of the First Amendment has been central to American political, cultural, and legal history from the beginning.

From the outset, the American debate over the meaning of "freedom of speech" has been a contest between two ideas, each elegant and compelling. The shorthand labels I give to these two ideas are the "order and morality" theory and the "marketplace of ideas" theory.

The "order and morality" conception of freedom of speech is grounded in the notion that freedom of speech cannot be elevated above the "social compact" that binds us as a society. A stable, decent, and just society may call on its citizens to obey certain elemental precepts of order. Examples might be "thou shalt not kill," or "thou shalt not wage war against the government." A stable, decent, and just society may also call on its citizens to respect certain precepts of morality. Examples might be "thou shalt not degrade or debase a person based on the person's racial, religious, or sexual identity." The order and morality theory posits that freedom of speech, while important, remains subordinate to values of order and morality. Speech that undermines order or morality may be punished by laws enacted through the democratic process. Freedom of speech is not freedom to subvert order or erode morality. This theory was sublimely articulated in one simple sentence in a 1942 Supreme Court opinion written by Justice Frank Murphy in *Chaplinsky v. New Hampshire*: "It has been well observed that such utterances are no essential part of any exposition of ideas, and are of such slight social value as a step to truth that any benefit that may be derived from them is clearly outweighed by the social interest in order and morality."[1]

The marketplace theory is the opposite. It is grounded in the notion that democracy is subordinate to free speech. The test of truth and morality should be the power of a thought to win in the competition of the marketplace of ideas. This should be an ongoing and unfettered competition, outside the heavy-handed authority of the law. Laws enacted by a majority vote through society's democratic processes may not suppress expression merely because the expression is deemed an affront to prevailing views of good order and morality. The government has no authority to declare political truth or orthodoxy. The Supreme Court justice Robert Jackson beautifully expressed this position in *West Virginia State Board of Education v. Barnette* (1943),[2] stating, "If there is any fixed star in our constitutional constellation, it is that no official, high or petty, can prescribe what shall be orthodox in politics, nationalism, religion, or other matters of opinion, or force citizens to confess by word or act their faith therein."

That the statements by Justice Murphy in *Chaplinsky* and Justice Jackson in *Barnette* would come just one year apart is enough alone to tell us something. The order and morality theory and the marketplace theory are both powerful, and both have long exerted significant force on American politics, law, and culture. Neither has ever entirely dominated, or squelched the other. (Several of the ensuing chapters in this book explore the victories and defeats of both ideas in modern cases.)

The American reverence for the marketplace is most famously embodied in one paragraph from a dissenting opinion of Justice Oliver Wendell Holmes. The "marketplace of ideas" metaphor, a notion that can be traced back at least as far as John Milton and his essay *Areopagetica*,[3] will forever be most powerfully represented in the American constitutional tradition by the words Justice Holmes wrote in his dissenting opinion in *Abrams v. United States* (1919):[4]

> Persecution for the expression of opinions seems to me perfectly logical. If you have no doubt of your premises or your power and want a certain result with all your heart you naturally express your wishes in law and sweep away all opposition. To allow opposition by speech seems to indicate that you think the speech impotent, as when a man says that he has squared the circle, or that you do not care whole heartedly for the result, or that you doubt either your power or your premises. But when men have realized that time has upset many fighting faiths, they may come to believe even more than they believe the very foundations of their own conduct that the ultimate good desired is better reached by free trade in ideas—that the best test of truth is the power of the thought to get itself accepted in the competition of the market, and that truth is the only ground upon which their wishes safely can be carried out. That at any rate is the theory of our Constitution. It is an experiment, as all life is an experiment. Every year if not every day we have to wager our salvation upon some prophecy based upon imperfect knowledge. While that experiment is part of our system I think that we should be eternally vigilant against attempts to check the expression of opinions that we loathe and believe to be fraught with death, unless they so imminently threaten immediate interference with the lawful and pressing purposes of the law that an immediate check is required to save the country.[5]

Holmes tells us to tolerate speech we *loathe*, speech we are convinced is *fraught with death*. It is the marketplace, not law, which will decide the value of speech. The government may intervene through the force of law only if there is an *immediate* need to check the speech *to save the country*.

Holmes's "marketplace of ideas" view, the nemesis of the "order and morality" theory, would be reinforced by Justice Louis Brandeis in a 1927 decision, *Whitney v. California*.[6] Justice Brandeis's concurring opinion in *Whitney* argued that efforts to stamp out hateful speech inexorably backfire. In driving hate speech underground, hate speech gathers increased strength. The framers of the Constitution, he wrote, "knew that order cannot be secured merely through fear of punishment for its infraction; that it is hazardous to discourage thought, hope and imagination; that fear breeds repression; that repression breeds hate; that hate menaces stable government; that the path of safety lies in the opportunity to discuss freely supposed grievances and proposed remedies; and that the fitting remedy for evil counsels is good ones."[7] Brandeis also counseled against surrender to fear and paranoia. "Fear of serious injury cannot alone justify suppression of free speech and assembly," he wrote. "Men feared witches and burnt women."[8]

The Holmes and Brandeis theory, later channeled by Justice Jackson in his famous statement in *Barnette*, was the *losing* theory throughout most of American history. Holmes's famous statement in *Abrams* came in a dissenting opinion, in which his was the losing side. The marketplace theory did not begin to emerge as the more dominant theory until the 1960s, when so much of American culture and law changed. Two decisions, *Chaplinsky* in 1942, and *Beauharnais v. Illinois*,[9] decided in 1952, exemplify the long-running dominance of the order and morality theory and support the notion that "hate speech" is *not* "free speech."

Walter Chaplinsky was a Jehovah's Witness. In 1940, he was distributing Jehovah's Witness literature and engaged in street preaching in Rochester, New Hampshire, near the town's city hall. Chaplinsky's purpose was to "preach the true facts of the situation of the Bible to the people," of "the Christian's permission."[10] His statements drew the ire of some of the residents of Rochester, and they complained to the city marshal. The marshal told the complainants that Chaplinsky had a right to distribute his literature and make his speeches, and that he should be left alone. The bystanders didn't leave him alone, however, and the situation grew increasingly tense. The marshal eventually approached Chaplinsky and told him that the crowd was getting restless and that Chaplinsky "better go slow."[11] But Chaplinsky, surely believing he was within his rights, did not go slow. Some in the angry crowd began threatening Chaplinsky with violence. The marshal then intervened, leading Chaplinsky toward the police station for his own protection. Resentful of how he had been treated by the crowd, and resentful of the marshal for leading him away, Chaplinsky allegedly blurted out to the marshal, "You are a God damned racketeer" and "a damned Fascist and the whole government of Rochester are Fascists or agents of Fascists."[12]

Chaplinsky admitted to accusing the marshal and the government of Rochester of being fascists but denied that he ever said, "God damned." Chaplinsky was convicted of violating a New Hampshire statute that read "No person shall address any offensive, derisive or annoying word to any other person who is lawfully in any street or other public place, nor call him by any offensive or derisive name, nor make any noise or exclamation in his presence and hearing with intent to deride, offend or annoy him, or to prevent him from pursuing his lawful business or occupation."[13]

Chaplinsky appealed his conviction all the way to the Supreme Court of the United States, asserting that his expressive activity, including the insult he uttered to the city marshal, was constitutionally protected free speech. Justice Murphy's famous opinion rejecting Chaplinsky's claim is the one of the great exemplars of the order and morality theory. It is worth reading the entire paragraph in which the theory was articulated:

> There are certain well-defined and narrowly limited classes of speech, the prevention and punishment of which has never been thought to raise any Constitutional problem. These include the lewd and obscene, the profane, the libelous, and the insulting or "fighting" words—those which by their very utterance inflict injury or tend to incite an immediate breach of the peace. It has been well observed that such utterances are no essential part of any exposition of ideas, and are of such slight social value as a step to truth that any benefit that may be derived from them is clearly outweighed by the social interest in order and morality.[14]

Justice Murphy in this passage admonishes us to take a stand against the demise of order and the disintegration of morality. Read it again: "It has been well observed that such utterances are no essential part of any exposition of ideas, and are of such slight social value as a step to truth that any benefit that may be derived from them is clearly outweighed by the social interest in order and morality." In this one sentence, he captured elegantly and economically the view that competes against Holmes, the view of all those who believe that, in the end, freedom of speech must always be measured against other vital societal interests in order and morality.

This is the "values conscious" view of freedom of speech, adhered to by those who believe society can and should draw lines between speech of high value and speech of low or no value. *Chaplinsky* is chock-full of certitude. Low-value speech, *Chaplinsky* tells us confidently, is "no *essential* part of any exposition of ideas." The court did not say that such speech plays *no* part, but no *essential part*. Thus, one need not say "Fuck the draft" in order to express the idea "oppose the draft."[15] One need not burn a flag to express the idea of dissent from the war effort. Reinforcing this theme, *Chaplinsky* speaks of *exposition*, connoting the use of language, reason, and argument—an *intellectual* enterprise, something more than burning two beams of wood to ignite a cross. Most profoundly, the *Chaplinsky* passage articulates with pristine clarity the theory that drives the balance it strikes: these examples of low-value speech are of such "slight social value as a step to truth that any benefit that may be derived from them is clearly outweighed by the social interest in order and morality."

This is decidedly not the stuff of the marketplace of ideas. For *Chaplinsky* does not leave the test of truth to the power of the idea to command the market. Rather, *Chaplinsky* contemplates that the test of truth has already been administered, and that these forms of speech have flunked the test. They have been certified already as truth deficient, as of only "slight social value as a step to truth," and perhaps more importantly, they have been certified already as unfit for decent society, as "outweighed by the social interest in order and morality." *Chaplinsky*, moreover, is not just about keeping order; it is about keeping morality. *Chaplinsky* is not limited to the speech that might breach the peace; it extends to speech that offends our moral sensibilities.

Joseph Beauharnais was an Illinois racist, the leader of a Chicago racial supremacist group that called itself the White Circle League of America. Beauharnais distributed leaflets in Chicago bearing the headline "Preserve and Protect White Neighborhoods!"[16] The leaflets declared that white neighborhoods needed protection from "the constant and continuous invasion, harassment and encroachment by the negroes." Beauharnais called for one million white people in the city of Chicago to oppose the national campaign supported by President Harry Truman's "Infamous Civil Rights Program." Beauharnais warned of efforts to amalgamate the black and white races with the object of mongrelizing the white race. "If persuasion and the need to prevent the white race from becoming mongrelized by the Negroes will not unite us," Beauharnais's leaflets asserted, "then the aggressions, . . . rapes, robberies, knives, guns and marijuana of the negro, surely will."[17]

Beauharnais was convicted of violating an Illinois law prohibiting hate speech.[18] The law made it a crime to publish "any lithograph, moving picture, play, drama or sketch" that "portrays depravity, criminality, unchastity, or lack of virtue of a class of citizens, of any race, color, creed or religion" or which "exposes the citizens of any race, color, creed or religion to contempt, derision, or obloquy or which is productive of breach of the peace or riots."[19]

While the Illinois statute did include punishment of hate speech "productive of breach of the peace or riots," no imminent threat of such violence was required to violate the law. The law made it criminal to engage in "group libel," the subjecting of a group to "contempt, derision, or obloquy." Beauharnais, like Chaplinsky, appealed his conviction all the way to the United States Supreme Court. Beauharnais, like Chaplinsky, lost.

The opinion of Justice Frankfurter in *Beauharnais* tracked the reasoning of *Chaplinsky v. New Hampshire* and represents the high-water mark of *Chaplinsky*'s influence on First Amendment law.[20] *Beauharnais* is grounded squarely in *Chaplinsky*'s solicitude for order and morality, and decidedly not in Justice Holmes's marketplace of ideas or his clear and present danger test.

Justice Felix Frankfurter, who was Jewish, plainly had in mind Hitler's Holocaust and the use of group libel against Jews when he wrote the opinion affirming Beauharnais's conviction, referring to the "the tragic experience of the last three decades." But "Illinois did not have to look beyond her own borders," Frankfurter observed, "to conclude that willful purveyors of falsehood concerning racial and religious groups promote strife and tend powerfully to obstruct the manifold adjustments required for free, ordered life in a metropolitan, polyglot community."[21] Illinois had its own long history of racist violence. In 1837, Elijah Parish Lovejoy, an abolitionist Presbyterian minister, journalist, and newspaper editor, was brutally murdered by a pro-slavery mob in downstate Alton, in an attack on a warehouse to destroy Lovejoy's printing press and abolitionist publications. In 1951, there were riots in Cicero, a suburb just west of Chicago. (Cicero would again be the center of violent racial tensions when Martin Luther King Jr. marched there, bringing the civil rights movement to the North.)

Echoing the reasoning of Justice Murphy in *Chaplinsky*, Justice Frankfurter concluded, "In the face of this history and its frequent obligato of extreme racial and religious propaganda, we would deny experience to say that the Illinois legislature was without reason in seeking ways to curb false or malicious defamation of racial and religious groups, made in public places and by means calculated to have a powerful emotional impact on those to whom it was presented."[22] Social scientists might debate whether an individual's sense of dignity and self-worth is diminished by attacks on the individual's racial or religious group, Justice Frankfurter argued, but the Illinois legislature was entitled to adopt the view that it was. It would "be arrant dogmatism, quite outside the scope of our authority in passing on the powers of a State," he concluded, "for us to deny that the Illinois Legislature may warrantably believe that a man's job and his educational opportunities and the dignity accorded him may depend as much on the reputation of the racial and religious group to which he willy-nilly belongs, as on his own merits."[23]

Under the reasoning in *Beauharnais*, drawing its sustenance from the order and morality theory of *Chaplinsky*, the supremacist speech of the alt-right and Ku Klux Klan in Charlottesville could be entirely banned by law. For many, inside Charlottesville and around the country, the reasoning of Justice Frankfurter in *Beauharnais* was right on target. The law, however, did not settle on the *Beauharnais* reasoning, but instead moved in a different direction. But did it move in the *right* direction?

As a young free speech lawyer and litigator, I was once an unabashed and unapologetic zealot for the marketplace theory. I constantly proclaimed that *Chaplinsky* and *Beauharnais* were misguided and unsound, should be regarded as repudiated and overruled, and banished from our thinking. But to quote the great singer-songwriter Joni Mitchell, "I've looked at life from both sides now."[24] I now see the battle of ideas as excruciatingly close, and for me the Charlottesville events make the choice even more excruciating. I am sure I am not alone.

Leslie Kendrick, who is Jewish, is a distinguished First Amendment scholar. She is the vice dean and a professor of law at the University of Virginia Law School and lives in Charlottesville. Reflecting on the events in her city and on her campus, particularly the August events that ended in death, she comes out in much the same place I do, which is to generally support the marketplace theory, but with skepticism and humility. "As a Jewish free speech lawyer living in Charlottesville," she has written, "I think about August 11 and 12 every day."[25] Kendrick is skeptical of several of the central arguments associated with the marketplace theory. The notion that that suppression of extremist speech actually strengthens it is a proposition that cannot really be empirically proven or disproven, for example. It is just as probable that allowing extremist speech to proliferate only helps it gather strength, as new members are recruited to join evil causes.[26] Yet Kendrick ultimately comes down in favor of the modern protection of hate speech, as better than any plausible alternative. Preventing government from deciding what speech is worthy of protection and what speech is not poses major problems of legitimacy, and the nation has a less than stellar track record in that regard. Modern marketplace of ideas principles exist to shelter unpopular views from the power of majorities. As Kendrick points out, this "is true whether the unpopular belief in question is white supremacy in 2017 Charlottesville or equality in 1964 Birmingham."[27]

If the meaning of freedom of speech in America may be seen as an ongoing mediation between the order and morality and marketplace conceptions, constitutional protection for freedom of speech has also always lived in complex tension with other constitutional rights and principles. In the context of hate speech, freedom of speech is in tension with values respecting religious liberty and tolerance, and values of equality and human dignity, particularly efforts to eliminate discrimination based on religious, racial, ethnic, national origin, or sexual identity.

Freedom of speech in America, like other civil liberties and civil rights guarantees, also navigates a complex relationship with the *structural* aspects of American constitutional law, including the system of separation of powers and checks and balances that distributes power among the branches of the federal government, as well as the system of federalism that allocates power between the national government and the states.

The wheels of history sometimes turn in unexpected ways. In the early battles over freedom of speech, advocates for "states' rights," asserting the power of states to resist actions of the national government, were also advocates for free speech. Yet the very "states' rights" arguments that emerged in the early days of the Republic to defend freedom of speech would later in American history be co-opted to defend slavery in the nineteenth century, and segregation in the twentieth.

The first profound test of the constitutional meaning of freedom of speech arose with the passage of the Alien and Sedition Acts in 1798, during the administration of President John Adams. While the phrases "order and morality" and "marketplace of ideas" had not yet entered the political and legal mainstream lexicon, the bitter American debate over the Alien and Sedition Acts was in fact an early version of the fight between those two ideas.

Even more broadly, the focus of the Alien and Sedition Acts, which attacked foreign immigrants and domestic dissenters, reflected impulses that have often powerfully asserted themselves in American history. These impulses have most recently surfaced with renewed vigor in the values and policies of President Trump.

The debate over the legality of the various executive orders issued by President Trump banning entry into the United States of aliens from certain designated countries, orders that were challenged as "anti-Muslim" bans in litigation that ultimately reached the Supreme Court in *Hawaii v. Trump* (2018),[28] posed a modern variant of this early delegation of power to the president over the presence of noncitizens deemed by the president as threatening to the nation's security. In a 5–4 decision, the Supreme Court held that despite Trump's anti-Muslim tweets and similar anti-Muslim rhetoric in campaign speeches and interviews, his actual executive order was neutral as to religion and should not be construed as a ban targeting Muslims. This holding was bolstered by the fact that by the time the third iteration of the ban reached the Supreme Court, it included Venezuela and North Korea, which did not have significant Muslim populations. The court went on to find that

Congress had indeed delegated to the president the power to exclude aliens, and upheld the ban.

What are often loosely called the Alien and Sedition Acts consisted of four separate pieces of legislation. The Naturalization Act increased the length of residency in the United States required to become a naturalized citizen from five to fourteen years. (The residency period today is back down to the original five years for most persons.) The Alien Enemies Act permitted the arrest and deportation of all male citizens of an enemy nation in the event of war. More profoundly, the ironically named Alien Friends Act gave the president the power to deport any foreign citizen in the United States suspected of plotting against the government.

The most extraordinary of the four laws was the Sedition Act. It made it a federal offense to "write, print, utter or publish" any "false, scandalous, and malicious writing against the government of the United States, or either House of Congress, or the President, with intent to defame, or bring either into contempt or disrepute, or to excite against either the hatred of the people of the United States, or to stir up sedition, or to excite unlawful combinations against the government, or to resist it, or to aid or encourage hostile designs of foreign nations."

Jeffersonian Republicans in the Congress argued that the Sedition Act violated the First Amendment. But the Federalist Party controlled both the Congress and the White House, and the law passed. Representative Matthew Lyon of Vermont was running for reelection in 1798 when he was charged with violating the Sedition Act for his campaign statements defaming the government and President John Adams. He was convicted and sentenced to prison for four months and fined $1,000. (Translated into contemporary players, imagine Senator Bernie Sanders jailed for railing against President Trump.) Another critic of President Adams, Thomas Cooper, was convicted of violating the act for distributing handbills in Philadelphia criticizing the president. (Imagine Alec Baldwin jailed for mocking President Trump on *Saturday Night Live*.) The most notorious conviction was that of James Callender, who was convicted in Richmond, Virginia, and sentenced to jail for nine months for statements he made in a newspaper, the *Richmond Examiner*, and a pamphlet titled *The Prospect before Us*, a tract supporting the nomination of Thomas Jefferson for president.

Seventeen persons were indicted under the Sedition Act, and ten convicted, all of them journalists, editors, activists, or politicians opposed to the policies and personalities of the Federalist Party. The passage of the Sedition Act and the prosecutions under it backfired on the Federalist Party. Republican newspapers supporting Thomas Jefferson and James Madison proliferated in response to the act, driven by outrage at the heavy-handed persecution of government critics.

The Sedition Act contained a "sunset" provision, expiring in 1801 with the end of Adams's presidency. Adams was succeeded by Jefferson, who was elected the third president of the United States. Upon assuming the presidency, Jefferson pardoned all those convicted under the act.

The Sedition Act episode reveals just how timid and tenuous notions of freedom and speech and press were at the founding of the Republic. John Adams and his fellow Federalists did not believe those freedoms included caustic critique of government or government officials. The Sedition Act story is shocking to our modern American sensibilities. It is beyond imagination that Americans today could be jailed for criticizing Bill Clinton, George Bush, Barack Obama, or Donald Trump for their actions as president.

The first lesson to be garnered from the Sedition Act story is sobering history. As much as we so often reflexively venerate the Framers of the Constitution as the American equivalent of Greek gods and demigods, the American counterparts to Zeus, Apollo, Hercules, and Achilles, they were human after all, filled with defects, contradictions, and ambiguities. The magnificent phrases they wrote in our founding documents, from Jefferson's proclamation in the Declaration of Independence that "All men are created equal," to the First Amendment's guarantee of freedom of speech, were real-world works-in-progress.

In opposition to the Alien and Sedition Acts, Jefferson and Madison championed resolutions at the state level, two of which, the Virginia and Kentucky Resolutions, were ratified by the legislatures of those two states. The resolutions asserted that the Alien and Sedition Acts were unconstitutional but asserted more broadly the proposition that states had the right to declare unconstitutional and legally nonbinding actions by the federal government in contravention of the Constitution. This "states' rights" position, usually described as "nullification" (by individual states) or "interposition" (by a collection of states), would ultimately come to be rejected in American constitutional law.

The states' rights position was one of the philosophical justifications for the secession of southern states from the Union, leading to the establishment of the Confederacy and the Civil War. In the words of slavery defender John C. Calhoun, "This right of interposition, thus solemnly asserted by the State of Virginia, be it called what it may—State-right, veto, nullification, or by any other name—I conceive to be the fundamental principle of our system."[29]

When I attended Yale in the 1970s, one of the residential colleges was named for this same John Calhoun, defender of slaves and the rights of states to interpose against federal law. I was oblivious of the possibility that the naming of Calhoun College at Yale might be offensive to African American students, or anyone opposed to the nation's history of slavery and oppression of people of color. By the time my daughter Corey attended Yale, there were open protests calling for the renaming of Calhoun College. While she was there, many students called the college "FKAC," for "Formerly Known as Calhoun." But when she graduated in 2016, the college was still called Calhoun. It was not until the uprisings following the Charleston massacre that Yale finally decided to change the name of the college, renaming it to honor Grace Murray Hopper, a Yale graduate and trailblazing computer scientist and navy rear admiral.

The states' rights position would be resurrected with a vengeance following the US Supreme Court's 1954 decision in *Brown v. Board of Education* ending school segregation. James J. Kilpatrick, one of the leading southern conservative intellectuals opposed to *Brown*, and editor of the *Richmond News-Leader*, called for southern states to enact resolutions of interposition resisting the authority of *Brown*.

"Massive resistance" became the southern watchword. Senator Harry Flood Byrd of Virginia thus declared, "If we can organize the Southern States for massive resistance to this order I think that in time the rest of the country will realize that racial integration is not going to be accepted in the South." Byrd was the most powerful Virginia politician of his time. He had been governor of Virginia from 1926 to 1930, at the height of the revival of the "lost cause" interpretation of the Civil War and the new proliferation of monuments to Civil War generals and leaders. He was the head of the legendary "Byrd machine," which held a grip on Virginia Democratic Party politics for most of four decades, from the 1920s to the 1960s.

Other states followed Byrd's suit—Mississippi, Georgia, North Carolina, South Carolina, Florida, Texas, Louisiana, Alabama, Arkansas—enacting various laws expressing opposition to *Brown*. In 1956, seventy-seven members of the US House of Representatives and nineteen members of the Senate signed on to the "Southern Manifesto," which pledged to use "all lawful means" to resist and overturn the decision in *Brown*.

MAY DAYS

While Judge Moore's ruling on May 2, 2017, enjoining the removal of the statues from the now-renamed Charlottesville parks guaranteed that Robert E. Lee and Stonewall Jackson would retain their symbolic presence in the city for at least six months, it did little to ease the underlying tensions over the two symbols of the Confederacy. If anything, the tensions took hold with growing intensity.

Richard Spencer and Jason Kessler, for example, were not about to let the City of Charlottesville off the hook. Spencer and Kessler still considered their alma mater UVA and the City of Charlottesville to be liberal, politically correct enemies. The city and the university remained ideal symbolic targets, and the moving of the monuments remained an ideal showdown issue.

Yet to imagine the plans that Spencer and Kessler began to make for a May rally in Charlottesville as "all about the monuments" would dramatically understate the breadth of their full agenda. Consider the links between their plans and the infatuation that many far-right American supremacist groups have long had with Adolf Hitler, an infatuation that had its perhaps most dramatic display in 1939, the day there were Nazis in the Garden.

Adolf Hitler became chancellor of Germany on January 30, 1933. That night Nazi storm troopers and columns of Hitler Youth staged a torchlight parade through Berlin to celebrate Hitler's rise. Brigades of torchbearers marched beneath the Chancellery as Hitler and the German president Paul von Hindenburg watched with approval.

On February 20, 1939, George Washington's birthday, twenty-two thousand Americans packed Madison Square Garden in New York for the largest Nazi rally in American history. The Madison Square Garden conclave was the brainchild of Fritz Julius Kuhn. Born in Germany, Kuhn fought in the Bavarian infantry in World War I. He migrated to the United States, got a job working in a Ford factory, and then entered the American political arena, joining the "Friends of New Germany," an American Nazi organization blessed by Germany's deputy führer Rudolf Hess.[1]

Hitler and Hess understood war as physical and metaphysical, the blood-and-soil stuff of shot and shell, the soul stuff of ideas. They advanced their war of ideas by seeding Nazi ideology throughout Europe and the United States, including my own hometown, Chicago, where Illinois Nazis were finding a sympathetic foothold. Kuhn joined the Chicago Nazis and ultimately became the leader of the "German-American Bund." The Bund was more than just a political movement sympathetic to Hitler and the rise of the Third Reich. The Bund was primal, spiritual, tribal, a swastika nation.

The Nazi rally staged by the Bund in 1939 in Madison Square Garden was a battle for the American soul. Osama bin Laden's 9/11 attack on the World Trade Center in New York just over six decades later was a battle over American soil. Both battles, over soul and over soil, struck at the core of what it means to be American.

The civilized and morally conscious world was at once perversely mesmerized by the images of massive Nazi rallies and repulsed by the evils those assemblies embraced. As Americans were learning of Kristallnacht, a November 1938 foretaste of Hitler's genocidal pogrom aimed at the extermination of Jews, here in one of the most famous forums in all American popular culture, the *Garden*, American Nazis were gathered in full virulent and terrifying force.

Isaac Newton's third law of physics states that "for every action there is an equal and opposite reaction." Newton's third law also works in politics. Concerned with both the raw power of the Nazi gathering and the backlash of counterprotesters that their power would unleash, the mayor of New York, Fiorello La Guardia, and the New York police commissioner, Lewis Valentine, ordered seventeen hundred New York police officers to surrounded Madison Square Garden, the largest presence at any event of New York's finest in the history of the city.

This show of overwhelming police force managed to prevent any physical violence at the rally. Yet New York's deployment of overwhelming force to prevent violence also had an unintended consequence. Perversely, the massive police presence seemed to empower, and almost legitimize, the Nazis' message. The *New York Times* story on the rally, for example, opened with the statement, "Protected by more than 1,700 policemen, who made of Madison Square Garden a fortress almost impregnable to anti-Nazis, the German-American Bund last night staged its much-advertised 'Americanism' rally and celebration of George Washington's Birthday."[2]

Charlottesville in 2017 was not linked in time or space to the 1939 Nazi rally at Madison Square Garden, but it was completely linked in mind and spirit. To begin, in the eyes of supremacists, one need not be Jewish to be a Jew.[3] In 2017, and throughout the history of Charlottesville and the history of America, the impulse to persecute Jews has been inextricably intertwined with the impulse to persecute the poor, women, Catholics, Muslims, African Americans, gays, lesbians, and immigrants from what President Donald Trump off-handedly described as "shithole countries."[4]

Many modern alt-right supremacists would extend what they regard as the epithet "Jew" to all of Hollywood, liberal academe, and the mainstream media. As the satirist Joe Raiola explained in a piece in the Huffington Post, "It's the Jews Fault—Still and Again."[5] When President Trump rallied supporters with a call to "take this country back," it was only the latest in a long line of "take back" rallying cries that have pockmarked the American experience.

One of the most famous echoes of this chant came on October 7, 1948, at the University of Virginia's Old Cabell Hall. Senator Strom Thurmond of South Carolina addressed the Charlottesville crowd to accept the Dixiecrat Party nomination for president of the United States. Thurmond had broken ranks with the Democratic Party that nominated Harry Truman as its candidate. Thurmond was angered by the insistence of the national Democratic Party that a plank endorsing progress in civil rights be included in the Democratic Party platform. He had declared at the Dixiecrat Party's earlier nominating convention "that there's not enough troops in the Army to force the Southern people to break down segregation and admit the *nigra* race into our theatres, into our swimming pools, into our homes, and into our churches."[6]

The impulse to once again take the country back, from Jews, Muslims, blacks, women, gays, and all liberals and moderates in general, surfaced with a vengeance in the lead-up to the hot Charlottesville summer of 2017.

It was 2016, inside the Ronald Reagan Building in the heart of Washington, DC. Richard B. Spencer, the self-proclaimed founder of the new American "alt-right," was addressing the National Policy Institute, over which he presided, which describes itself as "an independent organization dedicated to the heritage, identity, and future of people of European descent in the United States, and around the world." As he worked the crowd to a fever pitch, Spencer shouted, "Hail Trump, hail our people, hail victory!" His mesmerized followers responded with "Hail Trump!" salutes, raising their hands in the Nazi salute for "Heil Hitler!"

President Trump promised to make America great again. Spencer promised to make America white again. In Spencer's vision, the two were conflated. Trump wants America to be great again. Spencer wants the white race to be great again. The two are intertwined. As Spencer told the Washington crowd in his "Hail Trump" speech,

> To be white is to be a striver, a crusader, an explorer and a conqueror. We build, we produce, we go upward. . . . For us, it is conquer or die. This is a unique burden for the white man, that our fate is entirely in our hands. And it is appropriate because within us, within the very blood in our veins as children of the sun, lies the potential for greatness.
>
> That is the great struggle we are called to. We are not meant to live in shame and weakness and disgrace. We were not meant to beg for moral validation from some of the most despicable creatures to ever populate the planet. We were meant to overcome—overcome all of it. Because that is

natural and normal for us. Because for us, as Europeans, it is only normal again when we are great again.[7]

Months after his "Hail Trump" speech, in April 2017, Spencer met Jason Kessler at a meeting of conservative activists in Washington, DC. Both Spencer and Kessler were UVA graduates. Together, they began to collaborate on a rally to be staged in Charlottesville in May. For Spencer, events such as these were a time tunnel to the good old days of Nazis in Berlin and Madison Square Garden in the 1930s. As he once gleefully announced, "Let's party like it's 1933!"[8]

Spencer arrived in McGuffey Park in Charlottesville at noon on Saturday, May 13, joined by some one hundred supporters, many dressed in white polo shirts and khaki trousers, the informal uniform of the alt-right. Also present were other alt-right leaders, including Nathan Damigo, Matthew Heimbach, Mike "Enoch" Peinovich, and Sam Dickson.

Filing east in two lines on Jefferson Street, Spencer's group marched past Lee Park and its statue of Robert E. Lee, where Charlottesville's "Festival of Cultures" was being held. Many of the marchers were brandishing Confederate flags. The festival was an annual event celebrating "the cultural and linguistic diversity" of the Charlottesville community. Organizers boasted that some forty different cultures participated in the festival, celebrating diversity and inclusion. Those who gathered for the festival well understood the symbolism of holding it in a park bearing the name and statue of Robert E. Lee and appreciated the efforts to rename the park and remove Lee's statue.

Spencer's marchers did not overtly attempt to crash the party. They did not enter Lee Park that afternoon to directly confront the festivalgoers, but they surely did seek to make a statement, marching past the park in a bold affront to the festival attendees. The marchers then continued four blocks to Jackson Park and its statue of Stonewall Jackson.

In Jackson Park, several of the rally leaders spoke to their followers through a bullhorn. Sam Dickson, an Atlanta lawyer who had defended the Ku Klux Klan and white nationalists, called for a white "ethno-state."[9] Mike Enoch, the host of a popular alt-right podcast, claimed that the rally was more than about the removal of Confederate monuments.[10] Enoch argued that the rally was deeper than that, nothing less than a war of the races. These were "images of white heroes, images of white warriors being torn down to attack and demoralize our people." Enoch asserted that "they don't want us to have a future." "They want to destroy our future," he said, "they want to replace us with some mixed, muddy people that will be easy consumers and won't stand up for themselves." Enoch described the "ideology of the elite" as a war on everything white. "It's not going to stop with Robert E. Lee," Enoch argued, "it's not going to stop with Jefferson Davis. They're going to go after Andrew Jackson, they're going to go after Thomas Jefferson, they're going to go all the way back to Shakespeare, they're going to go after any white person that was a hero, that represented Europe, that represented white culture, that represented white civilization." Denouncing political correctness run amuck, Enoch argued that it is "going to be a hate crime to show pride in your race."[11]

Enoch then handed the megaphone to Richard Spencer. Spencer spoke of a "general unease" among "millions of white people" who are seeing "an image of a Confederate hero being removed in New Orleans" and seeing "an image of a portrait of Shakespeare being removed from an Ivy League college." Spencer proclaimed that "there is an angst among millions and millions of white people." He proudly proclaimed to his listeners, "We are the top of that spear, because we are putting into words what this is all about."[12]

"This is not like a genocide of yesteryear," Spencer said. "This is not a war with bullets and trenches, this is psychological war, a moral war." "We will fight it on the battlefield where the war is taking place. That is the battlefield of symbolism."[13] Whites, he argued, "have been subject to a giant demoralizing guilt trip." Those who sought to remove the statues of Lee and Jackson were like those who sought to remove the images of former communist leaders from formerly communist countries and place them in some isolated museum or distant park. Spencer said that their enemies wanted "a western world without us," a "neutered version" of the park.[14]

At one point, some counterprotesters heckled Spencer, which caused the entire group of marchers to scream and chant, "You will not replace us!" Spencer expressed his delight that so many of the marchers were young people. Older people felt the unease over attempts to remove the images of southern heroes, he said, but cannot articulate their feelings. He spoke of Robert E. Lee and George Washington and even Abraham Lincoln as "gods." At the mention of Lincoln, the crowd booed. Spencer laughed, and admonished, "Let's be honest, they're coming for Lincoln next." Spencer said they are "trying to take away our gods," "they are trying to take away our ideals" and replace them with a "monument to the holocaust," or a "monument to the black cloud that hangs over everyone's head, or perhaps quite literally, a statue of Lady Gaga."[15]

The rally ended with the leaders posing for cameras in front of a giant Identity Evropa banner proclaiming "YOU WILL NOT REPLACE US." The organizers, without providing any explicit details, encouraged attendance at another event that evening and reminded the group that dinner would be at five o'clock.

As the Jackson Park event wound down, an African American counterprotester arrived with several others and began chanting "Black Lives Matter!" They were quickly surrounded by Spencer's followers, who began chanting "Anti-white!" A brief scuffle broke out, and one of the counterprotesters fell. The alt-right marchers quickly left the scene.[16]

The afternoon rally in Jackson Park had been a "flash demonstration," modeled after "flash mobs," orchestrated gatherings in public places designed to create the appearance that they were not orchestrated but had sprung up spontaneously. In not openly promoting the demonstration in advance, Spencer's group was engaged in what amounted to a surprise attack. A Charlottesville ordinance appeared to require permits for organized events in which over fifty persons were anticipated to participate. The organizers of the Jackson Park event had not sought a permit, and the Charlottesville Police Department had no advance knowledge that the alt-right would even be in Charlottesville that day.

After dinner, the alt-right protesters gathered again, at 9 p.m. This time the venue was Lee Park.[17] Again led by Spencer and Enoch, the marchers formed two lines, carrying torches, marching up to the statue of Robert E. Lee, where they assembled in a five-rank formation.[18] The evening event at Lee Park was, like the afternoon event in Jackson Park, designed by Spencer as a flash demonstration. Once again, no permit was sought. Yet by now, word had spread throughout Charlottesville that the alt-right was in town. Officers of the Charlottesville police heading into the evening shift were briefed on the appearance of men in white polo shirts and khakis. Charlottesville police sergeant Bradley Pleasants spotted a mass of torches as he drove past Lee Park. An anonymous 911 call to the Regional Emergency Communications Center also reported the gathering.[19] As

Spencer and his one hundred torch-bearing followers conducted their ritual chants, they were confronted by an angry Charlottesville resident, Jordan McNeish, yelling at them to "get out of my town." Members of Spencer's group surrounded McNeish.[20]

Nine Charlottesville police officers arrived at Lee Park. Officer E. A. Maney moved quickly to quell any altercation between the torch-bearing protesters and McNeish. Officer Maney ordered Spencer and his minions to vacate Lee Park. No arrests were made, as the torch-bearing marchers, having made their point, left the grounds. Throughout their demonstration they had continued their chants: "We will not be overcome!" "Russia is our friend!" "You will not replace us!" and "Blood and soil!"

The next day, Sunday, May 14, was Mother's Day. It was also the day in which progressive activists and mainstream political leaders in Charlottesville moved quickly to counter the messages of Spencer's group the day before. Anne Coughlin, a law professor at the UVA Law School, circulated a Sunday morning e-mail calling for a response, admonishing that if no response was forthcoming, "God help us all."[21]

Erik Wikstrom, a Unitarian Universalist minister at the Thomas Jefferson Memorial Church, called for a gathering to show solidarity with those silenced by white supremacy. He forwarded an e-mail from a parishioner promoting an event organized by a group calling itself "Showing Up for Racial Justice in Charlottesville," which was planning a candlelight vigil that evening to "take back Lee Park." The message urged participants to "bring all the candles you can find, stating that "we will outshine their torches with our love, but we will also be sending a message that they will not come here to intimidate us unchallenged."[22] Just as Spencer's group had not sought any permits for their rallies, organizers of the candlelight vigil did not seek a permit from the city.

At nine o'clock on Sunday night, hundreds gathered in front of the Lee statue. Led by groups such as Black Lives Matter and Showing Up for Racial Justice, the counterprotesters draped the Lee statue with a banner proclaiming in black that "Black Lives Matter" and in red "Fuck White Supremacy." The event progressed peacefully for an hour. Only five Charlottesville police officers were present. One of the attendees was Don Gathers, the chair of the Blue Ribbon Commission on Race, Memorials, and Public Spaces that had been appointed to study the question of what to do about the Lee and Jackson memorials. "We will not let you come in and take over, and have your way," Gathers told the crowd. "I don't care who's in the White House, I don't care who's in Congress. . . . We are going to take control of this city and we are going to do it the proper way, the legal way. It might take six months to take care of this situation, but we're not going to give up the fight."[23] The peaceful vigil turned violent, however, around 10 p.m. when Jason Kessler arrived. Kessler walked up to the banner on the Lee statue and ripped it down. An altercation broke out. Jordan McNeish spat on Kessler. The police broke up the scuffles. One officer was hit by an object thrown from the crowd. McNeish and Kessler were charged with disorderly conduct. A third person, Charles Best, was allegedly the person who threw the object. He was charged with disorderly conduct, and while being searched incident to his arrest was discovered to be carrying a fully automatic-opening knife and was additionally charged with carrying a concealed weapon.[24]

12

CUE THE KLAN—STAGE RIGHT

On May 24, the Loyal White Knights of the Ku Klux Klan, based in Pelham, North Carolina, a town on the border between North Carolina and Virginia, got into the Charlottesville act. The Pelham Klan group on that date applied for a permit to hold a rally in Charlottesville on July 8. A married couple led the Loyal White Nights: Christopher Barker was the KKK group's "Imperial Wizard," and Amanda Barker was the "Imperial Kommander."[1] The Klan's purpose for holding the proposed rally was to protest Charlottesville's plan to remove the Robert E. Lee statue from what was now named Emancipation Park. In applying for a permit, the Klan asserted that it sought to "stop cultural genocide."[2]

Charlottesville's police chief, Al Thomas, had been frustrated by the lack of advance intelligence on Spencer's May 13 alt-right rally. Seeking to do better the next time around, he had assigned Captain Wendy Lewis to begin gathering intelligence on white nationalists. Chief Thomas also instructed Captain David Shifflett to serve as a liaison with the Pelham Klan in advance of the July 8 rally. Captain Shifflett contacted Amanda

Barker, who was handling the preparation from the Klan's side. Shifflett and Ms. Barker established a cooperative working relationship in negotiating logistics for the Klan rally. They agreed that the rally would take place between 3 and 4 p.m. in Justice Park, with about one hundred members of the Klan expected to attend.[3] Justice Park was the renamed Jackson Park, the site of the Stonewall Jackson statue, bordered by Jefferson Street, Fourth Street NE, High Street, and the Albemarle County Court building.

The imperial wizard Christopher Barker had curious credentials. In 2012, Barker had cooperated with the FBI in an investigation into a bizarre plan hatched by a Ku Klux Klan member in Albany, New York.[4] Glendon Scott Crawford, a New York Klan member, had invented a radiation-spewing "death ray" gun that he planned to use to kill Muslims. Crawford reached out to his fellow Klan leader in North Carolina, Christopher Barker. Rather than support Crawford, however, Barker went to the FBI. A meeting was arranged in which Crawford met with Barker and others—actually undercover FBI agents—and all of it was captured on a surveillance video. In the video Crawford, who was ultimately convicted on terrorism charges, was caught bragging about his death ray, asserting, "This will kill anything with respiration, anything with metabolism. It just shreds DNA."[5]

If Spike Lee is ever inclined to venture into a cross between science fiction and *BlacKkKlansman*, the story of imperial wizard Christopher Barker just might work.

Jason Kessler was displeased by the entry of the Pelham Ku Klux Klan and Christopher Barker into the Charlottesville arena. Kessler called Barker "an FBI informant and multiple felon" and claimed that he was "being paid by left-wing groups to discredit legitimate conservatives."[6] A few days after the Klan had applied for its rally, Kessler had filed a permit application for the "Unite the Right" rally on August 12. Kessler did not like the Klan's competition. "Someone is trying to discredit my rally by bringing in this jackass," Kessler claimed.[7] Richard Spencer also distanced himself from the Klan rally, stating the "KKK is not my scene."[8]

The Klan wanted to stage its rally in Charlottesville wearing traditional Klan regalia, including robes, hoods, and masks. The Charlottesville police were willing to allow the Klan to wear robes and hoods, as expressions of the Klan's identity and symbolic expression protected by the First Amendment. The police, however, would not allow the Klan members to wear masks.

Virginia is one of over a dozen American states with "anti-mask" laws, typically passed in direct reaction to the activities of the Ku Klux Klan. (The other states are New Mexico, Connecticut, Delaware, Georgia, Alabama, Florida, Louisiana, Michigan, Minnesota, Florida, North Carolina, Oklahoma, and West Virginia.)[9] The Virginia anti-mask law makes "unlawful for any person over 16 years of age to, with the intent to conceal his identity, wear any mask, hood or other device whereby a substantial portion of the face is hidden or covered so as to conceal the identity of the wearer, to be or appear in any public place, or upon any private property in this Commonwealth without first having obtained from the owner or tenant thereof consent to do so in writing."[10] The Virginia anti-mask law contains exceptions for persons "wearing traditional holiday costumes," or wearing protective masks for physical safety, or "engaged in any bona fide theatrical production or masquerade ball," or wearing masks for medical or public health reasons.[11] Violation of the law is a felony.

The Virginia statute was passed to "unmask the Klan." The law was passed in 1952, as part of anti-Klan legislative package that also banned cross burning. Given the history of the Virginia law, and its exceptions, which tend to reinforce the argument that Virginia's unmasking law, like those of other states, appears in part targeted against the Klan's identity and message, some legal commentators have questioned whether anti-masking statutes (in Virginia or elsewhere) are in tension with the First Amendment.[12]

In the early 1990s, Buddy Merci Hernandez, a Virginia Ku Klux Klan member, challenged the constitutionality of the Virginia law, claiming it violated the First Amendment. Hernandez was standing in front of a bank on a street in Fredericksburg, wearing a long white Klan robe, hood, and a mask covering his entire face except for his eyes. He had two companions. One was a woman wearing a long white robe and holding a hood but not wearing it. His other companion was a man wearing a camouflage jacket. Police arrested Hernandez for violating the mask law.

In *Hernandez v. Commonwealth* (1991),[13] Virginia's Court of Appeals, the state's intermediate appellate court, rejected the argument that the anti-masking law violated the First Amendment, distinguishing between the Klan's robes and hoods, which the court acknowledged were protected by the First Amendment, and the wearing of the mask, which the court held was not. The key was that the wearing of the mask concealed the wearer's identity, thereby emboldening and facilitating criminal violence and intensifying intimidation. The court noted that despite the law's anti-Klan history, the law on its face was a neutral measure aimed at crime deterrence, noting that "a potential rapist or bank robber wearing a mask could just as easily be prosecuted under this statute as a Klansman."[14] The court then distinguished between the robe and hood of the Klan and the mask, reasoning that while the robe and hood are identifying symbols of the Klan, the mask is not. "The mask worn without the robe and the hood would be meaningless," the court maintained. "The mask adds nothing, save fear and intimidation, to the symbolic message expressed by the wearing of the robe and the hood." Without the mask, the court held, "the social and political message conveyed by the uniform of the Ku Klux Klan is the same as it would be with the mask."[15] Hernandez tried a second time to challenge his conviction, filing a petition for habeas corpus in federal court, but lost again, as the federal court concurred in the Virginia Court of Appeals' reasoning that the anti-masking law did not violate the First Amendment.[16]

As with so much of the law surrounding the events in Charlottesville, the issue of unmasking is harder, on closer inspection, than it may at first seem, both as a matter of social or behavioral science and a matter of law.

Consider, first, the social dynamics of wearing or not wearing the mask. One of the pivotal moments in Harper Lee's masterpiece novel *To Kill a Mockingbird*, a moment given great dramatic emphasis in the movie *To Kill a Mockingbird*, is when Scout, the daughter of Atticus Finch, stands with her dad at the courthouse to confront the lynch mob that has gathered at the jail to abscond with and lynch Tom Robinson. Scout recognizes one of the members of the lynch mob, Mr. Cunningham, the father of her classmate Walter Cunningham. She starts talking to him about his "legal entailments" and asks him to tell his son Walter "hey" for her. In this simple moment of human connection, Mr. Cunningham is shamed. He tells Scout that he will say "hey" for her. Cunningham and the other members of the mob, called out by the little girl, are shamed, and they leave.

In counterpoint to that famous moment, consider what might be made of the fact that when Klan members choose *not* to wear masks, they may be asserting their dominance, or invulnerability. Just months after the unveiling of the Robert E. Lee statue in Charlottesville, the Jefferson Theatre, only two blocks from the Lee monument, conducted a rescreening of D. W. Griffith's epic 1915 silent film *The Birth of a Nation*, which glorifies the rise of the Ku Klux Klan. In the months following the rescreening, the Klan in Charlottesville engaged in a resurgence of activity, which included burning a cross in front of an African American church and setting off three explosions in the downtown.[17] The Charlottesville newspaper reported that the cross burning was attended by some fifty Klan members, only six of whom were masked.[18] The decision by so many of the Klan members in 1924 to appear unmasked may have signaled that they had no fear of public opprobrium. If anything, they were proud of their actions.[19] In the end, there were no masks worn by any of the supremacist marchers at any of the Charlottesville events in 2017. Perhaps they were proud of it as well.

Lest we gloss too superficially over the issue, however, it is worth pointing out that remaining masked—in the sense of disguising one's identity when one speaks—does have positive First Amendment traction in certain circumstances. Speaking anonymously, or "masked," is itself a First Amendment entitlement in many circumstances. In *Talley v. California* (1960),[20] the US Supreme Court held unconstitutional a Los Angeles ban on anonymous leaflets, observing that "anonymous pamphlets, leaflets, brochures and even books have played an important role in the progress of mankind." The court in *Talley* held that the First Amendment protected the distribution of unsigned handbills urging readers to boycott certain Los Angeles merchants who were allegedly engaging in discriminatory employment practices. In *McIntyre v. Ohio Elections Commission* (1995),[21] the court held that the First Amendment protected distribution of anonymous leaflets at a school board meeting. A major battleground in modern litigation involves attempts to discern the true identity of anonymous posts on the internet. State and federal courts have adopted a variety of tests to deal with the standards that should govern the digital "unmasking" of those who post material online.

As those who led the supremacist marches in Charlottesville would come to understand, the question of whether to mask or not mask one's true identity may not, in the digital age, be really so much about whether one wears a physical mask in a march staged on a public street or park. What may matter more is what one chooses to reveal or conceal in the online space leading up to that march.

13

THE RISE OF THE MARKETPLACE

The order and morality view of freedom of speech would have empowered Charlottesville to ban the proposed KKK rally. Everything the Klan planned to express was essentially identical to what Joseph Beauharnais had preached in Chicago, and the Supreme Court had declared the statements of Beauharnais outside the protection of the First Amendment.

The order and morality theory, however, was no longer the dominant constitutional position in 2017. It gave way to the marketplace theory, a casualty of one of the great tectonic shifts in American constitutional law. For most of the country's constitutional history, the order and morality theory was dominant. The positions advanced by Justices Oliver Wendell Holmes and Louis Brandeis were often praised by free speech advocates and scholars but never embraced by a majority of the United States Supreme Court. And then, in the 1960s, everything in free speech law changed, as so much in America changed.

This fundamental shift in the American constitutional doctrines of freedom of speech is best understood against a much broader story of the evolution of US constitutional law, a story of three epochs.

I think of the history of American constitutional law as embracing three broad historical epochs. The first, the "founding epoch," was dominated by the Marshall court, under the leadership of Chief Justice John Marshall, often called "the Great Chief Justice," from Richmond, Virginia. The "middle epoch," like the middle ages, was a dark period of about one hundred years, from the end of the Marshall court through the Civil War, extending to the start of President Franklin Roosevelt's New Deal. The "modern epoch" began midway through Franklin Roosevelt's presidency, extending into the Warren court of Chief Justice Earl Warren and its liberal revolution in the 1950s and 1960s, through the leadership of three successive chief justices appointed by Republican presidents, Warren Burger, William Rehnquist, and John Roberts. Each epoch has its distinct jurisprudential characteristics.

The founding epoch was dominated by Chief Justice Marshall's agenda. That agenda included (1) establishing the supremacy of the federal constitutional over state law; (2) ensconcing the supremacy of the Supreme Court as the final arbiter of the meaning of the Constitution—a supremacy that included the extraordinary power to declare the actions of Congress and the president unconstitutional; (3) an emphasis on unifying the nation as a national economic marketplace, overriding the parochial economic interests of individual states; and (4) an expansive approach to constitutional interpretation, in which the Supreme Court was willing to establish connotational principles that were not explicitly grounded in the language of the constitutional text but inferred from history and the Constitution's broad design and purposes.

The founding epoch did not accomplish much in the way of exposition of civil rights or civil liberties. This was before the Civil War and the passage of the Thirteenth, Fourteenth, and Fifteenth Amendments. The Bill of Rights during this period only applied to actions of the federal government, and not the states. There were no important cases involving issues of race, or gender, or freedom of religion, or freedom of speech. The founding epoch *did* include several profound cases involving the rights of American Indian nations. The Indians always lost. No litigation involving the Alien and Sedition Acts and the First Amendment reached the Supreme Court in the founding epoch, in part because Thomas Jefferson had pardoned all those convicted, and the Sedition Act expired in 1801. The founding epoch was thus a period in which there were no protections for equality or liberty but many decisions establishing the basic structures and principles of our constitutional life, structures and principles that would endure for two centuries with remarkable resiliency.

The middle epoch, stretching from before the Civil War to the New Deal, was marked by outright hostility to civil rights and civil liberties and a shift from federal power to states' rights. The middle epoch did have one affirmative goal: to ensure that the Constitution kept government small and off the backs of business. Using many different constitutional guarantees, the Supreme Court during the middle epoch consistently struck down labor laws, antitrust laws, and other forms of government regulation of the economic marketplace. The free enterprise system, the protection of entrepreneurial freedom, was the special franchise of the Supreme Court. Laissez-faire economic thought was not just an economic philosophy, it was American constitutional law. The Constitution was treated as a charter of capitalism, and any creeping socialism would be struck down. The most famous example was *Lochner v. New York*,[1] a 1905 decision striking down a New York law that limited the hours bakers could be required to work to ten hours a day and sixty hours per week. Finding the New York law to be nothing more than a "labor law," the court declared it an unconstitutional interference with the free market system, a violation of the rights of employers and employees to freedom of contract in deciding how long workers would work. In a dissenting opinion, Justice Oliver Wendell Holmes argued that it was wrong to treat free-market economic theory as ensconced in the Constitution. Holmes chided his colleagues, stating that "this case is decided upon an economic theory which a large part of the country does not entertain."[2] Whether laws regulating the hours or wages of workers were good or bad social policy, Holmes argued, should be left to the political process and not to judges purporting to interpret the Constitution. Some may favor unfettered economic freedom, others government intervention. "But a Constitution is not intended to embody a particular economic theory, whether of paternalism and the organic relation of the citizen to the state or of *laissez faire*."[3] Holmes, however, lost the argument in *Lochner*, just as he lost the argument in *Abrams* in opining on freedom of speech.

The middle epoch included the pro-slavery decision in *Dred Scott v. Sandford*,[4] written by Chief Justice Roger Taney. The centerpiece of Taney's *Dred Scott* was a passage that would go down in infamy:

> In the opinion of the court, the legislation and histories of the times, and the language used in the Declaration of Independence, show, that neither the class of persons who had been imported as slaves, nor their descendants, whether they had become free or not, were then acknowledged as a part of the people, nor intended to be included in the general words used in that memorable instrument. . . . They had for more than a century before been regarded as beings of an inferior order, and altogether unfit to associate with the white race, either in social or political relations; and so far inferior, that they had no rights which the white man was bound to respect; and that the negro might justly and lawfully be reduced to slavery for his benefit.[5]

Abraham Lincoln made an attack on *Dred Scott* a defining theme of his campaign for president. Invoking biblical imagery, Lincoln declared,

> "A house divided against itself cannot stand." I believe this government cannot endure, permanently, half slave and half free. I do not expect the Union to be dissolved; I do not expect the house to fall; but I do expect it will cease to be divided. It will become all one thing, or all the other. Either the opponents of slavery will arrest the further spread of it and place it where the public mind shall rest in the belief that it is in the course of ultimate extinction, or its advocates will push it forward till it shall become alike lawful in all the states, old as well as new, North as well as South.[6]

Lincoln was echoing the teaching of Christ, as recounted in the Gospel of Matthew, that "if a house be divided against itself, that house cannot stand."[7] America would remain a house divided, despite Lincoln's prophecy. A bloody Civil War would divide the nation, and Lincoln himself would fall to an assassin's bullet. The North would ultimately prevail, but the house would remain divided. The Thirteenth Amendment, abolishing slavery, the Fourteenth Amendment, guaranteeing the "equal protection of the laws," and the Fifteenth Amendment, prohibiting discrimination in voting on the basis of race, were passed with the hope and promise to reunify the nation and un-divide the house. The Supreme Court in the middle epoch largely eviscerated those amendments, however, leading to more than a century of intractable division. Two of the most malevolent Supreme Court decisions of the epoch dealt with equality. One, *Plessy v. Ferguson*,[8] dealt a blow to racial equality, enshrining the pernicious "separate but equal" doctrine. The other, *Bradwell v. Illinois*,[9] dashed any hope for equal rights for women, holding that women should be deemed both separate and unequal.

On June 7, 1892, Homer Plessy attempted to board a train traveling between New Orleans and Covington, Louisiana, a small town thirty miles to the north near the Louisiana-Mississippi state line.[10] He took a vacant seat in a coach designated as for whites only. Plessy was one-eighth African blood and seven-eighths Caucasian and, according to the allegations in the lawsuit he filed, a "mixture of colored blood was not discernible in him." He was ordered by a train conductor to vacate the coach and to take a seat in the coach "assigned to persons of the colored race," but he refused.[11] He was forcibly ejected with the aid of a police officer and thrown in the parish jail. Plessy had violated an 1890 Louisiana law providing for separate railway carriages for whites and blacks.[12] The passage of the 1890 Louisiana legislation was in some respects historically surprising, for it was passed against the backdrop of the peculiarly cosmopolitan and multiethnic New Orleans society. New Orleans was a racial bouillabaisse of French, African, Anglo-Saxon, and Indian stock unlike any other community in the nation, where "many no longer bothered to fret about how racially pure or polluted their blood was."[13]

Plessy, because he had at least "one drop" of African blood, was deemed colored. As the great writer Langston Hughes later remarked on the power of that one drop, "One drop—you are a Negro! Now, why is that? Why is Negro blood so much more powerful than any other kind of blood in the world? If a man has Irish blood in him, people will say, 'He's part Irish.' If he has a little Jewish blood, they'll say, 'He's half Jewish.' But if he has just a small bit of colored blood in him, Bam!—'He's a Negro!'; Not, 'He's part Negro.' . . . That drop is really powerful."[14]

The court in *Plessy v. Ferguson* held that relegating Homer Plessy to the car for blacks did not violate his constitutional rights.[15] While the cars were separate, they were equal. Under this "separate but equal" formulation, legally forced separation of the races—apartheid, to call it what it was—was not deemed to be discrimination against either race: "A statute which implies merely a legal distinction between the white and colored races—a distinction which is founded in the color of the two races, and which must always exist so long as white men are distinguished from the other race by color—has no tendency to destroy the legal equality of the two races, or reestablish a state of involuntary servitude."[16]

The court in *Plessy* insisted that the segregation law quite simply did not imply the inferiority of African Americans. If African Americans thought it did, it was their problem, a problem of their own sorry construction and making:

> We consider the underlying fallacy of the plaintiff's argument to consist in the assumption that the enforced separation of the two races stamps the colored race with a badge of inferiority. If this be so, it is not by reason of anything found in the act, but solely because the colored race chooses to put that construction upon it. The argument necessarily assumes that if, as has been more than once the case, and is not unlikely to be so again, the colored race should become the dominant power in the state legislature, and should enact a law in precisely similar terms, it would thereby relegate the white race to an inferior position. We imagine that the white race, at least, would not acquiesce in this assumption. The argument also assumes that social prejudices may be overcome by legislation, and that equal rights cannot be secured to the negro except by an enforced commingling of the two races. We cannot accept this proposition. If the two races are to meet upon terms of social equality, it must be the result of natural affinities, a mutual appreciation of each other's merits and a voluntary consent of individuals. . . . Legislation is powerless to eradicate racial instincts or to abolish distinctions based upon physical differences, and the attempt to do so can only result in accentuating the difficulties of the present situation. If the civil and political rights of both races be equal one cannot be inferior to the other civilly or politically. If one race be inferior to the other socially, the Constitution of the United States cannot put them upon the same plane.[17]

This passage was disingenuous on many levels. Most brazenly false was the lame claim that the forced segregation did not stamp blacks with a badge of inferiority. Of course it did. That the law implied inferiority was all but admitted in a strange digression in the court's opinion itself, in which the court speculated about whether the law injured the reputation of persons improperly classified as members of the wrong race. A white called a black, the court reasoned, might well have a cause of action for the damage to his "property" in the good reputation of the dominant race.[18]

The second claim of this infamous passage was that legislation is powerless to influence racial attitudes, and that if the races are not willing to meet on an equal plane, the law cannot place them there. This notion that the law cannot legislate racial harmony would be used as an excuse for decades to support the quite different proposition that it was therefore permissible for the law to legislate racial separation. *Plessy* gave aid, comfort, and encouragement to segregation, and to the erection of symbols such as the Robert E. Lee statue in Charlottesville, rubbing the noses of African Americans with the message, *you may not be slaves anymore but that does not mean we accept you.*

Plessy gave the Supreme Court's imprimatur to Jim Crow. The South took the cue, and spread Jim Crow laws with a vengeance. In the words of Juan Williams, "There were Jim Crow schools, Jim Crow restaurants, Jim Crow water fountains, and Jim Crow customs—blacks were expected to tip their hats when they walked past whites, but whites did not have to remove their hats even when they entered a black family's home. Whites were to be called 'sir' and 'ma'am' by blacks, who in turn were called by their first names by whites. People with white skin were to be given a wide berth on the sidewalk; blacks were expected to step aside meekly."[19]

It did not have to be so. One brave justice, John Marshall Harlan, dissented in *Plessy v. Ferguson*, in what would be recorded as one of the greatest dissents in the history of the Supreme Court. Speaking in a voice with the resonance of a prophet, Justice Harlan first exposed the duplicity of the majority's claim that the law was not aimed against blacks:

> Every one knows that the statute in question had its origin in the purpose, not so much to exclude white persons from railroad cars occupied by blacks, as to exclude colored people from coaches occupied by or assigned to white persons. Railroad corporations of Louisiana did not make discrimination among whites in the matter of accommodation for travellers. The thing to accomplish was, under the guise of giving equal accommodation for whites and blacks, to compel the latter to keep to themselves while travelling in railroad passenger coaches. No one would be so wanting in candor as to assert the contrary.[20]

This was Harlan's haunting appeal to candor and conscience, made all the more powerful by his lack of citation to evidence or authority. For, of course, it was true. Everyone did know the racist motivation underlying the law, and those who denied it—including Harlan's colleagues in the court's majority—were simply lacking in candor and anesthetized in conscience.[21] In a vain but valiant effort to awaken that conscience, Harlan wrote the most famous paragraph in his nearly thirty-four years on the Supreme Court—and indeed, one of the most famous passages in the entire history of American law:

> But in view of the Constitution, in the eye of the law, there is in this country no superior, dominant, ruling class of citizens. There is no caste here. Our Constitution is color-blind, and neither knows nor tolerates classes among citizens. In respect of civil rights, all citizens are equal before the law. The humblest is the peer of the most powerful. The law regards man as man, and takes no account of his surroundings or of his color when his civil rights as guaranteed by the supreme law of the land are involved. It is, therefore, to be regretted that this high tribunal, the final expositor of the fundamental law of the land, has reached the conclusion that it is competent for a State to regulate the enjoyment by citizens of their civil rights solely upon the basis of race.[22]

Harlan predicted that the decision in *Plessy* would "in time, prove to be quite as pernicious as the decision made by this tribunal in the *Dred Scott* case." Had Justice Harlan's view prevailed, America might have been one hundred years ahead of where it ended up, and much of the racial hatred that still vexes society today would have run its course through the system far earlier. "The destinies of the two races, in this country, are indissolubly linked together," Harlan wrote, "and the interests of both require that the common government of all shall not permit the seeds of race hate to be planted under the sanction of law."[23] Yet this is exactly what *Plessy* permitted. The decision, Harlan prophesied, would inevitably sanction racial hate and racial violence. It would "stimulate aggressions, more or less brutal and irritating."[24] And it would feed hate. "What can more certainly arouse race hate, what more certainly create and perpetuate a feeling of distrust between these races," Harlan wrote, "than state enactments, which, in fact, proceed on the ground that colored citizens are so inferior and degraded that they cannot be allowed to sit in public coaches occupied by white citizens?"[25]

The middle epoch was no kinder to women. In *Bradwell v. Illinois*, the Supreme Court upheld an Illinois law forbidding women from practicing law, rejecting the assertion of Myra Bradwell, who was undeniably qualified for admission to the bar, that the prohibition violated the equal protection clause of the Fourteenth Amendment. Of particular note was Justice Bradley's concurring opinion, declaring that "the civil law, as well as nature herself, has always recognized a wide difference in the respective spheres and destinies of man and woman."[26] Paternalism, Justice Bradley reasoned, was assumed in the Constitution, because women were unfit for the professions and needed the shelter and protection of men. "Man is, or should be, woman's protector and defender," Bradley wrote. "The natural and proper timidity and delicacy which belongs to the female sex evidently unfits it for many of the occupations of civil life." As Bradley saw it, this was not just the law of the land, it was the law of God: "The paramount destiny and mission of woman are to fulfil the noble and benign offices of wife and mother. This is the law of the Creator."[27]

It was not until the third epoch of American constitutional law, the modern epoch that we continue to inhabit, that everything changed.

In the early days of the New Deal of Franklin Roosevelt, the Supreme Court, clinging to the values of the middle epoch, struck down law after law proposed by the president and passed by the Democratic Congress. Frustrated, Roosevelt blasted the Supreme Court as "nine old men" and came up with a scheme to pack the court, proposing legislation to add new justices, up to a total of fifteen. The country, including his own party, rebelled at the court-packing scheme, handing Roosevelt a stinging rebuke. Yet while Roosevelt may have lost the battle, he won the war. Justices retired, Roosevelt replaced them with justices more in alignment with his thinking, and the modern epoch began.

The year 1937 was a key turning point, a year in which the court overruled *Lochner* and held that decisions over economic matters should be left to the political process. But the retreat from treating capitalism as a constitutional value was only one small part of the revolution that took place in the modern epoch. The court also recalibrated the balance between the power of the federal government and the power of the states, granting the federal government far more latitude in passing national laws dealing with pressing economic and social issues. The court held, for example, that the power granted to Congress under the Constitution to regulate interstate commerce was broad enough to justify passage of the Civil Rights Act of 1964, sweeping legislation designed to reverse a hundred years of discrimination in employment, travel, lodging, restaurants, and retail establishments.

The most profound hallmark of the modern epoch, however, was the explosion of protection for civil rights and civil liberties. Whereas the middle epoch had generated virtually no significant victories for equality or civil liberties, the modern epoch produced an avalanche of protections. In criminal law, the court created protections for the criminally accused, such as the requirement of *Miranda* warnings, or the right to court-appointed lawyers for indigent defendants, or the suppression of illegally obtained evidence. The court issued scores of opinions on religion, requiring separation of church and state, and protecting religious liberty.

In *Brown v. Board of Education*,[28] the court overruled *Plessy v. Ferguson*, declaring "separate but equal" schools unconstitutional. *Brown* was followed by many other decisions striking down segregation in all corners of public life. In *Loving v. Virginia*,[29] the Supreme Court struck down the conviction of Richard Perry Loving and Mildred Jeter Loving for violating a Virginia law stating that "if any white person intermarry with a colored person, or any colored person intermarry with a white person, he shall be guilty of a felony and shall be punished by confinement in the penitentiary for not less than one nor more than five years." In 1958 a Virginia judge had found the Lovings guilty, stating in his sentencing, "Almighty God created the races white, black, yellow, malay and red, and he placed them on separate continents. And but for the interference with his arrangement there would be no cause for such marriages. The fact that he separated the races shows that he did not intend for the races to mix."[30] In an opinion by Chief Justice Earl Warren, the Supreme Court rejected Virginia's reliance on the theories of *Plessy*, including the facile claim that no discrimination existed because the law applied equally to whites who wanted to marry blacks as to blacks who wanted to marry whites, concluding, "There can be no doubt that restricting the freedom to marry solely because of racial classifications violates the central meaning of the Equal Protection Clause."[31]

The Supreme Court finally recognized that women were also protected by the equal protection clause, rejecting *Bradwell*. While never willing to formally equate gender discrimination to race discrimination, the court repeatedly struck down laws discriminating on the basis of gender. Most famously, in the 1996 decision in *United States v. Virginia*,[32] the Supreme Court struck down the long-standing male-only admissions policy of the Virginia Military Institute, a state-supported college located in Lexington, adjacent to Washington and Lee University, about an hour from Charlottesville. In a 7–1 decision, the court, in an opinion written by Justice Ruth Bader Ginsburg, rejected Virginia's effort to defend the male-only admissions policy at VMI by opening of a parallel program at a small women's college about forty miles from VMI, Mary Baldwin College. VMI was founded in 1839 to produce "citizen-soldiers" fit for leadership in military service and civilian life. But its tradition of discrimination against women, dating back to its founding in a period in which women possessed no rights, could not justify continued discrimination in the modern epoch.

The modern epoch included recognition of a fundamental constitutional right to privacy on matters of procreation, sexual orientation, and ultimately same-sex marriage. The right of a woman to choose an abortion prior to the viability of a fetus was established in *Roe v. Wade*. The right of same-sex couples to marry was established in *Obergefell v. Hodges*,[33] in which the Supreme Court, in an opinion by Justice Anthony Kennedy, argued that the meaning of constitutional rights may evolve over history. "The nature of injustice is that we may not always see it in our own times," Justice Kennedy wrote. "The generations that wrote and ratified the Bill of Rights and the Fourteenth Amendment did not presume to know the extent of freedom in all of its dimensions, and so they entrusted to future generations a charter protecting the right of all persons to enjoy liberty as we learn its meaning."[34] The opinion concluded, "Their hope is not to be condemned to live in loneliness, excluded from one of civilization's oldest institutions. They ask for equal dignity in the eyes of the law. The Constitution grants them that right."[35]

If the Supreme Court in the modern epoch was ready to recognize new meaning in old constitutional clauses to advance positions cherished by liberals, it was also willing to find new meaning in old clauses for conservatives. In *District of Columbia v. Heller*,[36] the Supreme Court interpreted the Second Amendment to the Constitution, which reads, "A well regulated Militia, being necessary to the security of a free State, the right of the people to keep and bear Arms, shall not be infringed." This is a strangely worded sentence, beginning with the notion that a well-regulated militia is necessary to the security of a free state, and ending with the declaration of the right of the people to keep and bear arms.

For most of American history the Second Amendment was understood as a "collective" right protecting "militias," and not as an *individual* right guaranteeing a personalized entitlement to own, keep, and carry weapons. Not so, the court in *Heller* declared, in a 5–4 decision written by Justice Antonin Scalia. The *Heller* opinion would become prominent in debate over the events in Charlottesville in 2017, and in the national epidemic of episodic mass violence in public places, particularly American schools. The Supreme Court's rationale in *Heller* was that the Constitution precluded the entire elimination of the right to bear arms as a policy option in dealing with gun violence:

> We are aware of the problem of handgun violence in this country, and we take seriously the concerns raised by the many amici who believe that prohibition of handgun ownership is a solution. The Constitution leaves the District of Columbia a variety of tools for combating that problem, including some measures regulating handguns. . . . But the enshrinement of constitutional rights necessarily takes certain policy choices off the table. These include the absolute prohibition of handguns held and used for self-defense in the home. Undoubtedly some think that the Second Amendment is outmoded in a society where our standing army is the pride of our Nation, where well-trained police forces provide personal security, and where gun violence is a serious problem. That is perhaps debatable, but what is not debatable is that it is not the role of this Court to pronounce the Second Amendment extinct.[37]

The court in *Heller* did make clear that the Second Amendment right to keep and bear arms, like most constitutional rights, was not absolute. Its opinion was not to be read to prohibit all forms of gun regulation. "Although we do not undertake an exhaustive historical analysis today of the full scope of the Second Amendment," the court stated, "nothing in our opinion should be taken to cast doubt on longstanding prohibitions on the possession of firearms by felons and the mentally ill, or laws forbidding the carrying of firearms in sensitive places such as schools and government buildings, or laws imposing conditions and qualifications on the commercial sale of arms."[38]

The "weaponizing" of racist expression in Charlottesville drew new scrutiny over the meaning of this passage in *Heller*, including questions over whether it would empower cities to ban weapons at mass demonstrations and rallies. This became a significant focus of the Virginia task force formed in the wake of the events in Charlottesville, created by Governor Terry McAuliffe to study the summer's events and make recommendations for future policy. When I was asked to advise the task force, I expressed the opinion that Virginia *could*, if it had the political will, prohibit loaded firearms at mass demonstrations. I was less confident, however, that the state could prohibit *unloaded* weapons, which might, in their unloaded state, be symbols, not weapons, and thus come within the ambit of the free expression protected by the First Amendment. The puzzling out of how to deal with this confluence between First Amendment and Second Amendment rights remains a legal work in progress.

In describing the explosion of protection for civil rights and civil liberties in the modern epoch, I do not mean to imply that the Supreme Court's decisions during this epoch have been entirely consistent, unanimous, or uncontroversial. Many of the signature decisions of the time were close 5–4 judgments, extending or refusing to extend rights in areas such as criminal procedure, the death penalty, due process, privacy, guns, race discrimination, gender discrimination, sexual orientation, religion, or speech.

What I do mean to say, however, is that from the longer view of history, the epochs are in fact distinct. While there are ups and downs, frolics and detours, the modern epoch has witnessed an extraordinary advance in civil rights and civil liberties, when compared to roughly the first 150 years of the Republic.

In my lifetime in the law, from my years as a law student in the late 1970s through today, the Supreme Court has always been closely balanced. There have always been a handful of three or four ardent conservatives on the court, a handful of three or four ardent liberals, and one or two justices in the middle. Occupying that middle ground on the court at various times were justices such as Lewis Powell, Sandra Day O'Connor, and Anthony Kennedy. These "swing vote" justices have tended to exert extraordinary influence, often supplying the deciding vote that moves the court in one direction or another on a particular issue. With the retirement of Justice Kennedy, replaced by Justice Brett Kavanaugh, it is possible that the era of the swing vote is over, with no members of the court truly occupying the center.

While the composition of the Supreme Court has moved to the right, particularly given the retirement of Justice Kennedy and the confirmation of Justice Kavanaugh, there is *one* important area of modern constitutional law that does not appear likely to change, an area in which liberals and conservatives are remarkably aligned. That area is freedom of speech.

Free speech law was turned upside down in the modern epoch. And that turn has come to be embraced by most justices on both the liberal and conservative ends of the spectrum. Indeed, the most distinctive feature of the modern epoch has been the dramatic move away from the "order and morality" theory of freedom of speech to the "marketplace" theory of Holmes and Brandeis. Unlike some arenas of constitutional law, in which outcomes often divide on relatively predictable conservative and liberal fault lines, free speech has been different. The marketplace theory has been deeply internalized by justices of the Supreme Court, conservative and liberal alike. While occasionally there are nuanced free speech decisions that hang on 5–4 majorities, often the results are unanimous or near-unanimous 7–2 or 8–1 votes. This profound shift in the American law of free speech, and the still-lingering debate over whether the shift was good or bad for the country, would be visibly present throughout Charlottesville's long hot summer of 2017.

14

CUE THE COUNTERPROTESTERS — STAGE LEFT

In addition to gathering intelligence on the Klan, the Charlottesville Police Department prepared for the July 8 rally by gathering intelligence on the groups expected to protest against the Klan. The intelligence gathering included harvesting what was openly available on the internet, and interviews by Charlottesville police officers of community groups and individuals likely to stage counterprotests against the Klan. Captain Lewis's team conducted interviews by phone, knocking on doors, and showing up at meetings of activist groups such as Black Lives Matter, Equality and Progress in Charlottesville, and Showing Up for Racial Justice.[1] However well intentioned, the police tactic backfired. An attorney representing the groups sent a message to Chief Thomas accusing the police of engaging in "an intimidation tactic intended to curtail leftist speech and expressive conduct."[2] Pamela Starsia, a lawyer representing many of the activists, held a press conference in front of Charlottesville Police Department headquarters to protest the police inquiries. "We think it's disingenuous for CPD to pretend that these inquiries aren't arising in the context of

CPD aggression and disparate treatment of leftists and anti-racist activists in recent months," Starsia said.[3] As Starsia saw matters, the police were on the side of the forces of suppression. "There is a long history of police looking to preserve white supremacy and the current systems of power, and targeting those who seek to make change to the system," Starsia said. "I think what you're seeing is just a continuation of that pattern."[4]

The police denied singling out the left, insisting that they had been contacting activist groups from across the political spectrum, including right-wing groups such as Vanguard America and the League of the South, in order to prepare for the event and attempt to maintain order. Even so, the police effort to gather intelligence from human sources stopped, and the police gathered what intelligence they could online.

Among the counterprotest groups planning to oppose the Klan rally were two significant national movements, Antifa and Black Lives Matter.

Antifa—the term is short for "antifascist" or "antifascist action"—is a conglomeration of groups opposed to fascism, more a movement than a formal organization.[5] Antifa experienced a surge in support because of the presidency of Donald Trump, who is regarded by much of the left as encouraging racist and fascist impulses in America that are threatening to vulnerable minorities. Antifa members advocate meeting that racist and fascist threat with "direct action," which may include violence. Antifa, in short, is of the radical left. Many of its members are anarchists, who do not trust government and have no use for the system. When Richard Spencer was attacked during the inauguration of President Trump, it was an Antifa activist who attacked him.

While Antifa is decentralized, it is not disorganized. To the contrary, Antifa's activities are often well planned and carefully orchestrated. Antifa typically communicates with its members in secret, through internet sites that permit secure communication among members outside the access of the uninvited. Recall the last chapter's admonition that "masked speech" may or may not be constitutionally protected, depending on the circumstances. To the extent that Antifa's masking of its activity furthers its protest agenda, its care to remain anonymous deserves robust constitutional protection. In contrast, to the extent that Antifa, or the radical supremacist right, envelop communications in secrecy to facilitate violent conspiracies, the First Amendment ought not offer them any enhanced shelter.

The Black Lives Matter movement arose in reaction to incidents of unjust killings and beatings of African Americans by police. Although many members of the Black Lives Matter movement also support a broader progressive political agenda, such as economic redistribution, the heart and soul of the Black Lives Matter movement addresses the policing of minority populations.[6] On the national level, Black Lives Matter organizes protests in cities in which incidents of what appear to be racially motivated police abuses occur. The Black Lives Matter movement also lobbies for a ten-part agenda of reform of police practices and culture, known as Campaign Zero. The ten points of Campaign Zero call for stopping "broken windows" policing; more community oversight of police departments; stricter limits on the use of force; independent investigations of police misconduct; community representation in municipal governments; body cameras; better training; an end to "policing for profit"; demilitarization; and union contracts that don't protect misbehaving police officers from being held accountable.[7]

Views on Blacks Lives Matter are divided in American society. In the Reuters / Ipsos / University of Virginia Center for Politics poll taken in the aftermath of the Charlottesville events, almost two-thirds of African Americans (62 percent) voiced support for Black Lives Matter.[8] Yet only a quarter of whites (26 percent) supported the group. The split was also political. A slight majority of Democrats (52 percent) supported Black Lives Matter. Among Republicans 62 percent expressed opposition to the group.[9]

The Klan's rally application, coming close on the heels of the unsettling events of May 13 and 14, challenged Charlottesville's political, religious, and cultural leaders. There were, of course, racists and alt-right members and sympathizers in Charlottesville, but not many. The overwhelming majority of the people and leaders of Charlottesville hated the idea of the Klan staging a rally in the center of the city and wished that the Klan would just go away. But since the Klan would not go away, the debate among those who found the Klan disgusting shifted to a fundamental conundrum. Was it better to ignore the Klan, or confront the Klan?

Rev. Alvin Edwards was in the former camp. In an interview with Jonathan Blitzer, who wrote a thoughtful piece about the Charlottesville clergy in the *New Yorker*, Edwards explained, "My thought was that we should completely ignore the Klansmen."[10] These millennial Klan groups, he thought, did not appear to have anything near the potency of the Klan of the Old South that had run its reign of terror with bombings and lynchings. "The worst thing you can do to a person is to not listen to him. I hate when someone does that to me," Edwards said.[11]

Teresa Sullivan, president of the University of Virginia, also advocated ignoring the Klan. "I urge UVA community members to avoid the rally and avoid confrontation on July 8," Sullivan wrote.[12] "To listen and respond to these outsiders would only call more attention to their viewpoint and create the publicity that they crave."[13] Sullivan also recognized the Klan members' right to conduct their rally, stating, "We abhor their beliefs, yet we recognize their right to express those beliefs in a public forum, and the city of Charlottesville plans to protect their right to do so."[14]

Mayor Mike Signer asked city residents to refrain from engaging with the "ridiculous sideshow."[15] Signer stated, "This rump, out-of-state arm of a totally discredited organization will succeed in their aim of division and publicity only if folks take their putrid bait." He encouraged "everyone in C'ville to ignore this ridiculous sideshow and to focus instead on celebrating the values of diversity and tolerance that make us a World-Class City."[16]

In a letter to the editor published in the *Daily Progress*, Floyd Hurt also made a case for the power of ignoring the Klan. "If you disapprove of the KKK's message, don't attend the rally," Hurt wrote. "If no one shows up, all the noise and bombast will fall on deaf ears—receiving no support, no acknowledgment, no feedback. How demoralizing, how deflating, how delicious! Demonstrating against the KKK and its members only serves to give them exposure and, to a distorted degree, credibility . . . remarkably counterproductive."[17]

Josh Wheeler, the director of the Thomas Jefferson Center for the Protection of Freedom of Expression, noted that the First Amendment protected the Klan and that the city could not shut down the Klan's proposed rally because of its viewpoint, but then added that the "right of free speech includes the right to ignore."[18] Joining the chorus of leaders asserting that ignoring the rally was the best way to frustrate the Klan's goals, Wheeler stated, "My personal recommendation would be to ignore them. The attention that the Klan and these other groups are getting is exactly what they want."[19]

In a press conference held by Charlottesville's leaders, Police Chief Thomas urged staying away from the Klan rally and attending alternative unity events. "I hope that July 8 will be remembered as a day of unity—not a day of hate and fear," Thomas said. "Fear will not define this community." He elaborated, "Unfortunately, we have seen small fringe groups that have attempted to divide. . . . Please be mindful that extremists are not persuaded with calm reasoning or shouting. They attend these events to provoke responses."[20]

"We are not going to change their mind by simply saying they should leave and go home," city council member Wes Bellamy said. "And us confronting the Klan in a shouting match or a physical confrontation is not going to get us anywhere."[21]

Rev. Elaine Ellis Thomas of St. Paul's Memorial Church described the efforts of the Charlottesville Clergy Collective, a group of religious leaders that had come together to address divisions in the community. "We have been in conversation with representatives from the city and community about how we as faith leaders will be most effective in leading the way to address a resurgence of racism and white supremacist activity here," Thomas said.[22] Among other things, local clergy promised to "provide presence and prayer" on July 8. It would later become clear, however, that members of the Clergy Collective were themselves not unified as to the appropriate response to the racial supremacist rallies, with some urging peaceful alternative programming and others urging attendance at the supremacist rallies to actively confront the supremacists' message.

Alternative programming designed to counter the Klan rally and communicate counter-messages of inclusion and rejection of racism sprang up at venues throughout Charlottesville. A Unity Day Concert was scheduled for Sprint Pavilion on the Downtown Mall. At IX Art Park, a community potluck picnic was scheduled. Another program was set for the American Heritage Center at the Jefferson School, in the heart of what had once been Vinegar Hill, the center of the African American community before it was torn down by the city in a program of urban renewal.[23] The Jefferson School program included meditation, presentations on the history of the Klan and Charlottesville, and a gospel choir.

In a visit to the Clergy Collective, City Manager Maurice Jones and Mayor Signer urged the religious leaders to adopt the "ignore them" strategy in reacting to the Klan rally. Those who favored ignoring the Klan, like Rev. Alvin Edwards, embraced the message. But the split within the ranks of the clergy became apparent. Those who believed in confrontation, like Rev. Seth Wispelwey, found the "ignore them" message patronizing and began to grow impatient and wary of the leadership of Edwards, whom they regarded as an old-guard leader too close to the city's political leaders.

This division grew more significant as a growing number of city residents, including younger members of the clergy and many activist students and faculty at UVA, became increasingly vocal in their conviction that ignoring the Klan was exactly the wrong thing to do. Evil had to be confronted, this group maintained, not ignored. Edwards acknowledged that there were other clerics, many of them younger, who thought confrontation was important. Within the Clergy Collective, he said, "you had the ones who wanted to confront them, and I respect that."[24]

Jalane Schmidt was a professor at UVA who had been a leader in the movement to remove the Robert E. Lee statue. Schmidt told the *Washington Post* that it was important to confront the Klan, "because the Klan was ignored in the 1920s, and they metastasized." Schmidt explained, "I teach about slavery and African American history, and it's important to face the Klan and to face the demons of our collective history and our original sin of slavery. We do it on behalf of our ancestors who were terrorized by them."[25] "I don't think the 'ignore them' strategy is going to work," Schmidt told the *Post*, "because they're organizing. You don't just ignore evil and expect it to go away. That's the coward's way out."[26]

The religious groups within Charlottesville ended up taking two different approaches to the Klan rally. One wing of the Clergy Collective opted for participation in the various Unity Day alternative programming. Another wing advocated direct confrontation of the Klan by participation in the counterprotests at Justice Park (the renamed Jackson Park). Both groups gathered together for an interfaith service at the First United Methodist Church, just three blocks from Justice Park. When the service ended, the two groups split, with one heading for the Sprint Pavilion on the Downtown Mall and the other for Justice Park.

The debate between the "ignore them" and "confront them" camps was not unique to the Charlottesville clergy. The split reflected a larger debate within the Charlottesville community and, for that matter, across the country. Yet the intensity of this split should not be made out to be more than it was. The "ignore them" and "confront them" camps were allies, not enemies; they were united in their opposition to the racists. The debate was over means, not ends, over tactics, not principle.

The tensions in Charlottesville cannot be separated from the current of national tensions between minority communities and local governments, particularly local police forces, as most purely distilled in the Black Lives Matter movement. The point of Black Lives Matter is that too many police forces and local governments act as if black lives do not matter. As the loose collection of national and local activist groups converged on Charlottesville to oppose the Klan and the alt-right, it was only natural that many participants in that alliance would be wary of any within their midst who appeared too close to establishment authorities.

Several of the old guard religious leaders in the Clergy Collective saw the enemy as extremist supremacist radicals from outside Charlottesville who were descending on the city. For many in the new guard, however, the problem was more complex. Their enemies were broader, extending beyond the supremacists, to the police, to the government, to the entrenched patterns of systemic discrimination that they perceived as complicit in the oppression of marginalized populations. And therein was the asymmetry among the clerics. The old guard saw the new guard as a more aggressive wing of a generally united army. And undoubtedly, many members of the new guard saw it the same way. But some members of the new guard saw it in a fundamentally different sense. For some of them, the old guard was not just a more reticent or passivist wing of the one generally unified spectrum; instead, they viewed the old guard as complicit in the evil, part of the problem, collaborators, appeasers, the American equivalents of the Vichy collaborators of Nazi-occupied France.

If the division between these views was largely generational, a somewhat similar divide seemed to exist when it came to the meaning of freedom of speech. Many UVA students, for example, like many students at colleges and universities around the country, embraced a conception of freedom of speech akin to the order and morality theory and simply could not process why society should permit the supremacist marches of the Klan or the alt-right at all. As I travel across the country discussing free speech on campus, I often hear the lament that "this new generation does not understand free speech." I tend to push back on this. Instead, this generation includes many who have a different conception of free speech. Many in the current generation of university students may never have heard of the "order and morality theory," or the *Chaplinsky* or *Beauharnais* cases, but they are disciples of those conceptions of what free speech means. It is not that they don't understand freedom of speech. It is that they understand freedom of speech differently.

15

A ROLLING STONE GATHERS NO FACTS

Recall that in the lead-up to the alt-right rallies in Charlottesville's summer of 2017, UVA had been rattled, much as Duke had been rattled after the lacrosse team scandal, by the stunning account in *Rolling Stone* of the alleged gang rape of "Jackie" at a UVA fraternity. Yet just as events later proved that the rape accusations at Duke were false, so too the article in *Rolling Stone* turned out to be a fabrication. Richard Spencer had been steeled to his path of radical conservative activism by the Duke case. And in the lead-up to the summer of 2017, his undergraduate school, Virginia, now had gone through a similar experience.

The *Rolling Stone* story began to unravel as other news organizations began their own investigations of the alleged events and, as academics might put it, could not replicate *Rolling Stone*'s findings. The *Washington Post* took the lead, and before long it seemed that everyone was piling on.

Jackie, it was revealed, had told her story several different times, in several different ways. *Rolling Stone*'s reporter, Sabrina Erdely, responded by claiming that this was common among rape victims:

The fact that Jackie's description of the assault itself had evolved from a "bad run in" to forced oral sex to vaginal penetration did not concern me, nor did it cause me to doubt Jackie's credibility. To the contrary, I found this to be entirely consistent with the behavior of a victim of sexual assault or other trauma. In my experience writing about trauma victims and sexual assault victims, I know that their stories can sometimes evolve over time as they come to terms with what happened to them and work through their own shame and self-blame, and that this process can result in the victim revealing new or different details over time.[1]

Yet Erdely, it turned out, had never even attempted to contact the alleged mastermind behind Jackie's rape, Jackie's date "Drew." Moreover, as other journalists descended on Charlottesville to get Drew's side of the story, a mystery unfolded: No one could find him.

If Drew was missing in action, so were the identities of the other gang of eight rapists.

Also missing was any record of any social event on the night of September 28, 2012, at the Phi Psi fraternity house. The evidence showed instead that there had not been any function at Phi Psi that night.

Weeks after publication of the original *Rolling Stone* article, as reports in the *Washington Post* and other media outlets accelerated, some began to openly air the suspicion that the entire *Rolling Stone* article was fabricated. The Charlottesville Police Department conducted an investigation, which concluded that the events described in the *Rolling Stone* article did not happen. *The Columbia Journalism Review*, at the request of *Rolling Stone*, also conducted an investigation, which determined that the reporting on the story was deeply flawed. *Rolling Stone* ultimately retracted the story.

The *Rolling Stone* "Rape on Campus" article generated three libel lawsuits. In *Eramo v. Rolling Stone, LLC,*[2] Nicole P. Eramo, the associate dean of students at the University of Virginia, sued *Rolling Stone* for falsely depicting her as not appropriately responsive to the allegations of Jackie, the alleged victim. Dean Eramo's case was brought in federal court in Charlottesville, before District Judge Glen Conrad. Conrad would also become embroiled in the Unite the Right rally in Charlottesville, presiding over litigation involving an eleventh-hour effort to move the rally out of the downtown. In *Elias v. Rolling Stone LLC,*[3] individual fraternity brothers George Elias IV, Ross Fowler, and Stephen Hadford brought a libel suit in federal court in the Southern District of New York in Manhattan, where *Rolling Stone* had its headquarters. The third case, *Virginia Alpha Chapter of Phi Kappa Psi Fraternity v. Rolling Stone LLC*,[4] was the suit that Tom Albro, Evan Mayo, and I brought on behalf of the Phi Psi fraternity against *Rolling Stone*, in Circuit Court in Charlottesville, before Judge Richard Moore, the same judge who was handling the litigation over the moving of the Lee and Jackson monuments.

UVA's dean Nicole Eramo was the first to win. In a jury trial presided over by Judge Conrad, the jury returned a verdict in favor of Eramo for $2 million for the original published story, and an additional $1 million for the statements made following the story. *Rolling Stone* filed a token appeal but soon surrendered, settling the case rather than pursuing the appeal, obviously convinced that to continue to pay legal fees to defend a losing case was throwing good money after bad.

Rolling Stone won the first round in the New York litigation, convincing the trial judge that the case should be thrown out because none of the three individual fraternity brothers who brought suit were actually named in the article. That decision was reversed on appeal in the United States Court of Appeals for the Second Circuit. The Court of Appeals held that two individual fraternity brothers, George Elias IV and Ross Fowler, could sue *Rolling Stone*, because they could make out a case that while they were not named by name in the article, there were sufficient facts in the article from which many on the University of Virginia campus could have identified them as two of the alleged rapists. The court also held that the third plaintiff, Stephen Hadford, was too peripherally connected to the events to have been identified by anyone as one of the alleged assailants.

Rolling Stone attempted to get the Phi Kappa Psi lawsuit dismissed, on the theory that the "Rape on Campus" article was not about the fraternity itself but was instead about individual "rogue" students and a critique of the policies of the University of Virginia. I argued the case in Charlottesville in front of Judge Moore on May 17, 2016. Moore ultimately ruled in our favor, agreeing with our argument that the article was heavily focused on defaming the Phi Kappa Psi fraternity itself. Through the next year the case proceeded through discovery in preparation for trial. Just as the Ku Klux Klan was preparing to descend on Charlottesville in July 2017, *Rolling Stone* indicated that it was willing to settle the case rather than proceed to trial. Tom Albro and I, working in tandem, negotiated the terms of the surrender. Our case in Charlottesville ended just as the Klan's march though the city was about to commence.

16

THE MARKETPLACE DOUBLES DOWN

Sometimes a shift in constitutional law can be marked in one year—such as 1937, the year the US Supreme Court repudiated *Lochner*—or even one day. On May 17, 1954, the court in *Brown* declared school segregation unconstitutional. On June 12, 1967, the Supreme Court in *Loving* struck down bans on interracial marriage. On January 23, 1973, the court in *Roe* recognized a right to choose abortion. On June 26, 2008, the court in *Heller* recognized an individual right to keep and bear arms. On June 26, 2015, the court in *Obergefell* created a constitutional right to same-sex marriage.

When it comes to the free speech revolution, however, it is not possible to point to a single day, year, or decision. The shift from the order and morality theory to the marketplace theory took place in a series of landmark cases spanning decades. In *New York Times v. Sullivan* (1964), the court created First Amendment protections for critiques of public officials. In *Cohen v. California* (1971), the court held that a citizen had a right to wear a jacket proclaiming "Fuck the Draft." In three cases spanning twenty years, the court upheld the rights of racists to engage in rituals such as cross burning. In *Texas v. Johnson* (1989), the court held that the First Amendment protected the burning of the American flag. In *Hustler Magazine v. Falwell* (1988), the court held that crude sexual parodies of a preacher in a porn magazine were protected free speech.

In more recent years, the Supreme Court has upheld the right to express vicious homophobic messages while picketing at military funerals, convey gross depictions of small animals being crushed on internet videos, and make false claims to have received military honors. These are but a handful of the cases, but they capture the highlights. Several are particularly worth examining in greater detail, for what they reveal about the First Amendment principles of the modern epoch that exerted such powerful gravitational pull on the events in Charlottesville in 2017.

One of the early signs that the order and morality theory of *Chaplinsky* was waning came in 1971, in *Cohen v. California*.[1] Paul Cohen wore a jacket in the corridor of a Los Angeles courthouse, with women and children present, bearing the phrase "Fuck the Draft." Cohen was arrested and convicted for wearing the jacket, under an offense called "tumultuous and offensive conduct." Cohen appealed his conviction all the way to the Supreme Court of the United States. Cohen's lawyer was a hero of mine, UCLA law professor Melville Nimmer. Nimmer was famous as the nation's foremost authority on copyright law. When he died, his son David Nimmer took over his treatise, *Nimmer on Copyright*, which remains to this day the leading scholarly authority on copyright law. Mel Nimmer was also a fierce defender of freedom of speech. When he died in 1985 at age sixty-two of cancer, his family asked that I take over authorship of his free speech treatise, which is still called *Smolla and Nimmer on Freedom of Speech* in tribute to him.

As the case was being prepared for briefing and oral argument, an intense debate arose among the lawyers as to whether the briefs should spell out the word "fuck" or use some sanitized convention, such as "f---" Most on the legal team feared that writing the word "fuck" in the brief would offend the court, and that, most certainly, actually saying the word in open court during the argument would be deemed an offense to the court's dignity. Nimmer absolutely disagreed. To avoid writing or saying the word, he maintained, would be to concede that the word was so taboo it could not be written or spoken in civilized society. Much as Harry Potter refused to acquiesce in never referring to Lord Voldemort as anything other than "He-Who-Must-Not-Be Named," Nimmer refused to accept that "fuck" was the word that shall not be spoken. And so the brief used the word "fuck" in reciting the facts and legal issues.

The day came for the case to be heard in court. It happened that on that day, a group of students led by a nun from a Catholic school in Washington were attending the court session on a field trip. The court filed out to begin the argument. Chief Justice Warren Burger, eyeing the audience and the looking squarely at Mel Nimmer, stated as Nimmer approached the podium that the court was thoroughly familiar with the *factual* setting of this case and it was not necessary for him to dwell on the *facts*. Nimmer got the signal that there was no need to repeat the *facts*, as in "fuck." Nimmer was undaunted. Beginning his argument, Nimmer stated, "At the Chief Justice's suggestion, I certainly will keep very brief the statement of facts. What this young man did was to walk through the courthouse corridor wearing a jacket on which were inscribed the words 'fuck the draft.'" The lore is that the chief justice was outraged and voted against Nimmer and Cohen.[2]

But Nimmer won the case. In an opinion by Justice John Marshall Harlan, the Supreme Court rejected California's claim that it could use the law to preserve decency and decorum in society by banning public vulgarity and sheltering citizens from offensive language. No longer, the court made clear, could vulgar words be equated with *fighting words*, as that phrase had been used in *Chaplinsky*. Henceforth, the court made clear, to qualify as "fighting words," the statements must constitute "a direct personal insult" directed at a specific person. As to the crude use of the word "fuck," Justice Harlan's opinion quipped, "one man's vulgarity is another's lyric."[3]

Cohen involved graphic language. The shift to the marketplace theory would also embrace protection for the graphic use of symbols. Most pointedly, in 1989 the Supreme Court held in *Texas v. Johnson* that the First Amendment protected the burning and desecration of the American flag as a symbol of protest.[4] Gregory Lee Johnson was in Dallas in the summer of 1984 participating in the "Republican War Chest Tour" to protest against the Republican National Convention, which was about to nominate Ronald Reagan for four more years as president of the United States. Johnson and about one hundred fellow demonstrators made speeches criticizing Reagan, the military, and corporate America, distributed protest literature, and staged "die-ins" intended to dramatize the effects of nuclear war. Against the president they shouted, "Ronald Reagan, killer of the hour, perfect example of U.S. power."[5] They also screamed, "Reagan, Mondale, which will it be? Either one means World War III."[6] One of the protesters took down an American flag from a pole outside a downtown office building and handed it to Johnson. Johnson accepted it, and as the marchers reached the front of the Dallas City Hall, he unfurled the flag, doused it with kerosene, and set it on fire. While the flag burned, the demonstrators chanted, "America, the red, white, and blue, we spit on you, you stand for plunder, you will go under." Many onlookers to the flag burning were deeply offended. When the marchers dispersed, one of the witnesses solemnly collected the flag's charred remains and took them home for a respectful burial in his backyard.

There is no right to steal another person's flag and destroy it. The protester who stole the flag from the office building was a simple thief. But he was not caught or charged. Gregory Johnson was the only one of the hundred or so demonstrators to be arrested and charged with violation of a Texas criminal statute, titled "Desecration of a Venerated Object." The Texas law made it a criminal offense if a person "intentionally or knowingly desecrates" a "public monument," a "place of worship or burial," or a "state or national flag." The law defined the word "desecrate" as to "deface, damage, or otherwise physically mistreat in a way that the actor knows will seriously offend one or more persons likely to observe or discover his action."[7] Johnson was convicted of desecrating the American flag and sentenced to one year in prison and a fine of $2,000.

The Supreme Court overturned Johnson's conviction and struck down the Texas law, in an opinion written Justice William Brennan. Brennan stressed Johnson's burning of the flag was "overtly political."[8] The Texas statute was plainly designed to suppress unpopular views, singling out "only those severe acts of physical abuse of the flag carried out in a way likely to be offensive."[9] The law violated "a bedrock principle underlying the First Amendment," the court held, "that the Government may not prohibit the expression of an idea simply because society finds the idea itself offensive or disagreeable."[10]

No "American flag exception" existed to this principle. The government was not permitted to "ensure that a symbol be used to express only one view of that symbol or its referents."[11] The court understood the natural patriotic impulse to honor the flag and protect it. "It is not the State's ends," Justice Brennan wrote, "but its means to which we object."[12] He noted that "one of the proudest images of our flag, the one immortalized in our own national anthem, is the bombardment it survived at Fort McHenry."[13] The country and the flag, however, were tough enough to withstand graphic criticism. The court concluded, "It is the Nation's resilience, not its rigidity, that Texas sees reflected in the flag—and it is that resilience that we reassert today."[14]

The concluding theme of Justice Brennan's opinion emphasized the classic marketplace theory dictum that the best remedies for evil counsels are good ones. "We can imagine no more appropriate response to burning a flag than waving one's own," he wrote, and "no better way to counter a flag-burner's message than by saluting the flag that burns, no surer means of preserving the dignity even of the flag that burned than by—as one witness here did—according its remains a respectful burial." America, he admonished, does "not consecrate the flag by punishing its desecration, for in doing so we dilute the freedom that this cherished emblem represents."[15]

Chief Justice Rehnquist and Justices White, O'Connor, and Stevens all dissented. Quoting from the National Anthem and John Greenleaf Whittier, and invoking images from Iwo Jima, Korea, and Vietnam, the chief justice argued vehemently that the Constitution did not proscribe protection of our national symbol. Harking back to the language of *Chaplinsky*, Rehnquist argued that Johnson's flag burning was "no essential part of any exposition of ideas, and at the same time it had a tendency to incite a breach of the peace." As Rehnquist saw it, Johnson did not have to burn a flag to express his dissent. "Far from being a case of 'one picture being worth a thousand words,' flag burning is the equivalent of an inarticulate grunt or roar that, it seems fair to say, is most likely to be indulged in not to express any particular idea, but to antagonize others."[16]

These dissenting arguments all failed, however, and in that failure the marketplace theory of Holmes and Brandeis seemed firmly entrenched. The enduring strength of the marketplace theory throughout the modern epoch is illustrated by three decisions rendered since John Roberts became chief justice.

In *United States v. Stevens* (2010),[17] the court, in an opinion written by Chief Justice Roberts, struck down a federal statute barring trafficking in images of animal cruelty. Congress passed the law out of aversion to gruesome videos, sometimes called "crush videos," of horrific treatment of animals.[18] Crush videos often appealed to a sexual fetish in which viewers were aroused by the sight of women in stiletto heels crushing small helpless animals. If ever there was expression that appeared to be no serious exposition of ideas and an affront to order and morality, such depictions of animal cruelty would be high on the list.[19] As the court aptly put it, the government's claim was "not just that Congress may regulate depictions of animal cruelty subject to the First Amendment, but that these depictions are outside the reach of that Amendment altogether—that they fall into a 'First Amendment Free Zone.'"[20]

The Justice Department, represented at the time by Solicitor General Elena Kagan (who would later herself take a seat on the Supreme Court), defended the law prohibiting depictions of animal cruelty by relying on *Chaplinsky*. It appeared that the Justice Department didn't get the memo that the theory was now obsolete—or, if it got the memo, thought the memo was wrong. The government's theory was that "'whether a given category of speech enjoys First Amendment protection depends upon a categorical balancing of the value of the speech against its societal costs.'"[21]

In his opinion for the court rejecting the government's invocation of *Chaplinsky*, Chief Justice Roberts was uncharacteristically passionate and reproachful, admonishing the government that "as a free-floating test for First Amendment coverage, that sentence is startling and dangerous."[22] Such balancing of costs and benefits, the court lectured, is precisely what the First Amendment forbids, foreclosing deference to legislative judgments that some speech is just "not worth it."[23]

In *United States v. Alvarez* (2012),[24] the Supreme Court upheld the free speech right of Xavier Alvarez, a compulsive liar, to lie compulsively. Alvarez had falsely claimed to have played hockey for the Detroit Red Wings, to have married a starlet from Mexico, and to have been awarded the Congressional Medal of Honor—the last being the lie that got him into trouble.

Congress had passed a law, the Stolen Valor Act of 2005, making it a crime falsely to claim military honors. While it was hard, if not impossible, to see any constructive value to Alvarez's lies, the Supreme Court held that under the First Amendment, the government could not make lying alone a crime. Four justices—Kennedy, Roberts, Ginsburg, and

Sotomayor—joined in a plurality opinion written by Kennedy. Justice Breyer, joined by Justice Kagan, wrote a concurring opinion, supplying the extra two votes needed to reach the 6–3 result striking the law down. The key to the outcome was a distinction between falsehoods in the abstract and falsehoods that cause palpable harm. Defamation, for example, harms an individual's reputation. Perjury harms the pursuit of truth in trials. False advertising harms consumers. False statements on a business application or securities regulation may harm a creditor or investor. In contrast, some lies do not cause any demonstrable damage but are mere "lies in the abstract." These lies may evoke disgust but don't cause demonstrable, specific harm.

The lie Alvarez told about military honors surely outraged many, particularly those who had deservedly been awarded such honors for their service or valor, but this societal outrage at the content of a message, the majority of justices reasoned, was not enough to overcome the First Amendment free speech rights possessed by Alvarez, which extended even to the telling of lies. Invoking the imagery of George Orwell's classic novel *1984*, the plurality declared that our "constitutional tradition stands against the idea that we need Oceania's Ministry of Truth."[25]

Justice Alito, joined by Justices Scalia and Thomas, wrote a spirited dissent, praising the valor of those who are awarded the Congressional Medal of Honor and arguing that "the right to free speech does not protect false factual statements that inflict real harm and serve no legitimate interest."[26] Yet again, they lost, and yet again this signaled the demise of the order and morality theory, and the dominance of the marketplace theory.

The court in *Snyder v. Phelps* (2012)[27] again demonstrated the vigor of its commitment to the marketplace theory, upholding the exercise of free speech in circumstances far more harmful than crush videos. The Supreme Court, in an opinion by Chief Justice Roberts, ruled 8–1 that the speech of the Westboro Baptist Church of Topeka, Kansas, was insulated from liability by the First Amendment. The sole dissenting vote was Justice Samuel Alito, the one Supreme Court justice most inclined still to invoke the themes of *Chaplinsky* and its principles of order and morality.

In 1991, members of the Westboro church began a campaign against homosexuality through demonstrating, picketing, and distributing flyers at public and private events. Church members regularly picketed outside public buildings and churches, in parks frequented by gays and lesbians, and at funerals of people who died of AIDS. Among the church's most popular incantations were "God Hates Fags," "No Fags in Heaven," "Fags are Worthy of Death, Rom. 1:32," and "Turn or Burn." The Westboro church's real specialty, however, was the targeting of military funerals. Westboro members would descend on funerals in which families and friends had gathered to bury members of the US armed forces who had been killed in the service of their country. Church members would picket the funerals with signs such as "Thank God for Dead Soldiers," "Thank God for IEDs," and "God Hates Cripple Soldiers." The signs were accompanied by screaming at the bereaved family of the fallen soldier that their son or daughter is "rotting in hell" and that "God hates their tears." Fred Phelps, the leader of this hate-mongering cult, unapologetically preached hatred and embraced the condemnation of all he offended.

Phelps was often sued for these tactics, and finally one of the suits against him reached the US Supreme Court. By the time the test case, *Snyder v. Phelps*, reached the high court, the Westboro church had picketed nearly six hundred funerals. The *Snyder* case arose from a civil lawsuit brought by the family of Marine lance corporal Matthew Snyder, who was killed in Iraq in the line of duty. The funeral was set for a Catholic church in Westminster, Maryland, the Snyders' hometown. The time and location were printed in local newspapers. Phelps became aware of Matthew Snyder's funeral and decided to travel to Maryland with six other Westboro Baptist parishioners to picket the service. Two of the parishioners with Snyder were his daughters and four his grandchildren. On the day of the memorial service, Phelps and his group picketed on public land adjacent to public streets near the Maryland State House, the US Naval Academy, and Snyder's funeral. For the Snyder funeral they brandished signs proclaiming "God Hates the USA / Thank God for 9/11," "America is Doomed," "Don't Pray for the USA," "Thank God for IEDs," "Thank God for Dead Soldiers," "Pope in Hell," "Priests Rape Boys," "God Hates Fags," "You're Going to Hell," and "God Hates You."[28]

The Westboro church had, in advance, notified local law enforcement authorities of their protest plans. They complied with police instructions in staging their protests. The actual picketing took place within a ten-by-twenty-five-foot plot of public land adjacent to a public street, behind a temporary fence. This was a location approximately one thousand feet from the church at which the funeral service was conducted. The protest lasted about thirty minutes. The funeral procession passed within two to three hundred feet of the picket location. Albert Snyder, the father of Corporal Snyder, stated that he could see the tops of the picket signs but not read their content. No protesters entered the church property or went to the cemetery. There was no use of profanity, and there was no violence associated with the event.

There was also an internet element to the case. Several weeks following the funeral, a member of the Westboro church who had been one of the pickets at the Snyder funeral posted on the internet, on the Westboro website, an attack on the Snyder family. The message was laced with religious denunciations of the Snyders, interspersed among lengthy Bible quotations. When Albert Snyder discovered the posting, which came to be known in the litigation by the nickname "the epic," his distress and sense of offense were understandably intensified.

In *Snyder v. Phelps*, Snyder described the intensity of his emotional injury, testifying that he was unable to separate the thought of his dead son from his thoughts of Westboro's picketing, and that he often became tearful, angry, and physically ill when he thought about it. Snyder's personal testimony was in turn buttressed by expert witnesses, who explained that Snyder's emotional anguish had resulted in severe depression and had exacerbated Snyder's preexisting health conditions. A jury awarded Snyder $2.9 million in compensatory damages and $8 million in punitive damages. The trial judge sustained the $2.9 million compensatory damages award but reduced the punitive damages award to $2.1 million.

The award was overturned by the Supreme Court. The majority opinion of Chief Justice Roberts emphasized the right of Americans to express controversial and offensive views from public forums, such as streets, sidewalks, and parks. To be sure, the church was exploiting the occasion of the funeral to heighten the attention paid to its message. This no doubt was particularly hurtful to Albert Snyder and his family. Yet these factors, the court held, did not diminish the First Amendment protection that the Westboro church's speech would otherwise enjoy. The award to Snyder of damages for his emotional distress could not stand, the court held, because the jury was permitted to award liability merely on the finding that the picketing was "outrageous."

The leitmotif of the three opinions in *United States v. Stevens, United States v. Alvarez,* and *Snyder v. Phelps* was that society's judgment that a message was outrageous, deeply disturbing, or highly offensive is not enough, standing alone, to justify its censorship. These decisions built on prior decisions rejecting the order and morality theme of *Chaplinsky* and elevating the marketplace theories of Holmes and Brandeis. Perhaps no prior decision of the Supreme Court captured the principle more graphically than a case arising in Virginia from the United States District Court for the Western District of Virginia (the same federal court that would prove prominent as events unfolded in Charlottesville in 2017): *Hustler Magazine, Inc. v. Falwell.*[29]

Larry Flynt, the publisher of *Hustler,* had authorized the publication of a parody attacking the televangelist Jerry Falwell. The parody mimicked a popular ad campaign run in upscale American magazines by Campari liqueur. Campari, a bitter liqueur popular in Italy, was attempting to do better in the American market. The challenge for Campari, which is an acquired taste, was to get Americans to try Campari enough to acquire the taste. An ingenious ad campaign launched by Campari featured sexy American celebrities—famous movie or music stars, or athletes—musing about "their first time." The ads would feature an "interview" with a celebrity—Jill St. John, for example—wistfully reminiscing about her "first time," ostensibly her first time having sex. The memory was always awkward. The first time was not so great. But the second time was better, and after that, matters really took off. By the end of the interview, however, it was revealed that the "first time" was actually not about sex, but Campari liqueur. The clever, funny, sexy double entendre was that Campari, like sex, gets better with practice.

Larry Flynt and *Hustler* decided it would be a barrelful of yucks to do an exact replica of the Campari ads featuring Rev. Jerry Falwell talking about his "first time," which turned out to be with his mother, in an outhouse:

FALWELL: My first time was in an outhouse outside Lynchburg, Virginia.

INTERVIEWER: Wasn't it a little cramped?

FALWELL:	Not after I kicked the goat out.
INTERVIEWER:	*I see. You must tell me all about it.*
FALWELL:	I never *really* expected to make it with Mom, but then after she showed all the other guys in town such a good time, figured, "What the hell?"
INTERVIEWER:	*But your mom? Isn't that a bit odd?*
FALWELL:	I don't think so. Looks don't mean that much to me in a woman.
INTERVIEWER:	*Go on.*
FALWELL:	Well, we were drunk off our God-fearing asses on Campari, ginger ale, and soda—that's called a Fire and Brimstone—at the time. And Mom looked better than a Baptist whore with a $100 donation.
INTERVIEWER:	*Campari in the crapper with Mom . . . how interesting. Well, how was it?*
FALWELL:	The Campari was great. But Mom passed out before I could come.
INTERVIEWER:	*Did you ever try it again?*
FALWELL:	Sure . . . lots of times. But not in the outhouse. Between Mom and the shit, the flies were too much to bear.
INTERVIEWER:	*We meant the Campari.*
FALWELL:	Oh, yea, I always get sloshed before I go out to the pulpit. You don't think I could lay down all that bullshit *sober*, do you?[30]

Falwell was doing a gig at the Willard Hotel when he was shown a copy of the ad. He did not find it as funny as Flynt did, and sued. Falwell also launched an impressive counterattack against Flynt and *Hustler* magazine. Falwell's Moral Majority Inc. sent out two mailings over Falwell's signature. One was a mailing to 500,000 "rank and file" members, which described the *Hustler* parody and asked for contributions to help Falwell "defend his mother's memory." A second mailing to 26,900 "major donors" included a copy of the parody with eight of the most offensive words blacked out. A third mailing, signed by Falwell, under the auspices of his show, the *Old Time Gospel Hour*, was sent to 750,000 persons. Falwell also used his television program to discuss the parody and to counterattack Flynt, displaying the ad on national television. Within thirty days of the mailings, the Moral Majority received $45,000, and the *Old Time Gospel Hour* received $672,000 in contributions for the legal battle against Flynt. Falwell used Flynt's parody to make war on pornography and raise money for his cause. Falwell wrote, "Now pornography has thrust its ugly head into our everyday lives and is multiplying like a filthy plague. . . . And there, in my opinion, is clear proof that the billion dollar sex industry, of which Larry Flynt is a self-declared leader, is preying on innocent, impressionable children to feed the lusts of depraved adults. For those porno peddlers, it appears that lust and greed have replaced decency and morality."

The case was tried in federal court in Virginia. Falwell lost in his claim against Flynt for defamation. While it was of course "false" that Falwell had engaged in sex with his mother in an outhouse, or anywhere else, the accusation was not "actionable" as libel because no reasonable person could possibly believe that the parody was intended to be taken literally as an actual factual accusation against Falwell. But Falwell did win a verdict of $200,000 against Flynt for intentional infliction of emotional distress. That verdict was appealed by Flynt all the way to the US Supreme Court.

I became personally involved in the case. I gave a speech about the case in front of a group of lawyers, judges, and journalists in Richmond, Virginia, in which I argued that while most in the mainstream media would not want to align themselves with Larry Flynt and *Hustler*, the verdict against Flynt and *Hustler*, if allowed to stand, posed a major threat to all forms of parody and satire in America, from cartoons in the *New Yorker* to skits on *Saturday Night Live*. I was asked to author an amicus curiae brief. My clients for the brief were the *Richmond Times-Dispatch*, the *New York Times*, the *Fredericksburg Free Lance-Star*, the Times Mirror Company, the Virginia Press Association, the American Newspaper Publishers Association, and the Magazine Publishers Association. I later wrote a book on the entire case, titled *Jerry Falwell v. Larry Flynt: The First Amendment on Trial*.[31] A Broadway producer, Lewis Allen, whose many Broadway shows included *Annie*, *I'm not Rappaport*, *Master Class*, and *A Few Good Men*, invited me to try my hand at writing a Broadway script based on my book. I did, and we came close to producing the show. In a preview run staged on Broadway to attract investors, the actor William F. Macy played Jerry Falwell, and Peter Boyle played Larry Flynt. Lewis Allen took me around town introducing him as his new playwright, meeting people like Mike Nichols in the Russian Tea Room. I was ready to give up law teaching and practice and get my black turtleneck sweater and start the life of a writer in Greenwich Village. Just as we were about to sign the contracts for the show, movie producers Oliver Stone and Miloš Forman announced plans to do the movie *People v. Larry Flynt*, staring Woody Harrelson, Courtney Love, and Ed Norton. I was disappointed that our show didn't fly and gave up on the turtleneck, no hard feelings. When I went to see the movie, which I thought was terrific, I smiled when Woody Harrelson, who played Larry Flynt, snarled down at his lawyer, Alan Isaacman, played by Ed Norton, "I'm your dream client: I'm the most fun, I'm rich, and I'm always in trouble." I smiled because in real life Larry Flynt never said any such thing to his lawyer Alan Isaacman. It was, however, how I described Flynt in my writings. Years after the lawsuit was over, Jerry Falwell and Larry Flynt "reconciled" in a sense and did some college speaking engagements together. One of these occasions was at the University of Virginia in Charlottesville, where the two of them appeared onstage together with me as a moderator. Behind the scenes they joked and got along fine, and Flynt even referred to Falwell as "my preacher."

There was no such faith, hope, or charity between them when the lawsuit was in full gear, however, and certainly not as the case reached the Supreme Court of the United States. This was, to be sure, an ultimate test of the bounds of the marketplace theory, for however much Flynt may have wanted to deflate Falwell, it was hard to argue that he had to portray Falwell having sex with his mother in an outhouse to do the job.

Yet even so, the Supreme Court handed Flynt a resounding victory over Falwell, in what would prove to be one of the landmark cases in free speech history. The court ruled without dissent that the parody was protected under the First Amendment. Chief Justice Rehnquist conceded that the *Hustler* parody was at best a distant cousin of the conventional political cartoon, "and a rather poor relation at that."[32] The chief justice argued, however, that there was simply no way to draw a principled distinction between the *Hustler* parody and other satiric efforts. "If it were possible," he stated, "by laying down a principled standard to separate the one from the other, public discourse would probably suffer little or no harm."[33] The Supreme Court was doubtful, Rehnquist explained, that any reasonably concrete standard could ever be articulated. Amorphous pejoratives such as "outrageous" or "indecent" were too subjective to withstand First Amendment requirements. To permit a jury to impose liability for mere "outrageousness" would invite jurors to base liability on their tastes and prejudices.

The Day of the Klan

The first stirrings of activity at Justice Park began around noon. The Virginia State Police swept the park for explosives. Counterprotesters began to trickle into the park, some openly carrying firearms or knives. Very little happened until 1:20 p.m., when some of the counterprotesters began putting on Black Lives Matter shirts. Other opposition groups began to gather, and by 2:00 p.m. about two hundred counterprotesters were in the park.

A police command center was established in the conference room of the Charlottesville office of McGuire Woods, a large international law firm headquartered in Richmond. The Charlottesville office of the firm was located on Fourth Street, overlooking Justice Park.

Police had divided Justice Park into four zones. The designated area for the Klan to conduct its rally was zone 1, which included the Stonewall Jackson statue. To the back of the Klan's zone was the Albemarle County Courthouse, forming a natural physical barrier for one of the three sides of the Klan's designated zone. The other three sides of the Klan's zone were surrounded by double barriers, formed by two rows of bike-rack barricades positioned ten feet apart. Counterprotesters were allotted zones 2, 3, and 4, effectively allowing them to surround the Klan. The Klan's zone could be accessed only from High Street. The double barrier formed by the parallel bike racks ten feet apart were designed to create a buffer zone between the Klan and the counterprotesters, with police stationed inside the barriers to keep the groups separated.

The early planning for the event contemplated that only police would be allowed inside the buffer zone. A media staging area was established on East Jefferson Street, bordering the park. On July 8, however, police allowed members of the media to enter the buffer zone. The police believed they were required to permit such access under a Virginia law that contains a general prohibition making it illegal to cross police lines erected by authorities in situations involving fires, accidents, wrecks, explosions, crimes, riots, or other emergency situations where life, limb, or property may be endangered.[1] The same statute, however, contains an exception, which states, "Personnel from information services such as press, radio, and television, when gathering news, shall be exempt from the provisions of this section except that it shall be unlawful for such persons to obstruct the police, firefighters, or emergency medical services personnel in the performance of their duties at such scene. Such personnel shall proceed at their own risk." It does not appear that the "media exception" has ever been interpreted by a Virginia court. The literal wording of the law does not necessarily mean that reporters had a right to enter the buffer zone, because the law could be interpreted to treat the buffer zone as a corridor that needed to be kept free in order to avoid obstruction of the police in the performance of their duties. The media already appeared to have ample access to cover the event from the media staging area on Jefferson Street. The Charlottesville police, however, rightly or wrongly understood the Virginia law as requiring them to allow reporters into the buffer zones.

On July 8, Antifa's operations were sophisticated and well coordinated.[2] Antifa members arrived at Justice Park, highly prepared for potential physical confrontation, many wearing helmets, shields, body armor, padded clothing, and gas masks. They had walkie-talkies and even their own activist medics. Antifa members coordinated with other national and local counterprotest groups who were gathering to confront the Klan.

Antifa leaders scoped out the way in which the police had cordoned off Justice Park into zones and deduced that the Klan would have to enter the park from High Street in order to enter its designated zone, because the other sides of the Klan's zone were blocked by the buffer zone barriers and the courthouse.

By 3:00 p.m., when the Klan rally was scheduled to begin, the size of the counterprotest crowd had swelled to over six hundred people, and the atmosphere had become tense. The Klan had yet to arrive, and so counterprotesters and law enforcement, consisting of the Charlottesville Police Department and the Virginia State Police, were placed in adversarial roles. A group of about a dozen counterprotesters locked arms to block the entrance to the Klan zone on High Street. Lieutenant Joe Hatter had the principal command duty for crowd control. Lieutenant Hatter used a bullhorn to warn the counterprotesters to cease blocking the entrance to the Klan zone or risk arrest. After repeated warnings were ignored, the police moved in to arrest the counterprotesters blocking the entrance. As the arrests commenced, the crowd grew increasingly agitated. All the counterprotest zones were flooded with activists, and the crowd began to press against the barricades. Police officers who had been mingling within the crowed now all retreated to the safety of the buffer zones.

Meanwhile, the Klan was preparing to arrive. Klan members had gathered earlier in Waynesboro, Virginia, at the base of the Blue Ridge Mountains a little more than twenty-five miles west of Charlottesville. The Klan members donned their robes and regalia, conducted some preliminary rituals, and then drove toward Charlottesville. Two police squad cars escorted the Klan members, who were driving into the city in eighteen vehicles. The Klan drivers were instructed to ignore all red lights and stop signs and instead proceed through intersections following the police escorts. The original planning for the event had called for the Klan members to park their cars in a surface parking lot near Justice Park. As the size of the counterprotest gathering swelled and tensions escalated, however, the police realized that this arrangement would be too dangerous. A last-minute decision was made to instead divert the Klan motorcade to a parking garage at the Juvenile and Domestic Relations Court, a block from Justice Park. The Klan members parked in the garage, and at 3:45 p.m., dressed in robes and hoods, but with their faces exposed, they set off on foot, carrying Confederate flags.

The Klan had roughly a block to walk from the parking garage to Justice Park. By the numbers, the ratio was overwhelming. The Klan had only about sixty marchers. Counterprotesters now numbered between fifteen hundred and two thousand. The police formed a human barrier between the Klan and the counterprotesters, establishing a corridor through which the Klan members marched from the garage to the park. Yet despite police lining both sides of the gauntlet, they could not prevent the counterprotesters from tossing punches, hurling fruit and bottles, and berating the Klan with catcalls and insults. The Charlottesville and Virginia State Police labored to be professional and calm, trying not to project any bias toward either side. Even so, the raw fact that the police formed a corridor to protect the Klan's entrance to the park put them in the seeming symbolic position of protecting the Klan against the counterprotesters. Moreover, by having their backs to the Klan and their faces turned to the counterprotest crowd, the optics were that the police were there to protect the Klan against the counterprotesters. Yet the police were simply intending to keep the peace, not take sides. Yet to many, the physical deployment of the police, forming a protective corridor through which the Klan could march, with all police faces turned toward the counterprotesters, created a visual and symbolic impression that the police were there to protect the Klan and in effect had taken sides. This dynamic intensified over the next hour.

When the Klan finally reached Justice Park at 3:50 p.m., the "imperial kommander" Amanda Barker described Justice Park as a "zoo."[3] Counterprotesters sought to drown out the Klan speakers and tossed water bottles, apples, tomatoes, and oranges at the Klan. Some Klan members threw the projectiles back at the counterprotesters. Through it all, the police faced the counterprotesters with their backs to the Klan, inadvertently continuing to reinforce the impression that the police were protecting the "peaceful" Klan protest and wary of the "violent" counterprotesters.[4]

At 4:00 p.m., the crowd demanded that the police shut the Klan rally down, as the time allotted in the Klan's permit had expired. Police officials, however, decided to give the Klan an extra twenty minutes, a sort of First Amendment version of "stoppage time" in soccer, to compensate the Klan for the late start caused by the counterprotesters' attempts to block the Klan's entrance into the park. The extension of time added to the frustration of counterprotesters, who continued to perceive the police as siding with the Klan.

It was 4:22 p.m. when Lieutenant Hatter informed Barker that the Klan's time had run out. Barker and the Klan were ready to get out. The counterprotesters now shifted tactics, maneuvering to block the Klan's exit. The police again deployed in a corridor to enable the Klan's exit, forming a "human cop wall."[5] The Klan members were again spit on, punched, and hit with fruit and bottles as they ran the gauntlet back to the parking garage.

Hundreds of counterprotesters moved along Fourth Street, shadowing the Klan to the Juvenile and Domestic Relations Court parking garage. The Klan members reached the garage and headed to their cars. The counterprotesters blocked the vehicle exit from the garage, trapping the Klan inside. Police reinforcements arrived on the scene. Police announced over a bullhorn that the counterprotesters blocking the garage exit were an unlawful assembly. The police pushed the crowd away from the exit and across to the other side of Fourth Street, clearing a path for the Klan vehicles to exit. With a police escort car leading the way, the Klan caravan left the garage. Counterprotesters again surged forward to attempt to block the cars, hitting them with projectiles. The Klan vehicles made it out and headed to the Route 250 bypass out of Charlottesville.

The Klan was now gone, but the anger was not. As anger abhors a vacuum, frustrated counterprotesters turned their ire on the Charlottesville and Virginia State Police. Police became the enemy. Some counterprotesters took up the chant, "Cops and Klan go hand in hand!"

The police had staged an armored Bearcat vehicle in an alley next to the Juvenile and Domestic Relations Court. A large group of counterprotesters moved toward that alley. The police issued an order to disperse, announcing that if the crowd failed to vacate the area, chemical agents would be used. The Virginia State Police launched three canisters of tear gas. Screams of pain erupted in the crowd. Street medics helped the counterdemonstrators suffering from the tear gas with dousings of milk and water. The tear gas only fueled the crowd's anger.

The tear gas caught even some law enforcement personnel by surprise. Many officers in the street had no advance warning of the tear gas deployment and had not yet donned their gas masks. The release of the tear gas, which had not been ordered by Chief Thomas in the command center, also caused confusion and anger in the McGuire Woods conference room. The gas did cause the crowd to disperse but intensified the perception that the police had come to the scene to protect the Klan and not the counterprotesters and were using excessive force against the counterprotesters.[6]

18

WHEN SPEECH ADVANCES CIVIL RIGHTS

Lawyers who defend freedom of speech often find themselves defending people and causes that they personally find reprehensible. I have been in this position myself, representing speakers whom I find reprehensible and speech that I would not myself utter in a million years. Such is the fate of free speech lawyers. Flag burners are more likely than flag waivers to need the help of free speech lawyers.

When I get criticized for representing unsavory speakers, I often find myself resorting to a stock cliché. I may disagree with what my client says, I explain, but I defend my client's right to say it. As baseball player Crash Davis, played by Kevin Costner, teaches in the movie *Bull Durham*, "You're gonna have to learn your clichés. You're gonna have to study them, you're gonna have to learn them, you're gonna have to know them. They're your friends."

Drawing on stock free speech clichés, however, has its limits. It is not fully satisfying, either intellectually or morally. To dig more deeply, recall an enormously important point made by Virginia Law School professor

Leslie Kendrick, explaining that modern free speech principles exist to shield unpopular views from the power of majorities. Kendrick reminded us that this "is true whether the unpopular belief in question is white supremacy in 2017 Charlottesville or equality in 1964 Birmingham."[1]

Two cases arising from the struggle for civil rights buttress Professor Kendrick's point. One, *New York Times Co. v. Sullivan*,[2] involved efforts to defend Martin Luther King Jr. while he was in jail. The other, *N.A.A.C.P. v. Claiborne Hardware Co.*,[3] involved the protection of civil rights activists in the wake of King's assassination. These cases are not clichés, but rather powerful exemplars of how the robust protection for unpopular speech embraced by the marketplace theory may at times *advance* the cause of equality.

To be sure, the cases do not end the argument, because those who believe in the order and morality theory might take the position that free speech principles *should* protect those on the side of righteousness and justice—Martin Luther King during the 1960s civil rights movements and Black Lives Matter or Antifa in today's civil rights movements. The counter to this argument, however, is that if we are going to adopt a view of free speech that protects the "good" insurgents but not the "bad" insurgents, someone will have to decide who is good and who is bad. Those who, like me, generally come down in favor of the marketplace theory are not inclined to trust this job to government. The *New York Times* and *Claiborne Hardware* cases go a long way toward explaining why.

On February 29, 1960, Martin Luther King was arrested on trumped-up charges involving two counts of perjury in connection with the filing of his Alabama state income tax return. On March 19, 1960, three weeks after King's arrest, the *New York Times* ran an editorial in support of King's efforts. The editorial praised the efforts of blacks in the South to resist racism and admonished Congress to "heed their rising voices, for they will be heard." On March 29, 1960, a group called the "Committee to Defend Martin Luther King" paid for a full-page public interest advertisement in the *Times*, bearing a title lifted from the prior *Times* editorial, "Heed Their Rising Voices."

The ad began by proclaiming that black students in the South are "engaged in wide-spread non-violent demonstrations in positive affirmation of the right to live in human dignity as guaranteed by the United States Constitution and the Bill of Rights," and the efforts of those students are "being met by an unprecedented wave of terror." The ad claimed that four hundred students had been ejected from lunch counters in South Carolina, teargassed, soaked to the skin with fire hoses in freezing weather, and arrested en masse. According to the ad, after students in Montgomery, Alabama, sang "My Country, 'Tis of Thee" on the state capitol steps, "their leaders were expelled from school, and truckloads of police armed with shotguns and tear gas ringed the Alabama State College Campus." When the student body at Alabama State protested to state authorities by refusing to re-register, the ad alleged, their dining hall "was padlocked in an attempt to starve them into submission." The ad lauded the efforts of the students, praising them as "rising to glory," and stated that certain "Southern violators" had repeatedly answered Dr. King's peaceful protests with intimidation and violence. "They have bombed his home almost killing his wife and child," it stated. "They have assaulted his person. They have arrested him seven times—for speeding, loitering, and similar offenses." The ad then alleged that "now they have charged him with perjury—a felony under which they could imprison him for ten years." The ad asserted that it was obvious "that their real purpose is to remove him physically as the leader to whom the students and millions of others look for guidance and support, and thereby to intimidate all leaders who may rise in the South." The ad ended with a plea for funds to assist in the civil rights struggle and the defense of King, stating, "We urge you to join hands with our fellow Americans in the South by supporting, with your dollars, the combined appeal for all three needs—the defense of Martin Luther King—the support of the embattled students—and the struggle for the right-to-vote."

The *New York Times* was paid a little over $4,800 for running the advertisement. The total circulation of the issue was about 650,000, but only 394 copies of the *Times* were sent to Alabama news dealers, and only 35 copies found their way into Montgomery County, Alabama. The *Times* ad stirred up a whirlwind of bitter reaction in Alabama, with many prominent Alabama politicians, including Governor John Patterson, demanding apologies and retractions.

One of those demanding a retraction was an incumbent Montgomery city official, L. B. Sullivan, who as commissioner of public affairs was supervisor of the Montgomery departments of scales, cemeteries, fire, and police. The *Times* wrote back to Sullivan and told him it had investigated the matter and was "somewhat puzzled as to how you think the statements in any way reflect on you."[4] Without answering the letter, Sullivan sued the *Times* for libel in Montgomery County, seeking $500,000 in damages. The *Times* ad did not actually mention Sullivan by name, and much of the ad referred to events entirely outside of Alabama.

There were some trivial inaccuracies and exaggerations in the *Times* ad. Although black students in Montgomery did stage a demonstration on the capitol steps, the song they sang was not "My Country, 'Tis of Thee," but the National Anthem. Although nine black students had been expelled from college, they were not expelled for leading the demonstration on the statehouse steps but rather for demanding service at a lunch counter inside the Montgomery County Courthouse. Not the entire student body, only most of it, had protested the expulsions, and not by refusing to register for classes, but by boycotting classes on a single day. The dining hall was never literally padlocked, although some students who had neither registered nor obtained temporary meal tickets were barred from entering. Although police were called to the Alabama State campus in large numbers because of race-related protests on three occasions, the police never physically "ringed" the campus, and they were never actually deployed in connection with the state capitol demonstration. Martin Luther King had not been arrested seven times, only four; and although King claimed to have been physically assaulted by a Montgomery police officer in connection with an arrest for loitering outside a classroom, one of the arresting officers denied that an assault had occurred. King's home was in fact bombed twice when his wife and child were there, but both bombings took place prior to Commissioner Sullivan's tenure. The police were never implicated in the bombings and had actually made efforts to apprehend those who were. Three of King's four arrests antedated Sullivan's period as commissioner; and Sullivan was not personally involved in procuring the perjury indictments brought against King.[5]

Sullivan's theory was that the word "police" in the paragraph concerning Montgomery would be understood as referring to Sullivan, because Sullivan was the Montgomery commissioner who supervised the police department. He thus argued that the ad imputed to him the "ringing" of the Alabama State campus with police and the padlocking of the dining hall to starve students into submission. Sullivan further reasoned that since arrests are ordinarily made by the police, the statement "They have arrested [Dr. King] seven times" would be read as referring to Sullivan, and that the "they" who did the arresting would be equated with the "they" who committed the other described acts of the "Southern violators," thereby effectively accusing Sullivan himself of complicity in bombing Martin Luther King's home, assaulting his person, and charging him with perjury.

The trial judge was Walter B. Jones, the author of a manifesto titled "The Confederate Creed." Jones proclaimed in the Confederate Creed that "with unfaltering trust in God of my fathers, I believe, as a Confederate, in obedience to Him; it is my duty to respect the laws and ancient ways of my people, and to stand up for the right of my state to determine what is good for its people in all local affairs."[6] Judge Jones ordered the seating in the courtroom segregated, "in keeping with the common law of Alabama, and observing the time-honored customs and usages of our people." Jones stood by acquiescing as lawyers for Sullivan constantly used the word "nigger" in the courtroom. He allowed one of the lawyers to declare, in closing argument, "In other words, all of these things that happened did not happen in Russia, where the police run everything, they did not happen in the Congo, *where they still eat them*, they happened in Montgomery Alabama, a law abiding community."[7]

After a trial that lasted only three days, the jury returned a verdict of $500,000 against the *Times* and four individual black ministers. The award was affirmed by the Supreme Court of Alabama. The threat to the *Times* went well beyond the $500,000 verdict in Sullivan's case. A string of other libel suits against the *Times* had risen in Alabama in connection with its reporting on racial matters; and awards against the paper were piling up.

The Supreme Court, in an opinion by Justice William Brennan, reversed the libel judgment. Brennan's opinion was steeped in the marketplace theory. "The maintenance of the opportunity for free political discussion," the court said, "to the end that government may be responsive to the will of the people and that changes may be obtained by lawful means, an opportunity essential to the security of the Republic, is a fundamental principle of our constitutional system."[8] In a sentence that would become sacred scripture in the lore of the First Amendment marketplace theory, Brennan's opinion for the court stated the case must be considered "against the background of a profound national commitment to the principle that debate on public issues should be uninhibited, robust, and wide-open, and that it may well include vehement, caustic, and sometimes unpleasantly sharp attacks on government and public officials."[9] Criticism of official conduct does not lose its constitutional protection, Justice Brennan argued, merely because it is effective criticism and hence diminishes the reputations of the officials involved.

Brennan then spoke of the lessons to be drawn from the great controversy over the Sedition Act of 1798. Although no case challenging the validity of the Sedition Act ever reached the Supreme Court, Brennan noted (as had Justice Holmes several decades earlier) that "the attack upon its validity had carried the day in the court of history."[10] Brennan then stated the holding that would launch an entirely new era for the law of libel: "The constitutional guarantees require, we think, a federal rule that prohibits a public official from recovering damages for a defamatory falsehood relating to his official conduct unless he proves that the statement was made with actual malice—that is, with the knowledge that it was false or with reckless disregard of whether it was false or not."[11]

The *New York Times* case became the lodestar of all modern-epoch libel litigation involving public plaintiffs. History treats the case as the decision that forever changed the American law of defamation. The "actual malice" standard that the case established became the mainstay of libel suits brought by public officials and public figures ever since. It would be the critical fault issue, for example, in the Charlottesville lawsuit brought by the University of Virginia dean Nicole Eramo against *Rolling Stone*.

As a defamation lawyer myself, that is how I refer to and apply the *New York Times* case routinely in the libel litigation in which I am involved. But that workaday meaning of the case fails to capture the resonance of the case as a landmark civil rights suit, and it fails to capture the importance of this celebrated libel law decision as a powerful exemplar of the intersection of two of the great American constitutional law narratives— the story of the American struggle over the meaning of freedom of speech, and the story of the American struggle over the meaning of equality.

While the *New York Times* decision has taken on mythical stature as a landmark First Amendment decision, in fairness it should be pointed out that the case has also had its share of sharp critics. The most recent critic is Justice Clarence Thomas. In *McKee v. Cosby*,[12] Kathrine McKee publicly accused the actor and comedian Bill Cosby of forcibly raping her. Cosby, through his lawyer Martin Singer, denounced McKee. McKee then sued Cosby for defamation. A lower court held that in going public with her accusations, McKee became a "public figure" for defamation law purposes and was thus required to establish "actual malice" against Cosby. The Supreme Court refused to take the case, and Justice Thomas concurred in that refusal, agreeing that whether McKee was or was not a public figure was the sort of "fact bound" decision the court should not entertain. Thomas took the occasion, however, to condemn the decision in *New York Times v. Sullivan* and suggest that the court, at some future time, should take up the legitimacy of the decision and overrule it. "*New York Times* and the Court's decisions extending it were policy-driven decisions masquerading as constitutional law," he wrote. "We did not begin meddling in this area until 1964, nearly 175 years after the First Amendment was ratified," Thomas observed. He urged his colleagues on the court to look for a future opportunity to reconsider the decision and perhaps repudiate it.[13]

The decision in *New York Times v. Sullivan* arose from Martin Luther King's rise to prominence in the civil rights movement. The decision in *N.A.A.C.P. v. Claiborne Hardware Co.*[14] arose from events in the final years of his life, and events precipitated by his assassination.

In March 1966, black citizens of Port Gibson, Mississippi, part of Claiborne County, presented white elected officials with a list of demands for racial equality and justice. The effort was led by Charles Evers, the field secretary of the NAACP, and James Dorsey, the pastor of the First Baptist Church in Port Gibson. Their list of demands called for the desegregation of all public schools and public facilities, the hiring of black policemen, public improvements in black residential areas, selection of blacks for jury duty, integration of bus stations so that blacks could use all facilities, and an end to verbal abuse by law enforcement officers. It stated that "Negroes are not to be addressed by terms as 'boy,' 'girl,' 'shine,' 'uncle,' or any other offensive term, but as 'Mr.,' 'Mrs.,' or 'Miss,' as is the case with other citizens."[15]

When no favorable response to the demands was received, a meeting was held at the First Baptist Church, and those attending voted unanimously to commence a boycott against white merchants in Port Gibson and Claiborne County. In 1967, Port Gibson hired its first black police officer. Responding to this progress, the boycott was partially lifted from some of the white merchants.

Martin Luther King was shot in the early evening of April 4, 1968. His shooting triggered both peaceful demonstrations and violent riots across the United States. King's assassination caused the already tense situation in Montgomery to grow even more strained.

On April 19, Charles Evers spoke to a group assembled at the First Baptist Church and led a march to the courthouse, where he demanded the discharge of the entire Port Gibson police force. When this demand was refused, the boycott was reimposed on all white merchants. Evers that day gave an impassioned speech, which was recorded by sheriff's officers and would be used against him in the legal actions that followed. The speech minced no words. To black citizens, Evers was blunt in letting them know they must observe the boycott that the civil rights leaders had imposed. To white citizens, the speech was blunt in asserting that the boycott was going to do its damage. To whites who had joined with blacks in the civil rights marches, Evers stated, "Thank you for having the courage to walk down those streets with us. We thank you for letting our white brethren know that guns and bullets ain't gonna stop us."[16] Evers declared that "Port Gibson is all of our town," and that "black folks, red folks, Chinese and Japanese alike, that we are going to have our share."[17] He warned whites, "We are going to beat you because we know you can't trick us no more. You are not going to be able to fool us by getting somebody to give us a drink of whiskey no more. You ain't gonna be able to fool us by somebody giving us a few dollars no more. We are gonna take your money and drink with you and then we're gonna vote against you. Then we are going to elect a sheriff in this county and a sheriff that is responsible, that won't have to run and grab the telephone and call up the blood-thirsty highway patrol when he gets ready to come in and beat innocent folks down to the ground for no cause."[18]

Evers told white people that they did not need to fear being shot with bullets. He preached, "Oh, no, white folks, we ain't going to shoot you with no bullet. We are going to shoot you with our ballots and with our bucks. We are going to take away from you the thing that you have had over us all these years. Political power and economic power."[19]

Evers then took a more violent tone. "While you kill our brothers and our sisters and rape our wives and our friends. You're guilty. You're guilty because you don't care a thing about anybody," he said. "And when you go and let a big, black burly nigger like you get on the police force go down and grab another black brother's arm and hold it while a white racist stole him from us, and he's a liar if he says he didn't hold him," he continued. "We mean what we are saying. We are not playing."[20]

Evers was pointed in his message to blacks, arguing that they dare not fail to observe the boycott. His message was not just aimed at whites, admonishing them to cease their evil ways. It admonished blacks that they too were complicit if they failed to keep the pressure on whites. "Now, my dear friends, the white folks have got the message," Evers preached to the blacks in his audience. "I hope you have got the message and tell every one of our black brothers until all these people are gone."[21]

The Supreme Court, in an opinion by Justice John Paul Stevens, held that the boycott of white merchants, and the fiery rhetoric of Evers, were both protected by the First Amendment, stating that "mere advocacy of the use of force or violence does not remove speech from the protection of the First Amendment." "The emotionally charged rhetoric of Charles Evers' speeches did not transcend the bounds of protected speech," the court held.[22] No violence followed immediately after Evers's speech. "Strong and effective extemporaneous rhetoric cannot be nicely channeled in purely dulcet phrases," the court asserted.[23] "An advocate must be free to stimulate his audience with spontaneous and emotional appeals for unity and action in a common cause. When such appeals do not incite lawless action, they must be regarded as protected speech."[24] Quoting from the decision in the *New York Times* case, the court reasoned that "to rule otherwise would ignore the 'profound national commitment' that debate on public issues should be 'uninhibited, robust, and wide-open.'"[25]

DUKE AND THE DISCIPLES

David Duke would be one of the celebrity headliners of the Charlottesville Unite the Right rally. Yet Duke did not plan or lead the rally, nor did he create or lead the alt-right. Duke did, however, presage and inspire the alt-right, and his influence on the modern history of nationalist and supremacist movements in America ought not to be underestimated. Nor should Duke's influence on the election of Donald Trump as president of the United States. In the perverse worldview of some, Duke was John the Baptist to Donald Jesus Christ Superstar Trump, and the alt-right leaders who came after Duke and passionately endorsed Trump were the twelve apostles.

Russia's Vladimir Putin helped them all.

To understand the influence of David Duke is to understand how a perennial political election loser can turn his losses into ideological and cultural gains. To understand the influence of David Duke is to understand how, for a guerrilla information warfare insurrectionist, all bad news is really good news. And to understand David Duke is to understand how the real Russian collusion in the 2016 election was a far more deft sleight-of-hand than just sending Russian lawyers, oligarchs, and spies thinly disguised as diplomats to meetings with Michael Cohen or Trump advisers in the Trump Tower.

The story starts with what it means to be David Duke.

Duke was from Louisiana. He attended Louisiana State University, where he formed a white student group, the White Youth Alliance, affiliated with the National Socialist White People's Party. In 1970, the famed civil rights lawyer William Kunstler was speaking at Tulsa University and Duke showed up to protest Kunstler's talk wearing a faux Nazi uniform, complete with swastika armband.[1] Duke brandished a sign that said, "Gas the Chicago 7"—a reference to the antiwar protesters at the Democratic National Convention of 1968 that Kunstler had defended.

Forty-five years before Charlottesville's Unite the Right rally, Duke was involved in an altercation at another Robert E. Lee monument. In New Orleans in 1972, Duke organized with other segregationists a demonstration to place a Confederate flag at the city's Lee monument; they were confronted by Black Panthers who counterprotested and threw rocks at the segregationists. In 1974, shortly after graduating from LSU, Duke founded the Knights of the Ku Klux Klan, a Louisiana-based Klan organization, and became its leader, bearing the title "grand wizard." Presaging the hip fashion styles of Richard Spencer, Duke and his Klan attempted a style makeover in the 1970s. The title "grand wizard" was changed to "national director." The traditional Klan robes and masks were jettisoned for business suits. Duke accepted women members, encouraged Catholics to join the Klan, and argued for nonviolence. He shifted the emphasis from "anti-black" to "pro-white" and "pro-Christian." Duke left the Klan in 1980. Some Klan members at the time asserted that Duke had used funds to purchase and refurbish his private home in Metairie, Louisiana. Duke defended the expenditures by arguing that he used his home as the Klan headquarters and for Klan events and meetings. Duke finally parted ways with the Klan, he said, because of its associations with violence and his inability to prevent other Klan organizations around the country from engaging in what he called "stupid things."[2]

Duke often ran for political office, though he was successful only once. He raised losing to an art form. By constantly running for political office, for state representative and senator, for the United States Senate, for governor of Louisiana, for president of the United States, Duke consistently drew the attention of mainstream culture, gained "unearned media"—attention from news stories that he did not have to pay for—and ensconced himself as the single most significant persona of the extreme right until the arrival of Richard Spencer.

In repeatedly running for office, win or lose, Duke was a vivid example of the adage "All publicity is good publicity, as long as they spell your name right." Alan Sorenson, an economics professor at Stanford, was able to prove the adage more or less true. His research demonstrated that for books reviewed in the *New York Times*, sales jumped by at least one-third even if the review was bad.[3] Sorenson observed that there is a limit to this principle. Even bad publicity is good publicity for lesser-known people, such as a little-known author or a small business, but not necessarily good for a major brand. It didn't do Toyota stock or sales any good when it was hit with serial recalls.[4] David Duke was a person with social and political views on the fringe, so for him the whole idea of "bad publicity" is almost incoherent. If the *New York Times* features his nationalist views in an article, it is automatically good publicity for him, at least with his base, even if most of the readers of the article come away scornful.

An example of the dichotomy Sorenson observed was the revelation in January 2014 that US Representative Steve Scalise, a Louisiana Republican who had risen to the leadership position of House majority whip, had once given a speech at an organization Duke had created and led. The story was broken by a Louisiana blogger, Lamar White Jr., who manages a website on Louisiana politics.[5] Duke had created an organization called the European-American Unity and Rights Organization (EURO) in 2002. Scalise spoke at a EURO convention. When the news broke, Scalise claimed that he had no idea that EURO had racist or nationalist roots. This claim rang hollow, at least to Democratic rivals. "It's hard to believe, given David Duke's reputation in Louisiana, that somebody in politics in Louisiana wasn't aware of Duke's associations with the group and what they stand for," said Congressman Joaquin Castro of Texas.[6] Many others in Louisiana and Washington expressed skepticism of Scalise's story. Civil rights groups like the Southern Poverty Law Center called for his ouster or resignation as majority whip. Scalise apologized, admitting his error and expressing his regret.[7] Speaker of the House John Boehner acknowledged that Scalise had erred in judgment, but backed his staying on as majority whip. Scalise did manage to survive the scandal, but the bad news took its toll politically.[8]

On June 14, 2017, Scalise was shot and critically wounded during a mass shooting at a congressional baseball team morning practice in Alexandria, Virginia. Scalise recovered after several difficult surgeries and returned to Congress on September 28, 2018. In a poignant and emotive moment, Republicans and Democrats greeted Scalise with a standing ovation that lasted several minutes, before Speaker Paul Ryan gaveled the House to order, stating in a breaking voice, "Our prayers have been answered."[9]

The EURO scandal almost did in Scalise, though he did scrape through, and it is now behind him. If the EURO scandal hurt Scalise, however, it only helped Duke, who basked in the limelight of a sudden swarm of national attention, interviewed and quoted in most major news outlets, and appearing on television on CNN and Bill O'Reilly's *The O'Reilly Factor* on Fox. Once again, for Duke, bad news was good news.

Duke's political career thus cannot be judged simply by his won-loss record. At least with his base, he often won for losing, bringing a patina of legitimacy to his agenda, moving it from being a marginalized cultural joke in *The Blue Brothers* to a perceived legitimate threat to be taken seriously. Even rejection by his own Republican Party leadership did not really damage his agenda. "The Republican Party opposes, in the strongest possible terms, David Duke's candidacy for any public office," the chairman of the Louisiana Republican Party, Roger F. Villere Jr., stated when Duke announced a run for the United States Senate in 2016, adding, "David Duke is a convicted felon and a hate-filled fraud who does not embody the values of the Republican Party."[10] For Duke, such criticisms really didn't matter. His constituents had no brook for the likes of an establishment Republican leader's opinions anyway, and they were happy to see Duke drawing attention, letting Duke be Duke.

Duke ran for the Louisiana Senate from Baton Rouge in 1975, receiving about one-third of the votes. In 1979 he again ran for the state senate in Louisiana's Tenth District and finished second in a three-way race, with 26 percent of the votes. In 1979 Duke made his first run for president of the United States, which was aborted. When he left the Klan he formed a new group, the National Association for the Advancement of White People (NAAWP), an obvious play on the famous mainstay black civil rights group, the NAACP. Duke ran again for president in 1988, in the Democratic presidential primaries. He then switched to a new party, the Populist Party, and managed to get listed on the ballot for president in eleven states.

Back in Louisiana, Duke changed his political affiliation from the Democratic to the Republican Party and finally won an election, as he was voted to the Louisiana House of Representatives in 1989, where he served until 1982. Duke ran for the United States Senate from Louisiana in 1990 but was not successful.

Duke's run for governor of Louisiana in 1991 would become his most famous election. In the wake of convoluted primaries and a runoff, the general election ultimately pitted Duke as the Republican candidate against former governor Edwin Edwards, a Democrat. Edwards was a legendary, colorful, charismatic New Deal southern Democrat. Unfortunately, part of Edwards's legend was his reputation for corruption—and indeed he would ultimately be arrested and convicted on federal racketeering charges in 2001 and sentenced to ten years in prison. But in 1991 Edwards had not yet been shackled with any criminal convictions, though an atmosphere of corruption hung around him. Louisiana voters thus had a choice between Duke, with his history of racial supremacist views, and Edwards, with his reputation for corruption. In the late 1980s, a Louisiana journalist had quipped that the only way Edwards could make a political comeback was to run against Adolf Hitler. The joke proved prescient. The race between Duke and Edwards drew such bumper stickers as "Vote for the Crook: It's Important" and "Vote for the Lizard, Not the Wizard."[11] Edwards defeated Duke, by a vote of 61.2 percent to 38.8 percent. Duke declared victory for his own constituency, however, proudly touting the fact that he garnered 55 percent of the white vote in the election.

In 1992 Duke ran for the Republican nomination for president but garnered no delegates to the Republican National Convention. Duke ran unsuccessfully for the US Senate again in 1996, and for the US House of Representatives in 1999. He attempted a comeback in 2016, again running for the US Senate, and again failing to garner any substantial support, getting only 3 percent of the votes in Louisiana's November 2016 open primary.

An important component of David Duke's success in pushing his personal brand was that he did not look or usually talk like an archetypal

Klansman. He dressed sharply and, on several occasions, had plastic surgery. His biographer Tyler Bridges first reported on Duke's cosmetic surgery in 1990, which also led to a memorable campaign sign: "Nose Job Nazi."[12]

In many of his political campaigns, Duke soft-pedaled his racism, even trying to distance himself from his role as grand wizard of the Ku Klux Klan—a moniker that follows his name in almost all media reports that mention him. Yet Duke's spoken and published words on race stand as the best testament to his true beliefs. In an autobiographical book he published in 1998, *My Awakening: A Path to Racial Understanding*, Duke's virulent antisemitic and racist positions were on open display. His 2010 essay, "Will the White Race Survive?" succinctly captures his philosophy:

> Are facts racist too? Are white parents racist because they don't want their children to go to school where their children are ten times more likely to be robbed or abused, intimidated, beaten, or even killed or raped? A school where obscenity, drugs and violence and gangster rap are the dominant culture? Where sexual intimidation, obscene or crude language, or even sexual assault is pervasive? Schools that academically resemble more the third world than America? I know some of you don't worry about the white children in those environments. It's considered noble to concern yourself with the well being of minorities even at the farthest ends of the earth. But if you're white, and you concern yourself with the well being of your own people, even of your own children, you're deemed racist. The real racism today is not by white people, it's against white people.[13]

Duke's position here would be succulently repackaged by the alt-right through mantras such as "anti-racist is anti-white," a popular slogan shouted at many alt-right rallies when confronted with antiracist counterprotesters. As Mike Wendling notes in his excellent study of the alt-right,[14] this notion was taken from old-school white genocide racists such as Robert Whitaker, whose most famous line, blasted in all capital letters, was the lament that pro-diversity activists really mean "ASIA FOR THE ASIANS, AFRICA FOR THE AFRICANS, WHITE COUNTRIES FOR EVERYBODY!"[15]

"I don't think it's divisive for the vast majority of the American people to want to preserve our western, Christian heritage in this country," Duke claims.[16] Duke believes that the creators of the United States Constitution sought to limit citizenship to "European" and "Christian" people.[17] Duke once described the powerful financial firm Goldman Sachs as being the largest "gangster Zionist" bank in the world.[18]

While all publicity may be good publicity for the likes of David Duke, all criminal prosecutions are not. Duke has had repeated run-ins with the law, foreign and domestic.

Duke had been abroad for several years, in part to make international connections for his supremacist efforts, and in part to avoid facing arrest and prosecution in the United States. He first rented his apartment in Moscow in 1998 to write his antisemitic manifesto. In January 2000, as Duke was starting a speaking tour in Russia, federal agents, armed with a warrant, were searching his home in Mandeville, Louisiana.[19] Duke was accused of raising money for his political causes and diverting it to his own personal use, including luxury purchases, improvements to his home, and gambling trips. The claims, which were pretty much traditional charges of corruption leveled against a nontraditional movement leader, had surrounded Duke for decades, dating back to his early years as grand wizard of the Klan, and finally were coming home to roost. Duke negotiated a return to the United States with federal prosecutors, agreeing to voluntarily surrender and plead guilty to federal charges of filing a false 1998 tax return and mail fraud, for which he served a fifteen-month sentence and was fined $10,000. The prosecuting US attorney in Louisiana, Jim Letten, explained that Duke told his supporters his organization was in difficult financial straits, then used the money he raised for personal investments and gambling trips to the Mississippi Gulf Coast, Las Vegas, and the Bahamas.[20] Prosecutors did not require Duke to attempt to return the money, because the effort would have been "unwieldy," with so many contributors, often sending in amounts as small as five dollars. Though the amount Duke swindled was never disclosed, Jim Letten said it was in the "the six-figure area."[21]

Duke's international brushes with the law reveal the differences between the American conceptions of freedom of speech and assembly as reflected in the modern marketplace theory, and the theory that remains dominant in most other parts of the world, including Western Europe, which is much more akin to *Chaplinsky*'s order and morality theory.

Under the modern-epoch First Amendment marketplace theory, the government is not allowed to prohibit the mere existence of the Ku Klux Klan, or make Klan membership itself a crime. Nor does the modern First

Amendment permit making the wearing of a Nazi uniform or the brandishing of a swastika a crime. Nazi parties are free to form, and individuals are free to espouse Nazi ideology, as "abstract advocacy." David Duke's life provides a vivid exemplar of how this modern American view contrasts with the laws in many other civilized Western democracies, particularly in Europe.

Duke arrived in the Czech Republic at the invitation of Czech neo-Nazis in April 2009. The plan was for Duke to deliver three lectures in Prague and Brno to promote his book *My Awakening*. Czech authorities, however, had other plans. Czech law prohibits even the abstract advocacy of Nazi ideology and makes Holocaust denial a crime. Duke was arrested for "denying or approving of the Nazi genocide and other Nazi crimes." He faced up to three years in a Czech prison. As in an old American Western film in which the sheriff gives the bad guy a reprieve and a day to get out of town by sundown and never come back, the Czech police released Duke the day after his arrest, on the condition that he leave the country by midnight.[22]

In November 2011, Duke was arrested in Cologne, Germany, while on his way to give a speech to a right-wing extremist group.[23] As with his arrest in the Czech Republic, the charges against Duke were essentially based on his being David Duke. Germany, like many European countries, was experiencing a growth in nationalist groups opposed to minorities and immigration and had begun to crack down on neo-Nazi groups suspected of violence. Following his detention, Duke was once more released, on the condition that he "leave German territory without delay."[24]

Duke next tried Italy. In 2011 he moved to the Valle di Cadore mountain village after being granted a visa to study and write there by the Italian embassy in Malta.[25] Authorities in Italy subsequently discovered that in 2009, Switzerland had issued a travel and residence ban against Duke. Italy and Switzerland were both parties to the Schengen Agreement, a treaty among twenty-six European countries that facilitates free movement across their borders. Italy deemed the Swiss ban to be effective throughout the Schengen area (which encompasses most of Europe) and ordered Duke to leave Italy, where he had managed to live for a year and a half. Duke appealed to an Italian administrative court in Belluno, in the north of Italy. Once again, Duke was found guilty for being Duke. According to Belluno deputy police chief Luciano Meneghetti, the court affirmed Duke's expulsion, finding him "socially dangerous for his racist and anti-Semitic views."[26]

The Italian court's ejection of Duke was as fine a taste of vintage *Chaplinsky* "order and morality" theory as any fine taste of a vintage Barolo Monfortino Riserva Italian red wine. Duke was not expelled on grounds of actually being physically dangerous. He was living in a quiet village writing his book! He was expelled for being *socially* dangerous and for his mere *holding* of racist and antisemitic views.

None of this means that Duke is unwelcome whenever or wherever he ventures to foreign shores. There are countries that endorse and welcome his message. Like other alt-right leaders, he is always welcome back in mother Russia. And Duke was warmly greeted in Tehran, Iran, where he spoke at a 2006 Holocaust denial conference and voiced support for speeches denouncing the Holocaust and Nazi gas chambers as a myth.[27] Duke, however, is persona non grata in Europe, the very part of the globe whose "original" race he touts as supreme.

David Duke backed Donald Trump in the 2016 election, though with some ambivalence, given Trump's strong support for Israel. Duke plainly saw himself as Trump's precursor: "Until my candidacy in the 1990s," Duke bragged, none of this would have been possible.[28] "I mean I got over 60 percent of the European American vote for the U.S. Senate in my state, and later for governor of my state. The *New York Times* described it a few months ago, as, quote, 'David Duke's policies have become mainstream GOP policies today.'"[29] For the record, the exact quote from the *New York Times* to which Duke was referring was as follows: "Two decades later, much of his campaign has merged with the political mainstream here, and rather than a bad memory from the past, Mr. Duke remains a window into some of the murkier currents in the state's politics where Republicans have sought and eventually won Mr. Duke's voters, while turning their back on him."[30]

Here again the larger point may be proven. David Duke may have lost a boatload of elections, found himself constantly trashed by respectable political leaders of both major parties and the vast bulk of mainstream media, been given the bum's rush by Switzerland, the Czech Republic, German, Italy, and twenty-two other countries, yet his *mythology* grows and his *politics* gain traction. Duke might well say, yeah, you rejected me, but you elected Trump. Duke supported Trump, though he thought

Trump had maybe even out-Duked Duke. "As far as what I see, according to the candidates who are out there now, Republicans and Democrats, I think he's head and shoulders, right now, above the rest," Duke said. "I don't agree with everything he says. He speaks a little more . . . well, a lot more, radically . . . than I talk."[31]

If David Duke was Trump's John the Baptist, alt-right notables like Richard Spencer, Sam Dickson, Cameron Padgett, Nathan Damigo, Matthew Heimbach, Mike Enoch, Michael Hill, Don Black, Jason Kessler, Christopher Cantwell, Baked Alaska, and Johnny Monoxide were the twelve apostles.

The alt-right leaders all passionately rallied to Donald Trump. Their first choice may have been Vladimir Putin, but there was that sticky American constitutional "natural born citizen" thing that Trump had tried against Barack Obama, so that dog wouldn't hunt.

A diabolical alchemy formed among the alt-right's overt nationalist and racist impulses, the slightly more covert slogans of the impulsive candidate (and soon to be president) Donald Trump, and the coldly calculating influence of Vladimir Putin and Russia on both. That alchemy, a noxious mixture of xenophobia, racism, sexism, homophobia, antisemitism, mean ego, and testosterone, would explode in Charlottesville.

The August 12 Unite the Right rally officially entered the Charlottesville scene on May 30, when Jason Kessler filed a permit application for an event he described as a "free speech rally in support of the Lee Monument." When Kessler handed the paperwork to the city's receptionist, he signaled the controversy his request would trigger, saying to her that he expected the city council would "try to shut this down."[32] Kessler and the Charlottesville Police Department maintained wary but consistent communication. Captain Wendy Lewis represented the police. Kessler delegated Jack Pierce, a representative of Richard Spencer, as a principal security officer for the Unite the Right side.

Growing up in Chicago and attending games at old Wrigley Field and Comiskey Park, I remember hawkers shouting as we entered that you can't tell the players without a scorecard. I needed a scorecard to keep track of the players on the right whom Richard Spencer and Jason Kessler were trying to unite.

Samuel Glasgow Dickson was born in Atlanta in 1947, the son of a Presbyterian minister. The politics of race began early for Dickson. As a fourteen-year-old, he argued against the integration of his Presbyterian church. He attended the University of Georgia in Athens in the 1960s. As hippies, antiwar protesters, and civil rights activists were taking root on many college campuses, Dickson danced to an alternative beat. He was president of the university's Young Republicans and a leader in a campus group called Young Americans for Freedom, a national organization formed by William F. Buckley Jr. Dickson was a Goldwater Republican with extreme racist views mixed in. He believed that the white race needed to unite to save itself.[33] He went on to the University of Georgia Law School and then became a successful lawyer in Atlanta, finding a unique way to make a small fortune in the arcane world of tax liens and deed auctions.[34] He ran for lieutenant governor of Georgia and managed to garner 11 percent of the vote on a segregationist platform. Dickson made a name for himself representing members of the Ku Klux Klan. The notion of uniting various factions of the far right had been a pet cause of Dickson's for decades. He joined with Louisiana's David Duke in May 2004 to bring together a broad spectrum of white supremacists to endorse a document titled "New Orleans Protocol," a kind of right-wing Nicene Creed promising unity and an end to factionalist bickering.[35]

Cameron Padgett was a front man and booking agent for Richard Spencer on college campuses. Padgett claims not to identify as alt-right but as "Identitarian." The Identitarian movement began in France, through a group called Génération Identitaire, and spread throughout Europe and North America. It is a white nationalist movement that seeks to present itself as fashionable and hip, giving racism a modern makeover. In the United States, "Identity Evropa" would emerge as a group formed on Identitarian principles. As a graduate student at Georgia State University in Atlanta, Padgett also had connections to Sam Dickson. Padgett tried to book Spencer to speak at Auburn University, a public university, in September 2017. When Auburn denied the application, Padgett hired Dickson to sue the university.

Nathan Damigo grew up in Silicon Valley in California and attended a Christian private school before joining the Marines. He served in Iraq. According to his grandmother, he came back to the United States suffering from post-traumatic stress syndrome. Damigo allegedly attacked a cab driver that he thought was of Iraqi descent and was sentenced to prison for five years. In prison he began to read white supremacist material and was particularly influenced by David Duke's book *My Awakening*. He became interested in the Identitarian movement and the National Youth Front, a youth offshoot of the American Freedom Party. Damigo founded the group "Identity Evropa," which describes itself as an American Identitarian organization. The organization's "main objective is to create a better world for people of European heritage—particularly in America—by peacefully effecting cultural change."[36] Identity Evropa thus claims to be an "explicitly non-violent organization." In explaining Identitarian philosophy, Identity Evropa states, "we believe that identity matters, inequality is a fact of life, and ethnic diversity, as demonstrated by substantial historical and sociological evidence, is an impediment to societal harmony." The group claims that "unfortunately, the fetishization of diversity has resulted in a paradigm wherein 'less White people;—in academia, employment, and countries overall—is accepted as a moral imperative." Identity Evropa exists to counter this view "and instead demand that we, people of European heritage, retain demographic supermajorities in our homelands."[37] Following the Charlottesville violence, Damigo was disavowed by his father.[38]

Matthew Heimbach, a Maryland native, was twenty-six at the time of the Charlottesville events. He led a group called the Traditionalist Worker Party. Heimbach was a neo-Nazi. His protest regalia included a black combat helmet and black uniform with the insignia of his party on his arm. Heimbach first rose to national prominence in alt-right circles when he assaulted an African American protester, Kashiya Nwanguma, at a Louisville, Kentucky, rally for Donald Trump.[39] Heimbach's involvement in this event presaged the conflicts that would boil over in Charlottesville and the complex interactions among right-wing extremists, the political positions articulated by Donald Trump as a candidate and later as president, and counterprotesters passionately opposed to Trump and to the radical right who believe that, in his heart, Trump is simpatico with much of far-right ideology.

To depart momentarily from our scorecard, for some background: Kashiya Nwanguma, and her companions Molly Shah and Henry Brousseau attended the March 1, 2016, Louisville rally for the purpose of "peacefully protesting Trump." Nwanguma was carrying a sign with Trump's head on a pig's body.[40] A local broadcast station's video footage shows Nwanguma surrounded by a mass of pro-Trump attendees, being roughly poked and shoved as she is forced out of the rally.[41] Trump, speaking from the stage, can be heard on a video of the incident that was broadcast by CNN, appearing to endorse and encourage the actions of those shutting down the protesters.[42]

Nwanguma, Shah, and Brousseau filed a lawsuit against Trump, the Donald Trump for President Campaign, Heimbach, and another participant in the melee, seventy-five-year-old Alvin Bamberger, who is shown in the video wearing a Korean War Veterans hat and repeatedly shoving Nwanguma toward the exit. The lawsuit was filed in the US District Court for the Western District of Kentucky and assigned to the federal district judge David J. Hale.[43] In a preliminary ruling in the case, Judge Hale rejected an effort by Trump and the Trump campaign to have the case dismissed. Hale applied the modern-epoch marketplace cases, particularly the *Claiborne Hardware*[44] decision involving the violent rhetoric of civil rights leader Charles Evers—which, in an ironic turn of the legal karma wheel, Trump's lawyers had invoked in Trump's defense. But Judge Hale held that it was quite plausible that Nwanguma could prove that Trump—unlike Charles Evers in *Claiborne Hardware*—intentionally incited Heimbach and Bamberger to attack Nwanguma and the other protesters. Hale thus ruled that Trump had crossed the constitutional divide, though Evers had not. The key to Hale's ruling was that as the protest and ensuing violent disorder was occurring, Trump had said over the microphone, "Get 'em out of here!" and then added, "Don't hurt 'em. If I say 'go get 'em,' I get in trouble with the press." Judge Hale apparently thought this could have been code for *"get them out of here and go ahead and rough them up, but you didn't hear that from me."*

Judge Hale also pointed to a letter written by Bamberger to the Korean War Veterans Association, whose uniform he wore at the rally. Bamberger described the incident in a manner that appeared to demonstrate Trump's inciting power. "Trump kept saying 'get them out, get them out' and people in the crowd began pushing and shoving the protestors. . . . I physically pushed a young woman down the aisle toward the exit," Bamberger wrote. The judge also cited a blog later posted by Heimbach bragging of having helped push the anti-Trump protester out. Hale concluded that the suit could proceed because Nwanguma had "pointed to evidence that violence did in fact occur and that it was Trump's statement that prompted audience members—in particular, Bamberger and Heimbach—to engage in that violence."[45]

But back to the scorecard: Heimbach's attraction to Donald Trump was well within the mainstream of the extremist right—excuse the seeming oxymoron of "mainstream" and "extremist" in the same sentence.[46] Heimbach's rhetoric in his role as leader of the Traditionalist Worker Party, however, often darkly ranged far beyond anything Donald Trump would ever express.[47] Heimbach and his party often blame the woes of American workers on "the Jewish power structure."[48] They openly idolize Adolf Hitler, deny the Holocaust, and worship the former imperial wizard of the Ku Klux Klan David Duke. Heimbach's literary efforts include an essay titled "I Hate Freedom." Heimbach wrote, "homosexuality, sexual perversion, race mixing, abortion, and all other sorts of 'tolerance' all land at the feet of freedom. that doesn't sound like a very good thing for the survival of our folk, but maybe that's just me." Heimbach complained that "Americans are far too squeamish to admit that sometimes there are some things that just need a good ol' fashioned government boot heel to stomp out. While we tolerate homeschoolers and organic farmers being arrested and harassed by the federal authorities, people run in fear at the idea of breaking up a homosexual marriage ceremony, torching an abortion clinic, or doing any action that benefits the overall health and culture of their people." Heimbach was willing to describe his enemies as rabid animals deserving to be exterminated, stating "rabid dogs are put down, not allowed around the family kids. Our enemies are sick animals and we need to treat them as such."[49]

The extremist right has its internecine jealousies and rivalries. To quote from *A Lion in Winter*, what family doesn't have its ups and downs? And there was on-again, off-again tension between Heimbach and Richard Spencer. For years Heimbach and Spencer had been at odds, reportedly because Spencer thought that Heimbach was stupid, the kind of guy who gives racism a bad name. Yet in the lead-up to Charlottesville they were back working together.

In early April, Heimbach and other members of the Traditionalist Worker Party formed a security detail to provide security for Spencer as Spencer gave the talk that Cameron Padgett had booked for him at Auburn University. While it may take a scorecard to keep track of the right-wing players, it does not take a rocket scientist to connect the dots and see that they are all playing on the same team. As Spencer's talk ended, a group of Auburn students began to chase the neo-Nazis. Heimbach and his cronies pivoted and rushed headlong into the Auburn students, shouting "Sieg Heil!" Police broke up the scuffle and escorted Spencer and his minions away under escort.

Mike Enoch (or just "Enoch"), whose original name is Mike Peinovich, runs a blog and podcast platform called *The Right Stuff*, which includes "the Daily Shoah." Enoch is on the board of directors of the Foundation for the Marketplace of Ideas, an entity that funds right-wing causes and litigation. Enoch was embarrassed within the alt-right community when he was outed in 2017 for living in New York's Upper East Side with his Jewish wife, from whom he was later divorced. Enoch's podcast platform is brazenly open with racial slurs and violent antisemitic references, such as "Put 'em in the oven." Following his divorce, Enoch became more explicitly extreme, and Richard Spencer actively recruited him as a personality and speaker at events of the alt-right.

Eli Mosley is from Reading, Pennsylvania.[50] Mosley's original name was Elliott Kline. Mosley rose in the hierarchy of the alt-right during the events surrounding the inauguration of President Trump. Mosley took his name in homage to Sir Oswald Emald Mosley, a British member of Parliament who was once considered a possible candidate for Labour prime minister but who eventually split from the Labour Party to form other political parties in Britain, most notably the British Union of Fascists. In Charlottesville Mosley would emerge as a principal captain for logistics, in charge of making things happen. As Mosley explained to Emma Gott, a reporter for the *New York Times*, "I came to the realization around the inauguration that we must take this from an online activist movement to a real-life activist movement." Mosley added, "I decided that was my calling."[51]

A taste of Mosley's disposition is on display in a statement he made on an alt-right podcast, explaining that he was the person from HR who fires "niggers and spicks all day. Before that I was in the army and I got to kill Muslims for fun. I'm not sure which one was better, watching niggers and spicks cry they can't feed their little mud children or watching Muslims' brains sprayed on the wall. Honestly both probably suck compared to listening to a kike scream."[52] Mosley took a leadership position in Identity Evropa in 2017. He was introduced then to Richard Spencer, who was attracted to Mosley's "high level of energy and agency."[53] Even more revealing, however, is a long passage from an article on the Daily Stormer in which Mosley spoke at length of events and tactics at a pro-Trump rally in Philadelphia and confrontations with anti-Trump protesters. The Daily Stormer passage is especially illuminating for what it reveals about what Mosley and his fellow planners had in mind for Charlottesville:

> On both sides of the sidewalk shrieked accusations of racism and inbreeding from hooked-nose Philadelphians to a crowd of working class white Trump supporters displaying a bit of nationalism. Before being called out for her kikery, one filthy Jewess exclaimed, "Of course I am anti-white! So what?!" Quickly a chant arose from the entire crowd of "Open borders for Israel, Open Borders of Israel!" She quickly retreated away from the front of the pack after being named, but she would continuously return to be called a kike and repeat the process.
>
> Soon we came to within a few blocks of our intended destination of City Hall, but were stopped by the police as we were told that only a few hundred yards away antifa was attempting to break through the police line. A rather large crowd of spics, negros and hajis donning Black Lives Matter shirts had surrounded the crowd, chanting "down with white supremacy." In a sign of our new era, the Trump supporters roared back "You're anti-white, you're anti-white."
>
> The invader races stood there in awe at the sight of whites pushing back. . . .
>
> So what does this event mean in our struggle for total Aryan Victory? This is a sign that we have moved into a new era in the Nazification of America. Normie Trump supporters are becoming racially aware and Jew wise. They are willing to stick up for themselves side by side with Nazis without being adverse to violence. The police departments are begging for the return of law and order and love jokes about hooked-nose merchants, but need our help in getting strongmen elected so they can do their jobs. Antifa and the kike media are so dumb they can be tricked by a monkey in a police uniform. All of this while the media continues to cover antifa in a positive light while demonizing all Trump supporters and law enforcement, further pushing them into our arms.
>
> Moving forward we must continue to have a presence at these rallies or organize them ourselves to attract normies to redpill them in person. We need to continue to show the cops that the Nazis are the good guys, and help them elect local officials who will let them once again curbstomp undesirables.[54]

Mosley was proud of his military service, including his oft-repeated references to what he experienced in combat in Iraq. His military background gave him a special disposition for attention to detail and logistics. He would become the logistical master for the alt-right in Charlottesville. If his penchant for discipline and detail served the alt-right well in Charlottesville, however, his tendency to mythologize his military experience in Iraq—where apparently he had never set foot—would prove, later in the game, to hurt both him and his cause.

Perhaps the most improbable member of the team was Dr. J. Michael Hill, the only of the apostles with a PhD. Hill was educated at the University of Alabama and then went to work at historically black Stillman College in Tuscaloosa, Alabama, for eighteen years. While at Stillman he wrote two books romanticizing Celtic soldiers. Hill cofounded a group in 1984 called the League of the South. The league was a white nationalist, racial supremacist group that argued for secession of the former states of the Confederacy into a new South that would become a separate country.

How a person with Hill's views could teach for almost two decades at Stillman College is an unsolved mystery. Hill claimed that his black students loved him. It is hard to fathom that the love flowed both ways. Hill once wrote, "Yes, the South has a 'black' problem. It also has a 'yankee' problem. But our biggest problem—and one even Christian members within our own ranks refuse (or fear) to acknowledge—is the 'Jewry' problem. Indeed, organized Jewry has been at the root of most of the South's troubles for the past 100 years."[55]

Augustus Sol Invictus, born Austin Gillespie, was the leader of the "Fraternal Order of Alt-Knights, American Guard." A libertarian lawyer from Florida, Invictus ran on the Libertarian Party ticket for the US Senate in 2016, seeking to upset Florida senator Marco Rubio. Invictus is a member of the "Thelemite" occult sect, which engages in the sacrifice of goats and the drinking of goat blood. He considers himself more aligned with fascist groups than racist groups—he denies being a racist—and has been willing to lend his legal talents to defend members of extremist groups. He once defended a member of a skinhead group charged with illegal paramilitary training.[56]

Baked Alaska, otherwise known as Tim "Treadstone" Gionet, was born in Anchorage, Alaska. He was once a Buzzfeed social media strategist.[57] Baked Alaska was the tour manager for the British writer and commentator Milo Yiannopoulos. Yiannopoulos was also a former senior editor of Breitbart News, who was notable for the many college speaking engagements in which his invitation to speak sparked controversy and efforts to cancel his appearances. The most famous incident occurred at the University of California at Berkeley, which canceled an event at which Yiannopoulos was scheduled to speak, because of threats of violence and disorder posed by protest groups opposed to Yiannopoulos. Baked Alaska is openly antisemitic. He is a dedicated supporter of Donald Trump. While working at Buzzfeed, he posted a picture of himself on Twitter featuring a Donald Trump tattoo on his arm and Trump's signature tagline, "Make America Great Again." Baked Alaska drew intense criticism from followers of Buzzfeed, a liberal news organization. One early commentator posted on Twitter that Baked Alaska should have his arm cut off.

Christopher Cantwell had already played a major role in the events in Charlottesville in the summer of 2017. Cantwell grew up in Stony Brook, New York.[58] His father—like my own dad—was an air traffic controller. Unlike my dad, who had retired from a career of service in the navy and the FAA by 1981, Cantwell's father was fired when President Ronald Reagan made the dramatic decision to terminate all the federal air traffic controllers who had defied his presidential order for them to return to work.

Cantwell was the host of a popular alt-right podcast titled "Radical Agenda." In one media interview leading up to the events in Charlottesville, Cantwell stated, "Let's fucking gas the kikes and have a race war."[59] Cantwell stated in another interview, "My goal here is to normalize racism."[60] Cantwell has an emotional streak, and events in Charlottesville would stick him with the tag "the crying Nazi." Cantwell did not like to be underestimated, and he envisioned racism as a commercial growth industry. "I'm going to make a commercial enterprise out of saying things that people want to make illegal," he once stated. "I'm going to make a whole fucking bunch of money doing it. Anybody who gets in my way is going to find themselves in a very long list of people who regretted underestimating me."[61]

Cantwell questions Dylann Roof's life tactics in committing the horrific Charleston murders, but not his motive or morality. "I would go ahead and I would say that I don't know that Dylann Roof made the fuckin' best use of his life by fucking throwing it away on these fucking animals in the goddamn church. But I understand what he's going through, right?"[62]

Johnny Monoxide, formerly John Ramondetta, was born in 1972 and grew up in the greater Hartford, Connecticut, area in a family that was predominately Italian.[63] Monoxide claimed that his antisemitic views began to form in his childhood. He moved to Greenville, South Carolina, to attend Bob Jones Academy, a conservative fundamentalist Christian school, from 1994 to 1999.

Monoxide is an example of a radicalized rightist who started off on the left. In 2011, when he was living in the San Francisco Bay area, he joined the Oakland contingent of the leftist Occupy Wall Street movement. He attended a Black Lives Matter protest 2012 in reaction to the killing of Trayvon Martin. Monoxide joined progressive social justice Facebook groups such as "Cop Block" and "Police the Police."

Then his conversion experience began.

Monoxide was a longtime listener to Red Ice Radio, an online radio channel that began in Sweden and soon developed a substantial European and North American following. Red Ice Radio describes itself as "truly independent" and "supported by its members" and "an alternative to the mainstream, covering politics and social issues from a pro-European perspective." Following the shooting in Ferguson of Michael Brown, and the massive protests that ensued, Red Ice Radio began giving airtime to Holocaust deniers and World War II revisionists. These broadcasts appeared to influence Monoxide, whose views migrated to the conflation of diversity with white genocide. A key moment was a broadcast featuring Mike Enoch. This drew Monoxide to the Daily Shoah. One Daily Shoah episode featured several panelists speculating about the events surrounding Michael Brown's death, strongly cementing Monoxide's evolution to the right.

Monoxide ultimately became a podcast celebrity in his own (alt-)right. He began working on *The Right Stuff*, the blog created by Enoch that hosts the Daily Shoah, even getting his own show, which he called "the Current Year Tonight." Among Monoxide's broadcast gems was a program alleging that the Sandy Hook massacre was a hoax perpetrated by the Obama administration and that the children who supposedly died at Sandy Hook faked their deaths.[64]

The list of alt-right players above is not comprehensive or exhaustive, but evocative. These were among the most well known to descend on Charlottesville, and their biographies and ideologies tell a revealing story.

As the time for the Unite the Right rally approached, Vice News released a widely watched documentary on the Charlottesville rally leaders and participants. One clip from the documentary, quoting one of the alt-right participants, was especially telling, as he declared, "We'll fucking kill these people if we have to."[65]

THE RUSSIAN CONNECTION

Charlottesville's most notorious Russian connection—Anna Anderson as Anastasia—turned out to have been the stuff of fiction. Charlottesville's less known Russian connection—the link between the Donald Trump-supporting alt-right leaders and Russia, however, is the stuff of fact.

An incorrigible myth was that Charlottesville was the home of the sole survivor of the massacre of the Romanov monarchs during the Russian Revolution, Grand Duchess Anastasia of Russia. Anastasia was the youngest daughter Tsar Nicholas II and Tsarina Alexandra of Russia. The entire Russian royal family, including Nicholas II, Alexandra, and their children, were killed in Yekaterinburg, Russia, on July 17, 1918, by communist revolutionaries. (Yekaterinburg was renamed Sverdlovsk during the Soviet years, after communist leader Yakov Swerdlov.) Curiously, however, the body of young Anastasia was not found in Yekaterinburg with the other Romanov family members, leading to theories that she had somehow survived the massacre.

In 1920, a young woman attempted to commit suicide in Berlin and was admitted to a German mental hospital as Fräulein Unbekannt, German for "Miss Unknown." The woman spoke German with a Russian accent, and later adopted the name "Tschaikovsky." In a series of highly publicized legal actions in Europe that spanned decades, Tschaikovsky claimed, with some plausible credibility and verisimilitude, to be Anastasia, and her claim gained significant currency in Europe and the United States. The claim was contested by other surviving heirs of the Romanov family. Over the decades Tschaikovsky had many supporters and benefactors, including the brilliant pianist and composer Sergei Rachmaninoff, who arranged for Tschaikovsky to live at the Garden City Hotel in Hempstead, New York. In the late 1920s she was for a time the toast of New York society. She returned to Germany in 1932. She would eventually take on the name Anna Anderson. In a 1956 film *Anastasia*, the actress Ingrid Bergman won the Oscar for her starring role playing "Anna" and "Anastasia" in a film loosely based on Anna Anderson's claim to be Anastasia.

Anna Anderson moved to Charlottesville in 1968, with the help of history professor John Eacott "Jack" Manahan, himself a famous and beloved Charlottesville eccentric. Jack was twenty years younger than Anna when he married her in Charlottesville in 1968. Anna persisted in her claim to be Anastasia, and for years Jack and Anna were among Charlottesville's most colorful residents. Anna died in February 1984; Jack died six years later.

Just as DNA testing would eventually catch up with Thomas Jefferson, revealing his fathering of offspring through the slave Sally Hemings, DNA testing would eventually catch up with Anna. In 1991, the bodies of Nicholas II, Tsarina Alexandra, and three of their children were exhumed from their mass grave near Yekaterinburg. DNA testing was performed and matched against a DNA sample taken from tissue of Anna Anderson stored at Martha Jefferson Hospital in Charlottesville following surgery she had there in 1979. The tests established that Anna was not Anastasia but was actually Franziska Schanzkowska, born on December 19, 1896, in an area of what was then West Prussia and is now part of Poland. In 2007, the remains of the real Anastasia were discovered in a grave near Yekaterinburg.[1]

Anna Anderson's claim to be the Grand Duchess Anastasia of Russia thus came to be exposed as a prime example of what President Donald Trump would later come zestfully to call "fake news."

Not so fake, however, were the collusive connections between Russia and the American radical alt-right, including many figures prominent in the Unite the Right events in Charlottesville in 2017, figures who also strongly supported the candidacy and presidency of Donald Trump.

Whether or not the presidential campaign of Donald Trump colluded with the Russian government to skew the results of the 2016 presidential election, there can be no doubt that America's alt-right racial supremacists openly colluded with Russia to advance their supremacist agenda. Many on the alt-right idolize Russia's leader Vladimir Putin, seeing him as the sort of strong-willed authoritarian dedicated to "traditional values" that the world needs.[2]

Russia has been the hospitable home and host of American right-wing extremists. David Duke moved to Russia in 1999, renting an apartment in Moscow. He lived there for five years, writing his self-published book *Jewish Supremacism*, which he claimed was a best-seller in the Duma bookstore.[3]

In the interconnected network of the extreme right, Preston Wiginton, a white supremacist scholar from Texas, routinely sublets David Duke's Moscow apartment when he travels to Russia. Wiginton has argued that his "best friends" are in Russia and that Russia is "the only nation that understands RAHOWA," meaning "racial holy war."[4]

Following in Duke's footsteps, Richard Spencer also has strong Russian connections. Spencer describes Russia as the "sole white power in the world."[5] Spencer was married to Russian writer Nina Kouprianova, who often writes under the nom de plume "Nina Byzantina." Under her pen name, Kouprianova described herself as a "Kremlin troll leader." The Daily Beast described her as the "Moscow Mouthpiece" married to Richard Spencer.[6] Kouprianova was an apologist for Russia's invasion of Ukraine, calling it a "liberation war."[7] Defending Syria, Russia's client-state in the Middle East, Kouprianova described as "fake news" widespread credible news reports that thousands of civilians in rebel-held east Aleppo, Syria, were under siege by the Russian-backed Syrian government.[8] (I should disclose that my own wife, Anna Borisovna Smolla, was born in Siberia, migrated to the United States, and is now an American citizen, though she also carries, as she is entitled to carry, a Russian passport.)

Spencer's wife Kouprianova served as the translator for the works of Russian philosopher Aleksandr Dugin, an extreme-right Russian intellectual who advances theories of an expansive Russian ethnic state, a contemporary reincarnation of "Eurasianism," a geopolitical theory envisioning Russia as the inheritor of "Eternal Rome."[9] In much the same fashion that Adolf Hitler would embrace the German conception of *Volksgeist* and German theories of manifest ethnic destiny advanced by German thinkers such as Johann Gottfried von Herder and Carl Schmitt—theories that attracted Richard Spencer when he studied in Germany—the work of Aleksandr Dugin would be embraced by Vladimir Putin and would also attract Richard Spencer.[10] Dugin's work *Foundations of Geopolitics* is assigned reading for every member of Russia's General Staff Academy.[11]

Spencer's online publication Alternative Right published an article by Dugin. And Dugin himself recorded a speech titled "To My American Friends in Our Common Struggle," which was presented at a nationalist conference organized by Matthew Heimbach, held in California. Heimbach has praised Putin's Russia as "the axis for nationalists."[12] Heimbach and Spencer have adopted a strongly pro-Russia platform, asserting that the United States should abandon NATO, reset the Russia relationship, and embrace Syrian president Bashar al-Assad.[13]

In 2016, Russia was the host for a major supremacist convention in St. Petersburg, gathering extremist racist and antisemitic groups and leaders from the United States and Europe.[14] The sponsor was Russia's Rodina political party. Rodina, more formally Rodina Narodno-Patrioticheskiy Soyuz, is the "Motherland" or "Motherland National Patriotic Union" political party of Russia, a far-right political group generally supportive of Putin's government. The conference sponsored by Rodina included such American nationalist notables as Jared Taylor, Sam Dickson, and Matthew Heimbach. At the conference Taylor criticized the United States as "the greatest enemy of tradition everywhere."[15] Dickson echoed Taylor, calling for the preservation of the white race and civilization.[16] Heimbach asserted that the United States had "poisoned" traditional values.[17]

Many in the alt-right are also smitten by Putin's image as a "lion of Christianity." Putin has cultivated a close relationship with the Russian

Orthodox Church, recruiting the church as an ally against Western ideas of multiculturalism and gay rights, aligning faith with firepower.[18]

One of the great legacies of Thomas Jefferson was his commitment to religious liberty, expressed in his image of a wall of separation between church and state. Putin, in contrast, uses the church as an apparatus of the state. In a law Putin signed in July 2016, churches that are not aligned with the government are now banned from religious proselytizing.[19] Alt-right leaders such as Heimbach see Putin's move to establish the Orthodox Church as the official state orthodoxy as the sort of "nation building" that Heimbach adores. "To rebuild a nation, you have to be able to build up the people," Heimbach says. "And that requires having a strong moral foundation. Putin is fighting for faith, family, and folk. The fact that he's rebuilt tens of thousands of churches, allowed religious services to be broadcast on national television—all of that has been crucial to rebuilding Russia."[20]

Leaders and friends of the alt-right have well-documented and extensive ties to Russia. Friends and leaders of Donald Trump's campaign had well-documented and extensive ties to Russia. Yet where does that leave matters, and what do these connections signify? One need not indulge in wild conspiracy theories or fantastical assumptions to find the connections troubling. One need not fanaticize, for example, that during his five years in Moscow, David Duke was recruited as a Russian operative to act as an agent provocateur to disrupt American politics.

Duke needed no help from Russians to disrupt American politics; he had figured that out well enough on his own. Promising fictional plotlines for the gripping Showtime series *Homeland* might position the president of the United States as a stealth "Manchurian Candidate" operating as a puppet of Putin, or depict Russian operatives as directly involved in inciting the violence in Charlottesville that killed Heather Heyer.

But fiction is fiction, and fact is fact. Sticking to what is factually known, it is clear that Russian connections created currents of influence that contributed to the climate that made Charlottesville in the summer of 2017 ripe for confrontation and violence. In a piece published in *Newsweek*, Owen Matthews documented the ideological links between Russia's Aleksandr Dugin, whose thinking has strongly influenced Putin's vision for Russia, and America's Steve Bannon, whose thinking has strongly influenced Trump's vision for America.[21] Bannon has praised Dugin's vision of "Eurasianism," Russia's dream of a grand empire.[22] Dugin and Bannon share disdain for multiculturalism, egalitarianism, and secularism,[23] and they share a passion for nationalism—Russia First for Russia and America First for America. Putin and Trump each strive to make their nations great again.

This need not translate into direct collusion or conspiracy to be significant. Bannon has now left the White House, and reportedly thought the meeting in the Trump Tower between Trump's people and the Russians was unpatriotic and perhaps even treasonous.[24] What investigations such as special counsel Robert Mueller's probe, or various congressional inquiries, will establish or fail to establish, legally or politically, will be much debated and much litigated in courts of law, public opinion, and history.

Yet as the history of intellectual and cultural currents reveals, direct conspiracies and legal convictions are not the full story. Alignment and parallelism among the belief structures of Putin's Russia, Spencer's alt-right, and Donald Trump's presidency are too abundant to be ignored. Their simpatico orientations may not be attributable to direct "commanding" influence, in any palpable or linear sense. But ideas, convictions, and movements form through more subtle connections. The symbolic triangle of the Kremlin, Trump Tower, and downtown Charlottesville is real in its own right.

A Call to Conscience

The July 8 Klan event only served to further exacerbate the division among members of Charlottesville's clergy. The religious leaders who had gone to Justice Park to confront the Klan largely believed that the Charlottesville Police Department had effectively taken sides in favor of the Klan and against the counterprotesters. Like other counterprotesters, those religious leaders believed that the Charlottesville police should never have launched the tear gas against the counterprotesters.

Out of this experience a new clergy group emerged, calling itself "Congregate Charlottesville." It was led by Brittany Caine-Conley, who was designated the group's "lead organizer," and Rev. Seth Wispelwey, directing minister of Restoration Village Arts, designated the "consulting organizer." Congregate Charlottesville described itself as "less of a group and more of an instrument for organizing faith leaders."[1] The group strived "to equip folks to respond rapidly to community needs, bear public witness to (in) justice, and educate faith communities on issues of justice and liberation."[2]

Congregate Charlottesville was determined to take a more aggressive approach to the coming Unite the Right rally on August 12. The group issued a national appeal to clergy to come to Charlottesville to oppose the rally, calling "for 1,000 clergy and faith leaders to show up in Charlottesville . . . to confront a national white supremacist rally."[3] Describing the July 8 Klan rally, Congregate Charlottesville asserted that "nonviolent community members standing against racial hatred were met with chemical weapons, military vehicles, and hundreds of militarized police, some carrying grenade launchers and automatic weapons." The call for help explained that they group "concluded that there is an extremely high potential for physical violence and brutality directed at our community" and pleaded for support, because "we don't have the numbers to stand up to this on our own." The call was for "nonviolent direct action," asking fellow clergy to proclaim "with our bodies and our sanctuaries that God rejects white supremacy."[4] A coalition of other groups joined the call. The letter read,

Dear friends in faith across the United States,

Will you commit to counteract the narrative and agenda of white supremacy? In the aftermath of multiple deaths, we bear witness to the need for every American to understand that the isolation and divisiveness of white supremacy is the way of death for all people, and particularly for the most marginalized among us.

Therefore, we call on you to embody love over fear by proclaiming these truths, which are in stark contrast to the evil ideology of white supremacy:

Black Lives Matter
Queer Lives Matter
Indigenous Lives Matter
Differently Abled Lives Matter
Refugee Lives Matter
Jewish Lives Matter
Hispanic/Latinx Lives Matter
Trans Lives Matter
Muslim Lives Matter
Immigrant Lives Matter

As members of Congregate Charlottesville's clergy we thank you for your many demonstrations of love and solidarity since white supremacists and neo-Nazis attacked our city. As we said to the violent hate-mongers who pushed us to the ground and cursed us outside Emancipation Park, "Love has already won."[5]

As the August rally approached, Congregate Charlottesville held training sessions for counterprotesters in the tactics of nonviolent direct action. Among the trainers they brought in was Rev. Osagyefo Sekou, who had spent months leading protests and training in Ferguson, Missouri. "Martin Luther King ain't coming back. Get over it," Sekou said at a lecture he gave at Warner Pacific College in Portland, Oregon. "It won't look like the civil rights movement. It's angry. It's profane. If you're more concerned about young people using profanity than about the profane conditions they live in, there's something wrong with you."[6]

Congregate Charlottesville also invited Rev. Traci Blackmon, who also became nationally known as a voice for social change when Michael Brown was shot in Ferguson, near her church. Blackmon was one of the original organizers of the Black Lives Matter movement. Also invited to come to Charlottesville to confront the Unite the Right protesters was Cornel West, perhaps the most famous leftist American public intellectual speaking to issues of race of his time. In bringing in figures such as Sekou, Blackmon, and West, Congregate Charlottesville and the other counterprotest leaders were deliberately raising the ante, positioning Charlottesville as a great national showdown where the violent left, and the most aggressive advocates for social and racial justice, would rail against their enemies, which now included President Trump.

The Unite the Right rally and its counterprotest were no longer being viewed as an upcoming local skirmish, but rather as an incipient America race war. The war was intertwined with the substance and symbol of Donald Trump's ascendancy as president. As Cornel West argued after Trump's election, "White working- and middle-class fellow citizens—out of anger and anguish—rejected the economic neglect of neoliberal policies and the self-righteous arrogance of elites. Yet these same citizens also supported a candidate who appeared to blame their social misery on minorities, and who alienated Mexican immigrants, Muslims, black people, Jews, gay people, women and China in the process."[7]

"Solidarity Cville," as a principal counterprotest organizing movement was now calling itself, was "a community defense network of

Charlottesville activists acting in solidarity with communities of color locally and globally to fight all forms of white supremacy."[8] The group proclaimed that "everybody has a role in this struggle to creatively contribute our best gifts, and that White people have a particular responsibility to invest in the labor and risk-taking of dismantling white supremacist systems and cultures." As the Unite the Right rally approached, Solidarity Cville was "particularly focused on opposing the violent white supremacist terrorist groups who have targeted Charlottesville in what we are calling the #SummerofHate."[9]

While Congregate Charlottesville and groups like Black Lives Matter, Queer Lives Matter, and all the various other "Lives Matter" groups were urging greater confrontation and a national call for reinforcements, there were still voices in Charlottesville inclined to ignore the next invasion of supremacists and focus on constructive counterprogramming.

Most notably, UVA's vice-provost for academic outreach, Professor Louis P. Nelson, was urged in mid-July by city leaders to encourage UVA to develop alternative programming for city residents during the Unite the Right rally. Nelson took on the task with gusto and ultimately was able to assemble an astonishing forty-five programs to be put on by various members of the UVA faculty and community for August 12.

Nelson and his colleague Claudrena N. Harold would later edit a magnificent collection of short essays by UVA faculty members, reflecting on the aftermath of the Charlottesville violence in 2017.[10]

22

PREPARATIONS

As the August 12 Unite the Right rally approached, preparations were being made by many of the planned participants. Among the planners was Heather Heyer. "If you're not outraged, you're not paying attention," she wrote, in what proved to be her last Facebook post.[1]

Heyer was the great-granddaughter of coal miners.[2] She grew up in Greene County, Virginia, living in a trailer.[3] Greene County, named for the Revolutionary War hero General Nathanael Greene, is rural and sparsely populated, with only eighteen thousand residents. Greene County is directly north of Albemarle County, which encompasses Charlottesville. Heyer's mother, Susan Bro, worked in the Green County public schools, and after retiring worked for the Virginia Tech Extension Office in Standardsville, the Greene County seat.[4] Heather attended Greene County's William Monroe High School, which was founded by a bequest from an eighteenth-century immigrant from England, William Monroe, to provide free public education for white children.[5] As with all of Virginia's public schools, segregation separating white and black schools persisted for two more centuries, lingering on well after the 1954 decision in *Brown v. Board of Education* overturning the segregationist "separate but equal" doctrine of *Plessy v. Ferguson*. When Heather attended William Monroe High School, its motto was "Every child, every chance, every day."[6]

Heather and her mother moved to Charlottesville after Heather graduated from high school. Heather worked as a waitress, then as a bartender. Her mother said that the family had "always, our entire lives, been on the bottom end of the middle class, with not much hope of rising above that."[7] For Heather's family, middle class was working class.[8] While working as a waitress and tending bar, Heather lived with her mother, and they clashed often.[9]

In 2012 Heyer took a job as a paralegal in the Charlottesville law firm, the Miller Law Group. Her supervisor at the firm, Alfred Wilson, was African American. Sometimes Heyer would bristle when clients of the firm seemed to express surprise that one of its accomplished professionals was black.[10]

Heyer's personality was marked by two strong values—a sweet, kind-hearted disposition, and an intolerance for intolerance. She once broke up with a young man she was dating when he expressed surprise that her boss was African American. On another occasion she was overcome with tears and anger when a local Virginia sheriff's office offered a public seminar on the "Muslim religion" but labeled the title of the seminar "Understanding the Threat."[11]

James Alex Fields Jr., whose fate was to be closely connected to Heyer's, was also making plans. Fields was born in Kenton, Kentucky, to Samantha Lea Bloom. Fields's father died before he was born.[12] James Alex Fields Sr. died in a crash on December 5, 1996, after a vehicle in which he was a passenger struck a utility pole. The driver, who along with another passenger left Fields Sr. in the car to return to a bar they had left, was charged with murder. James Alex Fields's father was thirty-three when he was killed; Fields was born five months later. Fields's mother, Samantha, had also lived a violent and tragic life. When she was sixteen, on August 21, 1973, her father Marvin Bloom, who had recently divorced her mother, Judy Bloom, shot and killed Judy Bloom with a shotgun outside her apartment in Cold Spring, Kentucky, and then turned the shotgun on himself, taking his own life.[13]

Fields's domestic life with his mother, in a Florence, Kentucky, apartment, was marked by dysfunction and violence. Superb reporting by journalists at the *Cincinnati Enquirer* immediately following the murder of Heather Heyer revealed that on many occasions authorities from the Boone County Sheriff's Office and the Florence Police Department responded to distress calls from the residence. Samantha Bloom reported on at least two occasions that her son was attacking or threatening her. Police dispatcher notes revealed that Bloom had called in 2011 to report that her son "is being very threatening toward her. The mother is in a wheelchair and doesn't feel in control of the situation and is scared."[14] In November 2010, Bloom called police saying that Fields, after she told him to stop playing video games, took her phone and "smacked her in the head" and then "put his hands over her mouth." Bloom had to lock herself in the bathroom for safety.[15] In February 2011, Bloom called police at 5:20 a.m. to report that Fields had not come home and she was worried about him because he was wearing only a T-shirt and shorts. Bloom called police back two hours later to report he was home and acting "lethargic."[16] The next month, a woman called authorities to report that Fields had threatened Bloom. She told dispatchers that he had spat in Bloom's face, threatened her, and pushed her.[17]

Fields and his mother finally parted company five or six months prior to the Charlottesville violence. He then moved to his own apartment in Maumee, Ohio. His aunt, Pam Fields, described him as "a very quiet little boy." A former neighbor said he was a quiet teenager who "kept to himself a lot." "He had some trouble in school making friends," said a friend.[18]

In an interview with the Associated Press, Fields's mother said she knew her son was going to a rally, but that she tried to "stay out of his political views." She said that she thought the rally "had something to do with Trump," but added, "Trump's not a supremacist."[19]

Just as there were indications of Fields's propensity for impulsive violence, there were some clues to Fields's radicalization and sympathy for Nazi and supremacist causes. Fields attended Randall K. Cooper High School in Union, Kentucky. As a high school student, he wore a belt with swastikas on it, and he drew the symbol everywhere, several of his former classmates stated.[20] One of Fields's high school history teachers at Cooper High, Derek Weimer, said in an interview in the *Cincinnati Enquirer* that Fields was "a very bright kid but very misguided and disillusioned."[21] According to Weimer, when Fields was a freshman, he wrote a report that was "very much along the party lines of the neo-Nazi movement." Weimer thought that Fields's obsession with the Nazis was not normal. "A lot of boys get interested in the Germans and Nazis because they're interested in World War II," he said. "But James took it to another level."[22] "He was very infatuated with the Nazis, with Adolf Hitler," Weimer told a Cincinnati television station.[23] "He also had a huge [interest in] military history, especially with German military history and World War II. . . . He was pretty infatuated with that stuff."[24] Weimer recalled Fields seeming to fantasize about what a better world it might be if Hitler had won the war. "What if Hitler had won? What if we had this large white supremacist empire going into the modern world?" Weimer recalled Fields asking.[25] According to students at the high school, by his senior year Fields had come to be known as "the Nazi of the school."[26]

The Charlottesville police, the Albemarle County Police Department, the Virginia State Police, the Virginia National Guard, and the University of Virginia Police were all planning and training in advance of August 12. So were members of the alt-right. So were members of the counterprotesting left. Meanwhile, the Charlottesville community, some of whom just felt caught in middle, waited for what was coming.

Many Charlottesville police officers understood their instructions, either explicitly or to be read between the lines, as orders for passivity. The inclination toward passivity may have been animated by concern for the safety of officers, or may have been the product of not wanting to appear to pick sides between the opposing factions, or may have been born of a general concern over appearing antagonistic to citizens, particularly to groups like Black Lives Matter. Whatever the combination of motivations, the watchwords were caution and nonintervention. Photos and videos from the events of August 12 would make plain that officers followed those instructions.

Officer Tammy Shiflett was no front-line armed law enforcement officer. She was a school resource officer, who sometimes earned extra overtime money doing traffic patrol for the Charlottesville Police Department at special events, like concerts or big basketball or football games. For the Unite the Right rally it was all hands on deck, and Shiflett was available to work traffic. She was assigned to the intersection of Market Street and Fourth Street NE. Shiflett had been on the disabled list for much of June and July recovering from elbow surgery but was now back and ready for deployment. Officer Shiflett's assignment seemed mundane and straight-forward, not much different from most exercises in traffic control. Her job was to keep any traffic from moving down Market Street toward Emancipation Park. She was given a squad car, which she sensibly parked in the intersection to accomplish her principal task, blocking the flow of traffic on Market Street. There was also a token effort to block traffic down Fourth Street. A six-foot wooden sawhorse was positioned in the center of the intersection. The ramshackle sawhorse was a symbolic "do not enter" warning, but it posed no actual physical barrier to anybody on foot or in a vehicle intent on crashing through. The feeble impotency of the token barrier proved tragically fatal.

In advance of the rally, law enforcement officers in Charlottesville were provided with refresher training on the various offenses that might be committed by demonstrators or counterprotesters. Charlottesville police captain Victor Mitchell handled the briefing, informed by the Common-wealth's Attorney's Office, Virginia's name for the office of local criminal prosecutors. Among the offenses reviewed were "obstruction of free passage," "rioting," "failure to disperse," "injury to property or person," "crossing established police lines," "disorderly conduct," "curse and abuse," "wearing masks," "cross burning," "display of nooses," "conspiracy to commit crime," and "unlawful assembly."

This list of offenses is telling. Many of the offenses are fraught with subjective ambiguity. In some instances, "obstruction of passage" might be objectively cut-and-dried, and in others, subject to interpretation. Where does protest end and rioting begin? Many of the other offenses appeared to be triggered by the actions of police themselves. When does an assembly become "unlawful"? When the police judge it so? When can police make "failure to disperse" a crime? Whenever they like? Surely the First Amendment rights of free speech and assembly exert some gravitational pull on these offenses, constraining the exercise of police discretion. Some of the other offenses seemed to penalize certain symbols, pure and simple. Under what circumstances Virginia could or could not penalize cross burning, or the display of nooses, or swastikas, were questions of legal subtlety and depth. How could Virginia law enforcement officers, or the lawyers and trainers charged with briefing them, possibly make simple sense of the nuances of *Virginia v. Black* in a short training briefing?

What the briefings did communicate, to many of the officers who attended them, were that the marching orders were to be passive and non-interventionist. There was genuine concern that police might be caught in the middle, in harm's way, between the demonstrators and the counter-demonstrators.[27] The police had reports that Antifa members would bring soda cans filled with cement. Other rumors circulated that Antifa might use fentanyl, an opioid, to attack police.[28]

In the aftermath of the events in the summer of 2017, the City of Charlottesville commissioned an independent investigation of the events, hiring the distinguished Virginia attorney Timothy J. Heaphy, a lawyer at the Hunton & Williams law firm and former United States Attorney in Virginia, to lead the investigation. That investigation produced what became known as the "Heaphy Report." Lieutenant Tom McKean told Heaphy Report investigators that he was "not sending guys out there and getting them hurt."[29] One officer told the investigators that she was so concerned about the potential for violence, and the decision not to dress officers in riot gear at the commencement of the event, that she updated her will and left letters to both her children when she reported for duty on August 12.[30]

According to the Heaphy Report, Lieutenant Brian O'Donnell instructed his officers to avoid engaging attendees over "every little thing." Officer Lisa Best stated that she was instructed that police "were not going to go in and break up fights" or enter the crowd to make arrests "unless it was something so serious that someone will get killed." Sergeant Robert Haney understood the orders as "do not interrupt mutual combat" unless someone is seriously injured.[31]

The Charlottesville police appeared to treat the declaration of an unlawful assembly as the department's ace in the hole. If matters got dicey, the police intended to call the gathering an unlawful assembly and end it, disbanding the crowd. The planning document for the event asserted that the chief of police retained "the authority to issue the order for declaration of an unlawful assembly should circumstances warrant such action."[32]

A policy debate within the law enforcement community was whether police should wear their riot gear from the start of the rally, or instead have it nearby ready to don if necessary. Chief Thomas was still smarting from the criticism rained on the department for its decision to deploy tear gas after the Klan departed from its rally of July 8. As Captain Mitchell explained, the "optics are bad" when citizens see police wearing riot gear, because it sends the message that the police are "ready to fight."[33] Riot gear was instead packed into bags and stowed in a trailer on Jefferson Street north of Emancipation Park. Some officers would be near the stored gear. But others—those stationed at Market Street, for example—would need to traverse Market Street and cross Emancipation Park, the likely ground zero for violence, should the events turn violent.[34]

Besides the city's police, two other police departments were in the area—the Albemarle County Police Department and the University of Virginia Police Department. Agreements were in place among all three, establishing protocols for their coming to one another's assistance. In addition, the Virginia State Police was available to reinforce local police forces as needed. The Virginia National Guard was also available. The Guard would deploy a company of 115 military police officers to the area, to be kept in reserve at a staging area about 2.5 miles from Emancipation Park, at the National Guard Amory on Avon Street.[35]

"What we *got* here is a *failure* to *communicate*!" This was one of the most famous lines from the classic Paul Newman movie *Cool Hand Luke*, spoken by the penitentiary captain, played by actor Strother Martin. It could have been written for the law enforcement agencies responsible in the summer of 2017 for safety in Charlottesville, Virginia.

In the lead-up to the Unite the Right rally, the lines of communication and coordination among the four law enforcement agencies in and around Charlottesville were shockingly deficient. After the fact, there was finger-pointing on all sides. The Virginia State Police operational plan for August 12, for example, was never shared with the Charlottesville Police Department. It was only because a copy of the state police plan was inadvertently left behind at a staging area that the Charlottesville department later even became aware that there had been a state police plan.[36] More directly debilitating, the Charlottesville Police Department and the Virginia State Police failed to even establish communications on the same radio channels. Throughout August 12, commanders were able to coordinate with their own subordinates, but no radio communications were ever established between the Charlottesville police and the state police.[37] Whoever was to blame for failures to coordinate, the fact of a lack of communication was manifest and disastrous. It was an epic *failure to communicate.*

Among the leaders of the Unite the Right rally most concerned with logistics was Eli Mosley. The plan Mosley circulated had three contingency plans, color-coded green, yellow, and red.

Plan Green assumed that the rally would go forward in Emancipation Park as originally contemplated. Under Plan Green, the alt-right participants were to arrive at Emancipation Park at noon. There would be a rally point from which transport vans would bring the alt-right rally-goers to the park. The vans would get as close as police barricades would allow, and then the rally-goers would disembark and march en masse to the park.[38]

Plan Yellow contemplated that the permit to rally in Emancipation Park would be revoked at the last minute, or that police would fail in some other way to guarantee access to the park at noon. In this eventuality attendees were told to arrive at the park early, by 10 a.m.[39]

Plan Red contemplated outright hostility to the Unite the Right rally, in which police refused to secure the area and intended to arrest attendees. Under this scenario, the alt-right rally-goers would go to the park and engage in civil disobedience.[40]

Many of the private citizens, organizations, and businesses of Charlottesville were largely left to fend for themselves in figuring out how to cope with the contingencies posed by the rally.

Congregation Beth Israel was located only one block east of Emancipation Park. Beth Israel was the oldest standing Jewish synagogue in Virginia. Given the fierce currents of Nazi revivalism and antisemitism that permeated Charlottesville's summer invasion of hate, and given the synagogue's location so proximate to ground zero, just blocks from the Robert E. Lee and Stonewall Jackson statues, Congregation Beth Israel was on high alert during all the summer's protest confrontations.

When the alt-right had first come to Charlottesville in May, Congregation Beth Israel's president, Alan Zimmerman, was attending a bar mitzvah at the synagogue. When a loud noise from the alt-right rally at the Stonewall Jackson statue was heard within the synagogue, Zimmerman's son left to see what was up. He reached the rally, wearing his yarmulke. Immediately he was surrounded by the alt-right protesters, who mocked him and insulted him with anti-Jewish slurs.[41]

This recent memory, and historical memories of Nazi violence in Germany and cascading episodes of American Nazi violence in the United

States, were on the minds of the leadership of Beth Israel. In preparing for the August Unite the Right rally, rabbis at the synagogue removed its sacred scrolls. A security guard was hired and permitted to carry a firearm.

Charlottesville's Downtown Mall is a long pedestrian stretch of Charlottesville's Main Street, closed to vehicular traffic. The west end of the mall is anchored by the Omni Charlottesville Hotel and a plaza area. The mall then extends about a third of a mile, filled with restaurants, cafés, shops, and small businesses in restored buildings, until it ends at the east end, where it is anchored by the Sprint Pavilion.

The tumultuous events in the summer of 2017 were close to the mall. Market Street runs parallel to the mall, one block north. Lee Park, later Emancipation Park (and since again renamed "Market Street Park"), borders on Market Street, between First and Second Streets. Jackson Park, later Justice Park (and since again renamed Court Square Park), is just two blocks away from the mall, on East Jefferson Street, between Fourth and Fifth Streets. The mall has over 120 shops and 30 restaurants, many of the restaurants with outdoor seating. Street musicians and artists bring life up and down the mall, which is graced by many fountains and pleasant seating areas. It is, in short, a genuine urban success story, at once vibrant and peaceful.

The business owners with shops and restaurants on the mall were not enamored of the alt-right and supremacist rallies, to say the least. They feared that the events would be bad for business. They feared that any violence that might erupt from massive crowds just blocks away could spill into the mall, potentially resulting in vandalism, fires, or violent injury.

The business leaders in the mall repeatedly reached out to the Charlottesville police and other Charlottesville officials for advice on how best to prepare. They were given cordial general briefings but very little in the way of concrete recommendations or intelligence.

The nerves of the business owners in Charlottesville, like the nerves of leaders of religious institutions, nonprofits, and average citizens, were growing increasingly frayed.

23

The Day of the Cross

The call to conscience issued by Congregate Charlottesville, Black Lives Matter, and their allies, coupled with the ugly events in Charlottesville at the Ku Klux Klan rally on July 8, generated my own personal difficult crisis of conscience. I felt some personal accountability for the hate speech that Charlottesville had already endured in May and July and the massive storm of hate speech it was bracing to weather on August 12.

I grew up in the north, in Chicago, where we had plenty of issues involving racial polarization, and plenty of white supremacists, but no visible tributes to the Confederacy in our public squares. I went to law school in the South, at Duke in North Carolina, then clerked for a federal judge, Charles Clark of the United States Court of Appeals for the Fifth Circuit. Judge Clark had his chambers in Jackson, Mississippi, and the court had its headquarters in New Orleans. Later in my career I moved to Virginia, where I lived for twenty years as a law professor and lawyer, teaching at William and Mary, the University of Richmond, and Washington and Lee University. I then moved to Greenville, South Carolina, were I was president of Furman University. After that I taught as a visiting professor at Duke, and then the University of Georgia.

During all my time in the South, I was surprised at all the streets, towns, parks, monuments, and schools named for Confederate leaders. Tributes to Robert E. Lee seemed to be everywhere. According to the Southern Poverty Law Center, in 2016 there were 203 public commemorations of Robert E. Lee, including highways, cities, counties, parks, and monuments named for him. No fewer than fifty-two public schools were named for Lee. On the private side, the beautiful and distinguished Washington and Lee University in Lexington, Virginia, where I was once the dean of the law school, was named for George Washington and Robert E. Lee. The campus includes the Lee Chapel and the president's residence, the Lee House, where Lee lived when he was president of the university following the Civil War, and where he died.

When I was dean of the University of Richmond Law School, I lived just one block from Richmond's Monument Avenue, an elegant tree-lined boulevard divided by a grassy center mall separating eastbound and westbound traffic. The east end of the avenue originates in the heart of a historic residential district Richmonders call "the Fan," named for the way in which the streets spread from a base outward like spokes on a fan. Monument Avenue is the grand showcase street of the city, with many architecturally striking and historic mansions, churches, and museums. But what distinguishes Monument Avenue are the monuments for which it is named. From the base of the avenue in the heart of the fan and stretching westward, monuments to heroes of the Confederacy are placed in the center of traffic circles every few blocks. The monuments are massive. They include monuments to generals J. E. B. Stuart, Stonewall Jackson, and Robert E. Lee, the president of the Confederacy Jefferson Davis, and Matthew Fontaine Maury, a scientist and educator who resigned from the US Navy to join the Confederacy at the outbreak of the war. Lee's monument was placed in Richmond in 1890; Stuart's and Davis's in 1907, Jackson's in 1919, and Maury's in 1929. A crowd of some one hundred thousand was present for the unveiling of the Lee statue.

In 1996, a monument to Arthur Ashe, the famous African American tennis player who was from Richmond, was added to the series. The decision to add a monument to Ashe was controversial, exposing racial divisions within Richmond. The African American community supported the monument. Others opposed the addition of Ashe, arguing that Monument Avenue should retain its character as a tribute to the heroes of the Confederacy.[1]

My family's home was just a block from the Robert E. Lee statute, in a small park known as Lee Circle in the middle of Monument Avenue. It was common for me to play with my kids at the base of the statue, roughhousing with our dogs or throwing a Frisbee.

I look back now with some disorientation as to how I processed all these tributes to the Confederacy in those years. I would instinctively blanch anytime I saw the Confederate battle flag, which I viscerally associated with slavery and racism. But for reasons I don't now comprehend, the monuments did not engender the same reaction. Nor did streets or parks named after Lee or Stuart. Nor, later, did the idea of teaching at a university named "Washington and Lee." Somehow the monuments were a blind spot, and I don't find it easy to account for that. These statues were all erected during the Jim Crow years, in brazen defiance of the dignity of blacks. The monuments are suffused with the righteousness of the South's cause during the Civil War, and that cause was slavery. During the time we lived in Richmond there would be periodic parades in honor of the Confederacy, usually culminating with rallies in Lee Circle. When I walked past the marchers wearing their Confederate garb I would think to myself, "Dumb racist rednecks." But somehow the stupidity and racism of the marchers did not seep into the stone and metal of the monuments themselves. It just didn't register.

If we are to have honest conversations about race in America, we must admit to our blind spots. My inability to perceive the racism embedded in the monuments was typical of many whites. A poll conducted in the aftermath of Charlottesville's bloody summer in September 2017, conducted by Reuters/Ipsos in conjunction with the University of Virginia Center for Politics, was revealing.[2] There was no consensus as to what to do with Confederate monuments. There was, however, a distinct difference between the views of whites and blacks on the issue. In total, about three-fifths (57 percent) of those polled favored keeping Confederate monuments in public spaces. Slightly more than a quarter (26 percent) thought the monuments should be removed. Among whites, two-thirds

(67 percent) favored keeping the monuments in place, and 19 percent favored removal. Among blacks, in contrast, only 25 percent favored keeping the monuments in place, while 54 percent favored removal.[3]

There is no hate speech in America quite as intense as cross burning, the symbolic ritual long associated with the Ku Klux Klan. The Supreme Court of the United States has decided three landmark cross burning cases, *Brandenburg v. Ohio*,[4] *R.A.V. v. City of St. Paul*,[5] and *Virginia v. Black*.[6]

The third case and last word in this trilogy, *Virginia v. Black*, was "my case." It was a challenge to Virginia's cross-burning law that was ultimately decided by the Supreme Court of the United States, where I served as lead counsel and argued the case before the court. My client was the Ku Klux Klan.

Brandenburg v. Ohio involved a Klan rally conducted on a farm in Hamilton County, Ohio, outside Cincinnati. A local Cincinnati television station reporter had been invited to witness the rally, and he and a cameraman filmed the event, portions of which were later broadcast on the Cincinnati station and the NBC national network. Klan members shouted that the "the nigger should be returned to Africa, the Jew to Israel," and "if our president, our Congress, our Supreme Court, continues to suppress the white, Caucasian race, it's possible that there might have to be some revengence taken."[7] The word "revengence" is not in any standard dictionary, but the point was plain enough.

The state of Ohio prosecuted Clarence Brandenburg, the leader of the Klan group, under an Ohio "criminal syndicalism" law making it illegal to advocate "the duty, necessity, or propriety of crime, sabotage, violence, or unlawful methods of terrorism as a means of accomplishing industrial or political reform," or to assemble "with any society, group, or assemblage of persons formed to teach or advocate the doctrines of criminal syndicalism." Brandenburg was convicted, fined $1,000, and sentenced to one to ten years' imprisonment.

The Supreme Court held the Ohio law unconstitutional, overturning Brandenburg's conviction. No one was present at the Klan rally except the Klan members themselves, the television reporter, and his cameraman. Nothing in the record indicated that the racist messages of the Klansmen at the rally posed any immediate physical threat to anyone. In these circumstances, the court said, the Klan was guilty only of the "abstract teaching" of the "moral propriety" of racist violence. "The constitutional guarantees of free speech and free press," according to the court, "do not permit a State to forbid or proscribe advocacy of the use of force or of law violation except where such advocacy is directed to inciting or producing imminent lawless action and is likely to incite or produce such action."[8] This became known as the "*Brandenburg* test" governing prosecutions for incitement to illegal activity, a test that had three elements: an intent to incite lawless action, imminence, and likelihood.

In *Hess v. Indiana*,[9] the circumstances were different. Gregory Hess was leading an antiwar demonstration on the campus of Indiana University. The demonstration spilled into a public street, with roughly 150 demonstrators blocking traffic. The sheriff ordered the protesters to clear the street. As they obeyed, Hess stated, as the sheriff passed by, "We'll take the fucking street later."[10] Hess was immediately arrested, and convicted, for disorderly conduct. The Supreme Court reversed Hess's conviction, stating that he could not be convicted merely for having used the word "fucking." More importantly, the court held that Hess's statement could not properly be treated as a direct verbal challenge to fight the sheriff or his deputies. There was testimony in the case that Hess was facing the crowd, not the street, and that Hess did not appear to be addressing any particular person. Relying on the *Brandenburg* test, the court held that when Hess said "We'll take the fucking street later," he was not advocating immediate law breaking, but rather illegal action "at some indefinite future time."[11]

R.A.V. v. City of St. Paul, decided in 1992, involved a minor (whose initials were R.A.V.) who lit a small cross on the front yard of a black family in St. Paul, Minnesota. There was no doubt that what R.A.V. did was illegal and not protected under the First Amendment. There is no right to trespass on the property of another, and there is no right to threaten another person—as the act of burning a cross in the front yard of a black family quite arguably was. But R.A.V. was not charged with criminal trespassing, nor was he charged with making a threat. He was instead charged with violating a St. Paul ordinance that dealt specifically with brandishing a burning cross or a Nazi swastika, two of the most notorious symbols of hate known to the world. The ordinance read, "Whoever places on public or private property a symbol, object, appellation, characterization or graffiti, including, but not limited to, a burning cross or Nazi swastika, which one knows or has reasonable grounds to know arouses anger, alarm or resentment in others on the basis of race, color, creed, religion or gender commits disorderly conduct and shall be guilty of a misdemeanor."[12]

The Supreme Court overturned R.A.V.'s conviction, in an opinion written by Justice Antonin Scalia. The court concentrated not on the *criminal's act*, but on the "criminal act," the ordinance, under which the criminal was prosecuted. The court found that ordinance infected with "viewpoint discrimination," an exercise in legislative political correctness that penalized actions taken from one ideological perspective but not another.

Justice Scalia's opinion held that the ordinance violated the First Amendment because the government was taking sides—criminalizing racist or antisemitic messages communicated by burning crosses or swastikas because they arouse anger or resentment "on the basis of race, color, creed, religion or gender," but not criminalizing statements expressing opposing sentiments. The St. Paul ordinance only came down against what Scalia described as "one of the specified disfavored topics."[13] In the most famous passage in the case, Scalia argued that the ordinance licensed one side of the debate to "fight freestyle," while requiring the other to play by "Marquis of Queensberry Rules":

> Displays containing some words—odious racial epithets, for example— would be prohibited to proponents of all views. But "fighting words" that do not themselves invoke race, color, creed, religion, or gender—aspersions upon a person's mother, for example—would seemingly be usable *ad libitum* in the placards of those arguing in favor of racial, color, etc. tolerance and equality, but could not be used by that speaker's opponents. One could hold up a sign saying, for example, that all "anti-Catholic bigots" are misbegotten; but not that all "papists" are, for that would insult and provoke violence "on the basis of religion." St. Paul has no such authority to license one side of a debate to fight freestyle, while requiring the other to follow Marquis of Queensberry Rules.[14]

When the *R.A.V.* decision was announced, I considered it the clearest Supreme Court decision of its time demonstrating that the order and morality theory had been repudiated. It seemed to me that *R.A.V.*, when considered along with cases such as *Brandenburg*, had to be understood as essentially overruling *Beauharnais v. Illinois*. The racist messages for which Joseph Beauharnais was convicted were indistinguishable from the racist messages in *Brandenburg* and *R.A.V.*, and the St. Paul ordinance struck down in *R.A.V.* seemed indistinguishable from the Illinois law upheld in *Beauharnais.*

Brandenburg v. Ohio and *R.A.V. v. City of St. Paul* set the stage for *Virginia v. Black.* I stepped onto that stage.

Barry Elton Black was a Ku Klux Klan leader from Pennsylvania. Black organized a Ku Klux Klan rally, to be held on private property in rural Cana, Virginia, in the western part of the state, on August 22, 1998. Members of the local sheriff's office, concerned about the Klan's proposed rally, parked on a highway near the farm where the rally was scheduled, to keep an eye on things. The sheriff was a student of Virginia law, who would often read through the Virginia statutes in his spare time. He had a vague memory that Virginia law contained some sort of prohibition on cross burning. At the height of the rally, Klan members set fire to a giant thirty-foot cross, lighting up the night sky. Following a Klan custom, the Klan members played the sacred hymn "Amazing Grace" over a loudspeaker as they marched around the cross, shouting and chanting. Their statements included diatribes against blacks and Mexicans, and Bill and Hillary Clinton. The burning cross was visible from the nearby public highway. Several cars drove by the scene while the cross was lit, including one car with an African American family inside. The sheriff called into a dispatcher at headquarters, who had the Virginia Code on a computer disk, and asked the dispatcher to look up the state's cross-burning law. The dispatcher read the test of the statute over the radio:

> It shall be unlawful for any person or persons, with the intent of intimidating any person or group of persons, to burn, or cause to be burned, a cross on the property of another, a highway or other public place. Any person who shall violate any provision of this section shall be guilty of a Class 6 felony.
>
> Any such burning of a cross shall be prima facie evidence of an intent to intimidate a person or group of persons.[15]

The sheriff and his deputy drove up to where the Klan members were singing and shouting and observing the flaming cross. Barry Black identified himself as the person in charge. The sheriff stated to Black that burning a cross was against the law in Virginia and placed him under arrest. While in custody in the police car Black made racist statements, complaining about having seen interracial couples in the area.

The American Civil Liberties Union of Virginia decided it would offer to defend Barry Black. The ACLU asked me and defense attorney David Baugh to be the legal team for Black. Baugh would handle the trial work, I would handle any appeals. David Baugh, who was my friend, was African American. I had once actually been David's lawyer in a First Amendment case, *Baugh v. JIRC*,[16] defending his free speech rights in a case arising from ethical complaints he had filed against a sitting Virginia judge.

Baugh was one of the most successful criminal defense lawyers in Virginia, and indeed had a national reputation as a defense lawyer willing to defend highly unpopular clients. Among his clients was Mohamad al-Ohwali, whom he defended for the bombing of the United States Embassy in Nairobi, Kenya.

I foresaw one major problem with the ACLU plan, which was that I could not imagine that Klan leader Barry Black would accept an African American lawyer. Baugh and I agreed with the ACLU that this was Black's problem. We would offer to defend him as a team, and the choice was his, take it or leave it.

After the initial shock of seeing that the lawyer who arrived on his doorstep was African American, Barry Black took up the offer of free representation. When some folks in Virginia questioned Baugh on how he could represent a Klan leader, he replied that he was not taking the case to have some sort of "kumbaya moment" with Black. The point was to defend the principle of free speech.

At the trial, the prosecution's star witness was a woman named Rebecca Sechrist. Just prior to the rally, Mrs. Sechrist and her husband had had a mobile home delivered to the property adjacent to the field on which the rally took place. On the day of the rally, Sechrist had not yet moved into the home but was in the process of preparing it for occupancy. Mrs. Sechrist, who was related to the owner of the property where the rally occurred, did not approve of the Klan or the rally. Yet something drew her to watch it unfold, which she did, from the front porch of her new mobile home. Although on her own land, she was close enough to hear and see what was going on. At the trial, the prosecution produced her as its main witness. She testified,

> They talked a lot about blacks—and I don't call the word they called it—
> it started with an N and I don't, I don't use that word, I'm sorry—but they

talked real bad about the blacks and the Mexicans and they talked about how, one guy got up and said that he would love to take a .30/.30 and just random shoot the blacks and talked about how they would like to send the blacks and the Mexicans back from where they come from and talked about President Clinton and Hillary Clinton and about the government funding money for the, for the people that can't afford housing and stuff and how their tax paying goes to keep the black people up and stuff like that.

The prosecutor asked Sechrist how her witnessing the events at the Klan rally made her feel. "Oh, it made me feel awful," she responded:

They all walked around and then they would go in one circle and say things and then they would go around in another circle and say things and then they went up and all met at the bottom of the cross and lit it and played *Amazing Grace* and I tell you what, it was just terrible. It was terrible to see, that, when they were talking about random shooting black people and all, the guy that said it and everything talked about killing people and then get up there and said that he was a good Christian and when he died, he knowed he was going to heaven and then to burn the cross like that, I just couldn't begin to put in words how I felt. I sat there and I cried. I didn't know what was going to happen between everything going on. It was just terrible.

Sechrist testified that her feelings of fear and dismay lasted for a "couple months" after the rally. Sechrist, who was white, testified that "I think they were trying to scare me," but at the same time she admitted that no participant in the Klan ever did anything threatening directed at her. She conceded, indeed, that she would have felt much the same reaction had she witnessed video footage of the same rally on television.

The testimony of Mrs. Sechrist epitomizes what most people who witnessed the alt-right and Klan racial supremacist messages in Charlottesville felt in the summer of 2017. Her testimony likely captures what most Americans of goodwill would think and feel on witnessing a Klan cross-burning rally at close range. I remember feeling that what she said she felt was probably what I would have felt, had I been on the porch with her that night.

After the evidence was heard, the judge instructed the jury that to convict Black, they had to find that he burned the cross for the purpose of intimidating another person. The judge also instructed the jury, as the Virginia cross-burning law provided, that the jury could infer an intent to intimidate from the burning of the cross itself. The jury deliberated and found Black guilty. It was now my turn to begin arguing the appeals.

I began to research the history of the cross-burning statute. The law had been passed in 1952, before *Brown v. Board of Education*, at a time when Virginia was still heavily racist and heavily segregated. A wave of Ku Klux Klan violence erupted during that time. The Virginia governor and legislature reacted to the violence by passing the cross-burning statute, as well as its companion, prohibiting the wearing of masks. The legislation, though it did not name the Klan by name, was plainly targeted at the Klan.

I also had to learn more about the history of cross burning. The most succinct summary came from a case in which the Supreme Court justice Clarence Thomas had occasion to recount the history, in a concurring opinion he authored in a case called *Capitol Square Review & Advisory Board v. Pinette*.[17] The case involved Ohio's Capitol Square, the state-owned ten-acre plaza surrounding the Statehouse in Columbus. In 1993 Ohio placed a Christmas tree on the grounds during the holiday season and subsequently granted a permit to a local rabbi to also display a menorah on the grounds. The Ohio Ku Klux Klan then sought permission to erect a Latin cross on the grounds as well. The Klan did not seek to *burn* a cross, just to put up a cross during the holiday season, in apparent juxtaposition with the rabbi's menorah. Ohio would not let the Klan put up its cross, asserting that to do so would constitute an unconstitutional "establishment of religion." The United States Supreme Court overturned Ohio's ban, holding that the Klan's action would not amount to an establishment of religion, thereby allowing the Klan to put up its cross. The principal opinion in the case was written by Justice Scalia.

Justice Thomas wrote a fascinating concurring opinion, in which he discussed the meaning of the cross *to the Ku Klux Klan*. The court's opinion, he asserted, "should not lead anyone to think that a cross erected by the Ku Klux Klan is a purely religious symbol. The erection of such a cross is a political act, not a Christian one." The Klan's main reason for existence and its main objective, he asserted, "is to establish a racist white government in the United States." When the Klan engages in its cross-burning ceremony, he argued, "the cross is a symbol of white supremacy and a tool for the intimidation and harassment of racial minorities, Catholics, Jews, Communists, and any other groups hated by the Klan."[18] Justice Thomas then explained the historical accidents that led to the Klan's appropriation of cross burning as its signature ritual. As Thomas explained, the early Ku Klux Klan emerged in the South during Reconstruction. The practice of cross-burning was the product of Thomas Dixon, whose book *The Clansman* formed the story for the movie *The Birth of a Nation*. Dixon apparently believed that members of the South's Reconstruction Ku Klux Klan were the "reincarnated souls of the Clansmen of Old Scotland" and that in burning the cross they were engaged in an "old Scottish rite."[19] Cross burning did acquire some religious connotation, Thomas conceded, as the Klan was connected to certain southern white clergy in the 1920s—and indeed when the modern Klan lights the cross, Christian hymns are usually sung. Nevertheless, Thomas asserted, after World War II the Klan's burning cross had "reverted to its original function as an instrument of intimidation." Thomas concluded, "The Klan simply has appropriated one of the most sacred of religious symbols as a symbol of hate."[20]

When I read Justice Thomas's decision in *Pinette*, I thought it *helped* our case in Virginia in defending the Klan, and I thought it meant that if our case ever reached the Supreme Court, Justice Thomas would be on our side, because he would clearly see that cross burning was an exercise in *political* speech—even though that speech was racist and abhorrent. I *completely* misread Justice Thomas's point. My prediction that he would be a sure vote for us could not have been more wrong.

As Barry Black's case worked its way through the Virginia courts, my legal argument was straightforward. I conceded that the First Amendment did not protect incitement to violence, provided that prosecution was able to prove the standards required under *Brandenburg*, which were that the speech was directed to the incitement of imminent lawless action and likely to produce such action. No such jury instruction was given in Black's case, and there was nothing in the record to support the existence of those elements. Indeed, I pointed out, the cross-burning rally conducted by Black and the Klan in Cana was virtually identical to the rally in Ohio in *Brandenburg*. There was plenty of racist expression and abstract advocacy of violence at both rallies, to be sure, but no actual incitement to engage in imminent violence. If the First Amendment protected Clarence Brandenburg, I argued, it protected Barry Black.

I also relied heavily on the Supreme Court's decision in *R.A.V.* The Virginia statute, I pointed out, singled out one symbol, a burning cross, much as the St. Paul ordinance in *R.A.V.* had singled out cross burning and Nazi swastikas. Once again, I made an important concession. I agreed that the First Amendment did not protect real threats—what First Amendment cases call "true threats"—but there was no need, I argued, to single out burning crosses as a special kind of threat. On this point, I argued that the second sentence of the Virginia statute, which allowed a jury to *infer* an intent to intimidate from the mere act of cross burning itself, made the "intent" requirement of the law a "now you see it now you don't" illusion. Since cross-burning by itself supported an inference of intimidation, the law effectively made it illegal to burn a cross, period, whether there was any real threat to anyone or not.

At roughly the same time that these events were taking place in the western part of Virginia, another cross-burning incident was taking place in the eastern side of the state, in Virginia Beach. The two defendants were Richard Elliott and Jonathan O'Mara. They were having a dispute with their neighbors, the Jubilee family, arising from Elliott's and O'Mara's habit of shooting guns at targets in their backyard, a practice that scared the Jubilees, who had small children. After getting very drunk one night, Elliott and O'Mara decided to "get back" at the Jubilees for hassling them about their shooting. They took some sticks and lashed together a small cross. They managed to get it charred but were too drunk to get it to fully light. The next morning, James Jubilee, who was African American, found the charred cross in his backyard. Elliott and O'Mara were arrested and convicted of violating Virginia's cross-burning statute. Dahlia Lithwick, a trenchant and often brilliantly comedic reporter on the Supreme Court for the online Slate magazine, wrote that the facts in Elliott and O'Mara's case read like "outtakes from *A Charlie Brown Redneck Christmas.*"[21]

The Virginia Court of Appeals, the state's intermediate appellate court, affirmed the convictions. The stage was then set for oral argument in the Supreme Court of Virginia, which ordered the Barry Black case and the Virginia Beach case to be argued the same day, back to back. The date of the argument was September 10, 2001. The arguments were filled with back-and-forth among the justices and the lawyers over the connection between hate speech and hate violence, the history of the Klan, and the meaning of cross burning. I presented the argument in the Barry Black case; other lawyers argued the Virginia Beach case. I continued my mantra. A cross is an object or symbol of a particular shape: a vertical bar traversed by a horizontal bar. Nothing in this geometric configuration of the vertical and horizontal carries any peculiarly dangerous potency. It is not the fire that burns hotter when flaming sticks are crossed, but the passions that the fire inflames.

None of us in that courtroom that day could have known that within twenty-four hours all our lives would be profoundly changed. And none of us in that courtroom could have known that the events of the next day would hit the American consciousness with enough force to rattle the foundations of all certitudes. Like so many Americans on that September 11, I felt deep shock, grief, anger, and dismay, and I did what I could to provide assistance and comfort to those most directly affected by the terrorist violence. And like so many, as the immediate shock and sorrow gave way to participation in the national analysis, discussion, and debate over our society's proper responses to the events, I found myself, with others, beginning to reexamine many of the basic habits and premises of our national life. The role of free speech was part of that reexamination. Osama bin Laden, after all, had used speech to whip up the hysterical hatred for America that led the terrorists who hijacked the planes that day to strike the World Trade Center towers and their targets in Washington, DC. Bin Laden was a foreign terrorist. The Klan were domestic terrorists. On September 10, I felt confident that we would win and should win our free-speech arguments in the Virginia Supreme Court. On September 11, I was not so sure. I remember thinking of a quote from Oliver Wendell Holmes himself. "Certitude is not the test of Certainty. We have been cocksure of many things that were not so."[22]

The Virginia Supreme Court, by a 4–3 vote, in an opinion written by Justice Donald Lemons, struck down the Virginia cross-burning law, overturning all the convictions. But the case was far from over. The Commonwealth of Virginia appealed the decision to the Supreme Court of the United States, and the Supreme Court granted review.

When the Supreme Court agreed to take the case, the question became who, among the lawyers on our side, would argue the case. In the Virginia Supreme Court, the two Virginia Beach cross burners, Jonathan O'Mara and Richard Elliott, were represented by two superb Virginia defense lawyers, Kevin Martingayle and James Broccoletti, respectively. Because the fact patterns in the Virginia Beach case and the Cana Ku Klux Klan case were quite different, I thought it best if the Virginia Beach defendants had one lawyer in the Supreme Court and Klansman Barry Black a different lawyer. We filed a motion in the Supreme Court asking for permission to divide the argument, with me representing Black and another lawyer O'Mara and Elliott. The Supreme Court denied the motion, instructing us to pick one lawyer on our side to represent all three defendants. I was picked, and so I suddenly had two new clients, O'Mara and Elliott, along with Barry Black.

The day before the argument was to be heard, the lawyers on our side gathered for a luncheon meeting at the St. Regis Hotel in Washington. Among the attendees was a lawyer from Minnesota, Edward J. Cleary. Ed Cleary had argued the *R.A.V.* case in the Supreme Court a decade before. He had since gone on to become a Minnesota judge, ultimately becoming the chief judge of the Minnesota Court of Appeals. He was very proud of his victory in *R.A.V.*, and even went on to write a terrific book about the case, *Beyond the Burning Cross: A Landmark Case of Race, Censorship, and the First Amendment.*[23]

Judge Cleary and I became friends when he learned about *Virginia v. Black*. We corresponded and talked on the phone about constitutional law, arguing cases on appeal, and strategy. Although he was a sitting judge, he took time off and flew to Washington to watch the argument in *Black*, and I had invited him to the lunch. He was worried that the Supreme Court had granted review in *Black* because it was having second thoughts about the wisdom of its far-reaching decision in *R.A.V.* He joked with me that he was there to be sure I didn't mess up his case. I knew he was only half joking.

As an old football player warhorse competitor, I tend to get calm and focused before entering great contests. As the time for a noble battle nears, I like to be alone. Even so, I knew how much the case meant to so many, and while I was not too enthused about getting deeply into the nooks and crannies of the litigation, and don't like to over-rehearse, I understood that the group of lawyers connected to the case needed and deserved one last strategic conclave. We had lunch together, but for the most part I remained quiet. I left most of the chatter to others and sat fairly quiet, until suddenly a thought popped into my head, seemingly from nowhere. "Do any of you remember the page in the record that contains the actual jury instruction about inferring intent given to the jury at Barry Black's trial?" I asked. Of course, nobody could have been expected to remember a single page in a record several hundred pages long, so we looked it up. "I just want to be sure I have the wording in my head exactly correct," I explained, as we thumbed through the trial transcript. "Ah, here it is," I said, "page one hundred forty-six." Yup, I said to everyone, I was remembering it correctly. I read it aloud: "The burning of a cross by itself is sufficient evidence from which you may infer the required intent." It was right about then that the others, sensing I really was content to just focus and be left along, graciously wished me good luck, and the lunch meeting adjourned.

I believe that the oral argument in the United States Supreme Court on December 11, 2002, was one of the most illuminating and historically important moments in the history of the American struggle over race hate, symbols of racial violence, and freedom of speech. Dahlia Lithwick, who lives near Charlottesville, said in her report of the case in Slate, "Once in a while, a case comes along that makes a Supreme Court reporter proud to be involved, even tangentially, in the life of the high court. Oral argument in today's cross-burning case, *Virginia v. Black*, was most definitely one of those days."[24]

Strangely, in my view, the oral argument in the case is more important to the history of the country, and to the events that would later unfold in Charlottesville, than the actual opinions rendered by the justices when the case was decided. The opinions, discussed toward the end of this chapter, are in some ways opaque and confusing. They do not render any perfectly clear answers as to how much or how little of the speech and conduct of the alt-right in Charlottesville, or the speech and conduct of the counterprotesters who answered the "Call to Conscience," were protected under the First Amendment. The oral argument, however, was an extraordinary moment—perhaps more an extraordinary *cultural* moment than legal moment—for it laid bare all the conflicting values and crosscurrents at play in our national debate over race and speech with exquisite clarity.

It was also high drama, as the justices themselves entered the fray with exceptional passion and intensity. Justice Scalia, who lived for many years in Charlottesville as a professor teaching at the University of Virginia Law School, seemed to flip sides from his opinion in *R.A.V.* and attack the Klan and the Virginia Beach cross burners with pugnacious tenacity. His good friend Justice Ginsburg, the most liberal member of the court and the justice most likely to oppose Scalia in her opinions, displayed a poignant sympathy toward Virginia's cross-burning law, suggesting that there was a fundamental difference between flag burning, which attacks the government, and cross burning, which attacks people. There were probing questions on difficult points of law, and the history of the Ku Klux Klan, from Justices O'Connor, Breyer, Stevens, Kennedy, and Souter. And then, there was "He Who Never Speaks," Justice Clarence Thomas, the court's only African American. In this case, however, Justice Thomas spoke. He had plenty to say, and his words changed everything.

I argued the case in the Supreme Court of the United States against a fellow lawyer who was also a friend, William Hurd, the solicitor general of the Commonwealth of Virginia. Hurd began his argument before the court with a dramatic flourish. "Our Virginia cross-burning statute protects a very important freedom," he began confidently, "freedom from fear—and it does so without compromising freedom of speech."[25] Justice Sandra Day O'Connor was the first to interrupt. "There's a part of the statute that may be troublesome," she stated, "and that is the prima facie evidence provision. I suppose you could have a cross-burning, for instance, in a play, in a theatre, something like that, which in theory shouldn't violate the statute, but here's the prima facie evidence provision. Would you like to comment about that, and in the process, would you tell me if you think it's severable?"

Sitting at the counsel table as I processed this question, it struck me as good news and bad news for our side. The good news was that Justice O'Connor saw a First Amendment problem with the provision in the law that allowed a jury to draw an inference of an intent to intimidate from the mere act of cross-burning itself. The bad news was that perhaps O'Connor saw that as the *only* serious First Amendment problem with the law and was musing over whether the Supreme Court could strike that part down, by "severing it," and still uphold the rest of the statute.

The argument proceeded. Justice Ruth Bader Ginsburg asked Hurd where, in the record, was the jury instruction that had been given to the jury in Barry Black's case. I couldn't believe she was asking this question—the same one I'd asked the lunch crew the day before. My poor friend Bill Hurd was caught off-guard. He had no idea where the instruction was.

He reached for the thick bound volume that was the "record appendix in the case" and began nervously looking for it. But he could not find it. Finally, the awkward silence was broken, as he apologized for not being able to find the instruction.

Page one hundred forty-six, I thought to myself, feeling bad for Bill. *Page one hundred forty-six*. I took this all as a sign. Between the fact that the question had mysteriously popped into my head the day before, to it coming up so prominently in the middle of Bill Hurd's argument, it seemed plain that the intent provision of the law was going to figure prominently in the outcome of the case. Hurd's argument continued, with many justices posing questions. Up to this point, Justice Scalia, notoriously one of the most active questioners in oral arguments, had been quiescent. I had figured that Scalia was the single safest vote on our side of the case. He was, after all, the author of the *R.A.V.* opinion, the strongest precedent on our side.

Justice Scalia finally jumped into the fray with the observation, "I thought the key here is that this is not just speech," he stated. "It is not just speech. It's action that is intended to convey a message." This point puzzled me—it was not what I expected from the justice I had counted on for our side. Scalia continued, and more alarm bells went off inside my head. "Surely," he said, "your State could make it unlawful to brandish with the intent of intimidating somebody, couldn't it?"

Justice Scalia seemed to be equating burning a cross with brandishing a gun. Now I was getting worried. My friend Bill Hurd took Justice Scalia's cue and ran with it perfectly. "In fact," Bill said, "a burning cross is very much like a brandishing of a firearm."

"That's your point!" Scalia exclaimed.

That was Bill Hurd's point. It suddenly hit me that this was also Justice Scalia's point. I now got the point—that the justice I most counted as certainly in our column was actually with the other side. I got the point, but I could not fathom the principle. Many more questions between Hurd and the justices ensued, and in what seemed the time it takes between the flash of a camera and the image captured, his time expired.

Next to the podium stepped an advocate for the United States, Michael Dreeben, representing the Justice Department's Office of the Solicitor General. Dreeben, I am proud to say, is a fellow graduate of Duke Law School during my era at Duke. He has had an extraordinary legal career in the Justice Department, arguing over *one hundred* cases in the Supreme Court of the United States. Robert Mueller would later recruit Dreeben to join his team in investigating the charges of Russian collusion with the Trump campaign in the 2017 presidential election.

When Michael Dreeben argued against me in *Virginia v. Black*, however, it was not the force of Dreeben's arguments that emerged as important, but the force of the questions put to him by one Supreme Court justice, Clarence Thomas.

It is important to understand here that Justice Thomas never speaks. He falls within a certain band of Supreme Court justices who rarely, if ever, interject questions in oral argument. Justice William Brennan, perhaps the Supreme Court's most famous and quintessential liberal, was in this band. The judge I clerked for fresh out of law school, Judge (later Chief Judge) Charles Clark of the United States Court of Appeals for the Fifth Circuit, was of this school, never asking questions in oral argument. When I once questioned him on this, he told me two things. First, what mattered was what took place behind the scenes, how he interacted with the other judges, to exchange views and garner support. Second, he told me, with an impish smile, that for the sake of the media watching the argument, he preferred to remain inscrutable, "silent and smart."

Justice Thomas, silent and smart, had not spoken from the bench in seven years when he posed his first question to Michael Dreeben. In a resonant baritone voice, Thomas spoke.

"Mr. Dreeben, aren't you underestimating the effects of the burning cross?" he asked. "This statute was passed in what year?"

There was sudden silence in the courtroom. Thus spoke Justice Thomas. No one breathed. You could hear a pin drop.

"Nineteen fifty-two, originally," Dreeben replied. I am sure Dreeben registered the drama of Justice Thomas suddenly interjecting. I suspect that Dreeben was still momentarily clueless as to where this surprise was leading, like all the rest of us in the courtroom at that moment.

Thomas spoke again. "Now it's my understanding that we had almost one hundred years of lynching and activity in the South by the Knights of Camellia and the Ku Klux Klan, and this was a reign of terror. And the cross was a symbol of that reign of terror. Isn't that significantly greater than intimidation or a threat?"

"Well," Dreeben replied, "I think they're coextensive, Justice Thomas, because it is—"

"Well my fear is, Mr. Dreeben," Justice Thomas interjected, "that you're actually *understating* the symbolism and the effect of the burning cross. I indicated, I think, in the Ohio case that the cross was not a religious symbol and that it was intended to have a virulent effect. I think that what you're attempting to do is fit this into our jurisprudence rather than stating more clearly what the cross was intended to accomplish. Indeed, it is unlike any symbol in our society."

I believe everyone in the courtroom was stunned. Here was Justice Thomas, the only African American on the court and famous for his views of staunch conservatism and robust protection of freedom of speech, professing the reality that the burning cross had been a symbol of terror, a symbol like none other in our society. And Thomas had not spoken from the bench in ten years. It was a Shakespearean moment. Garrett Epps would later comment in the *Atlantic* that it was Justice Thomas's "most powerful moment on the bench."[26] Dahlia Lithwick described the moment more colorfully: "Out of nowhere booms the great, surprising 'Luke-I-am-your-father' voice of He Who Never Speaks. Justice Clarence Thomas suddenly asks a question and everyone's head pops up and starts looking madly around, like the Muppets on Veterinarian Hospital. 'Aren't you understating the effects . . . of 100 years of lynching?' he booms. 'This was a reign of terror, and the cross was a sign of that. . . . It is unlike any symbol in our society. It was intended to cause fear, terrorize.'"[27]

Thomas was making the case for Virginia. Michael Dreeben, a superb advocate, instantly seized the opening.

"Well, I don't mean to understate it," Dreeben deftly responded, "and I entirely agree with Your Honor's description of how the cross has been used as an instrument of intimidation against minorities in this country."

Thomas punctuated the point: "And I—I just—my fear is that there was no other purpose to the cross. There was no communication of a particular message. It was intended to cause *fear* and to *terrorize* a population."

In all my years as a lawyer I have never seen the atmosphere in an appellate courtroom change so suddenly and dramatically as at that moment. The convivial Justice Stephen Breyer, who sits next to Justice Thomas on the bench, but who rarely votes with Thomas in cases, placed his arm on his colleague's back as Thomas finished his soliloquy, a gesture of kinship, as if to say, "I feel your pain." At the other end of the bench, Justice Scalia was staring transfixed at his close friend Thomas, as if to say, "I'm with you, my friend, I got your back." Scalia then looked down at the counsel table and stared directly into my eyes, a scowl on his face. I could never prove this in a court of law, but I felt as if he was sending me a telepathic message: "Just wait to you get to the podium."

It was not a long wait. Dreeben sat down, and I got up.

"The heart of our argument is that when the State targets a particular symbol or a particular symbolic ritual, it engages in content and viewpoint discrimination of the type forbidden by the First Amendment," I began.

After just one sentence of argument, Justice Scalia interrupted, "What about the symbol of brandishing an automatic weapon in somebody's face?"

"Justice Scalia—"

"*You're next!*" Scalia cut me off. At first, I thought he meant that *I* was next, from the glower on his face, but I realized what he really meant was that the gun brandisher was signaling, "You're next to be shot," just as a cross burner was signaling, "You're next to get lynched."

I had to push back. "There is a fundamental First Amendment difference between brandishing a cross, and brandishing a gun," I replied. "The physical properties of the gun as a weapon add potency to the threat."

Justice David Souter, usually a foil to Justice Scalia, picked up Scalia's argument, seeming to agree with him and with Justice Thomas. "But is—isn't the—isn't your argument an argument that would have been sound before the cross, in effect, acquired the history that it has?" Souter asked. "If we were in the year 1820, and you had a choice between somebody brandishing the loaded gun, and somebody brandishing a cross and nobody knew how the cross had been used because it had not been used, your argument, it seems to me, would be—would be a winning one. How does your argument account for that fact that the cross has acquired a potency which I would suppose is at least as equal to that of the gun?"

I responded to Justice Souter by arguing that the burning cross had gathered meaning over the years communicating "a multiplicity of messages," including becoming a "trademark" of the Ku Klux Klan.

Souter countered with Pavlov. "But it—it carries something else, doesn't it? Isn't it not merely a trademark that has acquired a meaning?

Isn't it also a kind of Pavlovian signal so that when that signal is given, the natural human response is not recognition of a message, but fear?"

I thought this was a brilliant question. But I had to fight back. "No, Your Honor," I insisted. "Respectfully I think that that overstates what is being communicated. *Any* symbol in its pristine state that has gathered reverence in our society—the American flag, the Star of David, the cross, the symbols of government—is a powerful, emotional symbol in—in its revered state."

"But they don't make—they don't make you scared," Justice Souter rejoined. "And if you start with the proposition that the State can, in fact, prevent threats that scare people reasonably—for their own safety, this is in a separate category from simply a—symbol that has acquired a potent meaning."

"Your Honor," I replied, "the word scared is important in answering your question because it's—it's what we mean by being scared, or what we mean by being intimidated. If I see a burning cross, my stomach may churn. I may feel a sense of loathing, disgust, a vague sense of being intimidated because I associate it—"

Scalia jumped back in, asking about a burning cross on a lawn. "I dare say that you would rather see a man with a—with a rifle on your front lawn—If you were a black man at night, you'd rather see a man with a rifle than see a burning cross on your front lawn."

I conceded Justice Scalia's point, and then looked directly at Justice Thomas, to tell him that I also conceded the authenticity of all that he had said in his powerful earlier statement. I said, "As powerful as that point is—and I totally accept it, and totally accept the history that Justice Thomas has recounted, and that the United States recounts in its brief, as accurate. As powerful as all of those points are, there's not a single interest that society seeks to protect in protecting that victim that cannot be vindicated perfectly as well, exactly as well with no fall-off at all, by content-neutral alternatives, not merely general run-of-the-mill threat laws, or incitement laws, or intimidation laws which may have an antiseptic and sterile quality about them. You can go even beyond that—"

As much as I wanted to finish this sentence, I wasn't given that luxury. Justice O'Connor interjected, "But why isn't this just a regulation of a particularly virulent form of intimidation? And why can't the State regulate such things?"

"Your Honor, it is not a particularly virulent form of intimidation."

"Well, it is for the very reasons we've explored this morning. What if I think it is? Why can't the State regulate it?"

"Because, Justice O'Connor, it is also an especially virulent form of expression of ideas relating to race, religion, politics—"

Justice Kennedy broke in. "You were—you were saying that the State can go—doesn't have to have a sterile law on intimidation. It can go further, but not as far as this. What is this midpoint?"

I answered by trying to draw a distinction between laws that penalized conduct, and even racist intent, from laws that singled out certain symbols. Many of the justices jumped in on this issue, and the argument proceeded back and forth with jousting on this point for another ten minutes, until Justice Breyer jumped in with a deep study of linguistics and the philosophy of language.

"You have a very interesting point," Breyer started. "And as I've been thinking about it, it seems to me that the—a difficulty, possible difficulty with it is that the First Amendment doesn't protect words. It protects use of words for certain purposes. And it doesn't protect, for example, a symbol. It protects a thing that counts as a symbol when used for symbolic purposes."

"That's correct," I accepted.

"So just as it doesn't protect the words, 'I will kill you,' but protects them when used in a play, but not when used as a threat, so it doesn't protect the burning of the cross when used as a threat and not as a symbol."

"That is correct," I repeated.

"And now we have a statute that says you can use it as a symbol, but you can't use it as a threat," Breyer continued. "And therefore, the First Amendment doesn't apply. Now, if that's the right analysis, then what's your response?"

"Your Honor," I replied, "that everything you said up until the *very end* we would accept."

The entire courtroom burst into loud laughter. I added, "I have a— I have a hunch I have to at least say that much."

There was more laughter, which I let roll, before getting serious. "And Justice Breyer, it comes to this, that you cannot make the judgment that this law in its actual impact only penalizes those acts of cross burning that result in threat. It certainly chills, Justice Breyer, a wide range of expression, as it did in this case, that cannot plausibly be understood as a threat of bodily harm in any realistic sense. Every time the Ku Klux Klan conducts one of its rallies, at the height of its rally, it burns a large cross, and it plays a hymn such as the *Old Rugged Cross*, or *Onward Christian Soldiers* or *Amazing Grace*, and this is a ritual that it engages in. Now, it is inconceivable—there is absolutely nothing in this record that says that *every time* the Klan does that, that is, in fact, a true threat."

"No, it isn't," Scalia jumped in, "so long as the Klan doesn't do it in— in sight of a public highway, or on somebody else's property, there's not a chance that this statute would apply to them."

We were at a critical fulcrum. Scalia seemed to be saying that offensive speech is fine, as long as it is done in private for nobody else to witness. I attacked this view head-on. "The First Amendment value here," I insisted, "is that speech, particularly disturbing and offensive speech that runs contrary to our mainstream values that the majority of us embrace, is ineffective unless it is put out to the world where others can see it. And as Justice Brandeis said in *Whitney versus California* in his concurring opinion, you don't make the world safer by driving the speech of hate groups such as the Ku Klux Klan underground. In many societies in this world, you can ban racial supremacist groups."

Before I could finish the thought, Justice Breyer jumped in again, this time questioning me about the prima facie evidence provision of the cross-burning law. This time his line of questioning favored our position. Bob Dylan wrote that it doesn't take a weatherman to know which way the wind blows. I could see where the wind was blowing, and now clinging to the prima facie evidence provision as the Achilles' heel of the Virginia statute seemed like a good Plan B. I agreed with Justice Breyer that the prima facie evidence provision endangered protected speech.

I ended by emphasizing the power of the cross, whether sanctified or desecrated, as a symbol. The cross, I insisted, was a "symbol that you must concede is one of the most powerful religious symbols in human history. It is the symbol of Christianity, the symbol of the crucifixion of Christ. When the cross is burned, in much the same way as when the flag is burned, undoubtedly the burner is playing on that underlying positive repository of meaning to make the intense negative point, often a point that strikes us as horrible and as evil and disgusting, but that's—"

And this was when Justice Ginsburg quietly but firmly challenged me, in what I believe was one of the pivotal turning points in the argument.

"Mr. Smolla," Ginsburg pressed, "there's a huge difference between a flag and a burning cross, and it's been pointed out in the briefs. The flag is a symbol of our government, and one of the things about free speech is we can criticize the President, the Supreme Court, anybody, and feel totally free about doing that. It's the symbol of government. But the cross is not attacking the government. It's attacking people, threatening their lives and limbs. And so, I don't—I think you have to separate the symbol that is the burning cross from other symbols that are critical of government, but that don't—that aren't a threat to personal safety."

As Justice Ginsburg spoke, I felt our case slip-sliding away. Her point was compelling. It's one thing to criticize the government, burning the flag. It's another thing to hurt people, terrorizing them with a burning cross. If Justice Ginsburg, perhaps the most liberal member of the court, was about to rule against us, and if Justices Thomas and Scalia, the two most conservative members but also strong free speech advocates, had nothing but disdain for our position, I could see losing the case, 9–0.

"Justice Ginsburg," I replied, "I only partially accept that dichotomy. In fact, when the Klan engages in cross-burning, as it did in *Brandenburg versus Ohio*, and as it did here, it is—it is a mélange of messages. Yes, to some degree, it is a horizontal message of hate speech, the Klan members attacking Jews and Catholics and African-Americans and all of the various people that have been the point of its hatred over the years. But it's also engaged in dissent and in a political message. If you remember in *Brandenburg versus Ohio*, Brandenburg says if the Congress doesn't change things, some revenges will have to be taken. In this case, President Clinton was talked about by the Klan members. Hillary Clinton was talked about by the Klan members. Racial preferences and the idea that they're using taxes to support minority groups. There is a jumble of political anger."

Oral arguments flit back and forth among themes with lightning speed. Justice Kennedy opened a new line of questioning, suggesting that my argument would give evil speakers a "free ride" of protection when their real purpose is threat and intimidation. I replied that there is no free ride if the government simply polices threats and violence through neutral laws. "The First Amendment requires that we flip the question," I insisted. "It is not why can't the government single out this particular form of expression. It is why do you need to."

Justice Scalia got back in the battle, returning once more to his gun theme. I matched him by saying that a gun was a weapon, whereas a burning cross was not. Justice Scalia retorted, "It's an *unloaded* gun. This is an unloaded gun that's being brandished."

The courtroom erupted in laughter again—the kind of mocking laughter that I processed as "Scalia just got you, Smolla."

I started an attempted comeback but couldn't get a word in, between the rolling peels of laughter and Justice Scalia's continuing assertions—he was on a roll and loving it.

"So, once it's unloaded," he snarled, "it's nothing but a symbol."

I could not accept this. "It's still a weapon, Your Honor," I rejoined, "and it is gigantically different from a cross. If I take a torch. What would be the difference between brandishing a torch and brandishing a cross?"

"One hundred years of history!" interrupted Justice Kennedy, and again the courtroom crowd burst into laughter.

Gamely, I tried to come back. "Exactly, Justice Kennedy, that's the difference," I said. "And that one hundred years of history is on the side of freedom of speech, that it is one hundred years of history that a particular group has capitalized on this particular ritual to make not only points that are threatening, but to advance their agenda."

Justice Souter then thoughtfully brought us all back to his earlier observation that the last hundred years had made cross burning a kind of Pavlovian trigger for fear. My answer, looking back, anticipated *exactly* the event that would later transpire in Charlottesville, though I chose Richmond as the hypothetical setting.

"Imagine that you have two rallies going on side-by-side," I said. "The Klan is going to engage in a rally, and then a group that wants to counter the Klan's message, a Christian group, has a counter-rally in a public forum in Richmond. And imagine that at the height of those two rallies, the Klan ignites its cross. Under this statute, the Klan can be prosecuted, the other group cannot."

"What if the other group all are brandishing guns as Justice Scalia said?" Justice Souter asked.

"Then round them up, Your Honor." I replied. This time *I* got the entire courtroom laughing and, I felt, seeing my point.

Minutes later, the argument was over.

Years later, I went back over the transcript of the hearing. I'd been asked seventy questions in thirty minutes, a pace of a question every thirty seconds.

When the argument ended, we did the ritual thing of walking down the Supreme Court building's front steps, greeted by throngs of reporters and live broadcasts from CNN and Fox. When asked how I thought it had gone, I had nothing coherent to say. When asked how I thought it would come out, I also had nothing newsworthy to say.

Heading into the argument, I had been confident of two favorable votes, Justices Scalia and Thomas. Heading out of the argument, I was confident that those two votes were dead-set against us. Every other justice who spoke in the argument made observations strongly antagonistic to our position, though sometimes tempered. I thought about how Edward Cleary was concerned that his win in *R.A.V.* might be imperiled. I saw the possibility of an even greater sea change. Perhaps the move away from the *Chaplinsky* and *Beauharnais* "order and morality" theory and toward the Holmes/Brandeis marketplace theory was about to be reversed. *Chaplinsky* and *Beauharnais* could be on a comeback.

The Supreme Court announced its decision on the morning April 7, 2003. Within minutes I was flooded with phone calls from reporters. They all wanted to know one thing: Had I *won*, or had I *lost*?

The answer was not exactly obvious on a first quick read.

In the *Adventures of Huckleberry Finn*, Huck says of "Mr. Mark Twain" that he "told the truth, mainly." Huck inspired my answer to the inquiring reporters. "We won the case, mainly."

The Supreme Court overturned the conviction of the Klan leader, Barry Black, but did not overturn the convictions of the two Virginia Beach cross burners, Elliott and O'Mara.[28] The plurality opinion was written by Justice Sandra Day O'Connor, joined by Chief Justice Rehnquist, Justice Stevens, and Justice Breyer. Justice O'Connor seemed to breathe new life into *Chaplinsky*, noting that the "First Amendment permits 'restrictions upon the content of speech in a few limited areas,' which are 'of such slight social value as a step to truth that any benefit that may be derived from them is clearly outweighed by the social interest in order and morality.'"[29] O'Connor stated that "a State may punish those words 'which by their very utterance inflict injury or tend to incite an immediate breach of the peace.'"[30] O'Connor stated that the court had "consequently held that fighting words—'those personally abusive epithets which, when addressed to the ordinary citizen, are, as a matter of common knowledge, inherently likely to provoke violent reaction'—are generally proscribable under the First Amendment."[31]

Yet Justice O'Connor also acknowledged that under the *Brandenburg* standard, "the constitutional guarantees of free speech and free press do not permit a State to forbid or proscribe advocacy of the use of force or of law violation except where such advocacy is directed to inciting or producing imminent lawless action and is likely to incite or produce such action." Most importantly, the plurality held, the First Amendment permits the government to ban a "true threat."[32]

Such "true threats" encompass those statements "where the speaker means to communicate a serious expression of an intent to commit an act of unlawful violence to a particular individual or group of individuals."[33] In a key passage, Justice O'Connor elaborated: "Intimidation in the constitutionally proscribable sense of the word is a type of true threat, where a speaker directs a threat to a person or group of persons with the intent of placing the victim in fear of bodily harm or death."[34] O'Connor recounted in detail the history of cross burning and the history of the Ku Klux Klan, establishing that sometimes cross burning clearly was a "true threat," yet sometimes not.

In a passage that seemed to retreat from *R.A.V.*, O'Connor held that under *R.A.V.*, a state may choose to ban a particularly virulent form of threat, such as that posed by cross burning. Virginia's statute, O'Connor held, did not run afoul of the First Amendment insofar as it bans cross burning with intent to intimidate. Unlike the statute at issue in *R.A.V.*, O'Connor reasoned, "the Virginia statute does not single out for opprobrium only that speech directed toward 'one of the specified disfavored topics.'"[35] Elaborating, O'Connor argued that under the Virginia law "it does not matter whether an individual burns a cross with intent to intimidate because of the victim's race, gender, or religion, or because of the victim's 'political affiliation, union membership, or homosexuality.'"[36]

If in Justice O'Connor's view it would be possible under the First Amendment for a state to pass *some* kind of cross-burning law, the law that Virginia passed was not constitutional. The prima facie evidence provision of the law stated that "any such burning of a cross shall be prima facie evidence of an intent to intimidate a person or group of persons."[37]

This, O'Connor held, was beyond what the Constitution would allow, for it permitted a jury to find the intent to intimidate with no actual evidence of such intent beyond the burning cross itself. As the history of cross-burning indicates, the plurality elaborated, "a burning cross is not always intended to intimidate. Rather, sometimes the cross burning is a statement of ideology, a symbol of group solidarity. It is a ritual used at Klan gatherings, and it is used to represent the Klan itself."[38] Among other contexts, cross burnings have appeared in movies such as *Mississippi Burning*, and in plays such as the stage adaptation of Sir Walter Scott's *The Lady of the Lake*. In an important victory for freedom of speech, the plurality admonished that

> it may be true that a cross burning, even at a political rally, arouses a sense of anger or hatred among the vast majority of citizens who see a burning cross. But this sense of anger or hatred is not sufficient to ban all cross burnings. As Gerald Gunther has stated, "The lesson I have drawn from my childhood in Nazi Germany and my happier adult life in this country is the need to walk the sometimes difficult path of denouncing the bigot's hateful ideas with all my power, yet at the same time challenging any community's attempt to suppress hateful ideas by force of law." The prima facie evidence provision in this case ignores all of the contextual factors that are necessary to decide whether a particular cross burning is intended to intimidate. The First Amendment does not permit such a shortcut.[39]

Justice Souter, joined by Kennedy and Ginsburg, took an even stronger free speech position than Justice O'Connor, relying on *R.A.V.* Those three justices would have struck down the entire Virginia law, and all three convictions, because the law was tainted with the same kinds of viewpoint-based and content-based distinctions that the court had found constitutionally impermissible in *R.A.V.*

Justices Scalia and Thomas, apparently defecting from their positions in *R.A.V.*, would have gone well beyond the plurality. Thomas would have been willing to allow a state to attack all cross burnings, and to permit a state to employ a prima facie evidence provision and would have affirmed all three convictions. Scalia wrote primarily to express the view that the prima facie evidence provision is probably a mere permissible inference of the sort that in his view would not violate the First Amendment.

Translated, all this meant that Barry Elton Black was home free. His speech was not a true threat, and the jury instruction that was pivotal in convicting him violated the Constitution. No such jury instruction had been given in O'Mara's and Elliott's cases, however, and the Supreme Court sent their two cases back down to the Virginia Supreme Court to decide what to do with them. The Virginia Supreme Court, "on remand" (on "return" from the Supreme Court), upheld the convictions of O'Mara and Elliott.[40]

Where did *Virginia v. Black* leave the First Amendment rules governing the sort of hate speech planned by the alt-right leaders and the Klan for August in Charlottesville? My most honest answer is, "in a state of confusion." Clearly, absolute bans on the use of particular symbols, such as burning crosses or Nazi swastikas, remain unconstitutional after *Virginia v. Black*. So too, after *Virginia v. Black* a state may still not take a "shortcut" and enact rules that treat the use of certain symbols or the use of certain words as *automatically* constituting an "incitement" or a "true threat."

What *Virginia v. Black* may allow (even though *R.A.V.* did not) are laws that prohibit certain types of hate speech, *provided* they have built-in certain "hard" requirements, such as the *Brandenburg* incitement standard, or the "true threat" standard.

Years later, I had occasion to talk to Justice Thomas about *Virginia v. Black*. I was then dean of the Washington and Lee Law School. Justice Thomas had been invited to speak at Washington and Lee. He came and delivered an eloquent address on constitutional law in the Robert E. Lee Chapel on the campus, to a packed audience. After the event we had a dinner party in his honor, and I was seated with him, in a group that included faculty members and law students. Thomas was a convivial and gregarious dinner companion. The trip to Washington and Lee, located in Lexington, had been especially fun for him, because he was able to combine it with a trip to nearby Virginia Tech, where he watched his favorite football team, the University of Nebraska Cornhuskers, play the Virginia Tech Hokies.

Thomas's wife is a graduate of the University of Nebraska, and during football season he delights in driving his own large recreational vehicle across country to Nebraska games. He had driven his forty-foot Prevost

RV to Blacksburg for the game. To make the trip even more fun, Thomas had also attended a major NASCAR race at nearby Bristol Speedway. He had parked his RV in the camping and tailgating area for the NASCAR race the night before and had set up his site, including his barbecue grill. Thomas was quietly grilling the evening meal when a good old boy in a cowboy hat holding two Budweiser beers came up to him. "You that *judge*!" he exclaimed. "You that *judge*!" The man extended a friendly hand to offer Thomas a beer, but Thomas declined, as he does not drink. He introduced himself to the man, acknowledging that he was Clarence Thomas, from the United States Supreme Court. Warming to the conversation, the sociable stranger said to Thomas, "So tell me, how you think *Dale* gonna do?" He was referring to NASCAR driver Dale Earnhardt Jr. Justice Thomas now paused as he was telling us this story and looked squarely at me. "So, tell me, Dean Smolla," he said, "how do you think Ruth Bader Ginsburg would have answered that question?"

We burst out laughing at his story. A few minutes later, to my infinite chagrin, one of the law students asked Justice Thomas about *Virginia v. Black* and my oral argument in the case, and the fact that it had become famous for being one of the few times Justice Thomas ever spoke in the Supreme Court. I was mortified. I would never ask any justice or judge to talk about a case in which I had been an advocate—for me it was something just not done. And I was concerned that Justice Thomas would consider the question a similar breach of judicial propriety and etiquette. Once again, I could not have been more wrong.

Thomas paused for a moment, then broke into a gargantuan smile. He pointed a finger at me and cackled with a huge belly laugh, "I *GOT* you! I *GOT* you! I *GOT* you!"

There was more laughter. I laughed too, then immediately changed the subject. "So, Justice Thomas, how do you think Nebraska's gonna do?" That was all it took to move us on to college football for the rest of the dinner. But enough had been revealed. *He got me.*

24

THE IDEA OF THE UNIVERSITY

The University of Virginia, with the rest of Charlottesville, was bracing for the Unite the Right onslaught. As with many American universities, UVA's relationship to the city surrounding it was complicated. It is
not at all unusual for universities to be perceived as *in* the city in which
they reside, but not *of* the city. As I consider my two alma maters, Yale,
where I attended college, and Duke, where I attended law school, the
distance between town and gown was palpable. One of my daughters,
Erin, attended Duke as an undergraduate and a law student decades after
me. Another daughter, Corey, then attended Yale for college. As we compared family notes over our experiences, some progression in engagement
appeared to have taken place. Yale, which rests in the geographic center
of New Haven, Connecticut, had established more outreach and engagement programs with the city than existed when I was there. Duke had
made similar progress with Durham, North Carolina. Yet even so, parent and children were agreed that members of the university community
thought of themselves principally as citizens of Yale or Duke, not New

Haven or Durham. In her book *Becoming*, Michelle Obama makes a similar point about the University of Chicago. Michelle Robinson grew up in Chicago's South Side, where the University of Chicago is located, in the City's Hyde Park neighborhood. Yet to her, the university was an insular fortress, largely disconnected from the neighborhoods and city that surrounded it. Michelle Obama would, later in her professional career, be hired by Michael Riordan at the University of Chicago Medical Center to create programs to make the university more relevant to Chicago's South Side, and the South Side relevant to the university. My life would later intersect with Riordan's, as he moved from Chicago to take over the Greenville Hospital System in Greenville, South Carolina, at the same time that I moved to Greenville to become president of Furman University. We worked on similar programs to attempt to more deeply connect both Furman and the Greenville Hospital System to the community surrounding both institutions. While we made some progress, the task was not easy.

In Charlottesville, much the same dynamic existed. In the collection of essays edited by Professors Louis P. Nelson and Claudrena N. Harold on the events in Charlottesville in 2017, they observe that prior to the summer of 2017, the University of Virginia as an institution "generally positioned itself as separate from the city."[1] To be sure, many individuals within the UVA community were committed to the community, but this was not the institutional ethos of the university as a whole. As Nelson and Harold put it, "Faculty, staff, and some students understood themselves to be citizens of the city and participated in these conversations as individual activists, but the institution stood alongside the city disengaged."[2]

There were additional layers of complexity and intensity for UVA. Some of the layers were unique to UVA, arising from its founding by Thomas Jefferson, who owned slaves, to its complicity in the eugenics movement and the resurgence of racism in the 1920s. Other layers were not so unique, but rather partook of the shared culture of higher education in the United States. The conflicts of America's culture war and in the nation's constitutional unconscious have always played out with special intensity on public and private university and college campuses. Such conflicts put in play the very "idea of the university."[3] The unique position of the University of Virginia as a place that mattered in spirit and substance for the Unite the Right rally was surely registered by all sides.

The two principal organizers for the Unite the Right rally, Richard Spencer and Jason Kessler, were both UVA graduates. It was no accident that their initial alt-right rally in May 2017 had featured a nighttime torch march through the campus. Virtually all American conservatives, from the alt-right to the far-but-not-quite-alt-right to the mainstream right have for decades decried a perceived culture of leftist political correctness on American campuses. UVA was the ultimate higher education embodiment of all the crosscurrents of American culture. Thomas Jefferson, its founder, was a champion of freedom of speech and religion and the notion that "all men are created equal," yet he owned and had sex with his slaves. Over the course of two centuries, many famous world-class intellectuals, both conservative and liberal, taught at the University of Virginia. At the Virginia Law School, Justice Antonin Scalia had been among the professoriate. Yet no honest realist can contest that in more recent decades, the progressive left largely dominated UVA faculty politics, as it largely dominates the politics of many American colleges and universities. I personally had a friend on the UVA Law School faculty who told me a story of a faculty hiring committee rejecting a candidate on the grounds that he was "too pale, male, and Yale." While of course there were conservatives and liberals on the UVA faculty, and conservatives and liberals in the student body, in 2017 the liberals held the dominant genes and the conservatives the recessive. Richard Spencer and Jason Kessler were well plugged into this vibe, and their decision to stage the Unite the Right rally was not just about the *city* of Charlottesville, which had declared itself the "capital of the resistance" to all things alt-right and Donald Trump, but to the progressive politics of the University of Virginia and, by extension, virtually all American campuses.

None of this was lost on the leadership of the University of Virginia. At a dinner of vegetable pasta in the UVA president's residence at Carr's Hill, just a few days before the Unite the Right rally, President Teresa Sullivan confided in her friend, Professor Larry Sabato, one of the university's most famous scholars and political pundits, that the symbolism and history of the UVA campus might be too much for the supremacists to resist. Sullivan said to Sabato, "I'm just really worried that they might surprise us and show up at the Rotunda or on the Lawn."[4]

Faculty and administrative leaders at the University of Virginia played an important role in the lead-up to the counterprotests for the Unite the Right rally.

Walter Heinecke was an associate professor of educational research, statistics, and evaluation in the Department of Educational Leadership, Foundations and Policy at UVA's Curry School of Education, where he taught courses in qualitative research methods, program evaluation, and educational policy studies, as well as undergraduate courses on civic engagement and activism. Heinecke was disturbed by how events had turned out at the July 8 Klan rally. "I was a little disappointed with the Klan rally when the police declared it an unlawful assembly immediately after the Klan left," he told the UVA student newspaper, the *Cavalier Daily*. "I didn't know if that [the declaration] was appropriate."[5] As Heinecke saw it, "I think that part of the problem that occurred was that police were over-militarized." This added to the tension that day, and it contributed to the sense that the police were on the side of the supremacists. "I think that that kind of police presence leads to more problems and creates a situation of tension," Heinecke said. "I thought that maybe the next time around they could do a better job of thinking about the appearance of militarization that's going on here."[6]

When the Unite the Right rally was announced, Heinecke urged the city to reject the permit application and not allow the rally. Alternatively, he argued that the rally should be moved, or that better alternative forums for counterprotesters be created. "I wrote them an email and urged them to either cancel the permit based on safety and cost or if not, I thought that they should move it to a more secure location," Heinecke said. "Barring that, I urged them to get with the police department and ensure that . . . a space for lawful assembly was provided to protesters so we didn't repeat the mistakes of after the Klan rally."[7]

None of Heinecke's efforts drew any response from the city. And so he took a more aggressive approach, applying for permits in his own right to conduct counterdemonstrations. "My purpose in doing it is to provide a place for demonstrators to freely assemble, and the second purpose I have is to promote public safety and security," Heinecke said. "We saw what happened after the Klan left, and the police moved quickly to declare that an unlawful assembly. I learned something being at that protest and that rally about the police discretion to declare any group of three or more an unlawful assembly in terms of shutting it down."[8]

Heinecke's permits were approved by the city, but no police protection was promised. The Charlottesville Police Department explained to

Heinecke that there were no spare police assets available to protect the counterprotesters at the two parks for which Heinecke's permit requests had been approved, Justice and McGuffey Parks.[9]

Professor Anne M. Coughlin held the Lewis F. Powell Jr. chair at the UVA Law School and was one of the school's principal criminal law scholars. Besides criminal law, her specialties included feminist jurisprudence and law and the humanities. Coughlin had been active throughout the summer in urging Charlottesville's city and police officials to address more proactively the threats of violence posed by the supremacist elements descending on the city.

Lawton Tufts worked at the UVA Law School as the director of public service and alumni advising. Before joining UVA, Tufts had practiced law in Lexington, Virginia, where he litigated criminal and family law cases at a small firm and served as a guardian *ad litem* for children. He had also worked as an assistant public defender for the Charlottesville-Albemarle Public Defender's Office, a role in which he represented hundreds of indigent defendants, and served on the Charlottesville Police Citizens Advisory Board.

Tufts took on the role of ambassador, seeking to arrange a meeting among Blacks Lives Matter, Congregate Charlottesville, Rev. Alvin Edwards, and the Charlottesville Police Department. Black Lives Matter was not interested in attending if Police Chief Thomas attended, and so the city sent Mike Murphy, the assistant city manager, to the meeting instead. Anne Coughlin attended the meeting with Tufts.

Coughlin and Tufts were alarmed by what they learned at the meeting. The right-wing groups, they were told, would be attending the event armed with weapons. Yet the city of Charlottesville seemed to be adopting a laissez-faire attitude, which Coughlin thought "crazy and terrifying."[10] Tufts would later tell the Heaphy Report investigators that it appeared to him that the focus of the police was on restoring order after it broke down, not preserving order before conflict began.[11]

The University of Virginia's president in 2017 was Teresa Sullivan. Her take on the Unite the Right rally is especially illuminating. Having myself been the president of a university in the South, I begin this portrait of UVA's president with the qualification that I know it ain't easy.

In an interview with Julia Schmalz in the *Chronicle of Higher Education*, when Sullivan was asked about UVA's role in the events of the summer of 2017, she asserted that in Charlottesville "you see a clash of red and blue cultures in a way that you don't in a lot of places."[12] When challenged about the role of the university in the free-speech debate, Sullivan responded, "Well, our first responsibility is educational. Some current studies that have come out indicate that this generation of college students doesn't really understand or agree with free speech as it's been interpreted by the Supreme Court. And so making it clear what free speech is and is not, I think, is part of what our job is." Sullivan elaborated: "The Klan has the right to rally. We might not agree with what they say. We can publicly disagree with what they have to say. But they do have the right to be there and to say it. By the same point of view, I think our students have the right to hear different viewpoints. And they don't have to agree with those viewpoints. But they have the right to hear about it."[13]

Sullivan was also tuned into the agenda of the alt-right and its strategy of deliberate provocation. "I think that they exist in part to be provocative," she said. "I think they exist in part to have people take the bait." Sullivan then made a stronger point, which goes to the heart of whether the Unite the Right rally really was or was not appropriately deemed protected by the First Amendment. "I think that there is, *at some level, a desire for violence*," Sullivan said. And that is what I think we have to be on our guard about."[14] It was this insight that the alt-right *sought* reactive violence that led Sullivan to place herself in the "ignore them" camp.[15]

Yet as I knew well from my own tenure as a university president, taking the "ignore them" position inevitably leads to critics asserting that one lacks the moral compass or fortitude to confront evil.

Again, the job ain't easy. If it was, anyone could do it.

The real world of the modern college or university is what A. Bartlett Giamatti, former president of Yale (and later commissioner of baseball), described as "a free and ordered space."[16] The modern university reflects society itself. The most successful societies worldwide are those that have managed to achieve a healthy balance between freedom and order in the three great marketplaces of human endeavor: the political marketplace, the economic marketplace, and the marketplace of ideas. Our efforts to find this healthy balance are best guided by one overarching goal: to achieve the maximum freedom possible, consistent with our basic needs for stability and security.

This core tension between liberty and order extends far beyond "order" in the physical sense. The modern university is sometimes conceived of as a cauldron of fierce competition—for admission, for tenure and promotion, for athletic championships, for giant endowments—and as a "super marketplace of ideas," a no-holds-barred place where anything goes, nothing is censored, and only the strongest and fittest survive. Yet simultaneously, the modern campus is often conceived of as an orderly and moral space—a community of scholars and students organized around such values as respect for human dignity, cultural and religious pluralism, collegial civility, and rational discourse.[17]

At the University of Virginia in the summer of 2017, these were not just academic debates. The divisions ran increasingly deep, leading to distrust, a mutual skittishness about sharing information, and a tendency to blame the other side for anything that went wrong. In fighting the alt-right, the University of Virginia itself found itself a house divided.

25

HECKLER'S VETO

Charlottesville's city attorney Craig Brown and his deputy, Lisa Robertson, were the principal in-house lawyers providing legal counsel to the city manager and the city council. From the beginning, Brown and Robertson took the view that any attempt at outright cancellation of the Unite the Right rally would be immediately overturned by courts as a violation of the First Amendment. The growing concerns over the rally, they reasoned, arose from the possibility of clashes with counterprotesters. If by raising the rhetoric of defiance and confrontation counterprotesters could shut down the rally, this would be an example of what is known in free speech jurisprudence as the "heckler's veto." The First Amendment in modern times generally stands against acceding to the power of heckling counter-protesters to shut down messages with which they disagree.

When hecklers and protesters gather to express their disagreement with a speaker's message, the rights of the speaker, the rights of the audience that wishes to hear the speaker's views, and the rights of the protesters are in tension. In the parlance of free speech law, this is typically referred to as the heckler's veto problem. As the phrase suggests, the conundrum is whether to permit the heckler to "veto" the right of the speaker to speak and the willing listeners to listen.

An early Supreme Court opinion started the law down the wrong path in dealing with this conundrum. In *Feiner v. New York* (1951),[1] a college student named Irving Feiner was making a speech on a street corner in a black residential neighborhood in Syracuse, New York. Feiner was part of a group protesting the cancellation by authorities of a scheduled speech by a lawyer (a former assistant attorney general) on race discrimination and civil liberties. A crowd of about seventy-five or eighty persons, black and white, gathered around him. Feiner referred to President Truman as a "bum," to the American Legion as "a Nazi Gestapo," and to the mayor of Syracuse as a "champagne-sipping bum" who "does not speak for the Negro people." Feiner further proclaimed that "the Negroes don't have equal rights; they should rise up in arms and fight for their rights." Some of the people listening to Feiner's speech were upset by his message. One man in the crowd stated that if the police did not get "that S.O.B." off the stand, he would do it himself. Two police officers who arrived at the scene claimed they heard and saw "angry mutterings" and some "restless pushing, shoving, and milling." The police asked Feiner to stop speaking, but he refused. They then "told" him to get down off his soapbox, and ultimately "demanded" that he get down, but he kept on talking. He was arrested and charged with breach of peace.

The Supreme Court, in an opinion by Chief Justice Frederick Vinson, sided with the authorities and against Feiner, holding that his free speech rights were not violated. The court claimed to be "well aware that the ordinary murmurings and objections of a hostile audience cannot be allowed to silence a speaker" and claimed as well that it was "also mindful of the possible danger of giving overzealous police officials complete discretion to break up otherwise lawful public meetings." Even so, the court held that Feiner had passed the "bounds of argument or persuasion" and instead undertaken "incitement to riot." The police in such situations, the court held, are not "powerless to prevent a breach of the peace," and Feiner's speech constituted a "clear and present danger" of such a breach.

Three justices—Black, Douglass, and Minton—dissented. Justice Black was particularly passionate, describing the holding of the court as making "a mockery of the free speech guarantees of the First and Fourteenth Amendments."

Feiner was decided in 1951, and like many other cases of that epoch, it demonstrated precious little commitment to the protection of free expression. And like many other cases of that period, it has been passed by, both by time and law. Cases such as *Brandenburg* and *Hess* and *Claiborne Hardware* have created a standard for "incitement to riot" far more rigorous than the loose and easy conclusions reached in *Feiner*. Rather than arrest the speaker who is irritating listeners with unpopular views, modern First Amendment doctrine places the burden on the listeners to avert their eyes, close their ears, or simply walk away. The relatively low-grade uneasiness exhibited by the crowd in *Feiner* would simply not satisfy today's First Amendment requirements in our open public forum spaces. Even when crowd anger escalates to potentially dangerous levels, the soundest view of prevailing First Amendment principles is that it is incumbent on the police to quell the would-be rioters through reasonable crowd control measures, rather than suppress what would otherwise be considered protected speech.

I had been writing criticisms of the decision in *Feiner* for some time as a lawyer and scholar and devoted a fair amount of space criticizing the *Feiner* decision in a book I wrote titled *Free Speech in an Open Society*.[2] When the book came out, Irving Feiner tracked me down and called me. He was delighted with the critical treatment I'd given his case, and then he proceeded to tell me the real "inside story" of the grief and persecution that he had been subjected to for daring to speak out as a dissident. I was humbled, and wished I'd known enough to do his story better justice.

First Amendment scholar Frederick Schauer reflected on these conundrums in light of the events in Charlottesville. Schauer now teaches at the University of Virginia, where he is the David and Mary Harrison Distinguished Professor of Law. While the initial obligation of police is to protect the speaker who is delivering an offensive message provoking a hostile crowd, he observes, it is less clear "when, how, and on what basis the authorities can step in to restrict a speaker or force an end to a previously constitutionally protected event."[3]

There may, of course, be occasions in which the only feasible alternative is to remove the speaker from the scene. When a peaceful speaker's only "offense" is that his or her words are causing a hostile reaction, however, the better view is that the speaker should merely be taken into protective custody from the scene and transported to safety, but not arrested and charged. It is fundamentally antithetical to contemporary First Amendment principles to permit a "heckler's veto" of freedom of speech, in which persons who themselves violate the law by reacting with violence to speech that offends them are able to precipitate the arrest of a speaker who is obeying the law and exercising his or her constitutional rights.

What of situations that occur from time to time at public gatherings, including gatherings on university campuses, in which an invited speaker is peacefully delivering a message, and protesters and hecklers who oppose the speaker's position insist on counterdemonstrations? In such settings, the speaker, the audience wishing to hear the speaker's views, and the protesters all have legitimate First Amendment rights at stake. Our democracy would suffer if all heckling, protesting, and counterdemonstrations were shut down.

As a federal court put the point in *Landry v. Daley*, "Political campaigns, athletic events, public meetings and a host of other activities produce loud, confused or senseless shouting not in accord with fact, truth or right procedure to say nothing of not in accord with propriety, modesty, good taste or good manners. The happy cacophony of democracy would be stilted if all 'improper noises' in the normal meaning of the term were suppressed."[4]

These issues were placed in vivid focus during the tumultuous campaign rallies staged by Donald Trump, including the rallies in which counterprotesters were brusquely shoved away by Trump supporters.

Yet there may come a point in which the counterdemonstration so squelches the ability of an invited speaker to speak and a willing audience to listen that authorities are within their legitimate rights in forcing the hecklers to be quiet and let the speaker speak. In *Iowa v. Hardin*,[5] for example, the Supreme Court of Iowa addressed the constitutionality of a statute making it a misdemeanor to disturb or disrupt a lawful meeting of people. In upholding a conviction under the statute, the court held that purchasing a ticket to a political meeting does not give the defendant unlimited lawful authority to interrupt the meeting's speaker so as to disrupt the meeting and present objections to the speaker's comments. The case involved a group of protesters who paid the admission fee to see President George H. W. Bush speak at a political fund-raiser for two local Republican candidates. While Bush was giving his speech, the group began chanting slogans in opposition to the president's position on Iraq's invasion of Kuwait. After twice rejecting requests to cease their protest, the protesters were arrested and charged with disorderly conduct. The Iowa Supreme Court upheld the convictions, reasoning that if the hostility effectively prevents the speaker from speaking, and in that sense constitutes an outright bar to the speaker's exercise of his or her freedom to speak, the police are justified under *Brandenburg* in intervening against the audience. Until that threshold is reached, however, the First Amendment cautions us to indulge some degree of hostile chanting, sign-waving, booing, or hissing, though it may be disconcerting and offensive to the speaker or others in the audience.

In the lead-up to the Charlottesville Unite the Right rally, the classic heckler's veto problem was posed as dramatically as it ever has been. The possibility of imminent violence appeared quite likely. But was that violence the responsibility of the racist hate-mongers from the alt-right who sought to stage their demonstration, or the responsibility of those on the left who refused to let it go and ignore them but instead were intent on confronting the supremacists, even if violence ensued?

These questions would boil over into the federal district court of Judge Glen Conrad—the same judge who had decided the UVA assistant dean of students' suit against *Rolling Stone*—when the City of Charlottesville hit on the idea of not shutting down the Unite the Right rally but moving it.

If the city could not cancel the Unite the Right rally, might it not still be allowed to move the rally to a less dangerous location? By late July the "move the rally" idea was gaining momentum with the city council. The new location would be McIntire Park, which is not located in the downtown area near the Downtown Mall and UVA, but about a mile from the Downtown Mall and closer to the city's outer ring, in a vast forest-preserve type park, quite different from the small Emancipation Park, which was a tight urban plaza smaller than a square block. McIntire Park had the advantages of large open spaces, away from downtown shops, restaurants, courthouses, office buildings, churches, and synagogues, all of which might be damaged by unruly crowds. The legal mechanism would be to change the terms of the permit granted to Jason Kessler to hold the rally, dictating that the grant of the permit was conditional on a move to McIntire Park.

The First Amendment principles governing the terms on which permits may be granted for rallies were largely established in a 1992 decision arising from Georgia that also involved confrontations between white supremacists, including David Duke, and civil rights activists. The case was *Forsyth County, Georgia v. Nationalist Movement*.[6]

Forsyth County, a rural county located about thirty miles northeast of Atlanta, had a long history of racial troubles. In 1912, in a kind of ethnic purge, its entire population of African Americans, over one thousand people, was driven systematically from the county through a reign of terror. The racial violence ensued after the alleged rape of a white woman and the lynching of her accused African American assailant.[7] That purge lingered through history. In 1987, seventy-five years later, Forsyth County remained 99 percent white.

Hosea Williams, an Atlanta city councilman and civil rights activist, proposed a "March against Fear and Intimidation" for January 17, 1987, to remind people of this history and confront its lingering consequences. Led by Williams, some ninety civil rights demonstrators attempted to stage a parade in Cumming, Georgia, the Forsyth County seat.

The civil rights marchers were met by supremacist opponents—an essential reversal of the roles unfolding in 2017 in Charlottesville. The opponents included the local affiliate of the Ku Klux Klan, called the Forsyth County Defense League, a local branch of the Nationalist Movement. Other Cumming residents joined the Klan Nationalist Movement group, lining the parade route and peppering the marchers with racial slurs and throwing rocks and beer bottles. The local police were vastly outnumbered, and ultimately the racist counterprotesters forced the civil rights parade to a premature end.

Refusing to bow to this intimidation, Hosea Williams called for a massive new civil rights interracial "March for Brotherhood" demonstration, which he touted as the largest in the South since the heyday of the civil rights movement in the 1960s. Williams's plan was a remarkable success. On January 24, approximately twenty thousand marchers arrived in Cumming. Among those marching were Georgia's US senators Sam Nunn and Wyche Fowler; Congressman John Lewis, who had led the Bloody Sunday march decades before on the Edmund Pettus Bridge in Selma, Alabama; Coretta Scott King, the widow of the Dr. Martin Luther King Jr.; the Democratic presidential candidate and former senator Gary Hart; Mayor Andrew Young of Atlanta, Martin Luther King's protégé who was with King when he was shot; Rev. Jesse Jackson, who rose to prominence as a civil rights leader and ran for president; Rev. Ralph David Abernathy, a close friend of Martin Luther King and his roommate at the Loraine Hotel the day King was assassinated; the comedian and civil rights activist Dick Gregory; and Benjamin Hooks, the executive director of the NAACP.[8]

Their supremacist opponents numbered over one thousand and included David Duke. Many brandished Confederate flags and caps, wore Ku Klux Klan regalia, or appeared in camouflage combat fatigues, shouting at the marchers, "Nigger go home."[9] Some sporadic rock throwing and arrests occurred. David Duke was among those arrested or detained, for attempting to block a highway.[10]

No melees or other serious violence took place, however, because authorities were determined to police the demonstration and counter-demonstration with overwhelming force. More than three thousand state and local police and National Guardsmen were present to keep order.

That show of force probably saved lives, but it was expensive. The cost for security for the event was over $670,000. The state of Georgia paid $579,148, other governmental entities paid $29,759, and the City of Atlanta and Forsyth County itself paid most of the remainder.

The Forsyth County Board of Commissioners responded to these events by enacting a new ordinance on January 27, 1987, governing parades and demonstrations, requiring permits for all such activities. The ordinance required the permit applicant to defray the costs incurred by the county in handling such events by paying a fee, the amount of which was to be fixed "from time to time" by the board. A later amendment capped the total cost anyone could be charged at $1,000.

Two years later, in January 1989, the Nationalist Movement proposed to demonstrate on the County Courthouse steps in Cumming in opposition to the federal holiday commemorating the birthday of Martin Luther King. Following its new rules, the county imposed a seemingly token permit fee of one hundred dollars. Instead of paying the hundred bucks, the Nationalist Movement made a federal case out of it, claiming that the county's permit and fee process violated its First Amendment rights.

The American Civil Liberties Union joined the litigation, writing an amicus brief in favor of the Nationalist Movement racial supremacists.

The United States Supreme Court agreed with the Nationalist Movement, striking down the Forsyth County permit process, in an opinion written by Justice Harry Blackmun. The Supreme Court did not hold that government entities were barred from requiring permits, and it did not hold that government entities could not charge demonstrators fees to defray some of the costs of rallies and demonstrations. Rather, what the Supreme Court found objectionable was that the "Forsyth County ordinance contains more than the possibility of censorship through uncontrolled discretion."[11] In deciding how much to charge, the Forsyth County officials could take into account whether counterdemonstrators were likely to show up, thus driving up the costs. But taking the *reactions* of opponents into account, the Supreme Court held, made the government's decision a decision based on the *content* of the expression, not a mere content-neutral decision based solely on neutral logistical calculations, and this, coupled with the discretion the official was granted, rendered the Forsyth County permit system unconstitutional, *even with* the $1,000 overall cap and notwithstanding that the fee actually charged was just $100. "The fee assessed will depend on the administrator's measure of the amount of hostility likely to be created by the speech based on its content," the court explained. "Those wishing to express views unpopular with bottle throwers, for example, may have to pay more for their permit." This made the system unconstitutional, the court held, because "listeners' reaction to speech is not a content-neutral basis for regulation."[12]

The Supreme Court's decision in *Forsyth County* would prove enormously important as efforts to move the Charlottesville rally to McIntire Park gathered momentum.

Charlottesville's city officials sought advice from the city's lawyers. City Attorney Brown advised the city's leaders that any attempt to move the Unite the Right rally would likely face severe opposition in court.[13]

Mayor Signer was concerned that the advice the city was receiving from its in-house lawyers was too cautious, and so it was agreed to hire an outside law firm, Boies Schiller Flexner LLP, to evaluate the legality of moving the rally to McIntire Park.[14] In a closed city council meeting on August 2, the legal advice given to the city was that it could not legally move the rally unless it could demonstrate a "specific, credible threat" to public safety posed by the Unite the Right organizers.[15] The council was told that generalized threats of violence, promises to use violence in self-defense, and information that counterprotesters planned to use violence to quell a permit holder's speech were insufficient bases to move the event from Emancipation Park.

The council was also presented with logistical concerns by the Charlottesville police. All the police preparation had been based on the assumption that the rally would be held at Emancipation Park. While Police Chief Thomas agreed that a move to McIntire Park would be "marginally better" in terms of overall public safety, that margin was offset by the lack of planning for McIntire Park and by the fact that the counterprotesters had been granted permits for the downtown locations, which spread the police thin by forcing them to manage two fronts. There was also concern over keeping the groups separated in McIntire Park.[16]

By a vote of 4–1, the city council nevertheless voted to move the Unite the Right rally to McIntire Park. City Manager Maurice Jones was still not convinced that the move was the right thing to do, however, and asked for additional time to make a decision. In the end, Jones acquiesced in the council's decision.[17]

City officials invited Jason Kessler to a meeting to break the news to him about the planned move. On August 7, Kessler met with council member Michelle Christian, City Manager Jones, and Captain Wendy Lewis at the Parks and Recreation office. The pitch from the city officials was that media reports were now estimating that thousands would attend the rally, far more than Kessler's original estimate of four hundred in his permit application. Kessler pushed back, claiming that he still thought four hundred was the most realistic number, and that in any event he could not be responsible for how many ultimately showed. He also noted that Charlottesville had granted permits for the counterprotesters at the downtown McGuffey and Justice Parks. The meeting ended in an impasse. The city said that the Unite the Right rally could proceed, but only if moved to McIntire Park. Kessler said he and his group would be going to Emancipation Park no matter what.[18]

Kessler, much like the leaders of the Nationalist Movement in Forsyth County decades earlier, took his case to federal court, filing suit on Thursday, August 10, 2017, just two days before the scheduled event.[19] His litigation efforts were initially backed by a group called the Foundation for the Marketplace of Ideas Inc. This Michigan-based legal nonprofit had been formed in 2016 and was led by Kyle Bristow, who claimed that his foundation was "quickly becoming the legal muscle behind the alt-right movement." In April 2017, Bristow's group was behind the successful litigation that forced Auburn University to host Richard Spencer's talk. The group's board of directors include alt-right activist Mike Enoch; William Johnson, the chairman of the white nationalist American Freedom Party; and James Edwards, who runs the white nationalist *Political Cesspool* radio show.

Both the ACLU of Virginia and the Rutherford Institute, a public interest group located in the Charlottesville area, also joined with Kessler in the filing of his suit. "The ACLU of Virginia stands for the right to free expression for all, not just those whose opinions are in the mainstream or with whom the government agrees," said Claire Guthrie Gastañaga, executive director of the Virginia ACLU. "The city's action is unconstitutional in that it denies Mr. Kessler and his supporters the ability to fully express their views in the location most closely associated with their message while leaving in place permits granted other organizations with opposing views."[20] "Tolerance is a double-edged sword. It has to go both ways. This governmental exercise in intolerance and censorship of speech that may be distasteful to the majority of the populace is exactly what the First Amendment was intended to prevent," said constitutional attorney John W. Whitehead, president of the Rutherford Institute.[21]

Kessler alleged in his suit that the decision to revoke the permit for Emancipation Park was a violation of his civil liberties because it was based on the content of the speech that would be featured at the rally. The revocation of the permit, his suit asserted, was based on Kessler's viewpoint.

Backed by the ACLU, the Rutherford Institute, and the Foundation for the Marketplace of Ideas, Kessler's suit sought a federal court injunction preventing the city from moving the rally to McIntire Park and requiring the city to honor its original permit authorizing the rally to be held at Emancipation Park.

According to the Heaphy Report, some Charlottesville police officials were ambivalent about whether the rally should be moved to McIntire Park and may have been silently rooting for Kessler to win his lawsuit, keeping the rally at Emancipation Park.[22]

The case was assigned to Federal District judge Glen Conrad of the United States District Court for the Western District of Virginia, the judge who had presided over Dean Nicole Eramo's libel suit against *Rolling Stone*. Judge Conrad scheduled an emergency hearing on the motion for a preliminary injunction the next day, Friday, August 11. That Friday evening, in a six-page opinion, Conrad granted the motion and enjoined the revocation of the permit for Unite the Right rally at Emancipation Park.

Judge Conrad's six-page opinion recited the classic First Amendment proposition that "content-based restrictions—those that target speech based on its content—'are presumptively unconstitutional and may be justified only if the government proves they are narrowly tailored to serve compelling state interests.'"[23] Making a critical legal point, Conrad elaborated that content-based restrictions include not just government actions that are overtly based on the content of expression, but also those actions that cannot be justified without reference to the content of speech, or were adopted by the government because of disagreement with the message the speech conveys. It's not just what the government *says* its motivation is, but what the motivation of the government *actually* is. If government action against speech is motivated by disagreement with the message, that action presumptively violates the First Amendment. "Based on the current record," Conrad concluded, "Kessler has shown that he will likely prove that the decision to revoke his permit was based on the content of his speech."[24]

How could Judge Conrad reach such a conclusion? Was it not perfectly plausible that Charlottesville simply sought to move the demonstration to a place with greater open space, creating a safety valve release of the pressure-cooker hate steam that threatened to explode and spread dangerous shrapnel throughout the center of the city? Not so, Judge Conrad ruled. Charlottesville had revoked Kessler's permit, but not the permit of the counterdemonstrators. This disparity of treatment between the two groups, he ruled, suggested that it was the city's perception that Kessler's message was offensive, rather than a neutral application of safety concerns, that motivated the city's decision.[25] Concerns over the potentially explosive atmosphere, Conrad seemed to be saying, applied to both the Unite the Right side and the counterprotest side. But if that was the case, why move one rally and not the other? Charlottesville's actions had the appearance of banishing the bad guys to the boondocks while letting the good guys continue to enjoy the home field.

Judge Conrad also pointed to social media communications by members of the Charlottesville City Council indicating their disagreement with the views of Kessler and his alt-right crowd. And of course it was no secret that all of Charlottesville's leaders were disgusted and repulsed by the racism of the Unite the Right coalition. Of course they were, as most Americans of goodwill were. And they made no secret of that contempt. As Judge Conrad saw it, however, this rejection of the alt-right's message cast a pall on any decision made by the city's leaders that impacted negatively on the plans of the Unite the Right group. Given that the city's leadership plainly hated these hate groups, any action against them came to the court with a presumptive taint.

Charlottesville's efforts to base the decision to move the rally on raw numbers of attendees, Conrad held, was "purely speculative."[26] Nobody really knew how many people would attend the Unite the Right rally as supporters of the rally's causes, or for that matter how many counterprotesters would arrive in opposition.

Judge Conrad's opinion then turned to what may truly have been the heart of the matter. The real concern of the city, the judge suggested, was the potential for trouble when the alt-right demonstrators and counter-demonstrators clashed. Yet the counterprotesters who were bent on confronting Kessler and his alt-right compatriots were likely to seek him out wherever the Unite the Right rally was staged. The confronters were going to confront, whether at Emancipation Park or McIntire Park. Moving the rally to the edge of town would not ensure that confrontation would be skirted.

Weighing all these factors, Judge Conrad was convinced that the equities favored Kessler. One might ask, what would be the big deal to Kessler and the Unite the Right demonstrators if the rally were moved to McIntire Park? The big deal was that Emancipation Park was where the Robert E. Lee statue, facing impending removal, was located. A rally defending the Lee statue would not be the same without the Lee statue. And then there was the general principle of the thing. The Unite the Right organizers had obtained a permit for Emancipation Park. To push them elsewhere smacked of pushing them around because they were undesirable. On one level, the move may have seemed a trivial or fleeting inconvenience.

But under modern First Amendment marketplace principles, this was precisely the sort of seemingly trivial inconvenience that often counted a lot. Citing the maxim that "the loss of First Amendment freedoms, for even minimal periods of time, unquestionably constitutes irreparable injury,"[27] Judge Conrad granted the preliminary injunction.

The Unite the Right rally would not be moved.

Eli Mosley, in charge of Unite the Right logistics, would now execute Plan Green.

Channels of Communication

"The medium is the message."[1] So declared the celebrated Canadian philosopher Marshall McLuhan in 1964. I was eleven years old then, and though too young, immature, and insouciant to know or care who Marshall McLuhan was, I would have gotten the message. The medium was television. There were all sorts of messages—Elvis and the Beatles on *The Ed Sullivan Show* and the Cuban Missile Crisis and the assassination and funeral of President John F. Kennedy—moments I still remember almost minute by minute with total recall. Yet I also think I get, in some gauzy sense, what McLuhan meant. These were *shared* messages, *shared* moments. Everybody watched, on *television*. And though for news you had your pick of channels—there were NBC people and ABC people and CBS people for the nightly news broadcasts—the content of those broadcasts was not all that different. When some galvanizing moment took place, Elvis dancing with scandalizing moves of his pelvis or the Beatles harmonizing to early pop hits like "I Want to Hold Your Hand," with camera cuts to swooning teenage girls, it seemed like everybody in

America had seen it. And when we all thought we were heading for a duck-and-cover nuclear war with Russia over missiles in Cuba, or more profoundly, when President Kennedy was shot, all were glued to the television.

There are moments in modern American life in which this still happens. There are massive audiences for the Super Bowl, for presidential debates, for natural disasters such as Hurricane Katrina, for horrific mass shootings, for royal weddings and important funerals. But the *medium* no longer seems to be what it once was, as I sense Marshall McLuhan was striving to define it. That is because, in a certain sense, there is no one medium anymore. All messages are available everywhere, on flat screens, computer screens, phone screens, tablet screens. We expect everything to be at our fingertips at every moment and are largely agnostic as to how exactly the job gets done. This is not to say that nobody pays attention to whether some message comes over Twitter or Facebook or a Sunday morning YouTube repeat of the opening the prior night's *Saturday Night Live*. I just mean that there is no real magic to the medium anymore, as in the Marshall McLuhan 1960s there was magic to television, or at some vaguer cultural time marker in the early 1990s there was magic to the internet, or somewhere around 2000 there was magic to the newness of smart phones.

Now what matters are the messages, and now what matters is that as a culture, we no longer listen to the same messages. Setting aside the crisis or crescendo moments, such as the hours surrounding the attacks of 9/11 or the inauguration of a president, our listening and reading are now fragmented. The number of news and information "channels" available, all-in, counting every broadcast and cable television outlet, every print and online website, from the *New York Times* or the *Wall Street Journal* to the newest off-the-street-off-the-wall blogger in sweatpants, is now seemingly infinite—for none of us has the time or the patience to sample them all.

Scholars tell us that the proliferation of modern media has led to fragmentation and self-selection. Media outlets select their identity—Fox has its fans, MSNBC has its fans, CNN has its fans—and viewers tend to watch only those outlets with which they personally identify, reinforcing their own ideological and value preconceptions. Add in the hundreds of highly literate and entertaining online publications, and fragmentation becomes exponentially, hopelessly, and perhaps depressingly multiplied.

Those who read Breitbart read Breitbart, those who read the Huffington Post read the Huffington Post, and rarely the twain shall meet.

For my own part, I try, in my own puny and halfhearted way, to war against this. When a significant political story breaks, I prefer to switch around from CNN to Fox News to MSNBC. When I get the latest news on my computer or smart phone I try to sample from across the spectrum. What the experts say is that I'm the outlier. I am sure others do what I do, but apparently it is not so common. Most folks, apparently, zone in on their favorites and stick with them.

When a group has a highly iconoclastic identity, as the alt-right plainly does, the tendency toward fragmentation appears to get even more intensified. A few highly popular alt-right channels have emerged. Within the alt-right, those who read, listen, and watch have their preferences, of course, but within the narrowed band of the alt-right those preferences do not seem to matter so much, just as it once did not matter so much whether one watched the evening news with Walter Cronkite on CBS or Chet Huntley and David Brinkley on NBC.

In assessing the channels of the alt-right, it might matter who gets counted as an alt-right channel and who does not. Fox News is an easy no-brainer. It is not alt-right, not by any stretch. It may have its occasional alt-right hosts, panel participants, and guests, but by the measure I am using, it is no Nazi channel. The distinction I am drawing here—between being merely conservative and catering to vicious, violent, irrational hate—is akin to the difference between soft-core erotica and hard-core obscenity. Perhaps I do not have the sublime words to articulate with precision the difference between a biting conservative commentary on Fox and the routine stuff of alt-right channels such as Stormfront, but I am confident that, as Justice Potter famously explained in describing hard-core obscenity, "I know it when I see it." The American Spectator and the Daily Caller, two prominent conservative publications, fall within the same rough class as Fox.

Now to be precise, I am not saying that Fox does not have its extreme voices, or its embarrassments. Tucker Carlson, who founded the Daily Caller and then took over a prime time spot on Fox to replace Bill O'Reilly, was outed in March 2019 for statements he made on the shock jock *Bubba the Love Sponge Show* in Tampa, in which he openly used racist and homophobic language to describe gays, immigrants, African

Americans, and Iraqis. Carlson was caught on tape describing Iraq as a "crappy place filled with a bunch of, you know, semiliterate primitive monkeys." He added, "That's why it wasn't worth invading." That follows a 2006 segment on the show in which Carlson said he had "zero sympathy" for Iraqi people and their culture because they "don't use toilet paper or forks." When these and other remarks by Carlson were exposed, he took the air on his nightly program to defiantly defend himself, refusing to apologize or give in to "the mob." Yet Tucker Carlson, whatever one thinks of him, is not all of Fox News. Many other respected journalists and anchors play prominent roles at Fox, including Chris Wallace, Bret Baier, and Neil Cavuto, among others.

There are examples much closer to the border. The most famous of them on the right is Breitbart News. Some might call Breitbart "far right" but not "alt-right." Its conservative founder Andrew Breitbart envisioned it as a right-side counterpart to the left-leaning Huffington Post. If that were enough to tell the story, Breitbart would be akin to what Fox News is to MSNBC or CNN, and well short of far enough right to be alt-right. But that plainly is not enough to tell the story, because from its inception Breitbart has been heavily influenced by its cofounder and later leader Steve Bannon, who in 2016 openly declared Breitbart to be a "platform" for the alt-right in an interview he gave to *Mother Jones* magazine, in an article by Sarah Posner provocatively titled "How Donald Trump's New Campaign Chief Created an Online Haven for White Nationalists."[2]

Precise taxonomy here really does not matter. Academics may fuss over whether Breitbart is or is not "alt-right." Breitbart is plainly not the sort of extremist, vulgar, hate-spewing, propaganda machine for Nazis and white supremacists to be lumped into the same category as the pure extreme alt-right channels such as Stormfront and Daily Stormer.

It is not the label assigned to Breitbart that matters, but its function and influence. By that measure, Breitbart and Steve Bannon played a pivotal role in the election of Donald Trump, a pivotal role in Trump's early presidency, and a pivotal role in serving as a bridge between the violent hate-filled discourse of the alt-right—the discourse of David Duke or Richard Spencer or Matthew Heimbach or Eli Mosley—and the discourse of the less-extreme far-right conservative supporters of Donald Trump, and ultimately, of Donald Trump itself. By that measure, Breitbart, alt-right or far right, was right in the middle of all that ensued in Charlottesville.

Donald Trump made Steve Bannon his campaign chair and then brought him into the White House as chief strategist. As Sarah Posner put it, in elevating Bannon, "Trump was signaling a wholehearted embrace of the 'alt-right,' a once-motley assemblage of anti-immigrant, anti-Muslim, ethno-nationalistic provocateurs who have coalesced behind Trump and curried the GOP nominee's favor on social media. In short, Trump has embraced the core readership of *Breitbart News*."

Breitbart commenced operations in 2005 as the principal outlet for its namesake, Andrew Breitbart, a conservative publisher and commentator. Breitbart stated that he'd been initially radicalized by the confirmation hearings for Justice Clarence Thomas. He considered conservatives to be an invisibly victimized class, and he came to relish his role as a right-wing flamethrower in the nation's culture wars.[3]

Andrew Breitbart died of heart failure in 2012, and Steve Bannon became the organization's leader. Bannon's leadership, the rise of the alt-right, and the candidacy of Donald Trump all combined to elevate Breitbart's influence on American politics and culture. As Mike Wendling correctly points out, Breitbart News was surely not a traditional news source seeking objectivity and balance, yet it was also not a fake news outlet willing to just make things up to advance a strongly conservative partisan agenda.[4] However one labels Breitbart's peculiar hybrid, what matters is that it mattered. It was the crossover platform, where the hard alt-right met the more traditional far right and where they both pushed and influenced enough of the full right to help elect Donald Trump.

For the authentic hard-core alt-right supremacists, other channels of communication were more important. For example, 4chan is an internet "image based" bulletin board where anyone can post images and comments, free of charge.[5] It is divided into over a hundred specialized boards for specific topics. The titles of these boards are eclectic. There are multiple boards dealing with Japanese culture, including otaku (roughly translated from Japanese to include people with obsessive interests, including "geeks") and various forms of anime (Japanese cartoons and animation). There are numerous boards for video gamers, television, movie, sports, autos, guns, cooking, gardening, do-it-yourselfers, business, finance, fitness, music, literature, travel, animals, nature, games, toys, philosophy, science, math, advice, and the paranormal.[6] There are boards for sexuality, straight, and LGBT. There are boards on sex, including boards that feature the graphic amateur photographs of contributors engaged in oral, vaginal, and anal sex.

There is also a 4chan board about politics. And this is where it gets interesting. A 4chan board titled "Politically Incorrect" (or "/pol/") seems innocent enough. Its rules of engagement describe it as a board for "debate and discussion related to politics and current events." The rules admonish, "You are free to speak your mind, but do not attack other users. You may challenge one another, but keep it civil!"[7] The rules add, "Posting pornography is not permitted. This is a politics board, not a porn board." (For porn, users should go to other 4chan locations.)

The 4chan /pol/ site became the mecca for the alt-right, a principal alt-right digital forum for the spread of alt-right commentary and symbols. It was largely through the 4chan /pol/ board that the alt-right appropriated the cartoon image of "Pepe the Frog" as the movement's unofficial mascot.

Richard Spencer was being questioned by a reporter about the Pepe lapel pin he was wearing at the Trump inauguration when Spencer was suddenly rushed and punched in the face by an angry counterprotester—a punch seen round that world as it went viral on the internet. The punch propelled Spencer to even greater fame, or infamy, depending on whom you ask.

There are many hate platforms on the internet, and they vary widely as to their place on the continuum, from seemingly responsible to unabashedly racist and violent. Dylann Roof, the white supremacist murderer who slaughtered nine innocent African Americans at the Emanuel African Methodist Episcopal Church in Charleston, professed to have been radicalized by reading online material of the Council of Concerned Citizens, whose spokesperson was Jared Taylor, the person whose writings were among the early influences on Richard Spencer. The content of that site, quoted earlier (see chapter 9), was certainly not overtly violent. Whether the site was or was not overtly racist is a matter of debate. It was plainly sufficient to help radicalize Dylann Roof. As also chronicled earlier (see chapter 9), when it was revealed that Roof had been radicalized by the site, mainstream Republican politicians who had received contributions from the Council immediately severed ties with the group and returned or donated the money that had been contributed.

On the unabashedly extreme frequency of the spectrum are the sites Stormfront and Daily Stormer. Stormfront was founded by David Duke and Don Black. The site was originally founded to advance Duke's 1990 US Senate campaign. It was the first major hate speech site on the internet and remains one of the most popular. Stormfront is neo-Nazi, antisemitic, and white supremacist. In 2002 France and Germany ordered Stormfront to be "de-indexed" from search engines, and Google complied with the order.

Stephen Donald "Don" Black cofounded Stormfront with Duke. Black succeeded Duke as the grand wizard of the Knights of the Ku Klux Klan in Louisiana. Black also succeeded Duke as the husband of Chloê Eleanor Hardin, who had married Duke in 1974 and divorced him ten years later and married Black.

In yet other odd historical circumstances, Black, when he was seventeen, was shot in the chest and critically wounded while working on a political campaign for a segregationist candidate for governor of Georgia, J. B. Stoner. Stoner was defeated in the election by Jimmy Carter, who of course later became president of the United States. While working for Stoner, Black attempted to retrieve documents from the offices of the National States Rights Party. Jerry William Ray—the brother of James Earl Ray, the convicted killer of Dr. Martin Luther King Jr.—who was also working on behalf of Stoner, spotted Black absconding with the records. Black returned to the office for more records and was confronted by Ray. According to Ray, Black then pulled "a shiny object" from his pocket and pointed it at Ray. Ray then shot Black in the chest. Black spent nine days in critical condition in the hospital. No gun was found in Black's possession. Ray was charged with aggravated assault but was acquitted of the charges by a jury, which apparently believed his claim of self-defense. Black, however, entered a plea of guilty to charges of theft and was given a one-year sentence of probation.[8]

After assuming command of the Klan from David Duke, Black hatched a bizarre plan to invade the Caribbean island of Dominica, to establish a white supremacist nation there. In what turned out to be a kind of right-wing Bay of Pigs, the plot failed, and Black was convicted of violating an American statute, the Neutrality Act, for making war on a friendly nation. He served a sentence of two years in a minimum security federal prison. Black enlisted his son Derek, then a twelve-year-old, to run a companion website to Stormfront ("Stormfront.org for Kids") that explicitly targets youths and encourages them to enlist in supremacist movements and ideology.[9]

The online website Daily Stormer is a right-wing publication founded by Andrew Anglin. It had become the most popular English-language website of the radical right. Its name is a play on the name of the German Nazi Party newspaper that rose to prominence in the 1930s, *Der Stürmer*.[10] The Daily Stormer established various on-the-ground groups called "book clubs," many of which announced their intent to travel to Charlottesville for the Unite the Right rally. One superheated Daily Stormer acolyte excitedly proclaimed, "This will clearly be an earth-shaking day that will go down in the history books. It can really only be explained as a perfect storm."[11] The article that provoked this response explained that "everything has been leading up to this," and "our time has come."[12] In a chilling celebratory proclamation anticipating the launch of a new Holocaust, the article described Charlottesville as a "monumental turning point in the progression of our movement," confidently predicting, "Everything will be different afterwards" and ominously declaring, "Next stop: Charlottesville, VA. Final stop: Auschwitz."[13]

The alt-right has spawned its own lexicon of words and symbols. If you can't keep track of all the alt-right players without a scorecard, you can't keep track of their speech and tweets without a dictionary.

"Doxing" is not a term unique to the alt-right, but the alt-right makes heavy use of it. To be "doxed" originally meant to have one's anonymous internet identity unmasked, revealing a person's personal information, such as real name, address, phone number, or e-mail. Doxing was a form of digital outing. Now "doxed" is often used more generally to describe any revelation about an individual's personal life that is inconsistent with his or her projected public persona.[14] When it was revealed that the popular alt-right podcast personality Mike Enoch lived on the chic Upper East Side of Manhattan with a Jewish wife, many commentators wrote that Enoch had been doxed. "Doxed" is also sometimes used to describe hacking into a database to unveil embarrassing or compromising information,[15] as in "The Russians doxed the Democratic National Committee looking for dirt on Hillary Clinton."

The Right Stuff simply appropriates the title of writer Tom Wolfe's 1979 book about the early days of the space program and the original astronauts, made into a movie in 1983. The Daily Shoah is a play on *The Daily Show*, Comedy Central's popular evening political satire show hosted for many years by Jon Stewart and now Trevor Noah. In the darker wordplay at work, "shoah" is the Hebrew word for catastrophe and since World War II has commonly been used as the Hebrew term for the Holocaust.

Whenever a Jewish name was used on the Daily Shoah, a special sound-effect was superimposed on the name, making it echo ominously.[16] This generated a new alt-right symbol, called the "echo." When a Jewish name is used with the echo, three sets of parentheses surround the Jewish name, such as (((Goldberg))) or (((Rabinowitz))). The triple parenthesis echo can also be used to identify a person in a profession as Jewish, such as (((banker))) or (((Hollywood movie producer))). Enoch's Daily Shoah thus was the originator of one of the most popular antisemitic symbols of the alt-right.

There are countless terms in the alt-right language.[17] And new ones are constantly created. Here are some of the highlights: "Normies" are the masses, or more specifically the masses who are not hip to 4chan culture or the alt-right. A normie might move from normie-hood to the alt-right by taking a "red pill." The term "red pill," like the term "doxed," is not exclusive to the alt-right but is rather a popular internet term for a conversion experience, from normal to enlightened.[18] It most famously derives from a scene in the move *The Matrix*, in which the character Morpheus says, "This is your last chance. After this there is no turning back. You take the blue pill: the story ends, you wake up in your bed and believe whatever you want to believe. You take the red pill: you stay in Wonderland and I show you how deep the rabbit hole goes." For an alt-righter, taking the red pill might mean conversion from liberal or mainstream conservative to authentic alt-right. "Cucks" are feminized men. A "cuckservative" is a mainstream Republican conservative, such as Jeb Bush or Marco Rubio, loathed by the alt-right. "Cuckerservative" is an amalgam of "cuckold," the husband of an adulterous woman, and "conservative."[19] A "crybully" is an alt-right term for someone on the left who claims victimization and then uses that status to justify bossing others and infringing on the alt-right's freedom of speech. A "fashy" is a fashion term, denoting clothing or a "fashy haircut," with hair short on the sides and long on the top, conjuring a style popular in Germany in the 1930s. Hip alt-right leaders such as Richard Spencer sport "fashy" styles, seeking to set themselves apart from the cruder skinheads and Ku Kluxers who gave the extreme right such a bad rep.[20]

REDNECKS AND SAINT PAUL

Among the groups that traveled to Charlottesville on Friday, August 11, to participate in the weekend's events was the Silver Valley Redneck Revolt.[1] The Redneck Revolt is a national movement that, according to the group's web page, was founded in 2016 as "an anti-racist, anti-fascist community defense formation."[2] Redneck Revolt is a part of the "armed left" that emphasizes being armed in defense of leftist groups that seek to counter supremacist groups like the alt-right or the Klan—it's a militia of sorts aligned with the left. Redneck Revolt also has a class distinction—it is the armed left of workers and farmers, not the left of the wealthy elite. Redneck Revolt relishes its play on the word "redneck" and includes as one if its tag lines "putting the red back in redneck." According to Redneck Revolt, in 1921 the term "redneck" became synonymous with armed insurrection against the state, "as members of the United Mine Workers of America tied red bandanas around their necks during the Battle of Blair Mountain, a two week long armed multi-racial labor uprising in the coalfields of West Virginia."[3] What was originally a badge of honor, however, became a pejorative, a demeaning term often used "among upper class urban liberals who have gone out of their way to dehumanize working class and poor people." Redneck Revolt's use of the term "redneck" as a point of pride is a deliberate effort to counter the perceived views of those elites. Not all rednecks are racists, Redneck Revolt signifies, any more than they are "hillbillies" or "white trash."[4]

Redneck Revolt is openly ready to fight for what it believes in. It is plainly in the camp that is willing to move beyond abstract advocacy to physical action. Redneck Revolt's website thus explains that it is no longer possible to "constrain our desire for liberty within the abstract bounds of liberal discourse and polite debate." Instead, "The threat to ourselves and our neighbors, friends, and loved ones is clear and demands action. We have to organize and fight as if our lives depend on it," Redneck Revolt insists, "for indeed, they do."[5]

Among the members of Redneck Revolt to make the trip to Charlottesville was a professor at the University of North Carolina at Chapel Hill, Dwayne E. Dixon, an assistant professor in the Asian Studies Department. Dixon was an exceptionally well-informed student of the national Redneck Revolt movement, and like many of its participants, he defied traditional stereotypes. He was slight of build, a vegan, wore thick black horn-rimmed glasses, was an intellectual, had tattoos, self-identified as both "straight and queer," and carried an AK-47 rifle.[6] In an article published in the *Chronicle of Higher Education*, Dixon estimated that at least a third of the members of Redneck Revolt are people of color, women, and others with nonbinary gender identities and sexualities.[7]

Dixon was with his fellow members of Redneck Revolt on the evening of Friday, August 11, just as matters in Charlottesville were beginning to get really tense. Redneck Revolt had been asked by the Anarchist People of Color, another antifascist group, to help provide security for counterprotesters at the Unite the Right rally. Another member of the Sliver Valley Redneck Revolt, who called himself simply "Mitchell" to protect his privacy and safety, traveled from Davidson County, North Carolina, to Charlottesville to protect the counterprotesters gathering to confront the Unite the Right rally. Mitchell said that the activists organizing the Charlottesville counterprotest asked for the Silver Valley Redneck Revolt to assist with security.[8] Redneck Revolt obliged, arriving with assault rifles, pistols, and shotguns—all legal because of Virginia's open-carry laws. The group also sent members with first-aid training to help dress wounds and connect victims back to their group or family and friends.[9]

As they arrived in Charlottesville, the city was rife with rumor that something very bad was about to happen at St. Paul's Church.

Saint Paul, before he was figuratively knocked off his horse on the road to Damascus and still went by the name Saul, was a fighter. After his conversion, Paul preached peace, forgiveness, and forbearance toward enemies. He wrote to the Colossians, "Put on therefore, as the elect of God, holy and beloved, bowels of mercies, kindness, humbleness of mind, meekness, longsuffering; Forbearing one another, and forgiving one another, if any man have a quarrel against any: even as Christ forgave you, so also do ye."[10] And in a letter to the Galatians he chided, "Meekness, temperance: against such there is no law."[11]

There were both Pauls and Sauls gathered to pray together at St. Paul's Memorial Episcopal Church in Charlottesville on the evening of August 11. St. Paul's is located across the street from the University of Virginia campus, on the corner of University Avenue and Chancellor Street. St. Paul's associate rector, Rev. Elaine Ellis Thomas, was among the Charlottesville clergy allied with Congregate Charlottesville. Thomas asked her superior, St. Paul's rector, Rev. Will Peyton, if the church could be used on August 11 for an interfaith prayer service on the eve of the scheduled Unite the Right rally. She explained that a large crowd of those opposed to the rally was expected, and that national leaders such as Cornel West would be in attendance. Rector Peyton agreed to let St. Paul's be used as the site for the gathering. In Peyton's view, "an interfaith service is never the wrong thing to do."[12]

More than seven hundred people gathered at St. Paul's for the evening service on August 11. Among those in attendance was Mayor Signer. A local Charlottesville juvenile and domestic relations judge, Claude Worrell, was also in attendance. Judge Worrell had concerns for the safety of the crowd and asked a Charlottesville police officer present, Lieutenant Jim Mooney, if the police had a contingency plan to protect the gathering.[13] Four persons who appeared to be alt-right followers were spotted in the church gathering, and at 8:21 p.m. Mayor Signer sent a text message to City Manager Jones and Chief Thomas alerting them to the presence of the alt-right individuals inside the church.[14]

Also alerted to rumors that something nefarious might be afoot at St. Paul's, the members of the Redneck Revolt who had come to Charlottesville ringed the church to ward off any rush on the church by an alt-right mob.[15] The intelligence efforts of the counterprotesters included persons who had infiltrated the social media traffic of the alt-right. Someone allied with Congregate Charlottesville saw a Twitter message from an alt-right follower who said he was inside St. Paul's. The security detail inside the church was alerted and identified a suspect who they believed had probably sent the tweet. Security judged it was unlikely the suspect was armed and did not take any action to remove him.[16]

The Regional Emergency Communications Center received a 911 call at 8:43 p.m. from an anonymous male caller who said he had an AR-15 rifle and threatened to open fire inside the church in five minutes. Immediately eight additional Charlottesville police officers responded, joining the officers already at St. Paul's, to search for a potential active shooter.[17] Scanning the crowd inside the church, they spotted no one suspicious.

A second 911 call came into the Emergency Communications Center at 8:56 p.m., from an unidentified male who threatened to enter St. Paul's and engage in a mass shooting. With fear and tension rising from the repeated threats, security forces decided to place St. Paul's on immediate lockdown, barring entry to the church and also preventing anyone inside from leaving.[18]

No violence took place at St. Paul's, but the church remained on lockdown until around 10:30 p.m., when a disturbance at the Rotunda and Jefferson statue had ended and the Unite the Right torch marchers were dissipating.

THE LAWN AND THE ROTUNDA

On August 9, 2017, University of Virginia president Teresa Sullivan sent an e-mail to the university board that appeared to make light of the alt-right's intentions. "Of course we anticipate that some of them will be interested merely in seeing Mr. Jefferson's architecture and Lawn," she wrote.[1] It turned out however, that the alt-right members had a lot more in mind than sightseeing.

The organizers of the Unite the Right rally focused on a local Walmart as an initial staging area. Charlottesville itself does not have a Walmart, but north of the city on US Route 29 is the standard suburban fare of chain retail box stores and restaurants, including a Walmart Supercenter on Hilton Heights Road, in Albemarle County. This was the gathering spot selected by Unite the Right organizer Chris Cantwell as a first staging area for the weekend. Cantwell was the host of Radical Agenda, a podcast catering to right-wing interest. Cantwell had a sense of tradecraft, and to avoid infiltration by Antifa and other enemy provocateurs he had erected a paywall on his website.[2]

Emily Gorcenski was ahead of Cantwell's game, however, and through her own counterintelligence efforts had learned of the planned meeting of Cantwell and his supporters at the Walmart. Gorcenski and her counter-demonstrators were lying wait for Cantwell's assembly. Gorcenski posted pictures of Cantwell's gathering on Twitter, and within minutes officers from the Albemarle County Police Department arrived on the scene. Cantwell was carrying a firearm and was confronted by the county police. He explained that he had a lawful permit to carry his weapon and denied any inappropriate brandishing of it. Tensions abated. The police took no action, and Cantwell and his followers left the Walmart parking lot.[3]

The University of Virginia Police Department had received its first inkling of a possible Friday night Unite the Right event on campus on August 8, when university police captain Donald H. McGee learned in a meeting with the Charlottesville Police Department about a possible "tiki torch march" to be held on Friday.[4] But the university did not appear to register the full impact of what was planned. President Sullivan later seemed to place some blame on the activist students and faculty for failing to give the administration proper alerts of the warning signs the activists were reading. "Nobody elevated it to us," Sullivan complained. "Don't expect us to be reading the alt-right websites. We don't do that. Now you guys have responsibility here too. Tell us what you know."[5]

The activists saw it very differently. They believed they did in fact provide the administration with plenty of warning but never got the sense that they were being listened to. If anything, they felt "dismissed as social-justice crusaders crying wolf."[6]

On Friday afternoon, associate professor of religious studies Jalane D. Schmidt read online chatter planning the evening torch march. Schmidt, a well-known activist on campus, was concerned that a tip from her would not be treated seriously, and so she instead used an intermediary to convey what she had learned to UVA assistant professor of media studies Emily L. Blount, who just happened to be married to Mayor Signer. Schmidt later explained to the *Chronicle of Higher Education* that she figured the mayor's wife would appear more credible than "some brown-skinned, outspoken professor like me."[7]

Meanwhile, at 3:13 on Friday afternoon, Louis Nelson, the vice-provost for community engagement at UVA, received a phone call from an anonymous source that Jason Kessler and his alt-right followers would gather at UVA Friday evening to march with torches through the campus.[8] Senior officials at the university were notified, as were the Charlottesville and Albemarle County police. All involved treated the impending march across the campus with relative composure, apparently taking their cues from the UVA Police Department chief Michael Gibson, who did not appear overly concerned about the planned march and sought no assistance from the other agencies.[9] Gibson viewed the alt-right march as just like any other political gathering on the campus, and his department planned to intervene only if laws were broken.[10]

Kessler and Cantwell arrived at McIntire Park at five o'clock on Friday evening, to begin planning for their torch march. Cantwell asked if the local police would be alerted. Kessler told him no, because he wanted the march kept secret. Neither knew that police already had intelligence alerting them to the torch rally. However, given that the police had processed the intelligence with seeming indifference, it is not clear it would have mattered much either way.

Cantwell did not like the idea that Kessler was not going to call the police and insisted that Kessler inform them. Kessler relented and called Captain Lewis of the Charlottesville police. Lewis told Kessler to call Lieutenant Angela Tabler of the university police. He did, though the call did not appear to have any impact on the university police plans. According to an official timeline later released by the UVA police, at 8:15 p.m. a University Police Department official called a Unite the Right organizer, who passed the call on to the Unite the Right "security" person, who informed the university police that the likely staging location would be Nameless Field on the UVA campus.[11] (Yes, at a university in which virtually every building and every space has a name, often honoring a donor, UVA has a "Nameless Field").

The university made a decision not to sound any emergency alert to the UVA community that the Unite the Right group would be marching though the campus.[12] The decision not to issue an alert was grounded in concerns that an alert might "compromise efforts to contain the situation by drawing additional people to the area." The decision would later be criticized.[13]

Richard Spencer wanted the media to cover the Friday night torch march, and a few minutes after 8:00 p.m. Spencer sent a text to a reporter: "I'd be near campus tonight, if I were you. After 9 p.m. Nameless field."[14]

To further ensure that the torchlight march would have maximum public relations impact, the Unite the Right leaders used drones to film the rally for posting on the internet.

Nameless Field is a grassy expanse behind Memorial Gymnasium at UVA. For the night of August 11 it suited the alt-right's purposes well as a staging area where the marchers could gather with their torches, have them filled with kerosene by volunteer supporters from tables placed on the field, and then assemble themselves into orderly ranks.

As the evening sun went down, Charlottesville and Albemarle County police asked if the university needed reinforcements. "I think we are good for right now," Chief Gibson wrote at 8:11 p.m. to Charlottesville's Chief Thomas and Albemarle's Chief Lantz. "My folks are watching this closely."[15]

City Manager Maurice Jones, getting wind of the torch rally that evening, wrote an e-mail to UVA's chief operating officer Patrick D. Hogan, saying, "Pat, I just heard about Kessler March tonight. Do you need assistance?" Hogan responded, "I think Mike Gibson has ample coverage for University. But hopefully City will be available to help in surrounding areas."[16]

Like a general walking the battlefield one last time before hostilities, President Sullivan walked the University Lawn at 8:15 on Friday evening, talking with the "Lawnies."

The Lawn is part of what is known at UVA as the Academical Village. According to a policy adopted by the UVA board, the Academical Village is defined as the property bordered by the Rotunda, Hospital Drive, and McCormick Road, including the Rotunda, Pavilions, the Lawn and Range rooms, gardens, and the lower Lawn area.[17] Constituting the heart of the university, the Academical Village is one of the most celebrated open spaces in all of American higher education. It is recognized as a UNESCO World Heritage Site.[18]

The university had a policy involving "open burning," stating that "a person shall not kindle or maintain or authorize to be kindled or maintained any open burning" without obtaining formal special approval from the university's Office of Environmental Health and Safety or Medical Center Fire Protection Inspector's Office.[19] There were exceptions for cooking and warming food. And, since this was a university, after all, there were also exceptions for laboratory experiments.[20] As the Unite the Right marchers were assembling kerosene supplies and tiki torches at Nameless Field, it does not appear that anyone thought to invoke the open burning ban, perhaps because there was no precedent for applying it to a demonstration.

Dozens of senior undergraduate UVA students who had been selected for the prized rooms on the UVA Lawn had already moved in to get ready for the start of the fall semester. A resident assistant for the Lawn student housing stopped President Sullivan, to show her a post from social media describing the Unite the Right rally being planned that evening for the Rotunda.[21] Sullivan advised the resident assistant to contact Professor Sabato, who lived in a faculty pavilion on the Lawn and who had agreed at the dinner party two nights before to shelter students in Pavilion IV, where he lived, should the Unite the Right marchers descend on the campus.[22]

And indeed, Professor Sabato did take in some fifteen students soon thereafter, hosting them in the Pavilion IV basement, a congenial area with a kitchen and television. Though aware of the potentially bad optics of locking students in the basement, Sabato locked the pavilion doors as a precaution against attack. He did not view the situation as paranoid students afraid of offensive ideas, but rather as a genuine threat to security. "I can hear people say, 'Oh, the snowflakes, the snowflakes,'" Sabato said. "If you had seen these jackbooted thugs, you would understand why I took them down to the basement."[23]

President Sullivan claimed that the university would have prepared very differently if it had understood what was actually about to transpire. The university expected twenty or thirty people, not hundreds, and it was not expecting torches. "We would have prepared very differently if we had had any idea what this event was really going to be, Sullivan said. "For starters, 20 people is not the same as 250 to 300 people. Having torches is not the same as not having torches. There's just a lot of things that ended up being different about this. Walking up the street to the Rotunda is not the same as winding through our university and coming through the Academical Village to the Rotunda."[24]

Timothy A. Freilich, executive director of Madison House, a student volunteer center at the university, was among the eyewitnesses to the gathering storm. Freilich saw Unite the Right members unloading torches and approached a university police officer on the Lawn, to alert him as to what he'd seen. The reaction was ho-hum. "His response was along the lines of, 'Oh we know. They are everywhere,'" said Freilich.[25]

As the numbers of the Unite the Right contingent gathering at Nameless Field swelled, officials at the university were beginning to process the potential enormity of the situation. "I am being told social media is lighting up over this," Chief Gibson wrote to his colleagues at 8:30 p.m. "It is certainly no secret."[26]

Captain McGee replied to the chief's message, "Was afraid of that."[27]

Timothy Freilich, who had spoken to the university police officer on the Lawn after seeing the torches being unloaded, followed the action on Nameless Field. Freilich "did not see a single cop in the darkness other than the guy on the Lawn." Freilich watched "in horror" as the torches were ignited and the march began.[28]

The feelings were mutual. Unite the Right organizer Chris Cantwell was also taken aback by what seemed the complete absence any law enforcement presence on or around the University of Virginia campus that evening.

The Unite the Right's security official was Eli Mosley, the army veteran who described himself as "command soldier major of the 'alt-right." Mosley's objective was to execute the march on the University of Virginia Lawn "as a military operation." The use of drones by the alt-right to engage in aerial reconnaissance of the landscape before marching on the Rotunda was a mark of Mosley's military approach.[29]

By this point, President Sullivan had returned to Carr's Hill, the president's residence, where she was in communication with the dean of students Allen Groves and Professor Larry Sabato.

Emily Gorcenski, who had intelligence sources keeping her well informed, was at Nameless Field, as she had been at the Walmart earlier in the day, watching the alt-right group assemble. She would shadow the alt-right marchers that evening until they finally dispersed.

There were at least three hundred marchers.[30] One of the leaders shouted through a bullhorn, "Stay in formation! Two by two! Two by two!"

The march began around 9:30. Cantwell and several others were selected to walk in strategic positions as "guards" on the outside of the marching lines. The guards were selected as those willing to get rough with Antifa, should Antifa forces seek to physically disrupt the march. Cantwell was shocked that no law enforcement personnel were visible.[31]

The torchlight march began. The marchers proceeded past the Alderman Library, down McCormick Road, and onto the famous University of Virginia Lawn. Marchers shouted, "White lives matter!" "Blood and soil!" "You will not replace us!" "Jews will not replace us!" "Whose streets? Our streets!"

At 9:45 p.m. President Sullivan wrote to Dean Groves, "Lots of yelling west of us, but I can't see anything yet."

"We can hear it up here, too," Groves replied.[32]

At 10:07 p.m. the marchers reached the steps of the University of Virginia Rotunda, the university's most eminent edifice, the very soul and symbol of the university. They proceeded toward the statue of Thomas Jefferson.[33]

Counterprotesters, however, had beaten them to Jefferson. Kessler and Spencer had an intelligence leak—students at UVA had been tipped off on the alt-right plan. Some thirty UVA students, black and white, had gathered in front of the Jefferson statue and then circled the statue's base, locked arm in arm. The students had taken nonviolence training, and they would try to exercise control, not throw punches, or do anything physically aggressive. But they could sure as hell yell. As the Unite the Right group approached, the students chanted, "No Nazis! No KKK! No Fascist USA!"[34]

Emily Gorcenski watched as the supremacists approached the ring of counterprotesters. Some of the supremacists began making monkey noises, taunting the black students, while others took up the cheer "White lives matter!" The alt-right marchers encircled the Jefferson statue and the UVA students. They had the UVA students and Jefferson surrounded.

Devin Willis, a student and member of the college's Black Student Alliance, was one of the counterprotesters. Willis said the white supremacists approached while shouting "slurs and remarks."[35]

"I was very fearful for my life," Willis said. "It was very much a confrontational way that they approached us." he added. "It was very violently postured."

Professor Walt Heinecke was headed that evening to St. Paul's Church to participate in training events there for counterprotests at the next day's rally.[36] Heinecke parked at the architecture school a couple of blocks away. Walking from his car to St. Paul's, he ran into people who had seen Richard Spencer and his tiki-torch bearers assembling. Heinecke learned that St. Paul's was on lockdown because of reported threats. He then heard someone scream, "Your students are surrounded by Nazis in front of the Rotunda!"[37]

"I was shocked by the number of neo-Nazis," Heinecke said. "And I couldn't believe the police presence—I couldn't see any."[38]

Heinecke saw the UVA dean of students Allen Groves. He asked Groves where the university police were. Groves didn't know. Perhaps, Groves said, they were patrolling with Charlottesville police. "The violence and the temperature kept going up," Heinecke later told a reporter. "Some of my students were there."[39]

Heinecke approached his students, who were surrounded by the Nazis as they surrounded Jefferson, their backs to the statute. Heinecke could tell they were scared and asked them if they wanted to leave.[40] A torch, wielded like a spear, struck Groves. His arm bled as he tried to pull students out of the melee, eyewitnesses said.[41] The scene was "horrendous," Heinecke said. "I saw a neo-Nazi throw a torch at Allen, and then they started macing. I got hit with that."[42]

At 10:16 p.m., police assistance was requested. Physical skirmishes were breaking out. A UVA student tried to knock down a torch, creating a scuffle. Gorcenski claimed she saw Chris Cantwell deploy mace. Later, Gorcenski and Cantwell would both claim injury from the discharge of chemical agents.

At 10:22 p.m., Captain McGee wrote to his colleagues, "Do we need more help from CPD and County?"[43]

University police officer Scott Smallwood arrived and was soon assisted by Charlottesville police, who responded within one minute. But by that time the brief skirmishes were over and the alt-right marchers had already begun to retreat. Some of the UVA students were sitting or standing, dazed. Others were already leaving.

Gorcenski approached the Charlottesville and university police officers and demanded to know who was in command.[44] Charlottesville police sergeant Bradley Pleasants spoke to her. Gorcenski demanded to know Pleasants's badge number, which he provided to her. Gorcenski asked why police officers did not intervene during the confrontations. Sergeant Pleasants responded, "There was no brawl when we got here." Gorcenski called Pleasants a "fucking liar."[45]

By this time, the university police were treating people who had been pepper sprayed. Gorcenski, a blogger and activist who was among those sprayed, confronted the police on camera about not intervening sooner.

"My face is burning," Gorcenski said. "My face is burning. The cops did nothing."[46]

Dean Groves saw the confrontation as an attack by the Unite the Right marchers on his students. "I was with them when the attack came," he e-mailed Sullivan. "Totally unprovoked."[47]

At 10:24 p.m., using the public address microphone on a Charlottesville police squad car, the police declared the gathering of remaining persons near the Jefferson statue an unlawful assembly and ordered them to disperse. Charlottesville and university police formed ranks in a two-deep line to march through the area and clear it. Seeing this, Gorcenski asked for permission to assist a student in a wheelchair, which was granted.[48] The officers then drew out and extended their collapsible batons and began marching across the front of the Rotunda, causing the protesters to move away from the Jefferson statue.[49] The crowd was gone by 10:29. At 10:43 the police left the area.[50]

After the violence at the Jefferson statue in front of the Rotunda, Jalane Schmidt, who had warned Emily Blount earlier in the day, wrote Blount an e-mail asking, "Was the memo not received?"

"UVA has known about this since 3 pm," Blount answered. "I went to the top."[51]

Following the incident, President Sullivan called the chairman of the University Board of Visitors and the governor of Virginia, Terry McAuliffe, to report on what had transpired. She was told that the state would bump up police numbers and show force throughout the night.[52]

The events at the Rotunda alarmed Walt Heinecke, who had planned to take part in the counterprotests at McGuffey and Justice Parks. Heinecke fired off an e-mail to Chief Thomas, stating, "If this is a sign of things to come, the white supremacists will be violent tomorrow. I want police protection at McGuffey and Justice Parks."[53] Late that evening, Thomas responded to Heinecke that the Charlottesville Police Department would bring additional officers "to monitor McGuffey and Justice."[54]

That night, at 11:28, Larry Sabato wrote to President Sullivan, her husband, law professor Douglas Laycock, and Dean Groves: "In my

47 years of association with the University, this was the worst thing I have seen unfold on the Lawn and at the Rotunda. Nothing else even comes close."[55] Professor Sabato also tweeted, "This is the most nauseating thing I've ever seen. We will need an exorcism on the Lawn."[56]

At 1:00 a.m., President Sullivan was on a telephone call with the Virginia attorney general's office, exploring whether federal judge Glen Conrad might be persuaded to change his ruling and move the demonstration to McIntire Park, away from Emancipation Park, now that violence was not just hypothetical. "It did seem to me that it changed the situation," Sullivan stated. "Violence was no longer hypothetical. It had happened."[57]

But all seemed to realize that the momentum of events was now inexorable. The Unite the Right forces had descended on Charlottesville, and they were going to make their presence known again on Saturday, as they had on Friday night, no matter what any judge might rule.[58]

What may have been perceived as mere right-wing advocacy now appeared to impress President Sullivan as action laced with deadly threats. "If you listen to the chants, these were chants about killing people because of what groups those people were born into, or killing people because of their beliefs," Sullivan said.[59] This was not ordinary politics, the polarized America divided between conservatives and liberals, Republicans and Democrats, the red states and the blue states. For Sullivan, this had gone beyond normal. "The country is badly polarized, and people want to look at what's happening at the universities and put it into that narrative: It's red or it's blue," she said. "But that is not what's going on here; that's not what happened here. What happened here is infra-red and ultraviolet; it's beyond the spectrum of normal political discourse. Both Republican and Democratic elected leaders denounced what happened here. Seeking to normalize this as ordinary politics is the mistake."[60]

Free speech was one thing, violence was another. In Sullivan's eyes, the Unite the Right had crossed the line from speech to fight. "What happened here yesterday wasn't about ideas," she continued. "People weren't out there arguing with each other. They were clobbering each other. That's a very different situation. That's violence. Violence is not free speech."[61]

BLOODSHED

Charlottesville police began to report to their assigned locations in the city at 7:00 a.m. on Saturday. Virginia State Police arrived around 8:39 a.m.[1] As with the July 8 Ku Klux Klan rally, police had divided Emancipation Park into zones to which various groups were assigned.

An interfaith sunrise religious service was held early in the morning, at 6:00, at the First Baptist Church. Members of both the Clergy Collective and Congregate Charlottesville attended the prayer service. Once the sunrise service concluded, the attendees again split into two groups. Those opting to attend alternative programming headed toward the Jefferson School and planned later to march to McGuffey Park. Those who opted for "direct action" stayed behind to prepare to march to Emancipation Park to confront the Unite the Right demonstrators.[2]

At about 8:00, the Jefferson School group, now numbering some three hundred, began walking from the school to McGuffey Park, where they arrived at around 8:20. First aid and water stations were available. There were speeches and songs. Those assembled at McGuffey Park were too far

away from Emancipation Park or any of roads into Emancipation Park
to see the Unite the Right demonstrators, or the counterdemonstrators
who confronted them. From McGuffey Park that morning, Charlottesville
seemed a place of peace.[3]

For those near Emancipation Park, however, it was a very different
story. Tensions mounted by the minute as various contingents arrived. The
first two groups to arrive were the clergy and the armed militia.

The word "militia" has many different meanings in American law
and culture. Two self-proclaimed volunteer militia groups, the New York
Lightfoot Militia and the Pennsylvania Lightfoot Militia, entered the
Charlottesville dynamic. George Curbelo was the commander of the New
York group, and Christian Yingling was commander of the Pennsylva-
nians. The two militia groups had reached out to the Charlottesville police
to offer their assistance in keeping the peace and preserving the free speech
rights of all involved. The Charlottesville police, however, were not interested in any militia assistance and had advised them to stay away. Nevertheless, the police conceded that the militia groups had a right to travel
to Charlottesville and attend the rally if they chose to do so. They did.
The New York and the Pennsylvania Lightfoot Militias, armed and about
thirty in number, arrived at Emancipation Park at 8:20 a.m. A Virginia
State Police trooper surveyed the militia. "What are they, like military?"
the trooper asked a buddy. "They're more armed than we are."[4]

At 8:55 a.m., the clergy who had opted for direct action began to arrive
at Emancipation Park from the First Baptist Church. The armed militia
were already in place. The clergy members formed a line facing Emancipation Park at the north end of Market Street. The clergy members knelt,
locked arms, and began singing hymns.[5]

Not long after the clergy arrived, various elements of the Unite the
Right demonstrators began to appear. The police spotted Richard Wilson
Preston, the leader of the Confederate White Knights of Ku Klux Klan, in
Emancipation Park at around 9:00. The bulk of the Unite the Right dem-
onstrators, however, were gathering in their staging area at McIntire Park.
The Unite the Right leaders at McIntire Park included David Duke, Mike
Enoch, Jason Kessler, and Richard Spencer. Many of their followers were
dressed in their uniform of white polo shirts and khakis. Many carried
white flags. Vans arrived at McIntire Park to shuttle the demonstrators
into downtown Charlottesville.

A Unite the Right U-Haul truck pulled up at Emancipation Park at 9:00 to unload sound equipment. The equipment was unloaded, and the truck departed. A channel of communication had been established between one of the "security" leaders of the Unite the Right rally, Jack Pierce, and the Charlottesville police, represented by Sergeant Tony Newberry. Sergeant Newberry phoned Pierce a little after 9:00 to advise him that there would never be a better time to get the Unite the Right leaders into Emancipation Park.[6] Pierce said that he understood and would check with the leaders and get back to the sergeant. Pierce did call back shortly and said that the leaders preferred no special treatment in getting to the park but rather planned to join the marchers and walk to the park with their Unite the Right followers. Newberry, on hearing this, told his police partner, "They do not plan on this going well."[7]

The first wave of Unite the Right demonstrators arrived at the entrance to Emancipation Park at 9:42 a.m. Eli Mosley led the first group, Identity Evropa, brandishing its flag, heading to the southwest entrance to the park, chanting "You will not replace us!"[8]

Other passenger vans began rolling into the downtown, dropping off Unite the Right demonstrators in various locations. From whatever direction the demonstrators arrived, police directed them toward the southwest entrance to Emancipation Park. Consequently, that is where the counterdemonstrators also began to gather in growing numbers. The Unite the Right marchers and the counterdemonstrators traded insults and chants. From the counterdemonstrators came shouts such as "Love has already won!" From the alt-right came "You will not replace us!" "Commie scum!" "Off our streets!" and "Build the wall!"[9]

Throughout the Charlottesville downtown area, dozens of brawls erupted. As groups of Unite the Right marchers advanced toward Emancipation Park from various directions, counterdemonstrators would try to block them. The Unite the Right marchers would then try to force their way through, throwing punches, stabbing at the crowd with flagpoles, shoving people with shields. Fights would break out until somebody released pepper spray, causing the sides to disperse and move on.[10]

Some of the counterprotesters walked up to police to challenge them as to why they were not being more aggressive. Tanesha Hudson, a Charlottesville local, complained to Charlottesville police sergeant Lee Gibson that Unite the Right marchers were lowering their flags to use as weapons against counterprotesters and expressed frustration at the passivity of the police.[11] The two went back and forth over what the police should or should not be doing. Gibson finally said, "When things happen, we'll respond." Hudson retorted, "When they happen? You're supposed to *prevent* it from happening!"[12]

On Second Street NE near the First United Methodist Church, a group of Unite the Right marchers displaying swastikas and wearing white shirts ran into the peaceful black-shirted demonstrators returning from McGuffey Park—the counterdemonstrators who had sought to avoid direct confrontation with the Unite the Right forces. St. Paul's rector, Rev. Will Peyton, witnessed the clash from the parking lot of the Methodist church. The Unite the Right demonstrators appeared to be focusing their aggression on a middle-aged African American man. As fights broke out between the two groups, law enforcement officers stood and watched, not intervening. Only one of the law enforcement personnel on the scene, Diane Hueschen, was from the Charlottesville police. But Hueschen was not strictly a police officer; she was a department employee whose job was forensic technician. She was not armed, nor trained in police work, though she at times worked traffic at UVA football games. She had been told that if anything "went south" at her intersection, she was not to intervene but was instead to get out of the way and protect herself. Also nearby, however, were highly trained troopers of the Virginia State Police. They did nothing to intervene as the violence erupted. Finally, several of the state police did begin to walk toward the scuffle. This caused the Unite the Right demonstrators to break off, running out of the church parking lot, laughing and yelling "You want some more?"[13]

At 10:21 a.m., at the corner of East Market Street and Second Street NE, Unite the Right demonstrators entered a gauntlet of counterdemonstrators. The counterdemonstrators were wearing helmets and unfurled a banner declaring "Fascist Scum." As the Unite the Right marchers walked through them, one of the counterdemonstrators tried to grab one of the Unite the Right flags. A scuffle broke out. Charlottesville sergeant Larry Jones radioed his superiors, "We've got a disorder in middle of Market." But he was told, "Let's give them a second."[14]

As the scuffle continued, police did intervene—one of the only interventions of the day. Lieutenant Joe Hatter decided not to tolerate the escalating violence. Hatter jumped over a barricade and entered the street.

A Virginia State Police trooper followed him in. Hatter drew his baton and moved to separate the combatants. He moved the Unite the Right demonstrator with his flag away from the skirmish, with the state trooper assisting. Officer E. A. Maney then jumped the barrier to help them both. Members of the militia also rendered assistance, guarding the officers' rear. Hatter calmed the angry demonstrator down, and the situation de-escalated. Nobody was arrested.[15]

The locus of confrontation shifted to the entrance to Emancipation Park. The members of the clergy from Congregate Charlottesville who were most motivated to directly confront the Unite the Right marchers, including Rev. Seth Wispelwey, set out to block them from entering the park by forming a line at the top of the southeast stairs to the park, which Wispelwey thought was the only way for the Unite the Right marchers to enter the park. Wispelwey also wanted to draw a police response, seeking to "create a scene" that would provoke the police to act.[16] Ann Marie Smith and Rebekah Menning were among the clergy at the top of the stairs, and they fully expected to be arrested for their civil disobedience.[17] Cornel West was also part of the blockade.

Police did nothing at first, since no Unite the Right demonstrators were yet attempting to enter the park. But as the Unite the Right demonstrators got closer, the police realized that the clergy group and the Unite the Right demonstrators were heading toward a physical clash at the blocked entrance. Other counterprotesters were also beginning to gather at the bottom of the stairs. At 10:36 a.m., Rev. Osagyefo Sekou waded into the group gathering at the base of the stairs and urged them to walk away from the area. Antifa members assisted him. Sekou's motivation in clearing this space was unclear. Perhaps he wanted to avoid having innocents bearing the brunt of violence or arrest. Perhaps he wanted to create an unimpeded path between the approaching Unite the Right marchers and the clergy at the top of the stairs.

The stage for confrontation was set. As the crowd at the base of the stairs was cleared, a large column of Unite the Right demonstrators arrived from the east. They were wielding shields. The showdown moment had arrived. The Unite the Right marchers forged forward, shields first, determined to force their way through the opposition blockade. Behind the phalanx of shield wielders were columns of another hundred or so Unite the Right demonstrators. And then, bizarrely, the confrontation was defused, as everyone began to realize that the Unite the Right marchers had attempted entry from a different side of the park, thereby avoiding the counterdemonstrators' blockade. The Unite the Right demonstrators walked out of the park, along Market Street to the alternative entrance. The clergy scrambled and reformed their blockade at the new entrance.[18]

Once again, the defining moment of confrontation was set. A colossal column of Unite the Right demonstrators came thundering down Market Street. This wave was led by the League of the South and the Traditionalist Worker Party. The Unite the Right forces were wearing helmets and carrying shields, flagpoles, and pepper spray.[19] The counterdemonstrators surged to meet the Unite the Right formation. The counterprotesters blocked Market Street, locking arms to barricade the entrance to Emancipation Park.

The opposing groups engaged. A brawl erupted on Market Street. Unite the Right demonstrators smashed forward with their shields and flagpoles used as offensive weapons. The counterprotesters did not give. They flailed back, grabbing at the flagpoles and pushing against shields. Clouds of pepper spray swathed the combatants.[20]

Through it all, in surreal aplomb, law enforcement officers watched passively. They did not engage.[21] That passivity fueled more hostility among counterdemonstrators. One woman angrily shouted across a barrier to the police, "You tear-gassed us last time, what are you doing?"[22] The police did not respond, simply staring impassively like the guards at Buckingham Palace. The lack of reaction made the woman even madder. "This is shameful!" she screamed. "I am a teacher, I am a community member, take care of your people! What the fuck are you doing? I am the wife of a priest, I am a teacher, I love this city! Take care of your people!"[23]

Violence continued to escalate. People were crying "Medic! Medic!"[24]

Another woman approached Charlottesville police officer Earnest Johnson, asking "Are you going to engage the crowd at all?"

"Not unless I get a command to," he replied.

"Even if there are people physically hurting one another?"

"If I'm given the command to act, yes ma'am, I will."[25]

Tim Messer challenged a state police trooper, asking why the police were not breaking up battles. The trooper replied, "Our policy today is that we cannot get involved in every skirmish, and we are here to protect the public's safety." Messer was incredulous; he could not believe what he was hearing. The trooper coldly repeated, "That is our policy."[26]

A squad of state police troopers moved a short distance around a barricade. Officers from the Charlottesville Police Department asked the troopers, "What are we doing? Are we going in?" But another officer declared emphatically, "No, we're not. We're not going in. We need the riot squad, fast."[27] The formal Unite the Right program had not even begun, yet matters were rapidly unraveling. Objects were being thrown, clouds of pepper spray were enveloping the crowd. Charlottesville police officers on the street wondered if the entire assembly would be declared unlawful and the event shut down before it even started.[28]

Captain David Shifflett radioed from the street to the command center at 10:59 a.m. that the crowds at Second and Market Streets once more were "getting ready to erupt any second now." He then reported a fight of "about forty people going at it, they're using sticks." This was followed shortly by a radio report stating "Weapons are being used on Market and Second Street." Captain Shifflett had plainly seen enough. He radioed: "Recommend unlawful assembly."[29]

Shortly after 11:00, Charlottesville police officers withdrew from the streets to don their riot gear. This exercise did not go smoothly. For many of the officers, it was the first time they had used riot gear. The gear was not well organized, and officers had to waste critical time sifting through plastic bins for the right gas masks, helmets, and riot shields. While the Charlottesville police were suiting up, only the Virginia State Police remained on the streets.[30] They did not have riot gear. Meanwhile, civil disorder was accelerating. Whatever fragile semblance of order had existed in the morning now gave way to outright chaos. Unite the Right demonstrators grew increasingly aggressive, roaming from Emancipation Park outward to engage counterprotesters. Bottles, debris, and clouds of pepper spray filled the air.

At 11:31 a.m., Chief Thomas gave the order to declare the scene an "unlawful assembly." Police used bullhorns to announce the declaration of unlawful assembly to the crowd, ordering them to disperse.

With violence erupting in all directions, at 12:06 p.m. Virginia governor Terry McAuliffe declared a state of emergency. Neither the declaration of unlawful assembly nor the governor's declaration of emergency had any visible effect on ending the chaos and confrontation on the streets. To the

contrary, the declarations had the opposite effect. The zones and barricades that had been set up to establish boundaries and physically separate
the opposing sides now became meaningless, as the Unite the Right demonstrators and their counterprotesting enemies spilled randomly into the
streets of Charlottesville. The entire area seemed to descend into a melee
of marauding tribes, clashing as they made random hostile contact.

Someone lobbed a smoke grenade into the southeast corner of Emancipation Park, though it is not clear who launched it. Unite the Right
demonstrators and counterprotesters in turn picked up and tossed the
smoking grenade back and forth. With all the barriers now trampled
down, as police moved in unison to clear the park, their actions had the
perverse effect of pushing the warring factions into each other.[31]

A large contingent of Unite the Right demonstrators moved west from
Emancipation Park down Market Street. This retreat sent them directly
into a massive group of counterprotesters. One of those counterprotesters
was Corey Long. Holding an aerosol canister, Long ignited the canister's
aerosol spray, creating a makeshift flamethrower, and pointed it at the
passing Unite the Right demonstrators.[32] Seeing Long's homemade flame
thrower aimed at his compatriots, Ku Klux Klan leader Richard Wilson
Preston drew his handgun and pointed it at Long, screaming for Long
to stop. Long did not. Preston loaded a round into the chamber of his
gun and fired a shot in Long's direction. The bullet hit the ground at
Long's feet. Preston shouldered his weapon and walked away. Virginia
State Police troopers stood some twenty feet away from Long and Preston
but did not react. More chaos followed.

Unite the Right leaders Richard Spencer, Eli Mosley, Mike Enoch, and
David Duke retreated from downtown Charlottesville back to McIntire
Park. Many of their followers also arrived at McIntire Park with them.
A hurried rally was held in which Spencer, Enoch, and Duke gave brief
speeches. Mosley then told everyone to quickly get into their cars and
leave before the police and counterdemonstrators like Antifa chased them
down.

Back in downtown Charlottesville, the streets were a mess of confrontation and confusion. In front of a parking garage on Market Street, a
struggle over a flag led to counterdemonstrator DeAndre Harris rushing
into a scuffle, only to himself be turned on and beaten by Unite the Right
demonstrators, who pummeled him to the ground with sticks and shields,

splitting his head and causing profuse bleeding. Sheriff James Brown saw the altercation and managed to render aid to Harris, getting him in the hands of medics.[33]

As disorder consumed the streets of Charlottesville, Officer Tammy Shiflett maintained her tenuous watch on the corner of Fourth and Market Streets. Crowds pushed through the intersection, hurling profanities and insults at Shiflett. She felt isolated and endangered. With no riot gear, weapons, or fellow officers, she was a lone sentinel stationed at an intersection growing increasingly packed and volatile. Shiflett radioed Captain Lewis with alarm, "They are pushing the crowd my way, and I have nobody here to help me."[34] Lewis initiated efforts to extricate Shiflett and get her out of harm's way.[35] Shiflett began to move away from the intersection, then realized she had forgotten to lock her squad car. She ran back to the car, moved it out of the intersection, to a spot near the parking garage, and then joined with the officers who were helping DeAndre Harris. This left the intersection of Market and Fourth Street devoid of any police presence.[36]

In the swirling chaos, rumors spread like wildfires, some of them accurate and some of them false. Police received reports of a major breakout of violence at Justice Park, but when they arrived, there was no altercation going on.[37] There were constant fears that crowds would spill into the Downtown Mall, but no large groups ever materialized there.

Rumors spread among counterprotesters and law enforcement that a group of Unite the Right demonstrators were heading to attack Friendship Court, a public housing project near the downtown populated mostly by African Americans. The rumors arose from a misinterpretation of events arising from the fog of disorder. The Pennsylvania Lightfoot Militia "commander" Christian Yingling was told by Charlottesville police that his militia group had become a "lightning rod" and was asked to depart. Yingling complied with the request, and his group retreated to attempt to reach their vehicles, in the direction of the Downtown Mall. The militia members were confronted with angry counterprotesters as they tried to get to their vehicles. The militia members chose not to confront the counterprotesters, or even attempt, for the time being, to get to their vehicles at a parking lot but instead chose to head away from the counterprotesters. The counterprotesters, however, followed them. Some counterprotesters began throwing rocks at the militia members as they crossed railroad tracks on Garrett Street. One of the militia members was hit in the head with a rock. This caused the militia to stop and take a stand, near the Sultan Kebab restaurant at the corner of Garrett and Second Street SE. This spot happened to be directly in front of Friendship Court. The presence of the militia group there was interpreted by some as people staging for an attack on the housing project. The interpretation was wrong on two levels. The militia group considered themselves neutral peacekeepers, not an attack unit with designs on offensive action against anyone. And the group's presence in front of Friendship Court was pure happenstance—the product of their effort to retreat first from the disorder of the downtown and second from the counterprotesters who had cut them off and pursued them.

The rumor that Friendship Court was "under attack" spread through smart phones and radios, and suddenly other groups of counterprotesters began to make their way toward Friendship Court to come to its defense. Counterprotesters near Justice Park and McGuffey Park, hearing the story that Friendship Park was under attack, began moving to the rescue. Groups from the two parks converged at Water Street and Fourth Street SE. At about the time the two groups of counterprotesters merged, word came from Friendship Court that the "attack" story was a false alarm. Everything at Friendship Court was calm, and there was no point in the counterprotesters continuing on there.

The large crowd stalled for several minutes, uncertain where to go next. Two vehicles, a sedan and a minivan, were stuck in the middle of the intersection, surrounded by the pressing crowd of several hundred protesters milling about as they chose their next objective.

Dwayne Dixon and other members of Redneck Revolt say they saw a man, who they later found out was James Fields, driving his Dodge Challenger with tinted windows.[38] Dixon saw the car three times that day, but not the face of the driver. At first he assumed it was an undercover police officer. But the more the car came around, the more suspicious Dixon became. "One time he paused right in front of me," Dixon later said, "and I waved him off with my rifle," cursing him as well.[39]

It was 1:41 p.m. One block away from where the two stuck vehicles and hundreds of protesters were milling about on Water and Fourth Streets SE, James Alex Fields Jr. drove his silver Dodge Challenger through the flimsy sawhorse at the intersection at Market and Fourth

Streets SE, accelerating down Fourth Street toward the crowded inter-section. Fields's car smashed into the crowd and crashed into the two vehicles in the intersection, pushing them into pedestrians. Horrific video footage shows the car attack in graphic detail, as counterdemonstrators are tossed through the air from the impact of the crash. Fields slammed his car into reverse and accelerated wildly, driving in reverse back up Fourth Street to Market, and then turned east. The front bumper of the Challenger was hanging from the car's smashed grill. Counterprotesters gave chase on foot, trying to keep up with the Challenger. Above the scene, a Virginia State Police helicopter captured the license plate number and description of the car, directing law enforcement squad cars to give chase. Fields speeded down Avon Street to Monticello Avenue. The chase lasted only four minutes. Apparently realizing he could not outrun the police, Fields stopped the Challenger, dropped his keys out the window, and surrendered to police.

Emergency responders rushed to the intersection of Water and Fourth. Some five hundred people were there, many screaming or crying, in panic and shock. Street medics who had attended the rally in support of the counterprotesters were the first to provide aid, followed by a rush of fire department, police, and EMT personnel. The most severely hurt were tri-aged on the street, then loaded into transport to local hospitals.

Deia Schlosberg and Conrad Shaw, two eyewitnesses who were film-ing a documentary, were near the intersection. They said that the Chal-lenger hit a number of people before crashing into the two vehicles in the intersection.[40]

Nineteen people were injured. One person, Heather Heyer, was killed.

Heather Heyer was not the only person to die as a result of the Unite the Right rally.

Charlottesville leaders had planned a press conference at 4:00 p.m. in the immediate aftermath of Heather Heyer's death and the arrest of James Alex Fields Jr., but the time was postponed until later in the evening when Governor McAuliffe announced his intention to travel to Charlottesville.

As McAuliffe's motorcade approached Charlottesville, a Virginia State Police helicopter that had been providing intelligence in the area through-out the day of violence peeled away from the downtown to provide aerial cover for the governor's arrival. Then suddenly, at 4:49 p.m., a shocking report went out that the helicopter had crashed.[41]

The two Virginia state troopers aboard were killed in the crash. The pilot was forty-year-old Trooper Berke M. M. Bates. With him on board was forty-eight-year-old Lieutenant H. Jay Cullen.

A subsequent report of the National Transportation Safety Board indicated witnesses saw the helicopter hovering before it began a "rolling oscillation" and began to spin. The aircraft then "descended in a 40-degree nose down attitude" before it disappeared from view. Security camera footage corroborated those accounts. Witnesses then reported seeing a plume of smoke from the crash site.[42]

Governor McAuliffe was friends with Jay Cullen. McAuliffe spoke at Cullen's funeral, saying he considered Trooper Cullen a member of his family. McAuliffe said that he and his wife Dorothy were heartbroken over Cullen's tragic death. "It'll never be the same when I step into that helicopter and not see Jay in that front right seat with 'Cullen' on the back of his helmet."

Trooper Bates also had connections to the governor. He previously served on the governor's security detail and had only recently transferred to the aviation unit. The day before Bates died, he had contacted Governor McAuliffe about sending a care package to the McAuliffes' oldest son, a marine recently deployed to the Middle East.

30

AFTERMATH

There was a national outpouring of grief and anger over the death of Heather Heyer. As a sign of the fear and loathing that surrounded her death, Heyer's ashes were interred in a secret location, to protect the grave from desecration by neo-Nazis. Heyer's mother Susan Bro insisted on secrecy for the grave site, given the continued threats against both herself and her late daughter.[1]

"What I learned from my own surgery is that wounds cannot heal on the surface. You seal it over and it festers," said Bro, a cancer survivor. "You have to heal from the inside out, and that requires keeping the wound open. That's not a pleasant experience. That requires anesthetic. That requires pain."[2]

Susan Bro was not afraid to talk candidly about race and her daughter's death. "I think it's a damn shame that a white girl had to die for people to have to pay attention," she said. If a black person had died, she offered, the reaction would have been, "'Oh well, another person lost to violent protest.'"[3] When challenged as to why she let her daughter go to the counterprotest, Bro dismissed the question as ridiculous. Heyer was thirty-two years old, with a mind of her own, and was counterprotesting because of what she deeply believed in. "I'm glad she was there," Bro said. "I'm very proud of her."[4]

Susan Bro chose not to let any politicians speak at the funeral. When she spoke, she explained that she was unable to authentically endorse either love or hate. "I could have driven it to hate and vengeance, and I could have driven it to understanding and love and forgiveness and sweetness and light. And neither of those was what I wanted to say." Heather's death, she insisted, would not silence her cause. "They tried to kill my child to shut her up," she said at the funeral. "Well, guess what: you just magnified her."[5]

On August 18, 2017, Heather Heyer's name was placed on a memorial wall at the Southern Poverty Law Center in Montgomery, Alabama, honoring martyrs of the civil rights movement. Lecia Brooks, director of outreach at the center, noted the parallels between Heather Heyer's story and the story of another white woman civil rights activist killed by white supremacists fifty-two years before.[6]

In January and February of 1965, Martin Luther King Jr. and his civil rights organization, the Southern Christian Leadership Conference, staged demonstrations in Alabama.[7] Jimmy Lee Jackson, an African American participant in the protest demonstrations, was fatally shot on February 17, 1965, by a white Alabama state trooper, while Jackson was attempting to protect his mother, who was being clubbed by police.[8] Jackson's shooting is portrayed in the 2014 movie *Selma*.

Jackson's shooting galvanized the civil rights movement's focus on Alabama. The shooting led to a protest on Sunday, March 7, 1965, a date that history would register in infamy as "Bloody Sunday." John Lewis, then a youthful chairman of the Student Nonviolent Coordinating Committee, was among the civil rights leaders who organized six hundred marchers to walk from Selma to Montgomery. The marchers approached the Edmund Pettus Bridge, which crossed the Alabama River. They were met by a phalanx of Alabama state troopers and local police, commanding them to turn around. The marchers refused and continued to march forward to cross the river. The police violently responded, attacking the marchers with tear gas and billy clubs. Over fifty of the marchers were hospitalized.

The bridge at which the beatings took place was more than a physical bridge over the Alabama River. It was also a symbolic bridge spanning Alabama's racist past, named for one of Alabama's leading racist heroes. Edmund Pettus was a Confederate Civil War general. Pettus was also a "grand dragon" of the Alabama Ku Klux Klan. He was elected to the US Senate from Alabama in 1896. His successful campaign drew on his leadership of the Klan and his open opposition to the passage of the Thirteenth, Fourteenth, and Fifteenth Amendments to the Constitution, the "Civil War amendments" abolishing slavery, guaranteeing the equal protection of the laws, and prohibiting discrimination in voting on the basis of race.

"Bloody Sunday" was televised around the world. Civil rights leaders, led by Martin Luther King, were determined to march again, and this time to cross the Edmund Pettus Bridge. Calls went out for activists around the nation to join in more Selma marches.

Viola Fauver Gregg Liuzzo, a thirty-nine-year-old white woman from Michigan, a housewife, an activist, and the mother of five children, was among those who answered the call.[9] Liuzzo traveled from Detroit to Selma in March 1965 to join in the rallies and marches following Bloody Sunday.

When Liuzzo arrived in Selma on March 20, she met Leroy Moton, a nineteen-year-old African American and fellow marcher and organizer. Working in tandem, Liuzzo and Moton used Moton's Oldsmobile to transport demonstrators. On Wednesday, March 24, a celebration concert was held in Selma, featuring such celebrity luminaries as Sammy Davis Jr., Dick Gregory, Harry Belafonte, and Joan Baez. On Thursday, Martin Luther King spoke to a crowd of twenty-five thousand people at the Alabama state capitol building in Montgomery. King called the rally "a shining moment in American history." Later that day, when the rally had ended, Liuzzo worked with Moton to shuttle marchers who had participated in the rally from Montgomery back to Selma, where the march had begun. After having dinner and stopping for gas, Moton and Liuzzo were followed by a group of Klan members, who were agitated by the site of a white woman and a black man driving together. The Klan members chased Liuzzo and Moton at high speeds down winding country roads for nearly twenty miles, until the Klansmen's car finally drew even with the Oldsmobile. Several shots were fired into the car, and Liuzzo was instantly killed. Their car careened into a ditch, crashing into a fence. Moton lay still, pretending that he too had been killed. The Klansmen left the scene.[10]

One of the four Klansmen, Gary Thomas Rowe, was an FBI informant. The other three Klansmen responsible for the murders were arrested. Their state prosecutions ended in mistrials and acquittals, but federal prosecutors did manage to obtain convictions on federal charges, resulting in ten-year prison sentences. Liuzzo's family spent decades trying to uncover the truth surrounding the murder and the FBI's character assassination of Liuzzo. Based on congressional investigations into FBI abuses during the civil rights years, the family believed that the person who actually fired the shots that killed Viola was Rowe, the FBI informant.

Heather Heyer, like Viola Liuzzo, would be honored by many as a civil rights martyr. And Heyer, like Liuzzo, would also suffer scurrilous attacks even in death. Unite the Right organizer Jason Kessler tweeted on August 19, 2017, "Heather Heyer was a fat, disgusting Communist. Communists have killed 94 million. Looks like it was payback time."[11] In Liuzzo's case, the defamation campaign was led by none other than J. Edgar Hoover, director of the FBI. Hoover suggested that Liuzzo was a promiscuous woman who had traveled to Alabama to have sex with black men.[12]

In assigning accountability for Heather Heyer's death, and more broadly, for the deaths of the state police officers, and for all the physical and psychological injury the Unite the Right rally caused, there are many nominees to consider.

Alex Fields was plainly the person directly responsible for Heyer's death, and he was predictably and justifiably convicted of murder.

In ascribing blame for what happened in Charlottesville beyond Fields himself, there were many popular nominees. Some pointed fingers at Charlottesville leaders, University of Virginia administrators, and the law enforcement agencies, who in various ways could have done more to keep order. Many, of course, laid the principal blame on the alt-right leaders such as Richard Spencer, Jason Kessler, and their multiple disciples. President Donald Trump appeared to blame "both sides," the racists and the counterprotesters. In turn, many around the country blamed President Trump. While Heather Heyer died from a car, not a gun, the heavy presence of arms at the rally, which escalated tensions and contributed to the chaos, led some to apportion some of the blame to the Supreme Court and its interpretation of the Second Amendment that recognized the possession of guns as a personal right. And finally, there were those who argued that a piece of the blame should be placed on the First Amendment and the marketplace theory of free speech, which treated hate speech as free speech. I took this last criticism particularly personally, since I had long been, as both a scholar and a courtroom advocate, a champion of expansive protection for free speech. Was I, in some sense, personally complicit in Heather Heyer's death, and in the deaths of thousands of others killed by radicalized extremists who bought into the wild "white genocide" conspiracy theories that fueled the Unite the Right rally and other episodes of hate violence around the globe? I take up each of these in my concluding reflections.

The Authorities

As to Charlottesville officials, the university administrators at UVA, and the law enforcement agencies, there is no question, in hindsight, that mistakes were made. Law enforcement agencies failed to share information, did not have coordinated plans, and had poor lines of communication. In training for the rally, officers were encouraged to be passive, out of what may have been too much concern for not appearing to take sides or squelch free speech rights. Yet in my view, to assign any profound blame to UVA administrators, Charlottesville leaders, or law enforcement is unfair. I do believe that important things can be learned from the mistakes, but I am reluctant to go far beyond that.

Two major investigations took place to study the events and recommend reforms. One was the Governor's Task Force convened by Virginia governor Terry McAuliffe, which I assisted; the other was the Heaphy Report, independently commissioned by the City of Charlottesville, led by the superb Virginia lawyer and former United States Attorney Timothy J. Heaphy and the estimable Virginia law firm of Hunton & Williams.

The Governor's Task Force on Public Safety and Preparedness and Response to Civil Unrest issued a report with multiple recommendations. The recommendations of the task force's permitting working group graciously stated that the "products developed by the Work Group reflect significant discussion and deliberation by all members based on research and input from Task Force staff and Dean Rodney Smolla."[13] I deserve little personal credit, however, as the real work and real thought was performed by the task force members and staff.

My assistance to the Governor's Task Force focused heavily on existing First Amendment standards and the intersection of the First Amendment rights to freedom of speech and assembly, and the Second Amendment right to keep and bear arms, established by the Supreme Court's famous Second Amendment decision in *District of Columbia v. Heller*.[14] I expressed the somewhat controversial view to the task force that *Heller* should *not* be understood as preventing governments engaged in permitting for major events such as the Unite the Right rally, or the counterprotest rallies such events spurred, from prohibiting the possession of weapons at these events. The task force adopted my recommendation on this score, proposing that Virginia law be amended to include a provision stating, "Localities may prohibit the possession or carrying of firearms, ammunition, or components or combination thereof in public spaces during permitted events or events that should otherwise require a permit."[15]

Recall that the Supreme Court in *District of Columbia v. Heller* admonished, "Although we do not undertake an exhaustive historical analysis today of the full scope of the Second Amendment, nothing in our opinion should be taken to cast doubt on longstanding prohibitions on the possession of firearms by felons and the mentally ill, or laws forbidding the carrying of firearms in sensitive places such as schools and government buildings, or laws imposing conditions and qualifications on the commercial sale of arms."[16] Lower courts are divided over whether the individual right recognized in *Heller* encompasses *only* a right to possess guns for the purposes of self-defense inside one's dwelling, or also includes a right to carry weapons in public spaces. I suspect that the Supreme Court will eventually hold that given the Second Amendment's language expressing a right to both "keep" and to "bear" arms, and given the more conservative makeup of the court following Justice Kennedy's retirement and replacement by Justice Kavanaugh, who expressed strong pro–Second Amendment views while on the District of Columbia Court of Appeals, that the Second Amendment will eventually be interpreted to include a right to carry weapons in public spaces.

However, when it comes to large events on public property—events that require permitting—it does not follow that local governments would be barred under the Second Amendment from treating the sites of such events as "sensitive places" in which weapons may be prohibited for a set time. Critics of my position may say that Heather Heyer was killed by a car, not a gun. But this misses the point. But for the grace of God, the heavily armed attendees in Charlottesville at the Unite the Right rally could *well* have killed people with firearms, and the violently charged and heavily armed atmosphere was fraught with such menace and peril. Given the epidemic of violent episodes in American society over the last decade at mass gatherings that constitute "soft targets," and given the super-charged atmosphere of events such as the Unite the Right rally, I believe the policy judgments for banning weapons at such events are compelling. We do not know, of course, if the Supreme Court will eventually see it that way. In my view, however, the Virginia task force deserves great credit for its courage in recommending that society give it a try.

Law enforcement agencies and officials received a significant amount of critique in the Heaphy Report. I personally find it difficult to assign condemnation or blame against law enforcement at Charlottesville in any pointed sense, given the volatility the events presented, and the sense that police were constantly caught in the middle between opposing groups and were trying to respect the constitutional rights of both. There is a difference, however, between assigning blame, in a condemning sense, and *ascribing lessons to be learned*, in a constructive sense. On this score I have deep respect for both the Governor's Task Force and the Heaphy Report, and generally believe their future-looking recommendations on law enforcement strategies are sound.

Several lessons strike me as especially cogent.

Governments should not be afraid to use overwhelming force by assigning a massive presence of law enforcement personnel to events that pose the threat of violent clashes and civil disorder. For all the evils of the Nazis in Madison Square Garden in 1939, the massive presence of New York police at the event did prevent any physical violence. Following the Charlottesville violence, Boston used a massive presence of police to deter violence at a similar rally.

Governments should purchase and have readily deployable physical separators, such as barricades and fences, to block traffic and to keep opposing groups at sufficient physical distance that they cannot easily inflict physical harm on one another. First Amendment values dictate that opposing groups be close enough to see each other, to brandish signs and symbols criticizing each other, and to be able to yell and scream at each other. But the First Amendment does not require they be able to push, shove, or throw projectiles (at least at close range).

Governments should, as I have already opined, ban weapons at such permitted events.

When police are deployed, they should alternately face both groups. In Charlottesville, there was a tendency to treat the supremacists as the group "running the gauntlet" between counterprotesters. This was particularly the pattern at the KKK rally in Charlottesville in July. Police generally had their backs to the supremacists, who were moving in the protective corridor formed as police mostly faced outward, toward the counterprotesters. This creates the symbolic impression that the police are siding with the supremacists and protecting them from the counterprotesters. The police appear to be taking sides. This was clearly how the counterprotesters perceived the July KKK events, particularly after tear gas was released against the counterprotesters. Far better to alternate police officers facing outward and inward, with every other officer facing either the supremacists or those protesting against them. This protects each group against the other and does not send the inadvertent message that the police are choosing sides.

Finally, governments should not be hesitant to train police officers assigned to such rallies to *not* be inordinately passive when demonstrators go beyond vitriolic rhetoric and engage in physical action that is violent or illegal.

If I am reticent in assigning any deep moral culpability to Charlottesville and UVA authorities, I have no reticence in assigning full responsibility for all the death and destruction in Charlottesville to Richard Spencer, Jason Kessler, and their many radical supremacist disciples.

The Supremacist Leaders

Jason Kessler called a press conference in front of Charlottesville City Hall at 2 p.m. on Sunday, August 13. As Kessler began to speak, an outraged crowd began shouting "Say her name," in anger over the death of Heather Heyer.

Kessler sought to place the entire blame on the Charlottesville police. "What happened yesterday was the result of the Charlottesville police officers refusing to do their jobs," Kessler declared. "They stood down and did not follow through with the agreed upon security arrangements."

The crowd was in no mood for such apologetics. Jeff Winder, who was watching Kessler speak, lunged at Kessler and punched him. Others in the crowd followed, storming the podium where Kessler was trying to speak. Kessler ran from the podium. The crowed followed him as he ran up the street toward the Charlottesville Police Department. As Kessler reached the police headquarters, the police were able to separate him from the angry mob and escort him into the safety of the headquarters building. Jeff Winder later said that Kessler "had an incredible amount of nerve coming in front of the people of Charlottesville after the pain, suffering, and terror that he brought on the community. He should never be allowed to show his face in town again."[17]

Kessler sent a tweet commenting on the death of Heather Heyer, stating "Heather Heyer was a fat, disgusting Communist. Communists have killed 94 million. Looks like it was payback time." Kessler later repudiated the tweet and blamed it on Ambien, Xanax, and alcohol.

Whatever drugs or drink may have caused Kessler's tweet, they are no excuse for Kessler, Spencer, or the dozens of other leaders who orchestrated the Unite the Right rally. The message, the intent, the actions of these individuals were loathsome and fraught with death.

Multiple lawsuits were filed against Unite the Right leaders and participants by victims of the Charlottesville violence. The most formidable case, *Sines v. Kessler*,[18] was brought on October 12, 2017, by eleven plaintiffs against numerous individual Unite the Right leaders and their various supporting organizations, in federal court in Virginia.

The plaintiffs included Tyler Magill, who was surrounded and assaulted by various alt-right followers on the Friday night march to the Thomas Jefferson statue on the UVA campus, and who later suffered a trauma-induced stroke as a result of the assault. Two other UVA students present at the Friday night confrontation were also plaintiffs. One of them was Natalie Romero, who was not only at the Thomas Jefferson statute confrontation Friday night but was also hit by Fields's car when he slammed into the crowd on Saturday. Marcus Martin, an African American counterprotester, was another plaintiff. He too was hit by Fields's car and sustained a broken leg and ankle. Martin heroically pushed his fiancée, plaintiff Marissa Blair, out of the way of the car, but Blair still also suffered various physical injuries. Blair was a paralegal who worked and socialized with her fellow paralegal, Heather Heyer.[19] Chelsea Alvarado, another plaintiff, was yet another person hit by Fields's car, and she sued for her physical and emotional injuries. Elizabeth Sines, a graduate of Cornell University and a second-year law student at the UVA Law School, witnessed the events firsthand. She sued for her severe emotional distress and shock. Similarly, April Muñiz was nearly hit by Fields's car and sued for the acute stress disorder and trauma caused by the event.

Rev. Seth Wispelwey, one of the ministers who led Congregate Charlottesville, also joined the suit as a plaintiff. Wispelwey was a participant in the church service at St. Paul's the night of August 11. He alleged that he had been confronted by one of the defendants after the torchlight rally and in addition had been assaulted while counterprotesting on Saturday. Wispelwey alleged that the events caused him extreme emotional distress manifested in physical symptoms, including constricted chest pain, difficulty sleeping, and repeated nightmares concerning the events of August 11 and 12, interfering with his ability to return full time to work. Plaintiff Hannah Pearce, a dermatologist who lives in Charlottesville with her husband and four children, was an active member and leader of Congregation Beth Israel, the downtown synagogue near the epicenter of the violence. She alleged that throughout the events she was subjected to antisemitic harassment.

The suit was brought against many of the individuals who organized and led the Unite the Right rally, as well as many of their supporting participating organizations. The individual defendants included Jason Kessler, Richard Spencer, Christopher Cantwell, James Alex Fields Jr., Andrew Anglin, Robert "Azzmador" Ray, Nathan Damigo, Elliot Kline (alias Eli Mosley), Matthew Heimbach, Matthew Parrott (alias David Matthew Parrott), Michael Hill, Michael Tubbs, Jeff Schoep, Augustus Sol Invictus, and Michael "Enoch" Peinovich. The organizational defendants included Vanguard America, Moonbase Holdings LLC, Identity Evropa, the Traditionalist Worker Party, the League of the South, the

National Socialist Movement, the Nationalist Front, the Fraternal Order of the Alt-Knights, the Loyal White Knights of the Ku Klux Klan, and the East Coast Knights of the Ku Klux Klan (alias East Coast Knights of the True Invisible Empire).

David Duke was not named as a formal defendant but was named as a coconspirator.

The lawsuit was assigned to senior federal district judge Norman K. Moon. The journalist Dahlia Lithwick, writing for Slate, captured what was likely the sense of many people in Charlottesville as the suit commenced. Lithwick, who makes Charlottesville her home, observed, "Charlottesville is a city in pain, and for those who live there, it isn't just a set for the white nationalist edition of *The Apprentice*."[20] Lithwick slammed the defendants in the suit as cowards who just might be surprised at what the legal system had in store for them. "The alt-right cowards who sneak in with tiki torches by night, but not before alerting the press and fixing their hair," she wrote, "may not be quite as immune from litigation, discovery, and legal accountability as they believe."[21]

The lawsuit against the supremacists was based on multiple legal theories, but the two theories that carried the greatest weight involved a federal statute passed by Congress in 1871 specifically directed at organized terrorism against blacks in the Reconstruction South, and a Virginia law aimed at racial, ethnic, and religious intimidation.

The federal law, now codified and known as "Section 1985(3)," reads,

> If two or more persons in any State or Territory conspire or go in disguise on the highway or on the premises of another, for the purpose of depriving, either directly or indirectly, any person or class of persons of the equal protection of the laws, or of equal privileges and immunities under the laws; or for the purpose of preventing or hindering the constituted authorities of any State or Territory from giving or securing to all persons within such State or Territory the equal protection of the laws; or if two or more persons conspire to prevent by force, intimidation, or threat, any citizen who is lawfully entitled to vote, from giving his support or advocacy in a legal manner, toward or in favor of the election of any lawfully qualified person as an elector for President or Vice President, or as a Member of Congress of the United States; or to injure any citizen in person or property on account of such support or advocacy; in any case of conspiracy set forth in this section, if one or more persons engaged therein do, or cause to be done, any act in furtherance

of the object of such conspiracy, whereby another is injured in his person or property, or deprived of having and exercising any right or privilege of a citizen of the United States, the party so injured or deprived may have an action for the recovery of damages occasioned by such injury or deprivation, against any one or more of the conspirators.[22]

To prevail under this federal law the plaintiffs had to demonstrate five elements: (1) a conspiracy of two or more persons, (2) who are motivated by a specific class-based, invidiously discriminatory animus to (3) deprive the plaintiff of the equal enjoyment of rights secured by the law to all, (4) and which results in injury to the plaintiff as (5) a consequence of an overt act committed by the defendants in connection with the conspiracy.

The plaintiffs also invoked a Virginia law passed to provide a remedy for intimidation or harassment motivated by racial, religious, or ethnic animosity:

A. An action for injunctive relief or civil damages, or both, shall lie for any person who is subjected to acts of (i) intimidation or harassment or (ii) violence directed against his person; or (iii) vandalism directed against his real or personal property, where such acts are motivated by racial, religious, or ethnic animosity.

B. Any aggrieved party who initiates and prevails in an action authorized by this section shall be entitled to damages, including punitive damages, and in the discretion of the court to an award of the cost of the litigation and reasonable attorneys' fees in an amount to be fixed by the court.[23]

As would be expected, the defendants sought to have the claims against them dismissed, on the grounds that all their activities were protected by the First Amendment. In my view, the defendants were wrong. Despite my commitment to freedom of speech, and notwithstanding my own role in defending the Klan in *Virginia v. Black*,[24] in my view, the *facts* that have been revealed, and upon which the Charlottesville lawsuit was based, demonstrate that even under the robust protections for offensive speech embraced by the marketplace theory, these defendants crossed the line. They engaged in an actual conspiracy to descend on Charlottesville and the University of Virginia to plunge those communities into chaos and violence, and to intimidate and harass members of the community on the basis of race, ethnicity, and religion. Their actions were precisely the sorts of actions Congress sought to attack in 1871 in reacting against organized terrorism in the Reconstruction South, and their actions went beyond the protections of the First Amendment.

I was delighted when, on July 9, 2018, one year following Charlottesville's bloody summer of 2017, Judge Norman Moon agreed, holding that the actions of the Unite the Right leaders were not sheltered by the First Amendment, and the lawsuit could move forward. Judge Moon did not rule in favor of every plaintiff on every count against every defendant. His carefully analyzed and exhaustive opinion moved carefully and meticulously through each detailed count, person by person. Yet the overwhelming bulk of the case survived. Most of the defendants, Judge Moon ruled, had indeed engaged in a conspiracy to commit violence and intimidation against others, motivated by racial, ethnic, and religious hatred.

Judge Moon was very careful to distinguish between mere hate speech, which is protected by the First Amendment, and participation in hate crimes, which is not.

For example, Moon dismissed all charges against one of the individual defendants, Michael "Enoch" Peinovich, the host of a racist podcast, who was featured on a poster for the rally, and who interviewed followers after the events. "The podcast," Judge Moon ruled, "without more, is protected speech."[25] The plaintiffs had pointed to one of Peinovich's racist podcast statements, in which he said, "Now come on, beating up the wrong negro, is that even a possibility? Beat up the wrong nigger?"[26] Even this, Judge Moon ruled, was insufficient to demonstrate that Peinovich had entered an agreement to engage in racial violence at the events. Similarly, while Peinovich, through the promotional poster, may have been part of an agreement to promote the rally, mere promotion did not violate the law and was protected by the First Amendment, since the rally was "an event which many people attended for divergent reasons."[27] Judge Moon thus left Peinovich off the hook, reasoning that Peinvoich's racism alone was not enough to impose upon him liability for what happened.

Judge Moon also did not fully credit all the allegations of injury brought by all the plaintiffs. This is the mirror image of what is protected by the First Amendment. Bigots have a First Amendment right to hurl hateful insults, and the victims are barred by the First Amendment from suing for insults alone.

Setting these few caveats aside, however, Judge Moon allowed virtually all the claims to proceed against virtually all the defendants. In so doing, he pointedly rebuffed the argument that the actions of the defendants were absolutely protected by the First Amendment. Speaking of the torchlight parade across the UVA campus on Friday, August 11, for example, Moon observed, "Even if some of the torchlight march could be characterized as expressive conduct, the combination of the torches and this violence was not protected by the First Amendment." On this score, Moon properly invoked *Virginia v. Black*,[28] noting that the First Amendment permits a state to ban a true threat. Quoting from the Supreme Court's opinion in *Black*, Judge Moon concluded, "Intimidation in the constitutionally proscribable sense of the word is a type of true threat, where a speaker directs a threat to a person or group of persons with the intent of placing the victim in fear of bodily harm or death."[29] As an example, Moon observed that while lighted torches were being thrown at counterprotesters, Azzmador Ray shouted, "The heat here is nothing compared to what you're going to get in the ovens!"[30]

Judge Moon meticulously chronicled the evidence, pointing to advance orchestration and planning to engage in intimidation, threats, disruption, and violence. He noted the secretive online preparation platform, called "Discord," an "invite only" platform that allowed defendants and their chosen invitees to engage in their conspiratorial communications in the lead-up to the events. Moon noted that communications on Discord included mundane planning details, racist "jokes," and concrete threats of violence. Mosley posted "General Orders" for "Operation Unite the Right Charlottesville 2.0." Organizers also posted information about shuttle service, lodging, and carpools. "Other corners of Discord," Moon noted, "were significantly darker." One user posted a fake advertisement for a pepper-spray-look-alike called "Nig—Away," described as a "a no-fuss, no muss 'nigger killer,'" promised to "kill on contact" in order to "rid the area of niggers." Another frequent Discord user asked whether it was "legal to run over protestors blocking roadways?" This user specifically clarified that he was not joking, "I'm NOT just shitposting. I would like clarification. I know it's legal in North Carolina and a few other states. I'm legitimately curious for the answer." Elsewhere on Discord, Judge Moon noted, users made it clear they planned to fight at the events, saying things like "I'm ready to crack skulls." Jason Kessler told users on

Discord, "I recommend you bring picket sign post, shields and other self-defense implements which can be turned from a free speech tool to a self-defense weapon should things turn ugly." Vanguard America instructed its members "to arrive at the rally in matching khaki pants and white polos," with one member noting that this was "a good fighting uniform."[31]

Other social media platforms, including Facebook, were also used to incite and orchestrate violence. Michael Hill wrote, in a Defendant League of the South Facebook group, that he wanted "no fewer than 150 League warriors, dressed and ready for action, in Charlottesville, Virginia, on 12 August."[32]

As the plaintiffs in the case persuasively alleged, the violence in Charlottesville was no accident. Under the pretext of a rally to merely express their views within the safe confines of the First Amendment, the leaders of the alt-right exhorted each other to violence, with statements such as "If you want to defend the South and Western civilization from the Jew and his dark-skinned allies, be at Charlottesville on 12 August," and, "Next stop: Charlottesville, VA. Final stop: Auschwitz."[33]

Invoking the Supreme Court's decisions in cases such as *N.A.A.C.P. v. Claiborne Hardware Co.*, Judge Moon concluded that while the First Amendment protects vigorous advocacy, it does not protect violence. If the alt-right leaders engaged in only "abstract advocacy," Moon emphasized, that advocacy would be protected by the First Amendment. But if they crossed the line to engage in a conspiracy against the public peace and order, they had transcended the bounds of freedom of speech. While agreements to engage in illegal conduct do in a literal sense involve expressive association, society may ban conspiracies to form such illegal agreements without infringing on any right protected by the First Amendment.

Judge Moon also properly ruled that the facts alleged could constitute the sort of incitement to violence not protected under the Supreme Court's landmark decision in *Brandenburg v. Ohio*, which held that the First Amendment does not protect speech directed to the incitement of imminent lawless action and likely to produce such action. Among other actions, Moon noted, the defendants encouraged the throwing of torches at counterprotesters and ordered others to "charge!"[34]

Finally, Judge Moon had important things to say about the intersection of the Second Amendment's right to bear arms and the First Amendment's protection of free speech. The alt-right leaders argued that their encouragement to followers to bring their weapons to Charlottesville for the Unite the Right rally could not be used as evidence against them to demonstrate a conspiracy to encourage intimidation and violence. Judge Moon first noted that the plaintiffs in the case were not claiming that the mere *bringing* of the weapons was outside the protection of the Constitution, but rather that *using* them was not protected. Moreover, Moon ruled, even the *bringing* of the weapons was evidence of an intent to threaten or engage in violence that a jury could consider. Judge Moon correctly understood that the Supreme Court's Second Amendment decision in *District of Columbia v. Heller* was no magic talisman insulating the alt-right leaders from responsibility for encouraging their followers to come armed, while exhorting them to violent confrontation. Judge Moon held that the decisions of the alt-right leaders to encourage followers to bring substantial amounts of weapons to the rally were evidence of a plan to engage in violence. Among other specifics, Moon pointed to statements by Cantwell after the rally, such as, "I came pretty well prepared for this thing today," made while pulling out three pistols, two semiautomatic machine guns, and a knife.[35] Of the next alt-right protest, Judge Moon noted, Cantwell said, "'It's going to be tough to top but we're up to the challenge. . . . I think a lot more people are going to die before we're done here, frankly.'"[36]

President Donald Trump

As to the president of the United States, Susan Bro had little good to say. She told *Good Morning America*, "I'm not talking to the president. You can't wash this one away by shaking my hand and saying I'm sorry."[37] In a counsel that President Trump has undoubtedly heard hundreds of times from friend and foe alike, but that seemed especially poignant when spoken from the heart of a mother who had just lost her child, Susan Bro told the president, "Think before you speak."[38]

President Trump's role in the Charlottesville events of 2017 may be analyzed before, during, and after the traumas of August 12, 2017. The "before" analysis focuses on the synergy between the extremist views of the alt-right and Trump's run for the presidency. The "during" focuses on what he did and did not do while the events were unfolding. The "after" focuses on his response to the events once they transpired.

The deep philosophical and political connections between the alt-right and Donald Trump's candidacy have already been well documented in this book and need not be repeated here. Suffice it to say that while Donald Trump might or might not candidly admit the connection, his message to the American people was entirely congenial with the messages of the alt-right, which is why the alt-right exulted in his ascendency.

As American Renaissance leader Jared Taylor explained, "I'm sure he would repudiate any association with people like me, but his support comes from people who are more like me than he might like to admit."[39]

President Trump did nothing whatsoever during the summer of 2017 to address the growing racist tensions in Charlottesville. The president was entirely missing in action. Assessment of the president's role in Charlottesville thus devolves largely on his reaction to the events after Heather Heyer's death.

At 1:19 p.m. on August 12, President Trump tweeted, "We ALL must be united & condemn all that hate stands for. There is no place for this kind of violence in America. Lets come together as one!"

This Twitter post came after mounting criticism that the president had failed to condemn the Charlottesville violence, criticism that came from Republicans as well as Democrats. His response, however, was viewed by many as tepid. He did not mention the city of Charlottesville by name, and issued no specific condemnations.[40] Trump's tweet was contrasted with the condemnations of others, including his wife Melania, who nearly an hour before him had used the hashtag #Charlottesville on Twitter to condemn the violence.[41]

An hour later President Trump tweeted, "Am in Bedminster for meetings & press conference on V.A. & all that we have done, and are doing, to make it better-but Charlottesville sad!" This tweet too drew critique, as vague and failing to include any firm and direct condemnations.[42]

Trump then addressed the Charlottesville events in live remarks from his golf club in New Jersey. "We condemn in the strongest possible terms this egregious display of hatred, bigotry, and violence on many sides—on many sides," he said. Trump called on Americans to "cherish our history" which some interpreted as code for the preservation of the Robert E. Lee and Stonewall Jackson statutes that the alt-right members were defending.

A reporter shouted a question at Trump, asking him if he wants the support of white nationalists. Trump ignored the question. A White House spokesman later confirmed that the president meant what he said, asserting that "there was violence between protestors and counter-protestors today."[43]

President Trump's "many sides" remark generated a firestorm of rebuke, as persons across the political spectrum insisted there was no "moral equivalency" between the racist messages of the alt-right and the messages of the counterprotesters opposing racism. Among responses from Trump's own party, Republican senator Cory Gardner of Colorado tweeted, "Mr. President—we must call evil by its name. These were white supremacists and this was domestic terrorism." Republican senator Orrin Hatch of Utah, who lost a brother in the Second World War, similarly stated, "We should call evil by its name. My brother didn't give his life fighting Hitler for Nazi ideas to go unchallenged here at home." Republican senator Marco Rubio of Florida tweeted, "Very important for the nation to hear @potus describe events in #Charlottesville for what they are, a terror attack by #whitesupremacists." The Republican House Speaker, Paul Ryan, tweeted, "The views fueling the spectacle in Charlottesville are repugnant. Let it only serve to unite Americans against this kind of vile bigotry." The Senate majority leader, Mitch McConnell, tweeted, "The hate and bigotry witnessed in #Charlottesville does not reflect American values. I wholeheartedly oppose their actions." Mike Huckabee, the former Arkansas governor and father of the White House press secretary, Sarah Huckabee Sanders, tweeted, "'White supremacy' crap is worst kind of racism—it's EVIL and perversion of God's truth to ever think our Creator values some above others."[44]

Criticisms from Democrats were predictably even more pointed. The Democratic Senate minority leader, Chuck Schumer, said in a statement, "The march and rally in Charlottesville goes against everything the American flag stands for. President Trump must condemn this in the strongest terms immediately." Hawaii senator Brian Schatz offered a pointed comment on Twitter: "It is not too much to ask to have a president who explicitly condemns Nazis." Former presidential candidate Bernie Sanders tweeted at Trump, "No, Mr. President. This is a provocative effort by Neo-Nazis to foment racism and hatred and create violence. Call it out for what it is."[45]

Perhaps tellingly, however, David Duke thought even President Trump's pallid remarks were on the verge of betraying the alt-right sympathies that Duke believed had gotten the president elected, chiding the president,

"I would recommend you take a good look in the mirror & remember it was White Americans who put you in the presidency, not radical leftists."[46]

The backlash over President Trump's Saturday tweets and remarks escalated throughout the weekend. On Monday, August 14, Trump sought to cut off the criticism by calling out the KKK, neo-Nazis, and white supremacists by name and not stating that there was blame on both sides.

"Racism is evil," said President Trump, "including the K.K.K., neo-Nazis, white supremacists and other hate groups that are repugnant to everything we hold dear as Americans."[47]

The effort met with mixed reviews. Some thought that the president was obviously scripted and that his prepared statement was awkward, insincere, and did not reflect his true beliefs. "Trump faced a fork in the road today, and he took it," said Representative Nancy Pelosi, Democratic House minority leader from California. "He showed cowardice on Saturday by refusing to call out the racists and neo-Nazis, and on Monday he showed how uncomfortable he was in delivering another kind of message."[48]

Richard Spencer was among the skeptics who doubted that the message was the real Trump. "The statement today was more 'kumbaya' nonsense," Spencer told reporters on Monday. "He sounded like a Sunday school teacher."[49] Spencer seemed to signal that he thought the remarks were written by the president's handlers, and he doubted that Trump himself took his own remarks seriously. "I don't think that Donald Trump is a dumb person, and only a dumb person would take those lines seriously," Spencer quipped.[50]

Richard Spencer had it exactly right. On Tuesday, August 15, the real Trump, unscripted, spontaneously emerged. The president was in residence in Trump Tower, away from his White House staff, and away from family members. He addressed a group of about twenty reporters from behind a velvet rope line in the lobby at Trump Tower.[51] Because the president's remarks were so expansive and telling, it is best to report them with no substantive editing.

The president explained his delay in addressing the Charlottesville events as the product of wanting to be sure he had the facts:

> I didn't wait long. I didn't wait long. I didn't wait long. I wanted to make sure unlike most politicians that what I said was correct. Not make a quick statement. . . . It takes a little while to get the facts. You still don't know the facts

and it's a very, very important process to me. . . . You don't make statements that direct unless you know the facts. . . . When I make a statement I like to be correct. . . . Before I make a statement, I need the facts . . . so making the statement when I made the statement, it was excellent. In fact the young woman who I hear was a fantastic young woman . . . her mother wrote me and said, though I guess Twitter, social media, the nicest things and I very much appreciated that. . . . Her mother on Twitter thanked me for what I said. And honestly if the press were not fake and were honest, the press would have said what I said was very nice. I'd do it the same way and you know why? Because I want to make sure when I make a statement that the statement is correct.[52]

The president described a statement by David Duke made in Charlottesville as "beautiful":

I didn't know David Duke was there, I wanted to see the facts. . . . Everybody said "His statement was beautiful," he could've made it sooner. . . . There's still things that people don't know.

The president showed resistance to defining the alt-right and rejoined that there was also an alt-left, and placed blame for the violence as much or more on the alt-left as the alt-right:

When you say the "alt-right," define alt-right to me. You define it. What about the "alt-left" that came charging at, excuse me, what about the "alt-left" that came charging at as you say the "alt-right," do they have any semblance of guilt? They do. What about the fact that they came charging swinging, they had clubs in their hands. Do they have any problem? I think that they do. As far as I'm concerned, that was a horrible, horrible day. Wait a minute, I'm not finished, fake news. That was a horrible day. I will tell you something. I watch the shots very closely. You had a group on one side that was bad, and you had a group on the other side that was also very violent, and nobody wants to say that, but I'll say that right now. You had a group on the other side that came charging in without a permit, and they were very, very violent.

The president defended many of those who gathered for the Unite the Right rally, saying that they were not all neo-Nazis, and that many of the Unite the Right participants were "fine people." He defended the preservation of the statutes of Robert E. Lee and Stonewall Jackson. He suggested that removal of statutes of Lee and Jackson could next lead to the removal of monuments to Thomas Jefferson or George Washington, asking "where does it stop?"

> Not all of those people were neo-Nazis, believe me, not all of those people were white supremacists. By any stretch. Those people were also there because they wanted to protest the taking down of a statue of Robert E. Lee, and you take a look at it, many of those people were there to protest the taking down of the statue of Robert E. Lee. So this week it's Robert E. Lee. I noticed that Stonewall Jackson is coming down. I wonder is it George Washington next week and is it Thomas Jefferson the week after? You all, you really do have to ask yourself where does it stop. . . . You had some bad people in that group, but you also had very fine people on both sides.

Returning to his initial Saturday position assigning blame to both sides, the president made it clear that he thought both the right and the left were to blame, and made much of the left "violently attacking" the Unite the Right demonstrators:

> You had a group on one side and you had a group on the other, and they came at each other with clubs, and it was vicious and it was horrible, and it was a horrible thing to watch. But there is another side. There was a group on this side, you can call it the left . . . that came violently attacking the other group. So you can say what you want, but that's the way it is. I think there's blame on both sides . . . and I have no doubt about it, and you don't have any doubt about it either.

The president, returning to his "where does it stop" theme, centered on the fact that George Washington owned slaves:

> George Washington was a slave owner. Was George Washington a slave owner? So will George Washington now lose his statues? Are we going to take down statues to George Washington? How about Thomas Jefferson, you like him? . . . Because he was a major slave owner . . . you're changing history.

The president severely condemned James Alex Fields Jr.:

> The driver of the car is a disgrace to himself, his family, and this country. And . . . you can call it terrorism, you can call it murder. You can call it

whatever you want. I would just call it as the fastest one to come up with a good verdict, that's what I would call it. . . . The driver of the car is a murderer, and what he did is a horrible, horrible, inexcusable thing.

The president's press conference remarks on August 15 generated even more intense criticism than his original tweets and statements on Saturday. Senator Hatch reprised his earlier statement about the loss of his brother in World War II. "I was just eight years old when my older brother Jesse was killed in world war two," Hatch wrote in an Instagram post. "As I said on Saturday, Jesse didn't give his life fighting Hitler for Nazi ideas to go unchallenged here at home. I will never hesitate to speak out against hate—whenever and wherever I see it."[53]

Senator Rubio tweeted, "The organizers of events which inspired & led to #charlottesvilleterroristattack are 100% to blame for a number of reasons," adding, "Mr. President, you can't allow #WhiteSupremacists to share only part of blame. They support idea which cost nation & world so much pain." And he added, "the #WhiteSupremacy groups will see being assigned only 50% of blame as a win. We can not allow this old evil to be resurrected."[54] Speaker Paul Ryan called white supremacy "repulsive" and said "there can be no moral ambiguity."[55] Representative Ileana Ros-Lehtinen, Republican of Florida, tweeted, "Blaming 'both sides' for #Charlottesville?! No."[56] Republican senator Todd Young of Indiana wrote, "This is simple: we must condemn and marginalize white supremacist groups, not encourage and embolden them."[57] The president's remarks even drew a negative response from the General Robert B. Neller, the commandant of the Marine Corps. Such critique of the commander-in-chief, even though indirect, by a senior uniformed officer is extremely rare. General Neller stated in a Twitter message that there is "no place for racial hatred or extremism in @USMC. Our core values of Honor, Courage, and Commitment frame the way Marines live and act."[58]

President Trump's statements led to a rash of resignations by corporate leaders from the president's American Manufacturing Council.

The resignations began with Kenneth Frazier, the chairman and chief executive officer of Merck, who resigned from the council to protest the president's weak weekend statements, stating that "as a matter of personal conscience, I feel a responsibility to take a stand against intolerance and extremism." Trump caustically mocked Frazier, who is African

American, for his resignation, writing on Twitter, "Now that Ken Frazier of Merck Pharma has resigned from President's Manufacturing Council, he will have more time to LOWER RIPOFF DRUG PRICES!"

Executives from Intel, Under Armour, Campbell Soup, Walmart, 3M, and Johnson & Johnson were among others to resign, as well as Scott Paul, president of the Alliance for American Manufacturing, and Richard Trunka, deputy chief of staff of the AFL-CIO. Ever defiant, President Trump decided to simply disband the council and shut it down.[59]

Perhaps the best proof of the meaning and impact of the president's Tuesday remarks came from the leaders of the alt-right. They loved it. Richard Spencer on Tuesday told the *Atlantic*'s Rosie Gray he was "really proud" of Trump.[60] David Duke was almost giddy with delight. Duke tweeted, "Thank you President Trump for your honesty & courage to tell the truth about #Charlottesville & condemn the leftist terrorists in BLM/Antifa."[61]

It was all that was needed to be said. There can be no doubt that everything the president said on Tuesday reflected his sincere beliefs. And there can be no doubt that what he said gave tremendous aid and comfort to the alt-right. For some, that was giving aid and comfort to the enemy. For President Trump, it appeared more to be giving aid and comfort to what he considered to be an important part of his base.

Confessions of a Free Speech Lawyer

I end by taking up the indictment of what some may consider the ultimate culprit of the violence in Charlottesville. That culprit is not the expression and action of the radical supremacists, but the radical protection of supremacist speech represented by the domination of the marketplace theory of freedom of speech. What really caused the harm, many may think, is the contemporary First Amendment principle that hate speech *is* free speech. The Unite the Right rally in Charlottesville could never have happened if the order and morality theory of free speech continued to reign. What the alt-right leaders and participants advocated was *worse* than the speech of Joseph Beauharnais in *Beauharnais v. Illinois*, the argument goes, and it would be best for our nation and our constitutional tradition to resurrect *Beauharnais*, *Chaplinsky v. New Hampshire*, and the order and morality theory as the law of the land.

In my own introspection about the events in Charlottesville, I have struggled mightily with this argument. I have wondered if my own handiwork in advancing the marketplace theory in representing the cross burners in *Virginia v. Black* was wrong all along.

I will begin by saying that the events in Charlottesville have clearly convinced me that the marketplace theory cannot be defended on the naïve faith that allowing free speech to remain unfettered leads to the triumph of truth in the marketplace. Sometimes it does, and sometimes it doesn't. Often, as in the case of the irrational and hate-filled conspiracy theories of the far right, freedom of speech leads to the proliferation of death and destruction.

Take, for example, the core claim of so many supremacists, the "white genocide" conspiracy theory. The "you will not replace us" chant of the alt-right supremacists was an invocation of this white genocide conspiracy theory, an argument that governments worldwide, including the United States, are out to replace white people and European culture. The Unite the Right organizer Matthew Heimbach argued that the attempts by Charlottesville to remove Confederate statues were a form of this "white genocide."[62]

The white genocide theory has circulated the globe for years and has contributed to many terrorist attacks. In 2011, the white genocide theory was what animated Anders Behring Breivik, a white nationalist extremist who killed seventy-seven people at a summer camp in Norway. Breivik wrote, "I will know that I did everything I could to stop and reverse the European cultural and demographical genocide and end and reverse the Islamisation of Europe."[63] Robert Bowers, the killer who murdered Jews in the 2018 Pittsburgh synagogue shooting, was a believer in the white genocide theory, stating that the Jews were "committing genocide to my people. I just want to kill Jews."[64] Dylann Roof, the murderer who committed the Charleston massacre, claimed that blacks were "taking over the country."[65] Christopher Paul Hasson, the US Coast Guard lieutenant who was arrested in February 2019 for stockpiling weapons in preparation for an attack on Democratic politicians and liberal journalists, was a subscriber to the white genocide theory who drew on the Norwegian killer Breivik for inspiration.[66] Brenton Tarrant, the gunman who killed at least fifty-one worshippers in an attack on a mosque in Christchurch,

New Zealand, on March 15, 2019, published a white genocide manifesto on his Facebook page.[67]

The New Zealand killer Tarrant also expressed admiration for President Trump. On the same day of the New Zealand attack, Trump used his presidential veto power for the first time in his presidency, vetoing a congressional rejection of the national emergency Trump had called to justify his diversion of federal funds to build a wall on the Mexican border. Tarrant had labeled nonwhites as engaging in an invasion of New Zealand. President Trump constantly invokes the same "invasion" rhetoric, making such statements as, "It's an invasion of drugs and criminals and people," adding, "And in many cases, they're stone cold criminals . . . you have killers coming in and murderers coming in."[68]

If by the "search for truth" we mean that allowing the proliferation of hate speech leads in some sense to "truth," it is difficult to see how or why this is so. As UVA professor Leslie Kendrick, reflecting very personally on the Charlottesville events, wisely observed, as a society we have already reached consensus on fundamental values such as equality and human dignity. We do not have much need to subject these commitments to the marketplace of ideas.[69]

The events in Charlottesville also caused me to question the wisdom of the warning of Justice Brandeis in *Whitney v. California*,[70] that society should not enact laws out of fear, as when men feared witches and burned women, and that to suppress dangerous speech is often to strengthen it. Irrational fear is one thing. It was irrational fear that led to witch trials. And perhaps some of the trials against communists during the nation's red scares were akin to such witch hunting. But the fear engendered by the white genocide conspiracists hardly seemed irrational. Whether the evil speech of the alt-right supremacists would be made stronger or weaker by a return to the "order and morality" theory is difficult to calculate. Such supremacist speech has gone essentially uncensored on the internet. Under pressure, platforms such as Facebook have begun to shut down the worst supremacist sites. That may somewhat frustrate the proliferation of the supremacist messages. It certainly makes it more difficult for such groups to operate and gain converts. How much more difficult, or whether, on balance, the danger levels go up or go down when suppression of their message is successful, is extremely difficult to measure.[71]

So then, where does that leave us? I have come to the conclusion that it still leaves us with the marketplace theory, as the best of the bad options. I have two justifications for this conclusion. The first is a reality check on exactly what the marketplace theory does and does not protect. The second is an argument grounded in issues of legitimacy and trust.

Throughout this book I have noted that the marketplace theory does not result in absolute protection for freedom of speech. It protects speech that is *only* hateful, but it does not protect hateful speech that is also a true threat, an incitement, or part of a conspiracy to engage in either threats or incitement. Indeed, while I am a strong advocate of free speech, I have also represented plaintiffs against publishers when expression was intended to cause more palpable harm. In defamation cases, such as the lawsuit in Charlottesville against *Rolling Stone*, that palpable harm was damage to reputation. In yet another case, *Rice v. Paladin Enterprises, Inc.*,[72] cited by Judge Moon in his opinion in the civil lawsuit brought against the leaders of the Unite the Right rally, I argued that a book publisher could be held liable for publishing an instruction manual on how to embark on a career as a professional assassin. The *Rice* case is often referred to by its nickname, "the hit man case." I wrote a book about the case, called *Deliberate Intent: A Lawyer Tells the True Story of Murder by the Book*,[73] which was later made into an FX movie called *Deliberate Intent*, starring Timothy Hutton. Paladin Press, located in Boulder, Colorado, had published the book in question, titled *Hit Man: A Technical Manual for Independent Contractors*. It was a "how to" book explaining how to go into business as a professional assassin, and how to carry out murder for hire. Lawrence Horn, one of the original music producers and creators of the "Motown sound" with Motown Records, hired James Perry to murder Horn's disabled son Trevor and Horn's ex-wife, Mildred "Millie" Horn, so that Horn and Perry could split the millions Horn would inherit from a trust created from a medical malpractice award that had been established to care for Trevor's needs. Perry had never murdered anybody before, so he bought the *Hit Man* murder manual, as well as another Paladin publication, *How to Make a Disposable Silencer, Vol. II*, to plan, execute, and attempt to conceal the murders. Perry followed the instructions in *Hit Man* to kill three people: Trevor Horn, Millie Horn, and Janice Saunders, a nurse who was on duty the night of the murders, taking care of Trevor.

Both Horn and Perry were caught and convicted of murder. The families of the victims, however, also believed that Paladin Press was morally and legally complicit in the deaths. Paladin Press of course argued that *Hit Man* was nothing more than abstract advocacy, and that under the standards of cases such as *Brandenburg* and *Claiborne Hardware*, the book was protected by the First Amendment.[74]

We won the case, in a landmark decision, the only case in US history in which a book publisher was held liable for the actions of readers in following the instructions in the book. The case was highly controversial in its time and remains controversial today. I was described as a "traitor to the First Amendment." I did have some defenders, such as the famous jazz critic and civil liberties advocate Nat Hentoff, who nicely summarized in the *Village Voice* what we were up against. In an article titled "The Scorned Law Professor," Hentoff wrote, "Many lawyers with whom Smolla had worked on key First Amendment cases were shocked when he decided to sue a book publisher for complicity in three murders. He thereby became a heretic, scorned by practically every First Amendment attorney and journalist. Good lord, books can't kill people, they said. And they feared that if Smolla won the case, the creators and distributors of any book, movie, or TV show offering information on how to commit a crime could be hauled into court."[75] I argued that novelists, nonfiction writers, television producers, and moviemakers had nothing to fear. There was a world of difference, I maintained, between expression intended to inform and entertain and expression intended to train. Freedom of speech was not freedom to kill; nor was it freedom to incite and train killers.

The Fourth Circuit accepted my argument. The Fourth Circuit held, in an opinion by Judge Michael Luttig, that even though the publishers of *Hit Man* did not know that the specific murderers in our case would use the *Hit Man* book to commit the specific murders they perpetrated, the publishers did both know and intend that some of its readers would use the book to kill.

In litigating the case, I came to see that much of the book amounted to pure technical instruction in the arts and sciences of murder. Other parts of the book, however, seemed to possess a different quality—an element of psychological training, a kind of "argument," if you will, that paid assassins constitute an honorable profession and a socially worthy and valuable calling, while explaining the thrill, the sense of pride and accomplishment, the superiority, the manliness, the glory of a life as a professional assassin.[76] For the longest time I did not know what to make of this nontechnical material, did not know how to characterize it, did not know how to place it within the context of the First Amendment. My fear was that this psychological exhortation would form the "redeeming social value" of the book, the element of "abstract advocacy," the political or social "message" of the book that would save the publisher from liability.[77]

What I eventually came to see, however, was that it was the combination of the technical training and the psychological suasion that made the book so lethal.[78] Neither the technical material alone nor the brainwashing rhetoric of violence alone would have been nearly as dangerous as the explosive cocktail produced when the two ingredients combined. This conclusion seems obvious now. But it was a long time coming. The technical training is just part of the job—in fact probably the easiest part. You can teach just about anybody to shoot straight.[79] Yet obviously not every crack shot is a crackpot. Atticus Finch, the heroic attorney in *To Kill a Mockingbird*,[80] who may be the most morally honorable lawyer-character in American literature, was reputed to be the best marksman in the Alabama county where he lived.

No, to train a truly great assassin, a great terrorist, one must work on the killer's mind. The psychological training is the trick. Training the killer to believe in the righteousness of the cause, training the killer to carry forward his deadly task without flinching, without fear, without disabling remorse or guilt—that is the key. What made *Hit Man* so evil and so dangerous was not just that it taught the tricks of the trade; it was that it taught the tradesman to be so proud of them, to be so calm and composed during the execution.

Following the terrorist attacks on 9/11, I was invited to give a talk at the Loyola Law School in Los Angeles on the connections between violent advocacy and violent action. Western intelligence and law enforcement agencies have in their possession a copy of a manuscript titled "The Encyclopedia of Jihad," a comprehensive training manual and religious-political manifesto for Osama bin Laden's Al-Qaeda terror-ist network.[81] The manual was made available online, with some parts redacted, by the US Department of Justice, I suspect so that Americans would know what a sophisticated enemy we were up against.[82] And so to prepare for my Los Angeles speech, I began reading "The Encyclope-dia of Jihad."

I was shocked by how closely the bin Laden playbook appeared to track the writings of Paladin Press, including *Hit Man*. In my Los Ange-les talk and later essay I expressed thoughts, which I repeat here, that *Hit Man* and "The Encyclopedia of Jihad" are all but indistinguishable. I wouldn't be surprised if Osama bin Laden had read the Paladin books and ripped them off directly—it's not as though a little sin like copyright infringement was going to get in his way.

In their lawsuit against the leaders of the Unite the Right rally, the plaintiffs in the *Sines v. Kessler* litigation also relied on a case from the United States Court of Appeals for the Ninth Circuit that was a close jurisprudential cousin of the case I argued in *Rice*, titled *Planned Parenthood of Columbia/Willamette, Inc. v. American Coalition of Life Activists*.[83] It is popularly known among First Amendment lawyers and scholars by the nickname "the Nuremberg files case." The case was brought by Planned Parenthood, along with various women's health clinics and doctors who provided counseling on abortion services, against various members of a particularly violent and extreme faction of the antiabortion movement. The suit was brought in federal court in Portland, Oregon. The claim by the abortion providers was that the antiabortion activists had gone beyond mere advocacy against abortion into actions that posed a true threat to members of Planned Parenthood, the women's clinics, and the doctors. These alleged threats were com-municated through posters, pamphlets, and internet postings, accusing the abortion providers of committing "crimes against humanity" and offering rewards to persons who could provide information leading to the revocation of the abortion providers' medical licenses or to anyone who could persuade them to cease performing abortions. That much of the expression of the activists seemed to be mere advocacy. But the plot thickened. The activists also had a process for assembling dossiers on various abortion providers, judges, and political leaders deemed sup-portive of abortion rights. The activists, in some instances, got more up close and personal. For example, in one poster, a specific abortion provider, Dr. Robert Christ, was featured by name, along with his photograph and his work and home addresses. A website maintained by some of the antiabortion activists included the names and addresses of doctors who performed abortions and invited others to contribute additional names. In a macabre touch, the website denoted the names of those already victimized by antiabortion violence, striking through the names of those who had been murdered and graying out the names of the wounded. The antiabortion activists asserted that these abortion providers were guilty of crimes against humanity and should be prosecuted for those crimes just as the Nazis were prosecuted in the Nuremburg trials.

The case was difficult because neither the posters nor the website contained any *explicit* threats against the doctors. Yet the doctors knew that in the past, similar posters prepared by others had preceded clinic bombings and murders. There was evidence that the doctors took the "Nuremberg files" as serious threats: they began wearing bulletproof vests, drawing the curtains on the windows of their homes, and accepting the protection of United States marshals. What the defendants had done went beyond abstract expression, they claimed, and constituted real threats against their lives. A jury agreed and awarded the doctors $107 million in damages.

The case was heard twice on appeal. A three-judge panel of the Ninth Circuit originally held that the expression of the antiabortion advocates was merely violent advocacy and thus protected against liability by the First Amendment. But the full Ninth Circuit, sitting "en banc," held otherwise, and held that the expression of the antiabortion activists had gone beyond mere advocacy into the realm of action, constituting a true threat against the doctors. Most importantly, the Ninth Circuit held that it was permissible for the jury to consider *past acts* of violence against abortion providers in which the murderers had been spurred to action by violent antiabortion rhetoric in considering whether the *present* postings and posters constituted true threats. The messages, the Ninth Circuit held, "connote something they do not literally say, yet both the actor and the recipient get the message."[84] For those providing abortion services, that message was *Wanted, dead or alive.* As the court put it, "To the doctor who performs abortions, these posters meant 'You're Wanted or You're

Guilty; You'll be shot or killed.'" This deadly message was reinforced, the court reasoned, by "the scorecard in the Nuremberg Files." The message "was not conditional or casual," the court concluded. "It was specifically targeted."[85]

Against the backdrop of the *Rice* "hit man" decision and the *Planned Parenthood* "Nuremburg files" case, Judge Moon's decision in *Sines v. Kessler* to permit the lawsuit in Charlottesville to move forward against the leaders of the Unite the Right rally emerges as all the more sound and convincing. In considering the lead-up to Charlottesville, including the elaborate military-like logistical and training preparations of the alt-right, I am confident that the alt-right leaders crossed the constitutional divide and may be held accountable, even under the rules of the marketplace theory. In the chilling words of one of the participants planning for the rally that were carried on Vice News, "We'll fucking kill these people if we have to."[86]

In short, despite all its shortcomings, the marketplace theory largely *works*. It protects evil abstract advocacy, as it is designed to do. But it does not place society in a straitjacket. When proof of actual conspiracy to incite violence and intimidate exists, the rules of the marketplace theory permit accountability.

Moreover, in one sense, the marketplace theory worked as Holmes and Brandeis claimed it would, to advance the pursuit of truth by relying on "counter speech," on the answering of evil counsels with good ones. While it is likely that most supremacists who participated in the Unite the Right rally were unshaken in their commitments to racism, notwithstanding the severe criticisms they endured, there *was* a broad affirmation by American society at large of the evils of hate speech and the importance of equality and respect for human dignity. Democrats and Republicans, liberals and conservatives, roundly condemned the supremacists. President Trump, who was widely accused of engaging in a "false equivalency" between the supremacists and the counterprotesters, and who was perceived by many as secretly playing to the supremacists and their sympathizers, was also broadly condemned for his positions. Not everyone, of course, was convinced that either the supremacists or the president was wrong. But the marketplace theory does not presuppose that everyone will be convinced, or see the "truth" the same way.

Which leads to yet one final argument implicating questions of legitimacy and trust. The Achilles' heel of the order and morality theory is that it can work only if the government is empowered to decide when society's norms of order and morality have been transgressed. Those who advocate for the order and morality theory must, in the end, invite us to trust the government to make these decisions wisely. In the end, the best defense of the marketplace theory is that the government cannot and should not be trusted with this power.

It may well be that most of those opposed to hate speech are confident in the rectitude and truth of their positions. I fully share that confidence and rectitude. But the order and morality theory would empower the government to make such judgments on an infinite array of topics and viewpoints. Government majorities come and go. President Trump is, in a very real sense, a major governmental actor now, with the full powers of the presidency at his avail to issue executive orders on a wide variety of issues, many of which may venture into pronouncements on the limits of freedom of speech and freedom of expressive association. I suspect that many of those who today might be tempted by the attractiveness of the order and morality theory would not be so keen on having President Trump as the arbiter of what will be deemed orderly and moral. As the Supreme Court emphasized in *United States v. Stevens*, "the First Amendment protects against the Government; it does not leave us at the mercy of *noblesse oblige*."[87]

At any given moment, those who control majorities and wield power in our legislative and executive branches may well be wise and thoughtful judges of good order and morality. Yet much as the French philosopher Blaise Pascal argued that the best wager of a rational person is to bet on the existence of God, Oliver Wendell Holmes argued that the best wager is against the government, and in favor of the marketplace, to decide such issues. If we err on the side of trusting government, we may make short-term gains in the triumph of order and morality, but we risk the long-term danger of tyranny and oppression. "Every year if not every day we have to wager our salvation upon some prophecy based upon imperfect knowledge," Holmes warned.[88]

I am convinced that the expression of the alt-right supremacists was speech that we deservedly loathe and believe fraught with death. Yet for all that, I end up also convinced that we are better off leaving it to the legal tools available under the marketplace theory to hold the supremacist leaders accountable. Judge Moon's decision in *Sines v. Kessler* shows that such accountability is possible, even under the marketplace theory. As Holmes explained, "It is an experiment, as all life is an experiment."[89]

Yes, it is an experiment. That experiment remains, however, the best theory upon which to wager our salvation.

NOTES

1. A Call from the Task Force

1. The Widener University Delaware Law School is located in Wilmington, Delaware, and is Delaware's only law school.

2. Virginia v. Black, 538 U.S. 343 (2003).

3. James Baldwin, *I Am Not Your Negro*, ed. Raoul Peck (New York: Vintage Books, 2017), 70–71.

4. Baldwin, *Not Your Negro*, 70–71.

5. Adam Goodheart, "Regime Change in Charlottesville," Politico, August 16, 2017, https://www.politico.com/magazine/story/2017/08/16/regime-change-in-charlottesville-215500.

6. Eric Wallace, "Faulkner Left His Mark on UVA," *C-ville*, March 24, 2017, http://www.c-ville.com/faulkner-left-mark-uva/#.WpdNTUxFxZV.

7. William Faulkner, *Absalom! Absalom!* (New York: Random House, 1936), 146.

8. William Faulkner, *Requiem for a Nun* (New York: Random House, 1951), 73.

2. The Charleston Massacre

1. Michael Schmidt, "Charleston Suspect Was in Contact with Supremacists, Officials Say," *New York Times*, July 3, 2015, https://www.nytimes.com/2015/07/04/us/dylann-roof-was-in-contact-with-supremacists-officials-say.html.

2. Schmidt, "Charleston Suspect."

3. Schmidt, "Charleston Suspect."

4. Paul Lewis, Amanda Holpuch, and Jessica Glenza, "Dylann Roof: FBI Probes Website and Manifesto Linked to Charleston Suspect," *Guardian*, June 21, 2015, https://www.theguardian.com/us-news/2015/jun/20/dylann-roof-fbi-website-manifesto-charleston-shooting.

5. Lewis, Holpuch, and Glenza, "Dylann Roof."

6. Catherine Thompson, "Group That May Have Influenced Charleston Killer: 'He Had Some Legitimate Grievances,'" Talking Points Memo, June 22, 2017, https://talkingpointsmemo.com/livewire/ccc-dylann-roof-legitimate-grievances.

7. Schmidt, "Charleston Suspect."

8. Schmidt, "Charleston Suspect."

9. Schmidt, "Charleston Suspect."

10. Thompson, "Group That May Have Influenced Charleston Killer."

11. Thompson, "Group That May Have Influenced Charleston Killer."

12. Thompson, "Group That May Have Influenced Charleston Killer."

13. "Jared Taylor," Southern Poverty Law Center, https://www.splcenter.org/fighting-hate/extremist-files/individual/jared-taylor.

14. Jon Swaine and Jessica Glenza, "Four Republican Hopefuls Return Money after 'Dylann Roof Manifesto' Revelation," *Guardian*, June 22, 2015, https://www.theguardian.com/us-news/2015/jun/22/scott-walker-republican-dylann-roof-manifesto.

15. Brown v. Board of Education, 347 U.S. 483 (1954).

3. Becoming Richard Spencer

1. Devin Burghart, "Who Is Richard Spencer?," Institute for Research and Education on Human Rights, June 27, 2014, http://www.irehr.org/2014/06/27/who-is-richard-spencer/.

2. Graeme Wood, "His Kampf: Richard Spencer Is a Troll and an Icon for White Supremacists. He Was Also My High School Classmate," *Atlantic*, June 2017, https://www.theatlantic.com/magazine/archive/2017/06/his-kampf/524505/.

3. Burghart, "Who Is Richard Spencer?"

4. Taki, "High Life: Cult of Victimhood," *Spectator*, November 4, 2000, http://archive.spectator.co.uk/article/4th-november-2000/78/high-life.

5. Taki, "High Life."

6. Taki, "High Life."

7. Taki, "High Life."

8. Taki, "High Life."

9. Burghart, "Who Is Richard Spencer?"

10. Burghart, "Who Is Richard Spencer?"

11. Wood, "His Kampf."

12. William A. Wilson, "Herder, Folklore, and Romantic Nationalism," *Journal of Popular Culture* 6, no. 4 (Spring 1973): 819–35, at 24, citing *Sammtliche Werke*, 33 vols., ed. Bernhard Suphan (1877–1913; rpt. Hildesheim, Germany, 1967–1968), http://mysite.du.edu/~lavita/anth_3070_13s/_docs/wilsonw_herder_folklore%20copy.pdf.

13. Claudia Koonz, *The Nazi Conscience* (Cambridge, MA: Harvard University Press, 2005), 59.

14. Wood, "His Kampf."

15. Richard Spencer, "The Metapolitics of America," Radix Journal, July 4, 2014, https://radixjournal.com/2015/07/2014-7-4-the-metapolitics-of-america/.

16. Eli Sanders, "Searching for Richard Spencer: What I Found in a Small Montana Town at the Center of a White Nationalist Troll Storm," *Stranger*, January 11, 2017, https://www.thestranger.com/features/2017/01/11/24794084/searching-for-richard-spencer.

17. John Woodrow Cox, "'Let's Party Like It's 1933': Inside the Alt-Right World of Richard Spencer," *Washington Post*, November 22, 2016, https://www.washingtonpost.com/local/lets-party-like-its-1933-inside-the-disturbing-alt-right-world-of-richard-spencer/2016/11/22/cf81dc74-aff7-11e6-840f-e3ebab6bcdd3_story.html.

18. Sanders, "Searching for Richard Spencer."

4. Reverend Edwards

1. Jonathan Blitzer, "How Church Leaders in Charlottesville Prepared for White Supremacists," *New Yorker*, August 15, 2017, https://www.newyorker.com/news/news-desk/how-church-leaders-in-charlottesville-prepared-for-white-supremacists.

2. Mt. Zion First African Baptist Church, Charlottesville, VA, "Our Pastor," http://www.mtzionfabc.com/index.php?option=com.

3. Mt. Zion, "Our Pastor."

4. Gregory B. Fairchild, "How I Learned That Diversity Does Not Equal Integration," in *Charlottesville 2017: The Legacy of Race and Inequity*, ed. Louis P. Nelson and Claudrena N. Harold (Charlottesville: University of Virginia Press, 2018), 196.

5. Gary Orfield and Chungmei Lee, "*Brown* at 50: King's Dream or *Plessy*'s Nightmare?," Civil Rights Project of Harvard University, 2004, 1.

6. Fairchild, "How I Learned," 3.

7. Charlottesville Clergy Collective, "About Us," https://www.cvilleclergycollective.org/about.html.

8. Charlottesville Clergy Collective, "About Us."

5. The Charlottesville Monuments

1. John Edwin Mason, "History, Mine and Ours," in *Charlottesville 2017: The Legacy of Race and Inequity*, ed. Louis P. Nelson and Claudrena N. Harold (Charlottesville: University of Virginia Press, 2018), 20.

2. Mason, "History," 20.

3. Hawes Spencer, *Summer of Hate: Charlottesville, USA* (Charlottesville: University of Virginia Press, 2018), 55–57.

4. Mason, "History," 20.

5. Jenny Woodley, "Charlottesville, Virginia: The History of the Statue at the Centre of Violent Unrest," the Conversation, August 15, 2017, http://theconversation.com/charlottesville-virginia-the-history-of-the-statue-at-the-centre-of-violent-unrest-82476.

6. Woodley, "Charlottesville."

7. Elizabeth R. Varon, "The Original False Equivalency," in *Charlottesville 2017: The Legacy of Race and Inequity*, ed. Louis P. Nelson and Claudrena N. Harold (Charlottesville: University of Virginia Press, 2018), 42.

8. Varon, "Original False Equivalency," 42.

9. Varon, "Original False Equivalency," 42.

10. Mitch Landrieu, *In the Shadow of Statues: A White Southerner Confronts History* (New York: Viking, 2018).

11. A. C. Thompson, "A Few Things Got Left Out of the Daily Caller's Report on Confederate Monument Rally," ProPublica, May 31, 2017, https://www.propublica.org/article/things-got-left-out-of-the-daily-callers-report-confederate-monument-rally.

12. Thompson, "Things Got Left Out."

6. Blut und Boden

1. See Rodney A. Smolla, "The Trial of Oliver Wendell Holmes," *William & Mary Law Review* 36, no. 1 (1994): 173–233; Robert J. Cynkar, "Buck v. Bell: 'Felt Necessities' v. Fundamental Values?," *Columbia Law Review* 81, no. 7 (1981): 1418–61; Mary L. Dudziak, "Oliver Wendell Holmes as a Eugenic Reformer: Rhetoric in the Writing of Constitutional Law," *Iowa Law Review* 71 (1986): 833–67; Richard A. Estacio, "Sterilization of the Mentally Disabled in Pennsylvania: Three Generations without Legislative Guidance Are Enough," *Dickinson Law Review* 92, no. 2 (1988): 409–36; Stephen J. Gould, "Carrie Buck's Daughter," *Natural History*, July 1984, 14; "Recent Cases," *Harvard Law Review* 39 (1926): 767–70 (commenting on the decision of the Supreme Court of Appeals of Virginia in Buck v. Bell); "Recent Decisions," *Columbia Law Review* 27 (1927): 870–73 (commenting on the Supreme Court of the United States decision in Buck v. Bell).

2. Paul A. Lombardo, "Three Generations, No Imbeciles: New Light on Buck v. Bell," *New York University Law Review* 60, no. 1 (1985): 30–62.

3. Lombardo, "Three Generations," 54, quoting interview with Carrie Buck (December 27, 1982). See also Giametta, "They Told Me I Had to Have an Operation," *Daily Progress* (Charlottesville), February 26, 1980, A1.

4. Joshua D. Rothman, *Notorious in the Neighborhood: Sex and Families across the Color Line in Virginia, 1787–1861* (Chapel Hill: University of North Carolina Press, 2003), 68.

5. Chapter 394, Act to provide for the sexual sterilization of inmates of State institutions in certain cases [S B 281], Act of Mar. 20, 1924, ch. 394, 1924 Va. Acts 569, repealed by Act of Apr. 2, 1974, ch. 296, 1974 Va. Acts 445.

6. Harry H. Laughlin, *Eugenical Sterilization in the United States*, Psychopathic Laboratory of the Municipal Court of Chicago, 1922, 46–51, https://repository.library.georgetown.edu/bitstream/handle/10822/556984/EugenicalSterilizationInTheUS.pdf. See also Allan Chase, *The Legacy of Malthus: The Social Costs of the New Scientific Racism* (New York: Alfred A. Knopf, 1977), 135, 351n15.

7. Gregory Michael Dorr, *Segregation's Science: Eugenics and Society in Virginia* (Charlottesville: University of Virginia Press, 2008).

8. David McNair, "Erasing History: Wrecking Ball Aiming for DeJarnette?," the Hook, On Architecture, July 13, 2006, http://www.readthehook.com/79628/onarchitecture-erasing-history-wrecking-ball-aiming-dejarnette.

9. McNair, "Erasing History."

10. McNair, "Erasing History."

11. McNair, "Erasing History."

12. Lombardo, "Three Generations," 35–36.

13. Lombardo, "Three Generations," 36 (1985), quoting Special Report of the State Board of Charities and Corrections to the General Assembly of 1916, Mental Defectives in Virginia (1915), 8–9.

14. Lombardo, "Three Generations," 62n71.

15. Lombardo, "Three Generations," 61.

16. Lombardo, "Three Generations," 61.

17. Lombardo, "Three Generations," 51.

18. Lombardo, "Three Generations," 51.

19. Buck v. Bell, 143 Va. at 315.

20. Buck v. Bell, 274 U.S. at 207.

21. James Dickey, *The One Voice of James Dickey: His Letters and Life, 1970–1997*, ed. Gordon Van Ness (Columbia: University of Missouri Press, 2005), 312.

22. Buck v. Bell, 274 U.S. at 207–8.
23. Buck v. Bell, 274 U.S. at 207–8.
24. Jacobson v. Commonwealth of Massachusetts, 197 U.S. 11 (1905).
25. Buck v. Bell, 274 U.S. at 207.
26. Buck v. Bell, 274 U.S. at 207.
27. Buck v. Bell, 274 U.S. at 208.
28. Buck v. Bell, 274 U.S. at 208.
29. Lombardo, "Three Generations," 61.
30. Professor Lombardo's efforts culminated in a book-length treatment of the story: Paul A. Lombardo, *Three Generations, No Imbeciles: Eugenics, the Supreme Court, and* Buck v. Bell (Baltimore: Johns Hopkins University Press, 2008).
31. Lombardo, "Three Generations," 62.
32. McNair, "Erasing History."

7. Mr. Jefferson's University

1. Norman Mailer, *Tough Guys Don't Dance* (New York: Random House, 1984), 18.
2. "Joy to the World," released by Three Dog Night (1970), written by Hoyt Axton.
3. Reeves Wiedeman, "The Duke Lacrosse Scandal and the Birth of the Alt-Right," *New York Magazine*, April 14, 2017, http://nymag.com/intelligencer/2017/04/the-duke-lacrosse-scandal-and-the-birth-of-the-alt-right.html.
4. Wiedeman, "Duke Lacrosse Scandal."

8. Kessler v. Bellamy

1. K. Burnell Evans and Aaron Richardson, "It's Official: Fenwick to Be on Ballot for City Council," *Daily Progress*, June 14, 2013, http://www.dailyprogress.com/news/local/it-s-official-fenwick-to-be-on-ballot-for-city/article_926b3dd2-d547-11e2-bb67-0019bb30f31a.html.
2. "Jason Kessler," Southern Poverty Law Center, https://www.splcenter.org/fighting-hate/extremist-files/individual/jason-kessler.
3. "Wes Bellamy," City of Charlottesville Council Members, http://www.charlottesville.org/departments-and-services/departments-a-g/city-council/council-members/wes-bellamy.
4. "Supporters and Protesters as Bellamy Calls for Removal of Lee Statue," *Daily Progress*, March 22, 2016, http://www.dailyprogress.com/gallery/supporters-and-protesters-as-bellamy-calls-for-removal-of-lee/collection_2f92c2c2-f04a-11e5-8a3a-1b1bf4d90d66.html.
5. Anna Higgins and Tim Dodson, *Cavalier Daily*, "Homophobic, Sexist, Anti-white Language Abundant in Charlottesville Vice Mayor's Tweets," November 28, 2016, http://www.cavalierdaily.com/article/2016/11/wes-bellamy-charlottesville-twitter.
6. Higgins and Dodson, "Homophobic."
7. Higgins and Dodson, "Homophobic."
8. Higgins and Dodson, "Homophobic."
9. Higgins and Dodson, "Homophobic."
10. Higgins and Dodson, "Homophobic."

9. The Monuments Debate

1. City of Charlottesville, *Blue Ribbon Commission on Race, Memorials, and Public Spaces, Report to City Council*, December 19, 2016, 4, http://www.charlottesville.org/Home/ShowDocument?id=48999.
2. *Blue Ribbon Commission Report*, 4.

3. John Edwin Mason, "History, Mine and Ours," in *Charlottesville 2017: The Legacy of Race and Inequity*, ed. Louis P. Nelson and Claudrena N. Harold (Charlottesville: University of Virginia Press, 2018), 20.

4. Mason, "History," 20.

5. Derek Quizon, "Signer Declares City 'a Capital of Resistance' against Trump," *Daily Progress*, January 31, 2017, https://www.dailyprogress.com/news/politics/signer-declares-city-a-capital-of-resistance-against-trump/article_12108161-fccd-53bb-89e4-b7d5dc8494e0.html.

6. Chris Suarez, "Charlottesville Council's Vote on Statues Ends in Deadlocked Frustration," *Richmond Times-Dispatch*, January 19, 2017, http://www.richmond.com/news/virginia/charlottesville-council-s-vote-on-statues-ends-in-deadlocked-frustration/article_2347 9998-974e-5c81-9ad1-cc7c48b71fac.html.

7. Suarez, "Charlottesville Council's Vote."

8. Suarez, "Charlottesville Council's Vote."

9. Suarez, "Charlottesville Council's Vote."

10. Suarez, "Charlottesville Council's Vote."

11. Suarez, "Charlottesville Council's Vote."

12. Alexis de Tocqueville, *Democracy in America* (1835–1840; New York: Library of America, 2004), 310.

10. Competing Conceptions of Free Speech

1. Chaplinsky v. New Hampshire, 315 U.S. 568, 572 (1942).

2. West Virginia State Board of Education v. Barnette, 319 U.S. 624, 642 (1942).

3. John Milton, *Areopagetica: A Speech of Mr. John Milton For the Liberty of Unlicensed Printing, To the Parliament of England* (1644).

4. Abrams v. United States, 250 U.S. 616, 630 (1919) (Holmes, J. dissenting).

5. Abrams v. United States, 250 U.S. 630 (1919) (Holmes, J. dissenting).

6. Whitney v. California, 274 U.S. 357 (1927).

7. *Whitney*, 274 U.S. at 375.

8. *Whitney*, 274 U.S. at 376.

9. Beauharnais v. People of State of Illinois, 343 U.S. 250, 260 (1952).

10. State v. Chaplinsky, 91 N.H. 310, 18 A.2d 754, 757 (1941), aff'd sub nom. Chaplinsky v. State of New Hampshire, 315 U.S. 568 (1942).

11. State v. Chaplinsky, 18 A.2d at 757.

12. State v. Chaplinsky, 18 A.2d at 757.

13. State v. Chaplinsky, 18 A.2d at 757, *quoting* P. L., c. 378, § 2.

14. Chaplinsky v. New Hampshire, 315 U.S. at 571–72. See generally Rodney A. Smolla, *Smolla and Nimmer on Freedom of Speech* (New York: Thomson Reuters West, 2009; updated annually), § 2:70.

15. See Cohen v. California, 403 U.S. 15 (1971). The Supreme Court of the United States held that the First Amendment protected Paul Cohen from prosecution for wearing, in the public corridors of a Los Angeles courthouse, a jacket with the words "Fuck the Draft." Justice Hugo Black dissented, arguing that Cohen's actions were "conduct," not "speech," and thus outside the ambit of First Amendment protection.

16. People v. Beauharnais, 408 Ill. 512, 97 N.E.2d 343 (1951), aff'd sub nom. Beauharnais v. People of State of Ill., 343 U.S. 250 (1952).

17. People v. Beauharnais, 408 Ill. 512.

18. Ill.Rev.Stat.1949, chap. 38, par. 471.

19. Ill.Rev.Stat.1949, chap. 38, par. 471.

20. Chaplinsky v. New Hampshire, 315 U.S. 568 (1942).

21. Beauharnais v. People of State of Illinois, 343 U.S. 250, 260 (1952).

22. *Beauharnais*, 343 U.S. at 250, 261.

23. *Beauharnais*, 343 U.S. at 263.

24. Joni Mitchell, "Both Sides Now," A&M Records, 1969.

25. Leslie Kendrick, "The Answers and the Questions in First Amendment Law," in *Charlottesville 2017: The Legacy of Race and Inequity*, ed. Louis P. Nelson and Claudrena N. Harold (Charlottesville: University of Virginia Press, 2018), 72.

26. Kendrick, "Answers and Questions," 73.

27. Kendrick, "Answers and Questions," 74.

28. *Hawaii v. Trump*, 138 S.Ct. 2382 (2018).

29. John C. Calhoun, "The Fort Hill Address," July 26, 1831, in H. Lee Cheeck Jr., *John C. Calhoun: Selected Writings and Speeches* (Washington, DC: Regnery, 2003), 316.

11. May Days

1. Gordon F. Sandler, "When Nazis Filled Madison Square Garden," Politico, August 23, 2017, https://www.politico.com/magazine/story/2017/08/23/nazi-german-american-bund-rally-madison-square-garden-215522.

2. *New York Times*, "22,000 Hold Rally in Garden," February 21, 1939, https://timesmachine.nytimes.com/timesmachine/1939/02/21/94680980.html?emc=eta1&pageNumber=1.

3. Joe Raiola, "It's the Jews Fault—Still and Again," Huffington Post, August 17, 2017, https://www.huffingtonpost.com/entry/its-the-jews-fault-still-and-again_us_599510aee4b00dd984e37c6f.

4. Josh Dawsey, "Trump Derides Protection for Immigrants from 'Shithole Countries,'" *Washington Post*, January 12, 2018, https://www.washingtonpost.com/politics/trump-attacks-protections-for-immigrants-from-shithole-countries-in-oval-office-meeting/2018/01/11/bfc0725c-f711-11e7-91af-31ac729add94_story.html?noredirect=on&utm_term=.d47aaa2e9874.

5. Raiola, "It's the Jews Fault."

6. Jon Meacham, "American Hate, a History," *Time*, August 17, 2017, http://time.com/4904290/american-hate-a-history/.

7. Graeme Wood, "His Kampf: Richard Spencer Is a Troll and an Icon for White Supremacists. He Was Also My High School Classmate," *Atlantic*, June 2017, https://www.theatlantic.com/magazine/archive/2017/06/his-kampf/524505/.

8. John Woodrow Cox, "'Let's Party Like It's 1933': Inside the Alt-right World of Richard Spencer," *Washington Post*, November 22, 2016. https://www.washingtonpost.com/local/lets-party-like-its-1933-inside-the-disturbing-alt-right-world-of-richard-spencer/2016/11/22/cf81dc74-aff7-11e6-840f-e3ebab6bcdd3_story.html?utm_term=.9f12c3df11b9.

9. Michael Bragg, "Politicians Decry White Nationalist Torch Rally in Lee Park," *Daily Progress*, May 15, 2017, http://www.dailyprogress.com/news/local/alt-right-s-torch-rally-at-lee-statue-draws-condemnation/article_5cec3457-1861-5623-ab19-24117cca1958.html.

10. The rally at Jackson Park on May 13 was filmed and posted on YouTube: "Spencer & Enoch at Charlottesville, VA (13-May-2017)," https://www.youtube.com/watch?v=B-syXRg6TRE.

11. YouTube, "Spencer & Enoch at Charlottesville."

12. YouTube, "Spencer & Enoch at Charlottesville."

13. YouTube, "Spencer & Enoch at Charlottesville."

14. YouTube, "Spencer & Enoch at Charlottesville."

15. YouTube, "Spencer & Enoch at Charlottesville."

16. *Final Report: Independent Review of the 2017 Protest Events in Charlottesville, Virginia,* Hunton & Williams (the "Heaphy Report"), 27, http://www.charlottesville.org/home/showdocument?id=59691.

17. "Torch-Wielding Protesters Gather at Lee Park," *Daily Progress,* May 13, 2017, http://www.dailyprogress.com/news/local/torch-wielding-protesters-gather-at-lee-park/article_201dc390-384d-11e7-bf16-fb43de0f5d38.html.

18. "Charlottesville," AltRight.com, https://www.youtube.com/watch?v=vVFhC4kuYDU.

19. Heaphy Report, 28.

20. Heaphy Report, 28.

21. Heaphy Report, 28.

22. Heaphy Report, 29, citing "E-mail from Erik Wikstrom to a large distribution list (May 14, 2017, 12:09 p.m.)."

23. Allison Wrabel, "Candelit Counter-protest Follows 'Alt-right' Torch Bearers at Lee Park; Kessler among Arrested," *Daily Progress,* May 15, 2017, http://www.dailyprogress.com/news/candlelit-counter-protest-follows-torch-bearers-at-lee-park-kessler/article_37fe18f6-3916-11e7-ae38-0710fe91dea3.html.

24. Wrable, "Candlit Counter-protest."

12. Cue the Klan—Stage Right

1. Hawes Spencer, *Summer of Hate: Charlottesville, USA* (Charlottesville: University of Virginia Press, 2018), 125.

2. *Final Report: Independent Review of the 2017 Protest Events in Charlottesville, Virginia,* Hunton & Williams (the "Heaphy Report"), 32, http://www.charlottesville.org/home/showdocument?id=59691.

3. Heaphy Report, 32.

4. Spencer, *Summer of Hate,* 121.

5. Robert Gavin, "Secret Recordings Fill in Details in Death Ray Case: Klansman Shown Discussing Device, Plot to Kill Muslims," *Albany Times Union,* September 25, 2015, https://www.timesunion.com/local/article/Video-Glendon-Crawford-s-FBI-undercover-tapes-in-6522539.php.

6. Dean Seal, "KKK Leader Seeking Charlottesville Rally Has History as FBI Informant," *Daily Progress,* June 6, 2017, http://www.dailyprogress.com/news/local/kkk-leader-seeking-charlottesville-rally-has-history-as-fbi-informant/article_d4f743b0-4b0b-11e7-9b0d-bf585dde11ff.html.

7. Seal, "KKK Leader."

8. Seal, "KKK Leader."

9. See, for example, N.M.Stat.Ann. § 30–22–3 (1984); Conn.Gen.Stat. § 53–37a (1989); Del.Code Ann. tit. 11, § 1301(1)(g) (1987); Ga.Code Ann. § 16–11–38(a) (1988); Ala.Code § 13A–11–9(a)(4) (1982); Fla.Stat. §§ 876.12, 876.13 (1987); La.Rev.Stat.Ann. § 14:313 (West 1986); Mich.Comp.Laws § 750.396 (1979); Minn.Stat. § 609.735 (1990); N.C.Gen. Stat. §§ 14–12.7, 14–12.8, 14–12.11 (1986); Okla.Stat. tit. 21, § 1301 (1981); and W.Va. Code § 61–6–22 (1989).

10. Va. Code Ann. § 18.2–422.

11. Va. Code Ann. § 18.2–422.

12. See, for example, "Klan, Cloth and Constitution: Anti-mask Laws and the First Amendment," *Georgia Law Review* 25 (1991): 819–60 (Notes); Oskar E. Rey, "Antimask Laws: Exploring the Outer Bounds of Protected Speech under the First Amendment—State v. Miller, 260 GA. 669, 398 S.E.2d 547 (1990)," *Washington Law Review* 66, no. 4 (1990): 1139–58.

13. Hernandez v. Commonwealth, 12 Va. App. 669, 673, 406 S.E.2d 398, 401 (1991).

14. Hernandez v. Commonwealth, 12 Va. App. at 674.

15. Hernandez v. Commonwealth, 12 Va. App. at 673.

16. Hernandez v. Superintendent, Fredericksburg-Rappahannock Joint Sec. Ctr., 800 F. Supp. 1344, 1349 (E.D. Va. 1992).

17. Introduction to *Charlottesville 2017: The Legacy of Race and Inequity*, ed. Louis P. Nelson and Claudrena N. Harold (Charlottesville: University of Virginia Press, 2018), 10.

18. Nelson and Claudrena, Introduction, 10.

19. Nelson and Claudrena, Introduction, 10.

20. Talley v. California, 362 U.S. 60 (1960).

21. McIntyre v. Ohio Elections Commission, 514 U.S. 334 (1995).

13. The Rise of the Marketplace

1. Lochner v. New York, 198 U.S. 45, 53, 57 (1905).

2. *Lochner*, at 75 (Holmes, J., dissenting).

3. *Lochner*, at 75 (Holmes, J., dissenting).

4. Dred Scott v. Sandford, 60 U.S. 393 (1856).

5. *Dred Scott*, 60 U.S. 393.

6. Don E. Fehrenbacher, "The Origins and Purpose of Lincoln's 'House-Divided' Speech," *Journal of American History* 46, no. 4 (March 1960): 615–43, https://academic.oup.com/jah/article-abstract/46/4/615/714777?redirectedFrom=fulltext.

7. Mark 3:25.

8. Plessy v. Ferguson, 163 U.S. 537, 542 (1896).

9. Bradwell v. People of State of Illinois, 83 U.S. 130 (1872).

10. Rodney A. Smolla, "The Ghosts of Homer Plessy," *Georgia State University Law Review* 12, no. 4 (1996): 1037–88.

11. Smolla, "Ghosts," 1088.

12. Smolla, "Ghosts," 1088.

13. Richard Kluger, *Simple Justice: The History of Brown v. Board of Education and Black America's Struggle for Equality* (New York: Alfred A. Knopf, 1976), 72.

14. Langston Hughes, *Simple Takes a Wife* (New York: Simon & Schuster, 1953), 201.

15. *Plessy*, 163 U.S. at 542.

16. *Plessy*, 163 U.S. at 552.

17. *Plessy*, 163 U.S. at 551–52.

18. *Plessy*, 163 U.S. at 549. "It is claimed by the plaintiff in error that, in any mixed community, the reputation of belonging to the dominant race, in this instance the white race, is property, in the same sense that a right of action, or of inheritance, is property. Conceding this to be so, for the purposes of this case, we are unable to see how this statute deprives him of, or in any way affects his right to, such property. If he be a white man and assigned to a colored coach, he may have his action for damages against the company for being deprived of his so-called property. Upon the other hand, if he be a colored man and be so assigned, he has been deprived of no property, since he is not lawfully entitled to the reputation of being a white man."

19. Juan Williams, *Eyes on the Prize: America's Civil Rights Years, 1954–1965* (New York: Viking, 1987), 10.

20. *Plessy*, 163 U.S. at 557 (Harlan, J., dissenting).

21. Smolla, "Ghosts," 1048–50.

22. *Plessy*, 163 U.S. at 559 (Harlan, J., dissenting).

23. *Plessy*, 163 U.S. at 559 (Harlan, J., dissenting).

24. *Plessy*, 163 U.S. at 560 (Harlan, J., dissenting).

25. *Plessy*, 163 U.S. at 560 (Harlan, J., dissenting).

26. *Bradwell*, 83 U.S. 130 at 141 (Bradley, J., concurring).

27. *Bradwell*, 83 U.S. 130 at 141 (Bradley, J., concurring).

28. Brown v. Board of Education, 347 U.S. 483 (1954).

29. Loving v. Virginia, 388 U.S. 1 (1967).

30. *Loving*, 388 U.S. at 3.

31. *Loving*, 388 U.S. at 12.

32. United States v. Virginia, 518 U.S. 515 (1996).

33. Obergefell v. Hodges, 135 S. Ct. 2584 (2015).

34. *Obergefell*, 135 S.Ct. at 2598.

35. *Obergefell*, 135 S.Ct. at 2608.

36. District of Columbia v. Heller, 554 U.S. 570 (2008).

37. *Heller*, 554 U.S. at 63.

38. *Heller*, 554 U.S. at 626–27.

14. Cue the Counterprotesters—Stage Left

1. Derek Quizon, "Activist's Attorney Says Police Inquiries Are an Attempt to Stifle Protest," *Daily Progress*, June 23, 2017, http://www.dailyprogress.com/news/local/activists-attorney-says-police-inquiries-are-an-attempt-to-stifle/article_4d4ac5e6-587a-11e7-8400-b352d4520a81.html.

2. *Final Report: Independent Review of the 2017 Protest Events in Charlottesville, Virginia*, Hunton & Williams (the "Heaphy Report"), 34, http://www.charlottesville.org/home/showdocument?id=59691, citing letter from Pamela Starsia to Al Thomas, June 23, 2017.

3. Quizon, "Activist's Attorney."

4. Quizon, "Activist's Attorney."

5. Peter Beinart, "The Rise of the Violent Left," *Atlantic*, September 2017, https://www.theatlantic.com/magazine/archive/2017/09/the-rise-of-the-violent-left/534192/.

6. Connor Friedersdorf, "How to Distinguish between Antifa, White Supremacists, and Black Lives Matter," *Atlantic*, August 31, 2017, https://www.theatlantic.com/politics/archive/2017/08/drawing-distinctions-antifa-the-alt-right-and-black-lives-matter/538320/.

7. Friedersdorf, "How to Distinguish."

8. University of Virginia Center for Politics, Sabato's Crystal Ball, "New Poll: Some Americans Express Troubling Racial Attitudes Even as Majority Oppose White Supremacists," September 14, 2017, http://www.centerforpolitics.org/crystalball/articles/new-poll-some-americans-express-troubling-racial-attitudes-even-as-majority-oppose-white-supremacists/.

9. Sabato's Crystal Ball, "New Poll."

10. Jonathan Blitzer, How Church Leaders in Charlottesville Prepared for White Supremacists," *New Yorker*, August 15, 2017, https://www.newyorker.com/news/news-desk/how-church-leaders-in-charlottesville-prepared-for-white-supremacists.

11. Blitzer, "How Church Leaders in Charlottesville Prepared."

12. "Sullivan Urges UVA Community to Avoid July 8 Klan Rally," *Daily Progress*, July 27, 2017, http://www.dailyprogress.com/news/local/uva/sullivan-urges-uva-community-to-avoid-july-klan-rally/article_88a787e6-5b63-11e7-9425-23fdb7cc4b59.html.

13. "Sullivan Urges."

14. "Sullivan Urges."

15. Dean Seal, "KKK Leader Seeking Charlottesville Rally Has History as FBI Informant," *Daily Progress*, June 6, 2017, http://www.dailyprogress.com/news/local/kkk-leader-seeking-charlottesville-rally-has-history-as-fbi-informant/article_d4f743b0-4b0b-11e7-9b0d-bf585dde11ff.html.

16. Seal, "KKK Leader."

17. "Opinion/Letter: Two Fresh Ideas for Addressing Klan Rally," *Daily Progress*, June 18, 2017, http://www.dailyprogress.com/opinion/opinion-letter-two-fresh-ideas-for-addressing-klan-rally/article_d0db0db2-52cb-11e7-a82c-8ba488afc4c8.html.

18. Chris Suarez, "City Plans Alternate Events, Urges Ignoring Klan Rally," *Daily Progress*, June 20, 2017, http://www.dailyprogress.com/news/city-plans-alternate-events-urges-ignoring-klan-rally/article_2d77bef2-561a-11e7-9202-7fbf90d823a7.html.

19. Suarez, "City Plans Alternate Events."

20. Suarez, "City Plans Alternate Events."

21. Suarez, "City Plans Alternate Events."

22. Suarez, "City Plans Alternate Events."

23. John Edwin Mason, "History, Mine and Ours," in *Charlottesville 2017: The Legacy of Race and Inequity*, ed. Louis P. Nelson and Claudrena N. Harold (Charlottesville: University of Virginia Press, 2018), 20.

24. Blitzer, "How Church Leaders in Charlottesville Prepared."

25. Joe Heim, "Ku Klux Klan Rally Draws Loud Counterprotest in Charlottesville," *Washington Post*, July 9, 2017.

26. Joe Heim, "Charlottesville Prepares for a White Nationalist Rally on Saturday," *Washington Post*, August 10, 2017, https://www.washingtonpost.com/local/charlottesville-readies-for-a-white-nationalist-rally-on-saturday/2017/08/10/cff4786e-7c49-11e7-83c7-5bd5460f0d7e_story.html?nid&utm_term=.bf8b780714e9.

15. A *Rolling Stone* Gathers No Facts

1. Record in Virginia Alpha Chapter of Phi Kappa Psi Fraternity v. Rolling Stone LLC, Case. No. CL15000479-00 (Circuit Court of Charlottesville, Va.) (on file with author).

2. Eramo v. Rolling Stone, LLC, 209 F.Supp. 3d 862 (W.D. Va. 2016).

3. Elias v. Rolling Stone LLC, 872 F.3d 97, 100 (2nd Cir. 2017).

4. Virginia Alpha Chapter of Phi Kappa Psi Fraternity v. Rolling Stone LLC, Case. No. CL15000479-00 (Circuit Court of Charlottesville, Va.).

16. The Marketplace Doubles Down

1. Cohen v. California, 403 U.S. 15 (1971).

2. Thomas J. Krattenmaker, "Looking Back at Cohen v. California: A 40 Year Retrospective from Inside the Court," *William & Mary Bill of Rights Journal* 20, no. 3 (2012): 651.

3. *Cohen*, 403 U.S. at 25.

4. Texas v. Johnson, 491 U.S. 397 (1989).

5. Texas v. Johnson, 491 U.S. at 431.

6. Texas v. Johnson, 491 U.S. at 431.

7. Texas Penal Code Ann. § 42.09 (1989).

8. Texas v. Johnson, 491 U.S. at 412.

9. Texas v. Johnson, 491 U.S. at 411.

10. Texas v. Johnson, 491 U.S. at 419.

11. Texas v. Johnson, 491 U.S. at 419.

12. Texas v. Johnson, 491 U.S. at 418.

13. Texas v. Johnson, 491 U.S. at 419.

14. Texas v. Johnson, 491 U.S. at 419.

15. Texas v. Johnson, 491 U.S. at 420.

16. Texas v. Johnson, 491 U.S. at 432 (Rehnquist, C.J., dissenting).

17. 559 U.S. 460 (2010).

18. 18 U.S.C. § 48. United States v. Stevens, 559 U.S. at 464 ("Congress enacted 18 U.S.C. § 48 to criminalize the commercial creation, sale, or possession of certain depictions of animal cruelty. . . . Section 48 establishes a criminal penalty of up to five years in prison for anyone who knowingly 'creates, sells, or possesses a depiction of animal cruelty,' if done 'for commercial gain' in interstate or foreign commerce. § 48(a). A depiction of 'animal cruelty' is defined as one 'in which a living animal is intentionally maimed, mutilated, tortured, wounded, or killed,' if that conduct violates federal or state law where 'the creation, sale, or possession takes place'").

19. *Stevens*, 559 U.S. at 469 ("The Government argues that 'depictions of animal cruelty' should be added to the list").

20. *Stevens*, 559 U.S. at 469, quoting Board of Airport Commissioners of Los Angeles v. Jews for Jesus, Inc., 482 U.S. 569, 574 (1987).

21. *Stevens*, 559 U.S. at 469, quoting Brief for United States at 8.

22. *Stevens*, 559 U.S. at 469.

23. *Stevens*, 559 U.S. at 469 ("The First Amendment's guarantee of free speech does not extend only to categories of speech that survive an ad hoc balancing of relative social costs and benefits. The First Amendment itself reflects a judgment by the American people that the benefits of its restrictions on the Government outweigh the costs. Our Constitution forecloses any attempt to revise that judgment simply on the basis that some speech is not worth it. The Constitution is not a document 'prescribing limits, and declaring that those limits may be passed at pleasure.'") quoting Marbury v. Madison, 1 Cranch 137, 178, 2 L.Ed. 60 (1803).

24. United States v. Alvarez, 567 U.S. 709 (2012).

25. United States v. Alvarez, 567 U.S. at 723.

26. United States v. Alvarez, 567 U.S. at 739 (Alito, J., dissenting).

27. Snyder v. Phelps, 562 U.S. 443 (2010).

28. Snyder v. Phelps, 562 U.S. at 448.

29. Hustler Magazine, Inc. v. Falwell, 485 U.S. 46 (1988).

30. Rodney Smolla, *Jerry Falwell v. Larry Flynt: The First Amendment on Trial* (New York: St. Martin's, 1988), 313.

31. Smolla, *Jerry Falwell v. Larry Flynt.*

32. Hustler Magazine, Inc. v. Falwell, 485 U.S. at 55.

33. Hustler Magazine, Inc. v. Falwell, 485 U.S. at 55.

17. The Day of the Klan

1. Virginia Code § 15.2–1714.

2. *Final Report: Independent Review of the 2017 Protest Events in Charlottesville, Virginia*, Hunton & Williams (the "Heaphy Report"), 51, http://www.charlottesville.org/home/showdocument?id=59691.

3. Heaphy Report, 55.

4. Heaphy Report, 55.

5. Heaphy Report, 55.

6. Heaphy Report, 55.

18. When Speech Advances Civil Rights

1. Leslie Kendrick, "The Answers and the Questions in First Amendment Law," in *Charlottesville 2017: The Legacy of Race and Inequity*, ed. Louis P. Nelson and Claudrena N. Harold (Charlottesville: University of Virginia Press, 2018), 72–74.

2. New York Times Co. v. Sullivan, 376 U.S. 254 (1964).

3. N.A.A.C.P. v. Claiborne Hardware Co., 458 U.S. 886 (1982).

4. Rodney Smolla, *Suing the Press: Libel, the Media, and Power* (New York: Oxford University Press, 1986), 32.

5. New York Times Co. v. Sullivan, 376 U.S. 254 (1964).

6. Smolla, *Suing the Press*, 33.

7. Smolla, *Suing the Press*, 33.

8. New York Times Co. v. Sullivan, 376 U.S. at 269, quoting Stromburg v. California, 283 U.S. 359, 369 (1931).

9. New York Times Co. v. Sullivan, 376 U.S. at 270.

10. New York Times Co. v. Sullivan, 376 U.S. at 276.

11. New York Times Co. v. Sullivan, 376 U.S. at 280.

12. McKee v. Cosby, No. 17–1542, 2019 WL 659764, at *1 (U.S. Feb. 19, 2019).

13. McKee v. Cosby, No. 17–1542, 2019 WL 659764, at *1 (U.S. Feb. 19, 2019) (Thomas, J., concurring in the denial of the writ of certiorari).

14. N.A.A.C.P. v. Claiborne Hardware Co., 458 U.S. 886 (1982).

15. N.A.A.C.P. v. Claiborne Hardware Co., 458 U.S. at 899.

16. N.A.A.C.P. v. Claiborne Hardware Co., 458 U.S. at 934.

17. N.A.A.C.P. v. Claiborne Hardware Co., 458 U.S. at 934.

18. N.A.A.C.P. v. Claiborne Hardware Co., 458 U.S. at 935.

19. N.A.A.C.P. v. Claiborne Hardware Co., 458 U.S. at 935.

20. N.A.A.C.P. v. Claiborne Hardware Co., 458 U.S. at 935.

21. N.A.A.C.P. v. Claiborne Hardware Co., 458 U.S. at 938.

22. N.A.A.C.P. v. Claiborne Hardware Co., 458 U.S. at 927.

23. N.A.A.C.P. v. Claiborne Hardware Co., 458 U.S. at 928.

24. N.A.A.C.P. v. Claiborne Hardware Co., 458 U.S. at 928.

25. N.A.A.C.P. v. Claiborne Hardware Co., 458 U.S. at 928, quoting New York Times Co. v. Sullivan, 376 U.S. at 270.

19. Duke and the Disciples

1. Tyler Bridges, *The Rise of David Duke* (Jackson: University of Mississippi Press, 1995).

2. Tom Leonard, "David Duke: Nick Griffin Was 'Lynched' on Question Time," *Telegraph*, October 23, 2009, https://www.telegraph.co.uk/news/worldnews/northamerica/usa/6419715/David-Duke-Nick-Griffin-was-lynched-on-Question-Time.html.

3. Allyson Shontell, "Really, There's No Such Thing as Bad PR," Business Insider, February 28, 2011, http://www.businessinsider.com/there-2011-2.

4. Shontell, "Really, There's No Such Thing."

5. Robert Costa and Ed O'Keefe, "House Majority Whip Scalise Confirms He Spoke to White Supremacists in 2002," *Washington Post*, December 29, 2014, https://www.washingtonpost.com/politics/house-majority-whip-scalise-confirms-he-spoke-to-white-nationalists-in-2002/2014/12/29/7f80dc14-8fa3-11e4-a900-9960214d4cd7_story.html?utm_term=.27ca9a9d8dbf.

6. Costa and O'Keefe, "House Majority Whip."

7. Benjy Sarlin, "Steve Scalise: Speaking at Supremacist Event 'a Mistake I Regret," MSNBC, December 30, 2014, http://www.msnbc.com/msnbc/democrats-demand-answers-steve-scalises-ties-david-duke.

8. Sarlin, "Steve Scalise."

9. "Steve Scalise Returns to Capitol," CBS News, September 28, 2018, https://www.cbsnews.com/news/steve-scalise-returns-to-capitol/.

10. Alan Blinder, "David Duke, Ex-K.K.K. Leader, to Seek Senate Seat in Louisiana," *New York Times*, July 22, 2016, https://www.nytimes.com/2016/07/23/us/david-duke-senate-louisiana.html.

11. Peter Applebome, "An Epoch Is Ending But Why?," *New York Times*, June 8, 1994, https://www.nytimes.com/1994/06/08/us/an-epoch-is-ending-but-why.html.

12. Tyler Bridges, "David Duke's Last Stand," Politico, November 3, 2016, https://www.politico.com/magazine/story/2016/11/david-duke-louisiana-debate-214414.

13. "David Duke," Southern Poverty Law Center, https://www.splcenter.org/fighting-hate/extremist-files/individual/david-duke, quoting Duke, "Will the White Race Survive?," June 22, 2010.

14. Mike Wendling, *Alt-Right: From 4Chan to the White House* (London: Pluto, 2018), 77.

15. Wendling, *Alt-Right*, 77.

16. Scout Hough, "David Duke, Former Neo-Nazi, Ku Klux Klan Leader Says Donald Trump Speaks 'Radically,'" Inquisitr, December 15, 2015, http://www.inquisitr.com/2664950/david-duke-trump-former-kkk-leader-on-republican-poll-leader/.

17. Hough, "David Duke."

18. Hough, "David Duke."

19. "David Duke Pleads Guilty to Tax Charge and Fraud," *New York Times*, December 19, 2002 (Associated Press report), https://www.nytimes.com/2002/12/19/us/david-duke-pleads-guilty-to-tax-charge-and-fraud.html.

20. "David Duke Pleads Guilty."

21. "David Duke Pleads Guilty."

22. *New York Times*, "Czech Police Expel Ex-Leader of Klan" (Reuters), April 25, 2009, https://www.nytimes.com/2009/04/26/world/europe/26czech.html.

23. John Rudolf, "David Duke Arrested in Germany, Ex-Klan Leader Faces Deportation," Huffington Post, November 29, 2011, https://www.huffingtonpost.com/2011/11/29/david-duke-arrested-in-germany_n_1119010.html.

24. Rudolf, "David Duke Arrested."

25. "Italian Court Moves to Expel Former Ku Klux Klan Leader," Reuters, December 5, 2013, https://uk.reuters.com/article/uk-italy-kukluxklan/italian-court-moves-to-expel-former-ku-klux-klan-leader-idUKBRE9B40T120131205.

26. "Italian Court Moves to Expel."

27. Rudolf, "David Duke Arrested."

28. Hough, "David Duke."

29. Hough, "David Duke."

30. Jeremy Alford, "Much of David Duke's '91 Campaign Is Now in Louisiana Mainstream," *New York Times*, December 31, 2014, https://www.nytimes.com/2015/01/01/us/politics/much-of-david-dukes-91-campaign-is-now-in-louisiana-mainstream.html.

31. Hough, "David Duke."

32. *Final Report: Independent Review of the 2017 Protest Events in Charlottesville, Virginia*, Hunton & Williams (the "Heaphy Report"), 69, http://www.charlottesville.org/home/showdocument?id=59691.

33. John F. Sugg, "Cover Story: A Kinder, Gentler Racism," *Creative Loafing*, February 28, 2007, https://creativeloafing.com/content-185371-Cover-Story:-A-kinder,-gentler-racism.

34. Southern Poverty Law Center, "How Klan Lawyer Sam Dickson Got Rich," October 19, 2006, https://www.splcenter.org/fighting-hate/intelligence-report/2006/how-klan-lawyer-sam-dickson-got-rich.

35. "Sam Dickson," Southern Poverty Law Center.

36. Identity Evropa, "About Us," https://www.identityevropa.com/about-us.

37. Identity Evropa, "About Us."

38. Connor Gaffy, "Unite the Right Organizer Disavowed by Family after Charlottesville Violence," *Newsweek*, August 16, 2017, http://www.newsweek.com/unite-right-charlottesville-nathan-damigo-trump-651266.

39. Robert King, "Meet the Man in the Middle of the 'Unite the Right' Rally in Charlottesville," *Indianapolis Star* (USA Today Network), August 12, 2017, https://www.usatoday.com/story/news/nation-now/2017/08/12/meet-man-middle-unite-right-rally-charlottesville/562571001/.

40. Ray Sanchez, "Man Accused of Attacking Rally Protester Says Trump Inspired Him," CNN, April 16, 2017, https://www.cnn.com/2017/04/15/politics/donald-trump-rally-lawsuit/index.html.

41. "Woman Assaulted at Trump Rally," WLKY broadcast, March 1, 2016, https://www.youtube.com/watch?v=jvtqYeEms_0.

42. Sanchez, "Man Accused of Attacking Rally Protester."

43. Nwanguma v. Trump, No. 3:16-CV-247-DJH-HBB, 2017 WL 3430514, at *1 (W.D. Ky. Aug. 9, 2017).

44. NAACP v. Claiborne Hardware Co., 458 U.S. 886, 928 (1982).

45. Nwanguma v. Trump, at *2.

46. Rory McVeigh and Kevin Estep, *The Politics of Losing: Trump, the Klan, and the Mainstreaming of Resentment* (New York: Columbia University Press, 2019).

47. Vegas Tenold, *Everything You Love Will Burn: Inside the Rebirth of White Nationalism in America* (New York: Nation Books, 2018).

48. Nwanguma v. Trump, at *2.

49. Nwanguma v. Trump, at *2.

50. "Elliot Kline," One People Project, July 8, 2017, Rehttp://onepeoplesproject.com/2017/07/08/elliott-kline/ntokil (quoting Daily Stormer account by Eli Mosley).

51. Emma Cott, "How Our Reporter Uncovered a Lie That Propelled an Alt-Right Extremist's Rise," *New York Times*, February 5, 2018, https://www.nytimes.com/2018/02/05/insider/confronting-a-white-nationalist-eli-mosley.html.

52. Samuel Osborne, "Leading White Supremacist Eli Mosley 'Caught Lying about Fighting in Iraq,'" *Independent*, February 6, 2018, https://www.independent.co.uk/news/world/americas/elliot-kline-white-supremacist-caught-lying-iraq-fighting-killing-muslims-neo-nazi-unite-the-right-a8196846.html.

53. Richard Spencer and Evan McClaren, "A Statement on Eli Mosley," National Policy Institute, February 5, 2018, https://nationalpolicy.institute/2018/02/05/a-statement-on-eli-mosley/.

54. Daily Stormer, March 26, 2017, https://dailystormer.name/tag/make-america-great-again/feed/; "Elliot Kline," One People Project, July 8, 2017, http://onepeoplesproject.com/2017/07/08/elliott-kline/ (quoting Daily Stormer account by Eli Mosley).

55. "About Michael Hill," Southern Poverty Law Center, https://www.splcenter.org/fighting-hate/extremist-files/individual/michael-hill.

56. Spencer Sunshine, "A Guide to Who's Coming to the Largest White Nationalist Rally in a Decade," Political Research Associates, August 10, 2017, http://www.politicalresearch.org/2017/08/10/a-guide-to-whos-coming-to-the-largest-white-nationalist-rally-in-a-decade/#sthash.LJcbVU0u.dpbs.

57. Sunshine, "Guide to Who's Coming."

58. "Christopher Cantwell," Southern Poverty Law Center, https://www.splcenter.org/fighting-hate/extremist-files/individual/christopher-cantwell.

59. Sunshine, "Guide to Who's Coming."

60. "Christopher Cantwell," Southern Poverty Law Center.

61. "Christopher Cantwell," Southern Poverty Law Center.

62. "Christopher Cantwell," Southern Poverty Law Center.

63. "Johnny Monoxide AKA John Ramondetta," Southern Poverty Law Center, https://www.splcenter.org/fighting-hate/extremist-files/individual/johnny-monoxide-aka-john-ramondetta.

64. "Johnny Ramondetta Claims Murdered Sandy Hook Children Faked Their Deaths," Angry White Men (Tracking White Supremacy), https://angrywhitemen.org/.

65. "Charlottesville: Race and Terror," *Vice News Tonight* (HBO), August 14, 2017, https://www.youtube.com/watch?v=P54sP0Nlngg.

20. The Russian Connection

1. CNN, "Discovery Solves Mystery of Last Czar's Family," April 30, 2008, http://www.edition.cnn.com/2008/WORLD/europe/04/30/russia.czar/.

2. Natasha Betrand, "'A Model for Civilization': Putin's Russia Has Emerged as 'a Beacon for Nationalists' and the American Alt-right," *Business Insider*, December 10, 2016, http://www.businessinsider.com/russia-connections-to-the-alt-right-2016-11.

3. @DrDavidDuke, Twitter, February 16, 2017.

4. @DrDavidDuke, Twitter, February 16, 2017.

5. Casey Michael, "Meet the Moscow Mouthpiece Married to a Racist Alt-right Boss," Daily Beast, December 20, 2016, https://www.thedailybeast.com/meet-the-moscow-mouthpiece-married-to-a-racist-alt-right-boss.

6. Michael, "Meet the Moscow Mouthpiece."

7. Michael, "Meet the Moscow Mouthpiece."

8. Betrand, "'Model for Civilization.'"

9. Michael, "Meet the Moscow Mouthpiece."

10. Michael, "Meet the Moscow Mouthpiece."

11. Michael, "Meet the Moscow Mouthpiece."

12. Betrand, "'Model for Civilization.'"

13. Betrand, "'Model for Civilization.'"

14. Neil MacFarquhar, "Right-Wing Groups Find a Haven, for a Day, in Russia," *New York Times*, March 22, 2015, https://www.nytimes.com/2015/03/23/world/europe/right-wing-groups-find-a-haven-for-a-day-in-russia.html?_r=1.

15. Betrand, "'Model for Civilization.'"

16. Betrand, "'Model for Civilization.'"

17. Betrand, "'Model for Civilization.'"

18. Andrew Higgins, "In Expanding Russian Influence, Faith Combines with Firepower," *New York Times*, September 13, 2016, https://www.nytimes.com/2016/09/14/world/europe/russia-orthodox-church.html.

19. Fred Lucas, "Putin Goes to War with Russia's Free Churches," *Newsweek*, July 23, 2016, http://www.newsweek.com/putin-goes-war-russia-free-churches-482730.

20. Lucas, "Putin Goes to War."

21. Owen Matthews, "Alexander Dugin's and Steve Bannon's Ideological Ties to Vladimir Putin's Russia," *Newsweek*, April 17, 2017, http://www.newsweek.com/steve-bannon-donald-trump-jared-kushner-vladimir-putin-russia-fbi-mafia-584962.

22. Matthews, "Alexander Dugin's."

23. Matthews, "Alexander Dugin's."

24. Michael Wolff, *Fire and Fury: Inside the White House* (New York: Henry Holt, 2018).

21. A Call to Conscience

1. Congregate Charlottesville, "Welcome," https://congregatecville.com/home/.

2. Congregate Charlottesville, "Welcome."

3. Congregate Charlottesville, "Press Release about Clergy Call: Call to Clergy and Faith Leaders," https://congregatecville.com/home/.

4. Congregate Charlottesville, "Press Release about Clergy Call."

5. "National Call to Conscience," https://congregatecville.com/call-to-conscience.

6. Sarah van Gelder, "Rev. Sekou on Today's Civil Rights Leaders: 'I Take My Orders from 23-Year-Old Queer Women,'" *Yes!* magazine, July 22, 2015, http://www.yesmagazine.org/peace-justice/black-lives-matter-s-favorite-minister-reverend-sekou-young-queer.

7. Cornel West, "Goodbye, American Neoliberalism. A New Era Is Here," *Guardian*, November 17, 2016, https://www.theguardian.com/commentisfree/2016/nov/17/american-neoliberalism-cornel-west-2016-election.

8. Solidarity Cville, "About," http://solidaritycville.com/About/.

9. Solidarity Cville, "About."

10. Louis P. Nelson and Claudrena N. Harold, eds., *Charlottesville 2017: The Legacy of Race and Inequity* (Charlottesville: University of Virginia Press, 2018).

22. Preparations

1. Madeleine Sheehan Perkins, "New York Protester Holds Sign Quoting Charlottesville Victim's Last Public Facebook Post," Business Insider, August 14, 2017.

2. Louis Becket, "'A White Girl Had to Die for People to Pay Attention': Heather Heyer's Mother on Hate in the US," *Guardian*, October 1, 2017, https://www.theguardian.com/us-news/2017/oct/01/heather-heyers-mother-on-hate-in-the-us-were-not-going-to-hug-it-out-but-we-can-listen-to-each-other.

3. Terry Beigie, "Greene County Remembers Heather Heyer," *Green County Record*, August 17, 2017, http://www.starexponent.com/news/greene-county-remembers-heather-heyer/article_455aa566-3205-53fb-9446-f7792cef4c6a.html; Becket, "'White Girl Had to Die.'"

4. Beigie, "Greene County Remembers Heather Heyer."

5. Maev Kennedy, "Heather Heyer, Victim of Charlottesville Car Attack, Was Civil Rights Activist," *Guardian*, August 13, 2017.

6. Kennedy, "Heather Heyer, Victim of Charlottesville."

7. Becket, "'White Girl Had to Die.'"

8. Becket, "'White Girl Had to Die.'"

9. Kennedy, "Heather Heyer, Victim of Charlottesville."

10. Kennedy, "Heather Heyer, Victim of Charlottesville."

11. Kennedy, "Heather Heyer, Victim of Charlottesville."

12. Bob Strickley, Sarah Brookbank, Chris Graves, and Chris Mayhew, "911 Calls, Records Reveal Tumultuous Past for Accused Charlottesville Driver, Family," *Cincinnati Enquirer*, August 14, 2017, https://www.cincinnati.com/story/news/local/northern-ky/2017/08/14/mom-previously-accused-charlottesville-driver-james-alex-fields-jr-beating-her/566078001.

13. Strickley et al., "911 Calls."

14. Strickley et al., "911 Calls."

15. Strickley et al., "911 Calls."

16. Strickley et al., "911 Calls."

17. Strickley et al., "911 Calls."

18. Jonah Engel Bromwich and Alan Blinderaug, "What We Know about James Alex Fields, Driver Charged in Charlottesville Killing," *New York Times*, August 13, 2017, https://www.nytimes.com/2017/08/13/us/james-alex-fields-charlottesville-driver-.html.

19. Bromwich and Blinderaug, "What We Know."

20. Alexa Liautaud, "The Nazi of the School," Vice News, August 15, 2017, https://news.vice.com/en_us/article/kzgxmw/charlottesville-attack-james-alex-field-jr.

21. Bromwich and Blinderaug, "What We Know."

22. Bromwich and Blinderaug, "What We Know."

23. Hillary Lake, Abby Anstead, and Julie O'Neill, "Former NKY Classmate Said Charlottesville Attack Suspect 'Would Proclaim Himself as a Nazi,'" 9 WCPO Cincinnati, August 13, 2017, https://www.wcpo.com/news/local-news/i-team/former-classmate-said-char lotteville-suspect-would-proclaim-himself-as-a-nazi.

24. Lake, Anstead, and O'Neill, "Former NKY Classmate."

25. Lake, Anstead, and O'Neill, "Former NKY Classmate."

26. Liautaud, "Nazi of the School," https://news.vice.com/en_us/article/kzgxmw/charlot tesville-attack-james-alex-field-jr.

27. *Final Report: Independent Review of the 2017 Protest Events in Charlottesville, Virginia*, Hunton & Williams (the "Heaphy Report"), 97, http://www.charlottesville.org/home/showdocument?id=59691.

28. Heaphy Report, 97.

29. Heaphy Report, 98.

30. Heaphy Report, 98.

31. Heaphy Report, 98.

32. Heaphy Report, 98.

33. Heaphy Report, 98.

34. Heaphy Report, 98.

35. Heaphy Report, 106.

36. Heaphy Report, 103.

37. Heaphy Report, 120.

38. Heaphy Report, 79, citing Operation Unite the Right Charlottesville 2.0, https://www.unicornriot.ninja/2017/leaked-planning-meetings-led-neo-nazi-terrorism-charlottesville/.

39. Heaphy Report, 79.

40. Heaphy Report, 79.

41. Heaphy Report, 26–27.

23. The Day of the Cross

1. *New York Times*, "Richmond Approves Monument to Ashe," July 18, 1995, https://www.nytimes.com/1995/07/18/us/richmond-approves-monument-to-ashe.html?n=Top%2FReference%2FTimes+Topics%2FPeople%2FA%2FAshe%2C+Arthur.

2. University of Virginia Center for Politics, Sabato's Crystal Ball, "New Poll: Some Americans Express Troubling Racial Attitudes Even as Majority Oppose White Supremacists," September 14, 2017, http://www.centerforpolitics.org/crystalball/articles/new-poll-some-americans-express-troubling-racial-attitudes-even-as-majority-oppose-white-supremacists/.

3. Sabato's Crystal Ball, "New Poll."

4. Brandenburg v. Ohio, 395 U.S. 444 (1969).

5. R.A.V. v. City of St. Paul, 506 U.S. 377 (1992).

6. Virginia v. Black, 538 U.S. 343 (2003).

7. Brandenburg v. Ohio, 395 U.S. at 446.

8. Brandenburg v. Ohio, 395 U.S. at 447.

9. Hess v. Indiana, 414 U.S. 105 (1973).

10. Hess v. Indiana, 414 U.S. at 110.

11. Hess v. Indiana, 414 U.S. at 108.

12. St. Paul Bias-Motivated Crime Ordinance, St. Paul, Minn., Legis.Code § 292.02 (1990).

13. R.A.V. v. City of St. Paul, 506 U.S. at 391.

14. R.A.V. v. City of St. Paul, 506 U.S. at 392.

15. Virginia Code § 18.2–423 (1996).

16. Baugh v. Judicial Inquiry & Review Commission (JIRC), 907 F.2d 440, 441 (4th Cir. 1990).

17. Capitol Square Review & Advisory Board v. Pinette, 515 U.S. 753, 770–71 (1995) (Thomas, J., concurring).

18. Capitol Square Review & Advisory Board v. Pinette, 515 U.S. at 770 (Thomas, J., concurring).

19. Capitol Square Review & Advisory Board v. Pinette, 515 U.S. at 770 (Thomas, J., concurring).

20. Capitol Square Review & Advisory Board v. Pinette, 515 U.S. at 771 (Thomas, J., concurring).

21. Dahlia Lithwick, "Virginia Burning: Are Cross-Burnings Speech or Violence?," *Slate*, December 11, 2002, http://www.slate.com/articles/news_and_politics/supreme_court_dispatches/2002/12/virginia_burning.html.

22. Oliver Wendell Holmes, "The Natural Law," in *The Collected Legal Papers* (New York: Harcourt, Brace and Howe, 1920), 311.

23. Edward J. Cleary, *Beyond the Burning Cross: A Landmark Case of Race, Censorship, and the First Amendment* (New York: Random House, 1994).

24. Lithwick, "Virginia Burning."

25. Transcript of Oral Argument, Virginia v. Black, 2002 WL 31838589 (December 11, 2002). Except where noted in text, all the following courtroom quotations from Virginia v. Black are taken from the court transcript of the oral arguments.

26. Garrett Epps, "Clarence Thomas Takes on a Symbol of White Supremacy," *Atlantic*, June 18, 2015, https://www.theatlantic.com/politics/archive/2015/06/clarence-thomas-confederate-flag/396281/.

27. Lithwick, "Virginia Burning."

28. Virginia v. Black, 538 U.S. 343 (2003).

29. Virginia v. Black, 538 U.S. at 359 quoting R.A.V. v. City of St. Paul, 506 U.S. at 382–83.

30. Virginia v. Black, 538 U.S. at 359 quoting Chaplinsky v. New Hampshire, 315 U.S. 568, 572 (1942).

31. Virginia v. Black, 538 U.S. at 359 quoting Cohen v. California, 403 U.S. 15, 20 (1971).

32. Virginia v. Black, 538 U.S. at 359 quoting Watts v. United States, 394 U.S. 705, 708 (1969).

33. Virginia v. Black, 538 U.S. at 344.

34. Virginia v. Black, 538 U.S. at 344.

35. Virginia v. Black, 538 U.S. at 345.

36. Virginia v. Black, 538 U.S. at 345.

37. Va. Code Ann. § 18.2–423 (1996).

38. Virginia v. Black, 538 U.S. at 367.

39. Virginia v. Black, 528 U.S. at 367.

40. Elliott v. Commonwealth, 267 Va. 464, 593 S.E.2d 263 (2004).

24. The Idea of the University

1. Louis P. Nelson and Claudrena N. Harold, eds., introduction to *Charlottesville 2017: The Legacy of Race and Inequity* (Charlottesville: University of Virginia Press, 2018), 11.

2. Nelson and Harold, *Charlottesville 2017*, 11.

3. Rodney A. Smolla, *The Constitution Goes to College: Five Constitutional Ideas That Have Shaped the American University* (New York: NYU Press, 2011).

4. Jack Stripling, "Beyond a President's Worst Fears, A Mob with Torches Arrived," *Chronicle of Higher Education*, August 13, 2017, https://www.chronicle.com/article/Beyond-a-President-s-Worst/240914?cid=rclink.

5. Kate Bellows, "Curry Prof. Walt Heinecke Submits Applications for Aug. 12 Counter-rallies," *Cavalier Daily*, July 19, 2018, http://www.cavalierdaily.com/article/2017/07/curry-prof-walt-heinecke-submits-applications-for-aug-12-counter-rallies.

6. Bellows, "Curry Prof. Walt Heinecke."

7. Bellows, "Curry Prof. Walt Heinecke."

8. Bellows, "Curry Prof. Walt Heinecke."

9. *Final Report: Independent Review of the 2017 Protest Events in Charlottesville, Virginia*, Hunton & Williams (the "Heaphy Report"), citing letter from Pamela Starsia to Al Thomas (June 23, 2017), 77–78, http://www.charlottesville.org/home/showdocument?id=59691.

10. Heaphy Report, 73.

11. Heaphy Report, 74.

12. Schmalz, "In Charlottesville, UVa Grapples with Its History and the Alt-right," *Chronicle of Higher Education*, July 30, 2017, https://www.chronicle.com/article/In-Charlottesville-UVa/240747?cid=rclink.

13. Schmalz, "In Charlottesville, UVa Grapples."

14. Schmalz, "In Charlottesville, UVa Grapples." Emphasis is mine.

15. Stripling, "Inside the U. of Virginia's Response."

16. Smolla, *Constitution Goes to College*.

17. Smolla, *Constitution Goes to College*.

25. Heckler's Veto

1. Feiner v. New York, 340 U.S. 315 (1951).

2. Rodney A. Smolla, *Free Speech in an Open Society* (New York: Alfred A. Knopf, 1992).

3. Frederick Schauer, "In the Shadow of the First Amendment," in *Charlottesville 2017: The Legacy of Race and Inequity*, ed. Louis P. Nelson and Claudrena N. Harold (Charlottesville: University of Virginia Press, 2018), 67.

4. Landry v. Daley, 280 F.Supp. 969 (N.D. Ill. 1968).

5. Iowa v. Hardin, 498 N.W.2d 677 (Iowa 1993).

6. Forsyth County, Georgia v. Nationalist Movement, 505 U.S. 123, 124–25 (1992).

7. Forsyth County, Georgia v. Nationalist Movement, 505 U.S. at 124–25, citing Hackworth, "Completing the Job," in Forsyth County, 8 Southern Exposure 26 (1980).

8. Dudley Clendinen, "Thousands in Civil Rights March Jeered by Crowd in Georgia Town," *New York Times*, January 25, 1987, https://www.nytimes.com/1987/01/25/us/thousands-in-civil-rights-march-jeered-by-crowd-in-georgia-town.html.

9. Clendinen, "Thousands in Civil Rights March."

10. Clendinen, "Thousands in Civil Rights March."

11. Forsyth County, Georgia v. Nationalist Movement, 505 U.S. 123, 133 (1992).

12. Forsyth County, Georgia v. Nationalist Movement, 505 U.S. at 133.

13. *Final Report: Independent Review of the 2017 Protest Events in Charlottesville, Virginia*, Hunton & Williams (the "Heaphy Report"), 155, http://www.charlottesville.org/home/showdocument?id=59691.

14. Heaphy Report, 81–82.

15. Heaphy Report, 81–82.

16. Heaphy Report, 82.

17. Heaphy Report, 82.

18. Heaphy Report, 82.

19. Chris Suarez, "City Sued over Rally Permit Decision," *Daily Progress*, August 10, 2017, http://www.dailyprogress.com/news/local/city-sued-over-rally-permit-decision/article_5255aa5e-7e1f-11e7-8a16-e37d2241f987.html.

20. Suarez, "City Sued."

21. Suarez, "City Sued."

22. Heaphy Report, 83.

23. Kessler v. City of Charlottesville, Civil Action No. 3:17CV00056, (W.D. Va., August 11, 2017), quoting Reed v. Town of Gilbert, 135 S.Ct. 2218, 2226 (2015).

24. Kessler v. City of Charlottesville.

25. Kessler v. City of Charlottesville.

26. Kessler v. City of Charlottesville.

27. Kessler v. City of Charlottesville, quoting Elrod v. Burns, 427 U.S. 347, 373 (1976).

26. Channels of Communication

1. See Marshall McLuhan, *Understanding Media: The Extensions of Man* (New York: McGraw-Hill, 1964), 8–13.

2. Sarah Posner, "How Donald Trump's New Campaign Chief Created an Online Haven for White Nationalists," *Mother Jones*, August 22, 2016, https://www.motherjones.com/politics/2016/08/stephen-bannon-donald-trump-alt-right-breitbart-news/.

3. Connor Friedersdorf, "Andrew Breitbart's Legacy: Credit and Blame Where It's Due," *Atlantic*, March 8, 2012, https://www.theatlantic.com/politics/archive/2012/03/andrew-breitbarts-legacy-credit-and-blame-where-its-due/253953/.

4. Mike Wendling, *Alt-Right: From 4chan to the White House* (London: Pluto, 2018), 110.

5. 4chan website, http://www.4chan.org/.

6. 4chan website, http://www.4chan.org/.

7. 4chan website, "Rules," http://www.4chan.org/rules.

8. "Man Acquitted of Shooting Nazi," *Dispatch* (Lexington, NC), November 25, 1970, https://news.google.com/newspapers?nid=1734&dat=19701125&id=ok4qAAAAIBAJ&sjid=rFEEAAAAIBAJ&pg=4424,2011459.

9. Tara McKelvey, "Father and Son Team on Hate Site," USAtoday.com, July 15, 2001, https://usatoday30.usatoday.com/life/2001-07-16-kid-hate-sites.htm.

10. Spencer Sunshine, "A Guide to Who's Coming to the Largest White Nationalist Rally in a Decade," Political Research Associates, August 10, 2017, http://www.politicalresearch.org/2017/08/10/a-guide-to-whos-coming-to-the-largest-white-nationalist-rally-in-a-decade/#sthash.LJcbVU0u.dpbs.

11. Benjamin Garland, "Charlottesville 2.0: Be There or Be Square," Daily Stormer, August 5, 2017, https://www.dailystormer.com/charlottesville-2-0-be-there-or-be-square.

12. Garland, "Charlottesville 2.0."

13. Garland, "Charlottesville 2.0," citing "Andrew Anglin," Southern Poverty Law Center, https://www.splcenter.org/fighting-hate/extremist-files/individual/andrew-anglin; Lee Rogers, "Join Daily Stormer Staff at the 'Unite the Right' Rally in Charlottesville, Virginia!," Daily Stormer, July 30, 2017, https://www.dailystormer.com/join-daily-stormer-staff-at-the-unite-the-right-rally-in-charlottesville-virginia; Keegan Hankes, "Eye of the Stormer," Southern Poverty Law Center, February 9, 2017, https://www.splcenter.org/fighting-hate/intelligence-report/2017/eye-stormer; Garland, "Charlottesville 2.0."

14. Urban Dictionary, "doxed," https://www.urbandictionary.com/define.php?term=doxed.

15. Urban Dictionary, "doxed."

16. Amanda Hess, "For the Alt-Right, the Message Is in the Punctuation," *New York Times*, June 10, 2016, https://www.nytimes.com/2016/06/11/arts/for-the-alt-right-the-message-is-in-the-punctuation.html?_r=0.

17. Wendling, *Alt-Right*, 76–101.

18. Urban Dictionary, "red pill," https://www.urbandictionary.com/define.php?term=red%20pill.

19. Alan Rappeport, "From the Right, a New Slur for G.O.P. Candidates," *New York Times*, August 13, 2015, https://www.nytimes.com/2015/08/13/us/from-the-right-a-new-slur-for-gop-candidates.html.

20. Wendling, *Alt-Right*, 84.

27. Rednecks and Saint Paul

1. Ben Coley, "Local Resident Recounts Charlottesville," *Dispatch* (Lexington, NC), August 15, 2017, http://www.the-dispatch.com/news/20170815/local-resident-recounts-char lottesville.

2. Redneck Revolt, Putting the Red Back in Redneck, https://www.redneckrevolt.org/.

3. Redneck Revolt, Putting the Red Back in Redneck.

4. Redneck Revolt, Putting the Red Back in Redneck.

5. Redneck Revolt, Putting the Red Back in Redneck.

6. Julian Wyllie, "A Professor Brought His Guns to Protect Protesters at White-Supremacist Rallies. Then His Troubles Started," *Chronicle of Higher Education*, May 28, 2018. https://www.chronicle.com/article/A-Professor-Brought-His-Guns/243516?cid=at&utm_source=at&utm_medium=en&elq.

7. Redneck Revolt, Putting the Red Back in Redneck.

8. Coley, "Local Resident Recounts Charlottesville."

9. Coley, "Local Resident Recounts Charlottesville."

10. Colossians 3:12–13 (King James Version).

11. Galatians 5:21 (King James Version).

12. *Final Report: Independent Review of the 2017 Protest Events in Charlottesville, Virginia*, Hunton & Williams (the "Heaphy Report"), 113, http://www.charlottesville.org/home/showdocument?id=59691, citing letter from Pamela Starsia to Al Thomas, June 23, 2017.

13. Heaphy Report, 115.

14. Heaphy Report, 115.

15. Wyllie, "Professor Brought His Guns."

16. Heaphy Report, 116.

17. Heaphy Report, 116.

18. Heaphy Report, 116.

28. The Lawn and the Rotunda

1. Jack Stripling, "Inside the U. of Virginia's Response to a Chaotic White-Supremacist Rally," *Chronicle of Higher Education*, November 20, 2017, https://www.chronicle.com/article/inside-the-u-of-virginia-s/241832.

2. *Final Report: Independent Review of the 2017 Protest Events in Charlottesville, Virginia*, Hunton & Williams (the "Heaphy Report"), 112, http://www.charlottesville.org/home/showdocument?id=59691.

3. Heaphy Report, 112.

4. Stripling, "Inside the U. of Virginia's Response."

5. Stripling, "Inside the U. of Virginia's Response."

6. Stripling, "Inside the U. of Virginia's Response."

7. Stripling, "Inside the U. of Virginia's Response."

8. Heaphy Report, 112.

9. Heaphy Report, 112.

10. Heaphy Report, 113.

11. "University Police Department (UPD)—Timeline: August 11, 2017," posted September 11, 2017, https://response.virginia.edu/system/files/public/upd-timeline.pdf.

12. "The University's Response to August 11, 2017: Observations and Improvements," September 11, 2017.

13. "University's Response to August 11, 2017."

14. Heaphy Report, 113.

15. Stripling, "Inside the U. of Virginia's Response."

16. Stripling, "Inside the U. of Virginia's Response."

17. Caroline Newman, "Resolutions Address Academical Village, Open Flame and Rotunda Memorials," *UVA Today*, September 15, 2017, https://news.virginia.edu/content/resolutions-address-academical-village-open-flame-and-rotunda-memorials.

18. Newman, "Resolutions Address Academical Village."

19. Newman, "Resolutions Address Academical Village."

20. Newman, "Resolutions Address Academical Village."

21. Jack Stripling, "Beyond a President's Worst Fears, a Mob with Torches Arrived," *Chronicle of Higher Education*, August 13, 2017, https://www.chronicle.com/article/Beyond-a-President-s-Worst/240914?cid=rclink.

22. Stripling, "Beyond a President's Worst Fears."

23. Stripling, "Beyond a President's Worst Fears."

24. Stripling, "Beyond a President's Worst Fears."

25. Stripling, "Beyond a President's Worst Fears."

26. Stripling, "Beyond a President's Worst Fears."

27. Stripling, "Beyond a President's Worst Fears."

28. Stripling, "Beyond a President's Worst Fears."

29. Stripling, "Beyond a President's Worst Fears."

30. Stripling, "Inside the U. of Virginia's Response."

31. Heaphy Report, 116.

32. Stripling, "Inside the U. of Virginia's Response."

33. "University Police Department (UPD)—Timeline."

34. Stripling, "Inside the U. of Virginia's Response."

35. Michael Vasquez, "Why Did UVa Allow Banned Torches during White-Supremacist Rally?," *Chronicle of Higher Education,* August 25, 2017, https://www.chronicle.com/article/Why-Did-UVa-Allow-Banned/241019?cid=rclink.

36. Lisa Provence, "Defense Strategy: UVA Prof Fends Off White Supremacy Invasion," *C-Ville Weekly*, August 23, 2017, http://www.c-ville.com/defense-strategy-uva-prof-fends-off-white-supremacy-invasion/#.Wpn_yUxFxZU.

37. Provence, "Defense Strategy."

38. Provence, "Defense Strategy."

39. Provence, "Defense Strategy."

40. Provence, "Defense Strategy."

41. Stripling, "Inside the U. of Virginia's Response."

42. Stripling, "Inside the U. of Virginia's Response."

43. Stripling, "Inside the U. of Virginia's Response."

44. Heaphy Report, 118–19.

45. Heaphy Report, 119.
46. Stripling, "Inside the U. of Virginia's Response."
47. Stripling, "Inside the U. of Virginia's Response."
48. Stripling, "Inside the U. of Virginia's Response."
49. Stripling, "Inside the U. of Virginia's Response."
50. "University Police Department (UPD)—Timeline."
51. Stripling, "Inside the U. of Virginia's Response."
52. Stripling, "Inside the U. of Virginia's Response."
53. Heaphy Report, 78.
54. Heaphy Report, 78.
55. Heaphy Report, 78.
56. Hawes Spencer, *Summer of Hate: Charlottesville USA* (Charlottesville: University of Virginia Press, 2018), 27.
57. Stripling, "Beyond a President's Worst Fears."
58. Stripling, "Beyond a President's Worst Fears."
59. Stripling, "Beyond a President's Worst Fears."
60. Stripling, "Beyond a President's Worst Fears."
61. Stripling, "Beyond a President's Worst Fears."

29. Bloodshed

1. *Final Report: Independent Review of the 2017 Protest Events in Charlottesville, Virginia*, Hunton & Williams (the "Heaphy Report") 120, http://www.charlottesville.org/home/showdocument?id=59691.
2. Heaphy Report, 121.
3. Heaphy Report, 122–23.
4. Heaphy Report, 123.
5. Heaphy Report, 123.
6. Heaphy Report, 124.
7. Heaphy Report, 124.
8. Heaphy Report, 124.
9. Heaphy Report, 132.
10. Heaphy Report, 132.
11. Heaphy Report, 125.
12. Heaphy Report, 124.
13. Heaphy Report, 126–27.
14. Heaphy Report, 128.
15. Heaphy Report, 128.
16. Heaphy Report, 129.
17. Heaphy Report, 124.
18. Heaphy Report, 129.
19. Heaphy Report, 129.
20. Heaphy Report, 130.
21. Heaphy Report, 130.
22. Heaphy Report, 131.
23. Heaphy Report, 131.
24. Heaphy Report, 131.
25. Heaphy Report, 132.
26. Heaphy Report, 132.

27. Heaphy Report, 131.

28. Heaphy Report, 131.

29. Heaphy Report, 132.

30. Heaphy Report, 132.

31. Heaphy Report, 135.

32. Heaphy Report, 136.

33. Heaphy Report, 138.

34. Heaphy Report, 139.

35. Heaphy Report, 139.

36. Heaphy Report, 139.

37. Heaphy Report, 140.

38. Julian Wyllie, "A Professor Brought His Guns to Protect Protesters at White-Supremacist Rallies. Then His Troubles Started," *Chronicle of Higher Education*, May 28, 2018, https://www.chronicle.com/article/A-Professor-Brought-His-Guns/243516?cid=at&utm_source=at&utm_medium=en&elq.

39. Wyllie, "Professor Brought His Guns."

40. Jonah Engel Bromwich and Alan Blinderaug, "What We Know about James Alex Fields, Driver Charged in Charlottesville Killing," *New York Times*, August 13, 2017, https://www.nytimes.com/2017/08/13/us/james-alex-fields-charlottesville-driver-.html.

41. Heaphy Report, 146–47.

42. Lori Aratani, "NTSB Releases Preliminary Report in Charlottesville Helicopter Crash That Killed Two Virginia State Troopers," *Washington Post*, September 5, 2017, https://www.washingtonpost.com/news/dr-gridlock/wp/2017/09/05/ntsb-releases-preliminary-report-in-charlottesville-helicopter-crash-that-killed-two-virginia-state-troopers/?utm_term=.cc4e84757bdc.

30. Aftermath

1. Andrew Buncombe, "Heather Heyer Was Buried in Secret Grave to Protect It from Neo-Nazis after Charlottesville, Mother Reveals," *Independent*, December 15, 2017.

2. Louis Becket, "'A White Girl Had to Die for People to Pay Attention': Heather Heyer's Mother on Hate in the US," *Guardian*, October 1, 2017, https://www.theguardian.com/us-news/2017/oct/01/heather-heyers-mother-on-hate-in-the-us-were-not-going-to-hug-it-out-but-we-can-listen-to-each-other.

3. Becket, "White Girl Had to Die."

4. Becket, "White Girl Had to Die."

5. Becket, "White Girl Had to Die."

6. "SPLC Honors Heather Heyer at Civil Rights Memorial Center," Southern Poverty Law Center, August 18, 2017, https://www.splcenter.org/news/2017/08/18/splc-honors-heather-heyer-civil-rights-memorial-center.

7. David J. Garrow, *Protest at Selma: Martin Luther King Jr. and the Voting Rights Act of 1965* (New Haven, CT: Yale University Press, 1978), 31–34.

8. Christopher Klein, "Remembering Selma's 'Bloody Sunday,'" *History Channel*, March 6, 2015, https://www.history.com/news/selmas-bloody-sunday-50-years-ago.

9. Mary Stanton, *Viola Liuzzo and the Gendered Politics of Martyrdom from Selma to Sorrow: The Life and Death of Viola Liuzzo* (Athens: University of Georgia Press, 1998).

10. Stanton, *Viola Liuzzo*.

11. Stanton, *Viola Liuzzo*, 54–55.

12. Stanton, *Viola Liuzzo*, 54–55.

13. *Governor's Task Force on Public Safety Preparedness and Response to Civil Unrest: Final Report and Recommendations, December 1, 2017,* https://www.policefoundation.org/wp-content/uploads/2018/08/Governors-Task-Force-on-Public-Safety-Preparedness-and-Response-to-Civil-Unrest.pdf 2.

14. District of Columbia v. Heller, 554 U.S. 570 (2008).

15. *Governor's Task Force,* 9.

16. District of Columbia v. Heller, 554 U.S. 570 (2008) at 626–27.

17. "Jason Kessler Punched, Chased from Press Conference at Charlottesville City Hall," NBC29.com, August 13, 2017, http://www.nbc29.com/story/36124649/jason-kessler-chased-from-press-conference-in-front-of-charlottesville-city-hall.

18. Sines v. Kessler, 324 F. Supp. 3d 765 (W.D. Va. 2018).

19. Spencer Hawes, *Summer of Hate: Charlottesville, USA* (Charlottesville: University of Virginia Press, 2018), 15.

20. Dahlia Lithwick, "Lawyers vs. White Supremacists," Slate, October 12, 2017, https://slate.com/news-and-politics/2017/10/two-new-lawsuits-against-the-organizers-of-charlottesvilles-unite-the-right-rally.html.

21. Lithwick, "Lawyers vs. White Supremacists."

22. 42 U.S.C. § 1985(3).

23. Va. Code Ann. § 8.01–42.1 (West).

24. Virginia v. Black, 538 U.S. 343 (2003).

25. Sines v. Kessler, 324 F. Supp. 3d at 794.

26. Sines v. Kessler, 324 F. Supp. 3d at 794.

27. Sines v. Kessler, 324 F. Supp. 3d at 794.

28. Virginia v. Black, 538 U.S. 343.

29. Sines v. Kessler, 324 F. Supp. 3d at 794, quoting Virginia v. Black, 528 U.S. at 360.

30. Sines v. Kessler, 324 F. Supp. 3d at 794, citing Virginia v. Black, 528 U.S. at 360.

31. All quotes in this paragraph from Sines v. Kessler, 324 F. Supp. 3d at 777.

32. Sines v. Kessler, 324 F. Supp. 3d at 777.

33. Complaint, Sines v. Kessler, Case No. 3:17—CV—00072 (W.D. Va., October 12, 2017).

34. Sines v. Kessler, 324 F. Supp. 3d at 779, 803.

35. Sines v. Kessler, 324 F. Supp. 3d at 805.

36. Sines v. Kessler, 324 F. Supp. 3d at 805.

37. Becket, "White Girl Had to Die."

38. Becket, "White Girl Had to Die."

39. Evan Osnos, "The Fearful and the Frustrated," *New Yorker,* August 31, 2015, https://www.newyorker.com/magazine/2015/08/31/the-fearful-and-the-frustrated.

40. Jackie Calmes, "Trump Responds to Charlottesville Violence with Vague Statements Blaming 'Many Sides,'" *Los Angeles Times,* August 12, 2017, http://www.latimes.com/politics/la-pol-updates-trump-tweets-charlottesville-violence-htmlstory.html.

41. Calmes, "Trump Responds."

42. Calmes, "Trump Responds."

43. Benjamin Hart, "Trump Blames 'Many Sides' for Virginia Violence," *New York Magazine,* August 12, 2017, http://nymag.com/daily/intelligencer/2017/08/trump-blames-many-sides-for-charlottesville-violence.html.

44. "Donald Trump under Fire after Failing to Denounce Virginia White Supremacists," *Guardian,* August 13, 2017. All quotations in this paragraph are from the *Guardian* article. See https://www.theguardian.com/us-news/2017/aug/12/charlottesville-protest-trump-condemns-violence-many-sides.

45. "Donald Trump under Fire." All quotations in this paragraph are from the August 13 *Guardian* article.

46. "Donald Trump under Fire."

47. Glenn Thrush, "New Outcry as Trump Rebukes Charlottesville Racists 2 Days Later," *New York Times*, August 14, 2017, https://www.nytimes.com/2017/08/14/us/politics/trump-charlottesville-protest.html.

48. Thrush, "New Outcry."

49. Thrush, "New Outcry."

50. Thrush, "New Outcry."

51. Michael D. Shear and Maggie Haberman, "Trump Defends Initial Remarks on Charlottesville: Again Blames 'Both Sides,'" *New York Times*, August 15, 2017, https://www.nytimes.com/2017/08/15/us/politics/trump-press-conference-charlottesville.html.

52. Tom McCarthy, *Guardian*, "Key Moments from Trump's Most Extraordinary Press Conference Yet," August 15, 2017. All the subsequent quotes from Trump's August 15 press conference are from this article. See https://www.theguardian.com/us-news/2017/aug/15/donald-trump-charlottesville-trump-tower-white-supremacists.

53. "Charlottesville: Trump Reverts to Blaming Both Sides Including 'Violent Alt-left,'" *Guardian*, August 16, 2017, https://www.theguardian.com/us-news/2017/aug/15/donald-trump-press-conference-far-right-defends-charlottesville.

54. *Guardian*, "Trump Reverts."

55. Shear and Haberman, "Trump Defends."

56. Shear and Haberman, "Trump Defends."

57. Shear and Haberman, "Trump Defends."

58. Shear and Haberman, "Trump Defends."

59. Kristina Monllos, "Trump Shuts Down Manufacturing Council after More CEOs Resign in Protest," *Adweek*, August 15, 2017, https://www.adweek.com/brand-marketing/trump-shuts-down-manufacturing-council-after-more-ceos-resign-in-protest/.

60. Sam Levine, "Ex-KKK Leader David Duke Is Absolutely Thrilled with Trump Blaming 'Both Sides' in Charlottesville," Huffington Post, August 15, 2017, https://www.huffingtonpost.com/entry/david-duke-donald-trump_us_59936199e4b009141640bd7b.

61. Levine, "Ex-KKK Leader."

62. Benjamin Goggin, "A White Nationalist Conspiracy Theory Was at the Heart of the New Zealand Shooting. This Isn't the First Time It's Been Associated with Terror Attacks," Business Insider, March 14, 2019, https://www.businessinsider.com/white-genocide-racist-conspiracy-theory-fueled-new-zealand-shooting-2019-3.

63. Goggin, "White Nationalist Conspiracy Theory."

64. Goggin, "White Nationalist Conspiracy Theory."

65. Goggin, "White Nationalist Conspiracy Theory."

66. Goggin, "White Nationalist Conspiracy Theory."

67. Goggin, "White Nationalist Conspiracy Theory."

68. Amy Gutman and Denis Moynihan, "In New Zealand, Violent Echoes of Trump's White Conspiracy," *Cap Times* (Madison, WI), March 22, 2019, https://madison.com/ct/opinion/column/amy-goodman-and-denis-moynihan-in-new-zealand-violent-echoes/article_ea49f1ff-2f4f-5f1f-a33c-45b15f63fd9f.html.

69. Leslie Kendrick, "The Answers and the Questions in First Amendment Law," in *Charlottesville 2017: The Legacy of Race and Inequity*, ed. Louis P. Nelson and Claudrena N. Harold (Charlottesville: University of Virginia Press, 2018), 73.

70. Whitney v. California, 274 U.S. 357 (1927).

71. Kendrick, "Answers and the Questions," 72.

72. Rice v. Paladin Enterprises, Inc., 128 F.3d 233, 241 (4th Cir. 1997).

73. Rodney A. Smolla, *Deliberate Intent: A Lawyer Tells the True Story of Murder by the Book* (New York: Crown, 1999).

74. Smolla, *Deliberate Intent.*

75. Nat Hentoff, "The Scorned Law Professor," *Village Voice*, January 25, 2000, archive. is/EkK5X.

76. Rodney A. Smolla, "From Hit Man to Encyclopedia of Jihad: How to Distinguish Freedom of Speech from Terrorist Training," *Loyola Los Angeles Entertainment Law Review* 22 (2002): 479–490.

77. Smolla, "From Hit Man," 490.

78. Smolla, "From Hit Man," 490.

79. Smolla, "From Hit Man," 490.

80. Harper Lee, *To Kill a Mockingbird* (Philadelphia, J. B. Lippincott & Co.,1960), 98.

81. Steve McKenzie, "Laden's Blueprint to Destroy West," *Sunday Mail* (UK), January 6, 2002; see also John Cloud, "What Is Al-Qaeda without Its Boss?," *Time*, November 26, 2001, 50.

82. "The Encyclopedia of Jihad," US Department of Justice, 2001, accessed XXXXXXXX, XX, 2002, http://www.usdoj.gov/ag/trainingmanual.htm; see also Rodney Smolla, "From *Hit Man* to *Encyclopedia of Jihad*: How to Distinguish Freedom of Speech from Terrorist Training," *Loyola of Los Angeles Entertainment Law Review* 22 (2002): 479–80.

83. Planned Parenthood of Columbia/Willamette, Inc. v. American Coalition of Life Activists, 290 F.3d 1058 (9th Cir. 2002).

84. *Planned Parenthood*, 290 F.3d at 1085.

85. *Planned Parenthood*, 290 F.3d at 1085.

86. "Charlottesville: Race and Terror," *Vice News Tonight* (HBO), August 14, 2017, https://www.youtube.com/watch?v=P54sP0Nlngg.

87. United States v. Stevens, 559 U.S. 460 (2010).

88. Abrams v. United States, 250 U.S. 616, 630 (1919) (Holmes, J., dissenting).

89. Abrams v. United States, 250 U.S. at 630 (Holmes, J., dissenting).

INDEX